BUDDHA'S NOT SMILING

BUDDHA'S NOT SMILING

*Uncovering Corruption at the Heart of
Tibetan Buddhism Today*

ERIK D. CURREN

MOTILAL BANARSIDASS PUBLISHERS
PRIVATE LIMITED ● DELHI

First Indian Edition : Delhi, 2008
First Published : USA, 2006

In Association With
ALAYA PRESS
217 E. Beverley Street, Suite A
Staunton, VA 24401
United States

ISBN: 978-81-208-3331-9

MOTILAL BANARSIDASS
41 U.A. Bungalow Road, Jawahar Nagar, Delhi 110 007
8 Mahalaxmi Chamber, 22 Bhulabhai Desai Road, Mumbai 400 026
203 Royapettah High Road, Mylapore, Chennai 600 004
236, 9th Main III Block, Jayanagar, Bangalore 560 011
Sanas Plaza, 1302 Baji Rao Road, Pune 411 002
8 Camac Street, Kolkata 700 017
Ashok Rajpath, Patna 800 004
Chowk, Varanasi 221 001

Printed in India
BY JAINENDRA PRAKASH JAIN AT SHRI JAINENDRA PRESS,
A-45 NARAINA, PHASE-I, NEW DELHI 110 028
AND PUBLISHED BY NARENDRA PRAKASH JAIN FOR
MOTILAL BANARSIDASS PUBLISHERS PRIVATE LIMITED,
BUNGALOW ROAD, DELHI 110 007

Do not accept my dharma merely out of respect for me,
but analyze and check it the way a goldsmith analyzes gold,
by rubbing, cutting, and melting it.

—*Sutra on Pure Realms Spread out in Dense Array*

CONTENTS

ACKNOWLEDGMENTS

Thanks to Ed Worthy for his detailed comments and suggestions on my manuscript. Thanks to Karine Le Pajolec, Harrison Pemberton, and Thule Jug of Vienna Dharma Photos for use of photographs. Thanks also to others who helped in various ways along the way: Terry Burt, Derek Hanger, Brett and Amanda Hood, Carol Gerhardt, Jay Landman, Hannah Nydahl, Harrison Pemberton, and Stephanie Yang. I am grateful to Gerry Stowers for her friendship and support during the process of revising my manuscript and producing this book. All errors are solely the responsibility of the author.

CAST OF CHARACTERS

The Karmapa

THE 16TH GYALWA KARMAPA, RANGJUNG RIGPE DORJE (1924-81)
The spiritual leader of the Karma Kagyu school of Tibetan Buddhism
until his death. He led the Karma Kagyu lamas' escape from Chinese
forces in 1959 and established his headquarters in exile at Rumtek
monastery in Sikkim, now a state of northeastern India.

The Candidates for 17th Karmapa

OGYEN TRINLEY DORJE ALSO KNOWN AS URGYEN THINLEY (1985-)
Recognized by Tai Situ and supported by both the Dalai Lama and the
Chinese government. Born of a nomad family in eastern Tibet, he was
enthroned in Tibet in 1992 and resettled in 2000 in Himachal Pradesh
state in northwestern India.

TRINLEY THAYE DORJE (1983-)
Recognized by Shamar Rinpoche. He was born in Lhasa, escaped Tibet
in 1994, and is now completing his education in Kalimpong in the
Himalaya foothills of northeastern India.

Supporters of Ogyen Trinley

THE 14TH DALAI LAMA, TENZIN GYATSO (1935-)
The spiritual leader of the Gelugpa school of Tibetan Buddhism and
the political leader of the Tibetan people living in exile. Since winning
the Nobel Peace Prize in 1989, he has become the international face
of human rights, nonviolence, and Buddhist teachings. He is based

at Dharamsala in Himachal Pradesh state, located in the Himalayan foothills of northwestern India.

THE 12TH TAI SITU RINPOCHE ALSO KNOWN AS THE SITUPA (1954-)
The third-ranking spiritual leader of the Karma Kagyu school. Tai Situ is the primary supporter of Ogyen Trinley and originally presented the boy on the basis of a prediction letter that became the subject of dispute. He served on the Council of Regents and then on the Karmapa Search Committee at Rumtek. His monastic seat is located in Bir, in Himachal Pradesh in northwestern India.

THE 12TH GOSHIR GYALTSAB RINPOCHE (1954-)
The fifth-ranking lama in the Karma Kagyu hierarchy. He is the second main supporter of Ogyen Trinley after Tai Situ. He served on the Council of Regents and then on the Karmapa Search Committee at Rumtek. He is based in India's northeastern state of Sikkim, near the sixteenth Karmapa's monastery at Rumtek.

KHENCHEN THRANGU RINPOCHE
The abbot of Rumtek monastery in Sikkim and head philosophy teacher there until he left to establish his own monasteries in 1975.

TENZIN NAMGYAL
Assistant secretary of Rumtek monastery until dismissed in 1988. A layman, he was married to the sister of Thrangu Rinpoche until his death in 2005.

AKONG RINPOCHE
The aide of Tai Situ. With a Swiss follower, he runs the Rokpa Foundation, dedicated to relief work in the Himalayan countries. He is based in Scotland.

NAR BAHADUR BHANDARI
Chief minister of India's northeastern state of Sikkim during the years 1979-84 and 1985-1994.

Supporters of Thaye Dorje

THE 14TH SHAMAR RINPOCHE ALSO KNOWN AS THE SHAMARPA (1952-)
Traditionally known as the "Red-Hat Karmapa," the Shamarpas are the second-ranking spiritual leaders in the Karma Kagyu school. The current Shamar is the primary supporter of Thaye Dorje and is based in Kalimpong, in northeastern India. He served on the Council of Regents and then on the Karmapa Search Committee at Rumtek.

TOPGA YUGYAL RINPOCHE
General secretary of the Karmapa's administration from 1983 until his death in 1997.

JIGME RINPOCHE
The elder brother of Shamar Rinpoche. Since the mid-1970s he has run two large monasteries established by the sixteenth Karmapa in France.

KHENPO CHODRAK TENPHEL RINPOCHE
The abbot of Rumtek from 1978 until the monastery was taken over by followers of Karmapa candidate Ogyen Trinley in 1993. He is now based in New Delhi.

OLE AND HANNAH NYDAHL
A Danish couple who became some of the first Western students of the sixteenth Karmapa and went on to start more than four hundred Buddhist centers in Europe and throughout the West.

MAP

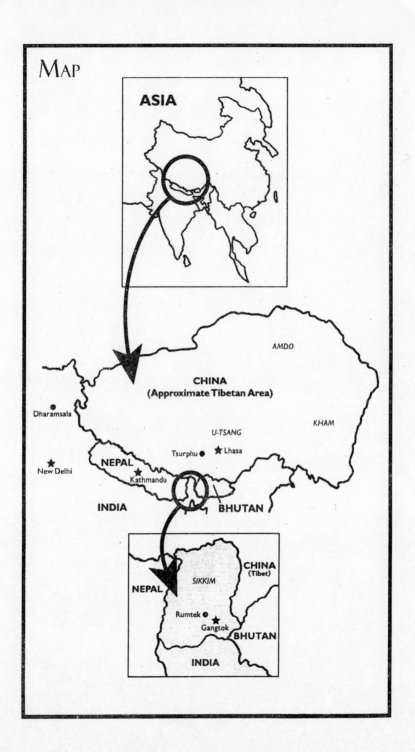

PREFACE

T his book is about corruption in Tibetan Buddhism, but not about sex scandals. We have already seen discussions about Buddhist teachers, particularly well known Zen masters and Tibetan lamas, having romantic affairs with their students, especially those from Western countries.[1] This is nothing new, and it afflicts Buddhism as it does all other major religions. Here, I do not touch on this topic.

Instead, I explore a type of corruption that I believe is much more insidious, and whose exposure can be of much greater benefit to people seeking to find meaning in their lives through a spiritual path, or just trying to understand the massive phenomenon that Tibetan Buddhism has become in the past thirty years. This book is a history of a dispute among the highest lamas with roots centuries in the past and a present of deep shame. It is a dispute over the identity of a lama called the Karmapa.

I have been a student of Buddhism for a decade. I was inspired by this ancient path's time-tested methods to escape suffering, and by the example of compassionate living offered by Tibetan lamas. A few years ago, when I first heard how spiritual leaders who stand for love, peace, and nonviolence had behaved in this dispute I was shocked and disillusioned. Were Tibetan lamas just hypocrites and charlatans? If this was so, I would have been ready to give up Buddhism altogether. The only way I could remain was to discover the facts for myself.

So that's what I set out to do. In the process, I discovered a dark side to some Tibetan lamas. But I also developed a confidence in the basic teachings of a spiritual tradition that was more mature, based on my own investigation, rather than merely on hopeful faith. I believe that this journey did me much good, and helped me grow intellectually and spiritually. I hope the reader will take much the same journey in these pages, and discover some of the same benefit along the way.

For the past three years, I have been a student of one of the main lamas involved in the controversy, Shamar Rinpoche. Thus I cannot claim to be a disinterested outsider. Shamar even suggested that I write this book. Four books have already come out in the last few years sympathetic to the views of his opponents.[2] These books raised many questions for me about the purity of Tibetan Buddhism, and I am sure they raised the same questions for many others. So it seemed only fair to investigate Shamar's claims and give him a chance to tell his story. The following pages try to disentangle the many knots in the web of claims, counterclaims, and outright deceptions that have come to enshroud the topic of the Karmapa today.

Two young men are at the center of our story, and both of them claim to be the Karmapa. The four most recent books on the subject all refer to one of the young men as "the Karmapa" while calling the other by his enthronement name, the equivalent of a personal name. Here, I begin from the premise of an authentic controversy, so I do not presume to know which candidate is the genuine reincarnate. Accordingly, I do not call either candidate "the Karmapa." Instead, I refer to each young lama by his enthronement name. I hope this will make for a fairer presentation that is also clearer for the reader.

I would like to invite you, the reader, to make your own judgment on the specific issue of this book—the story of the Karmapa. Considering the evidence, whom do you believe and whom do you trust? After that, it may be fruitful to consider how this connects to your attitude about Tibetan Buddhism and spiritual teachers in general. Finally, if you follow a spiritual tradition, or if you know someone who does, then I encourage you to meditate on what it means to follow a spiritual teacher with maturity, as an intelligent person in the modern world. Is it possible to balance faith and logical thinking? Does rationality conflict with faith, or can rationality enrich faith? When should we just believe, and when should we ask questions?

If you can prove any of my claims wrong please contact me directly, I will correct them in future editions.

INTRODUCTION

Reincarnating Lamas

Near the beginning of Martin Scorsese's 1997 film *Kundun*, a search party from Lhasa arrives at a small village in the dusty northeastern borderlands between Tibet and China. The time is the late 1930s. The visitors are looking for a boy who they think might be the reincarnation of the thirteenth Dalai Lama Thubten Gyatso (1876-1933), who died a few years earlier.

Before his death, the Tibetan leader had left a letter, written in an obscure poetic style, indicating the family and place of his rebirth. Following their late lama's instructions, and consulting intelligence reports, the Dalai Lama's administration in Lhasa had put together a list of likely boys—candidates for the Dalai Lama's reincarnation.

Now, the Lhasa lamas have come to a remote province to investigate one of these boys, the son of a peasant family. Disguised as traders, they have not divulged the purpose of their mission to the small boy or to his parents. The lamas have brought personal items of the deceased Dalai Lama to test the boy. Inside the family's rustic house, they spread these items out on a table and mix them together with newer, fancier versions of each object.

The parents bring in their boy and the disguised lamas invite him to choose "his" belongings—those which belonged to the thirteenth Dalai Lama. Unprompted, the boy correctly chooses the Dalai Lama's rosary, ritual drum, and walking stick, leaving the more attractive, newer ones on the table. The boy has passed the test: he is the genuine reincarnation of the thirteenth Dalai Lama. Convinced, the lamas prostrate to the boy, and address him as "Kundun," a title of respect for the Tibetan leader.

Buddhists everywhere believe that humans and all other beings die and then are reborn again and again in endless reincarnations, until they reach the state of enlightenment. Enlightenment, or nirvana, is the end of all suffering and the goal of Buddhism. Buddhists believe that enlightenment is reached by developing perfect wisdom and compassion through following the Noble Eightfold Path of correct view, goal, speech, action, livelihood, effort, mindfulness, and meditation.

Siddhartha Gautama, a prince of the Shakya clan that ruled one of the small kingdoms in the Himalayan foothills of northern India in the sixth century B.C., set the example when he renounced palace life and took to the road as a wandering ascetic. After years of fruitless practices, one day the young man sat down on a pile of grass under a large leafy tree by the Naranjana River. He determined not to rise from his seat until he surmounted all craving, thus liberating himself from the need to be reborn again in the physical world. He meditated through the night, resisted all the blandishments and threats of Mara, the lord of death, and as the sun rose, the young man reached enlightenment, thus becoming the Buddha or Enlightened One.

Known as Shakyamuni or the Sage of the Shakyas, the Buddha spent the next forty years traveling around northern India, giving sermons on the way out of suffering, and gaining disciples. He formed a community of monks, and later, an order of nuns, creating the Buddhist *sangha* of ordained practitioners. As needed, the Buddha came up with rules to ensure the harmony of the sangha, and his disciples codified these as the Vinaya. At age eighty, he died at Kushinagara, giving a final teaching on the impermanence of all beings and things, including the Buddha himself. After his death, the Buddha's disciples carried on the work of the monastic sangha and passed along the Buddha's teachings as the sutras.

After a couple of centuries, Buddhism began to divide into three main approaches, or paths. Much like Catholic, Orthodox, and Protestant Christianity, each path of Buddhism is defined by its religious practice as well as by the geographical areas it came to occupy.

The Theravada, or "Teaching of the Elders," developed out of one of the early Buddhist schools of India, and taught the value of ascetic monastic practice in order to become an *arhat*, a "worthy one" who has freed him- or herself from all worldly craving and from the endless cycle of birth and death known as *samsara*. Theravada Buddhism can be traced to the third century B.C. and is found today in the nations of south and Southeast Asia, including Sri Lanka, Thailand, and Burma.

Some early Buddhists criticized a focus on one's own salvation, not explicitly thinking of others, as inherently selfish and dubbed it the Hinayana or "Narrow Path." As an alternative, in the first century B.C. teachers began to present the Mahayana or "Great Path," in which altruism became the path to enlightenment. Mahayana practitioners sought to become *bodhisattvas*, beings whose every thought, word, and deed was dedicated to saving all beings from suffering. Today, the Mahayana is found in East Asian countries including China, Japan, Korea, and Vietnam.

The path of the bodhisattva was said to be a sure path to enlightenment, but was also said to take millions of lifetimes to achieve. In the middle of the first millennium A.D., adepts in north and northwestern India came upon a more powerful approach, one they said could bring enlightenment in one lifetime, the Vajrayana, or "Diamond Path." Vajrayana or Tantric practitioners sought to save themselves and all beings by realizing the enlightened qualities in their own cravings and illusions. Indian missionaries brought this supercharged version of the Mahayana over the Himalayas to Tibet beginning in the eighth century.

While all Buddhists believe in rebirth, only in the Himalayas did people come to believe that their highest spiritual teachers consciously chose to return to teach their students, lifetime after lifetime.

According to Vajrayana belief, after death, these teachers were reborn as reincarnate lamas, or *tulkus*, whose boundless compassion led them to postpone the bliss of enlightenment until all living beings would be liberated as well. The tulku is the Himalayan embodiment of the Mahayana ideal of the bodhisattva, but the tulku system is found in no other branch of Buddhism and in no other major religion. It is unique to Vajrayana Buddhism, and since its origin in the thirteenth century, the tulku ideal has been an important source of power, purity, and authenticity in the Diamond Path.

One practical advantage of the tulku system at its inception was to take politics out of deciding who would lead a monastery after its last leader's death. Previously, in Tibet, powerful aristocratic patrons would use their influence to get one of their sons appointed to lead a monastery. This effectively put the cloisters under the control of local landowners and warlords and made the religious centers subject to the rivalry of competing families. These families involved lamas in their political conflicts and disrupted the monasteries' spiritual work. The tulku system promised to solve this problem. Over eight centuries that followed, reincarnate lamas became the bedrock of Tibetan religion and the foundation of the largest monastic system on earth.

The First Tulku of Tibet

Today, in Tibetan Buddhism, there are hundreds of lamas reputed to be tulkus. The Dalai Lama—the current incarnation Tenzin Gyatso is the fourteenth of his line—is the most famous tulku of Tibet. But he and his thirteen predecessors were not the first lamas said to take rebirth intentionally to continue their work as bodhisattvas. The first tulku of Tibet was a lama known as the Karmapa.

In the twelfth century, the first Karmapa Dusum Khyenpa predicted that he would return to teach his students and manage his monastery in his next lifetime. And sure enough, when Dusum Khyenpa died, his students located a boy who showed signs that he was the reincarnation of the Karmapa. The boy was named Karma Pakshi and when he was old enough, he inherited control over the Karmapa's cloister and his activities. From then on, the Karmapa's monastery was relatively free of control by local noble families. Being able to choose their own leader, the Karmapa's lamas became masters of their own destiny.

Impressed by the success of this system, other monasteries copied it as a means to choose their own top lamas. Thus, over a period of a couple centuries, power shifted in Tibet from land-owning families to the lamas who managed the most powerful monasteries. The most revered tulkus attracted donations and students, developing monastic empires and political power of their own. As tulkus became major political leaders in their regions, lama-rule in Tibet reached its apex. In the late fourteenth century, nearly three centuries after the first Karmapa, the Dalai Lamas would appear. Two centuries after that, in 1642, the fifth Dalai Lama would take over the throne of central Tibet from a dynasty of secular kings.

Outsiders might think that tulkus were always chosen according to set procedures laid down to ensure the accuracy of the result—that the child located would be the genuine reincarnation of the dead master, as in the scene from the movie *Kundun*. But in Tibetan history, tulku searches were not always conducted in such a pure way. Because reincarnating lamas inherited great wealth and power from their predecessors they became the center of many political disputes.

Tulkus were often recognized based on non-religious factors. Sometimes monastic officials wanted a child from a powerful local noble family to give their cloister more political clout. Other times, they wanted a child from a lower-class family that would have little leverage to influence the child's upbringing. In yet other situations, the desires of the monastic officials took second place to external politics. A local warlord, the Chinese emperor, or even the Dalai Lama's government in Lhasa might try to impose its choice of tulku on a monastery for political reasons.

Only the strongest monastic administrations had the ability to resist such external pressures, and the Karmapa's monastery was one of these. Sixteen Karmapas were recognized by the Karmapa's own monastery without participation from outsiders. Only in one instance, when the sixteenth Karmapa was recognized in the 1920s, did the Tibetan government of the thirteenth Dalai Lama try to intervene in choosing a Karmapa. In that case, as we will see later, the government ultimately had to back down.

When the highest lamas fled Tibet along with nearly a hundred thousand refugees from Chinese rule in 1959, the lamas reestablished their monasteries in exile. The sixteenth Karmapa built the monastery of Rumtek in the tiny Himalayan kingdom of Sikkim, which became a state of India in 1975.

After the sixteenth Karmapa died in 1981, the lamas who ran Rumtek clashed with other lamas from the Karmapa's Karma Kagyu school of Buddhism over finding his reincarnation, the seventeenth Karmapa. In 1992, two high-ranking lamas enthroned a boy of their choosing in Tibet against the wishes of the previous Karmapa's administration at Rumtek. To his credit, this boy had powerful friends and enjoyed the support of the Dalai Lama and, surprisingly, the Chinese government as well. But this was not enough to convince the administration of Rumtek to accept him. So, with the help of local state police and paramilitary forces, the two renegade lamas and their followers took over the monastery in 1993, replaced the administration with their own people, and then proclaimed their boy the new Karmapa.

In response, the lama who had been in control of Rumtek but was ousted in 1993 installed his own boy in India the following year. Thus there came to be two Karmapa candidates, two boys taking their places in a struggle to control the largest school of Tibetan Buddhism that has continued to the present day.

Loyalty vs. Religious Freedom

The dispute over the identity of the Karmapa is a bewildering mix of religion, geopolitics, and infighting among exiled Tibetan lamas. It is a complex story, not easy to untangle from the outside. For outsiders, the story is troubling from the beginning. It shows Tibetan lamas in a very negative light. It also shows Tibetans disagreeing with the Dalai Lama. We are used to hearing the Dalai Lama described as the "spiritual leader of Tibet." Given that, do the claims of the Tibetans who dispute his selection of the Karmapa have any merit? And, if so, should their story affect the way we view the Dalai Lama?

Since the first Dalai Lama appeared, his successors have been the effective leaders of the Gelug, one of the five religious schools of Tibet.[1] Starting in 1642, the Dalai Lamas were also the political rulers of the central provinces of the huge area now called Tibet, an area I will refer to as Central Tibet. This gave the Dalai Lamas a mix of religious and political authority that has been difficult for historians to sort out. Were the Dalai Lamas the recognized leaders of all the religious groups of Tibet? And is the current Dalai Lama the religious leader of all Tibetans today? His supporters say yes. But many Tibetans disagree. They hold that the four religious schools outside of the Dalai Lama's own Gelug governed themselves autonomously back in Tibet—and that they continue to run their own affairs today, without reference to the authority of the Dalai Lama.

In 1959 the Dalai Lama fled Tibet for exile to India and he took his government ministers with him. Ever since, he and his officials have run an exile government in India whose main goal has been to regain influence in Tibet. Until the late eighties, the Dalai Lama demanded independence for his people from China. After that goal came to seem unattainable, he moderated his demand to autonomy for Tibetans within China. Over nearly half a century living in the free world, the Dalai Lama has learned much about the grim realities of geopolitics. He has also imbibed concepts such as human rights and religious freedom. These ideas were unknown in old Tibet, yet the Dalai Lama has skillfully adopted these modern concepts in his own quest to gain more freedom for Tibetans.

"When we demand the rights and freedoms we so cherish we should also be aware of our responsibilities. If we accept that others have an equal right to peace and happiness as ourselves, do we not have a responsibility to help those in need?" the Dalai Lama asked in a speech at the World Conference on Human Rights in Vienna in 1993. "The rich diversity of cultures and religions should help to strengthen the fundamental human rights in all communities. Because underlying this diversity are fundamental principles that bind us all as members of the same human family. Diversity and traditions can never justify the violations of human rights."[2]

In perhaps his biggest challenge, the Dalai Lama has had to walk a fine line to maintain his integrity as a Buddhist lama while also running an exile government. As there are chauvinists of Chinese nationalism, or of any other group's attempts to advance itself, so there are chauvinists of Tibetan nationalism. And as there is dissent among any group, so Tibetans in exile hold a range of views on how best to advance Tibetan nationalism and preserve Tibetan Buddhism.

Some exiled Tibetans fear that Tibetan religion will die without a Tibetan national state to actively promote the Tibetan language along with Tibet's distinctive culture and customs. These Tibetans are most likely to argue that Buddhism should serve politics, and that bringing Tibetans together into a coherent, united people is more important than ensuring that the variety of lineages and practices of Tibetan religion can flourish in the contemporary world. For many Tibetans, loyalty to the Dalai Lama effectively trumps religious freedom, though they might not put it so bluntly. Instead, they might speak of "unity"—how important it is to unify all Tibetans behind the Dalai Lama.

Yet other Tibetans feel that Buddhism can live on in Chinese Tibet as long as there can be a separation of church and state. Still others see a bright future for Buddhism in the world outside of Tibet. In our exploration of the Karmapa issue, we will meet Tibetans and outsiders who embrace each of these views. We will also consider the purpose of Tibetan Buddhism. Important questions arise: Should religion bring all Tibetans together and promote a free Tibet and world peace in general? Or does religion have another purpose, to help people reach their individual happiness through their own faith and diligence, irrespective of race, culture, and language?

Digging up Skeletons

Sometimes Tibetans and their foreign supporters tend to project an image of old Tibet and Tibetan exiles today as relatively free of sectarian strife. This is understandable, since a positive image has gone a long way towards creating worldwide interest in the Tibetan cause, interest that other refugee groups have not been able to garner for themselves. "Unity of the Church is ideally and practically valued in exile, and great efforts are made by the Tibetan [exile] government to display unity, especially through the Private and Information Offices [of the Dalai Lama in India]."[3] Criticisms, whether from Tibetans or outsiders, are often strongly rejected as harmful to the cause of Tibetan unity and thus, of Tibetan freedom and human rights in China.

Many writers have discussed the problems of Tibet under the Chinese and the Tibetan freedom movement that arose in response. Our story is more concerned with how politics within the Tibetan community has affected Buddhism. However much we may sympathize with the Dalai Lama or the plight of the Tibetan people under Chinese rule, we should not be too quick to smooth over serious conflicts among the leading Tibetan lamas themselves.

This book explores the Karmapa controversy as a case study of the corruption that has infected Tibetan Buddhism in exile, as normal human emotions have been unleashed without the traditional strictures of life in Tibet to restrain them. It is a story of spiritual leaders involved in violence, deceit, murder—and even litigation. Should this story affect how the world views Tibetan Buddhism?

Tibetan lamas boast that they have passed down an unbroken lineage of oral teachings from Shakyamuni Buddha in the fifth century B.C. to the current day. Thus, Tibetans claim that theirs is perhaps the purest form of Buddhism, having been isolated behind their Himalayan wall from corrupting, modernizing influences well into the twentieth century. But does the shocking history of the Karmapa fight belie this claim? Indeed, considering the corruption that the controversy reveals among the lamas, is it possible that Tibetan Buddhism is rotten to the core? To find out, I made my way to the main scene of the Karmapa controversy over a period of years by a circuitous route.

First, I walked the streets of Lhasa, the ancient capital of Tibet and the holy city of Vajrayana Buddhism, the religion of the Himalayas. There I learned how seamlessly and cozily religion, commerce, and politics have always wrapped every Tibetan from birth until death. The great monasteries of Lhasa, once masters over thousands of acres of fields and hundreds of peasants and herders—each cloister now a mere shell for tourists, manned by a skeleton crew of show-monks—showed me how much power the lamas had exerted in old Tibet. The new roads, shops, and military bases of the last four decades showed me how strong the Chinese grip on Tibetan life is today.

Afterwards, in India, I started to uncover the truth about the controversy over the reincarnation of the Karmapa. I discovered that the version that the Dalai Lama's supporters have told to Westerners was an incomplete story at best. In New Delhi, I toured a Buddhist school that had been attacked to support the Dalai Lama's Karmapa candidate. I learned how Buddhist converts from the United States and Europe had played key roles on both sides of that attack. In the old British hill town of Kalimpong I met the other young man who claimed the title of Karmapa—not the Dalai Lama's choice. I found that he had an interest in the philosophy of Immanuel Kant, the science of black holes, and the film versions of *The Lord of the Rings*.

I also learned about an investigation that had been conducted by a team of journalists from four Asian countries that revealed the deepest, darkest secret of the whole Karmapa affair.[4] This team had put together a film in the early days of handheld video cameras that documented a covert operation involving the Karmapa, Chinese state security, and perhaps even the American CIA. It would take more than a year to track down the filmmaker, who turned up in Bangkok, and get a copy of this remarkable film.

Finally, I entered the disenchanted kingdom of Sikkim and made my way to the Karmapa's headquarters in exile: Rumtek monastery. For decades, Sikkim was a flash point for border tension between nuclear-armed rivals India and China, and until recently it had been nearly off-limits to foreigners. I questioned monks who lived at Rumtek now and those who had left as a result of the dispute over the seventeenth Karmapa. They were helpful, but they knew only a handful of "facts" about the Karmapa dispute, most of them untrue. It was not until I started digging through old newspapers, legal documents, and manifestoes written by both sides in the dispute—scattered on three continents and all over the Internet—that the story behind the Karmapa issue slowly emerged.

A volume put out in New Delhi in 1996 detailed a meeting where ordinary monks and Buddhist devotees testified to their experiences before and after the dispute became violent.[5] Their voices spoke with heartbreaking poignancy of betrayal, fear, and loss that was only made bearable by deep religious faith.

A decision by a court in Sikkim revealed the depth of distrust that had developed between high lamas who had been raised together as children under the eye of the previous Karmapa.[6] An affidavit in another case, this time in far-away New Zealand, raised serious questions about the historical claims of the Dalai Lama's candidate.[7] A memoir of a Tibetan general from the eighteenth century painted a picture of sectarian religious conflict in old Tibet as brutal and bigoted as anything from the European Reformation and its bloody wars of religion.[8] Tibetans are not proud of this history, and it is largely unknown to followers of Tibetan Buddhism in the West. But this legacy of conflict remains alive to today's high lamas and to the politicians of the Tibetan exile government of the Dalai Lama.

The main players in this drama are two young men, each claiming to be one of the highest masters in Tibetan Buddhism, and each with a compelling story. But the two boys are not the only characters in this behind-the-scenes tale of religion, politics, violence, and greed.

They are surrounded by people with stories as vivid and compelling as their own: the previous incarnation of the Karmapa, who ruled over Rumtek as a jolly autocrat until his death in 1981; his nephew Shamar Rinpoche, whose previous reincarnations were banned by the Tibetan government and who, in his current lifetime, became an amateur attorney, taking the case for Rumtek all the way to the Indian Supreme Court; Tai Situ Rinpoche, the first Tibetan lama to win a Grammy Award and Shamar's ambitious rival for dominance at Rumtek, who brought in three governments to make the case for his boy; and of course the Dalai Lama, an international celebrity and a presence always in the background at Rumtek.

Surprisingly, all these men, born in the medieval society that was Tibet before 1959 and raised as monks in a rarefied world of butter-lamps, sacred chanting, and mandarin protocol, had become cosmopolitans at ease with adoring foreign devotees from Hong Kong to London, from Biarritz to Beverly Hills. Most of them were used to dealing with, and sometimes manipulating, the international press as well.

Another irony: The principal lamas of Tibetan Buddhism fled from the Chinese occupation of their homeland in 1959. Yet, a couple of decades later, many of them had begun to shuttle back and forth between China and "exile," restoring their monasteries in Tibet and helping to revitalize Buddhism there. The line between enemy and friend began to blur considerably in politics as played by Tibetan lamas.

Buddha's Not Smiling is the anatomy of a crisis. Buddhism, and particularly its Tibetan variety, has begun to spread long, leafy branches out into the West, placing our spiritual landscape under its expanding shadow. But if we dig beneath the topsoil, do we find that its roots are infected with incurable rot? As Buddhism is now the fastest growing major religion in the West, so the Tibetan variety, known as the Vajrayana, has become Buddhism's most popular path.[9] In turn, of the five religious schools of Tibet, the most widespread is the Karma Kagyu, whose leader is the Karmapa. The dispute behind his recognition exposes deep corruption at the heart of Tibetan Buddhism today.

The Chinese Communists tried to destroy the practice of Buddhism in Tibet. But confronted with the stubborn piety of the Tibetan people, the Communists failed. For more than a decade, the battle for Rumtek has raised rancor among supposedly compassionate Tibetan lamas and their students. It has led allegedly non-violent Buddhists to insult, to denounce, and to physically attack each other. Will the lamas, living in exile, now kill off Buddhism themselves, finishing the job that the Chinese started?

1 BAYONETS TO RUMTEK

This story begins with a violent attack on a Buddhist monastery. It is a scene that could have been replayed hundreds of times in Tibet after the Chinese took full control in 1959. Government officials, soldiers, and police enter the cloister. The officials demand the keys to the main temple, with its huge Buddha statue, a thousand smaller statues, and images of saints and sages painted by the great masters of centuries past. A mob of hundreds of angry local people shouts at the monks. Women beat the monks and try to pull off their red and yellow robes. Police and local bullies herd the monks into the monastery kitchen. There, the bullies and police line the monks up and force them to hold large knives. The police shoot photographs to create a bogus criminal file for each monk.

At gunpoint, officers order the monks to perform prostrations in front of a photograph of a boy-lama. The lama was approved by the government and was supposed to be the reincarnation of a famous lama who died a decade earlier. The leaders of the crowd continue to occupy the monastery. They give the monks three days to sign a statement saying that the boy-lama is their true leader. Afterwards, those who do not sign are thrown out by bullies. The monks have no time to collect their things and find themselves out in the woods with no other possessions than their torn and bloody robes. Some villagers curse and harass them. Others, at great risk to themselves, feed and shelter the hungry, tired monks.

Yes, the scene described above could have happened in occupied Tibet. But in this case, it did not. Shockingly, this drama took place in a free country, India, the very haven to which nearly a hundred thousand Tibetans had fled for safety in 1959.

Nothing in this scene makes sense. The monastery was not in Tibet; it was located in the tiny state of Sikkim nestled among the high peaks and valleys of the eastern Himalayas in India. The government officials who entered the monastery were not Communist cadres from Lhasa or Beijing; they were appointees of the democratically elected state government of Sikkim. The angry mob was not seeking revenge for centuries of supposed class oppression; its members were dozens of local Buddhist families whose devotion had led them to the monastery for a religious ceremony. The police and soldiers were not crack troops of the People's Liberation Army brought in from faraway areas in China; they were young men from the local community, and many of them were Buddhists.

Perhaps most confusingly—because this monastery was not in China—the boy-lama in the photograph was indeed approved by the Communist Chinese government, like so many figurehead lamas in occupied Tibet since 1959. But unlike these lamas, the boy was also approved by the local state government, in India. India is a secular nation, whose constitution guarantees freedom to all religions while prohibiting government interference in spiritual matters. Yet, the local state government had most decidedly interfered at the monastery. The leader of this government was a Hindu. But many of his officials were Buddhists.

Finally, the biggest enigma of all.

The boy-lama was also approved by the Dalai Lama.

What Did the Dalai Lama Know?

The monastery is called Rumtek. It was attacked in August 1993 by supporters of the boy in the photograph. And, to the Dalai Lama, as to the Chinese government and the state government of Sikkim, the boy was one of the highest lamas of Tibetan Buddhism. To his supporters, he was the Karmapa. His name was Ogyen Trinley Dorje.

Normally, the Dalai Lama and the Chinese government agree on very little. But in the case of this boy, they both agreed that not only should he be the head of Rumtek monastery; as the Karmapa, the boy would also lead the particular sect of Tibetan Buddhism—the largest one worldwide, with two million or more devotees—which had its headquarters at Rumtek monastery.

To most Tibetans, whether living inside China or in exile, the Dalai Lama embodies their aspirations for national identity. For centuries back in Tibet, the Dalai Lamas were known as the spiritual leaders of Tibet. After the current Dalai Lama fled Tibet in 1959 and even more so after he won the Nobel Peace Prize thirty years later, the exiled high lama has become known worldwide as the moral and spiritual leader of all Tibetans.

So, if the Dalai Lama had recognized the boy, why did it require Sikkimese soldiers and police, and a mob of angry local devotees, to try to make the monks at Rumtek accept the boy in the photograph as the Karmapa? Even then, most of the monks would rather fight than switch, at least figuratively speaking. Clearly, the word of the Dalai Lama, even when backed up with armed force, was not enough to legitimize the boy-lama for the monks of the Karmapa at Rumtek.

The monks insisted that they were loyal to the Dalai Lama. They also said that they had nothing against the boy in the photograph. But they objected, respectfully, that the boy was not recognized as Karmapa by traditional means, and that the Dalai Lama had no right to choose their leader. The monks claimed that the Tibetan exile leader had overstepped his authority in trying to choose a leader for their group. Neither his political role nor his position as a lama in his own Gelug tradition entitled him to choose the Karmapa, who is the leader of a different tradition, known as the Karma Kagyu.

In history, the Karmapas originated nearly three centuries before the Dalai Lamas. The monks said that their own lamas have always chosen the Karmapa without help from the Dalai Lama and the government he led in Tibet until 1959, and in exile ever since. It was thus for eight centuries in Tibet and the monks did not see why things should be any different in exile.

The Case of Dorje Shugden

Outsiders are used to thinking of Tibetans as united in solidarity behind the Dalai Lama on all issues, whether spiritual or political. How could they not be? We know the Tibetan leader for his gentle manner and engaging laughter, his patience and goodwill in the face of overwhelming power, and his generosity in spreading Buddhist teachings on non-violence and compassion around the world.

But some Tibetans in exile have disagreed with the Dalai Lama on religious matters. The most famous example may be the dispute over worship of the tantric protector deity Dorje Shugden. "A Dharma Protector is an emanation of a Buddha or a Bodhisattva whose main functions are to avert the inner and outer obstacles that prevent practitioners from gaining spiritual realizations, and to arrange all the necessary conditions for their practice," say Dorje Shugden devotees. "In Tibet, every monastery had its own Dharma Protector, but the tradition did not begin in Tibet; the Mahayanists of ancient India also relied upon Dharma Protectors to eliminate hindrances and to fulfill their spiritual wishes."[1] As in practices for other dharma protectors, Shugden worship involves various rituals including chanted liturgies, ritual offerings, and visualizations.

And like other wrathful deities or dharma protectors, Shugden is scary, but with a purpose. "His round yellow hat represents the view of Nagarjuna, and the wisdom sword in his right hand teaches us to sever ignorance, the root of samsara, with the sharp blade of Nagarjuna's view... Dorje Shugden rides a snow lion, the symbol of the four fearlessnesses of a Buddha, and has a jewel-spitting mongoose perched on his left arm, symbolizing his power to bestow wealth on those who put their trust in him...His wrathful expression indicates that he destroys ignorance, the real enemy of all living beings, by blessing them with great wisdom; and also that he destroys the obstacles of pure Dharma practitioners."[2] Nagarjuna was an Indian philosopher of the second or third century A.D. whose views on Buddhism were influential in Tibet.

Since the sixteenth century, monks in the Dalai Lama's own Gelug school of Tibetan Buddhism have performed rituals calling on the fearsome figure of Dorje Shugden to protect their spiritual practice and help them in worldly matters. The current Dalai Lama learned these practices from his junior tutor before fleeing Tibet in 1959. But beginning in 1976, the Tibetan exile leader started to discourage his people from supplicating Shugden, saying in part, that such practice would be harmful to the Nyingma order. Historically, Shugden practice was popular among lamas of the Gelug school ("Yellow Hats") who resisted mixing their school's philosophy and practice with those of other Buddhist schools, particularly the original Buddhism of Tibet, the Nyingma, as a traditional prayer to Shugden shows:

Praise to you, violent god of the Yellow Hat teachings,
Who reduces to particles of dust
Great beings, high officials and ordinary people
Who pollute and corrupt the Gelug doctrine.[3]

In exile, the Dalai Lama has said, all Tibetans need to unite in a common front against the Chinese. Shugden practice could be an obstacle to such unity, as it could alienate followers of schools outside the Gelugpa, particularly the Nyingma. Indeed, lamas of other schools often look cautiously on those who also follow Dorje Shugden, fearing that they might be Gelugpa chauvinists. Therefore, on March 7, 1996, the Dalai Lama's exile government in India decreed a ban on Shugden practice. Of course, this writ did not carry the force of law, since India guarantees religious freedom in its constitution. But, like a Papal Bull among followers of the Catholic Church, the Dalai Lama's decree carried weight among Buddhist Tibetans, whenever they resided. After the ban, loyalists to the Dalai Lama echoed their leader in denouncing Shugden practice.

Longtime Shugden followers have denied that their tradition discriminates against the Nyingma or other Tibetan religious traditions. They took the ban as a blow to their religious freedom and the prelude to persecution. "I felt the ground slipping under my feet," said Kundeling Rinpoche (Rinpoche is a title of respect for high lamas), a leading Shugden practitioner, when he heard of the ban while traveling in Europe. "What followed was even more shocking—the persecution of and propaganda against respected masters of the Dorje Shugden spiritual practice." An Indian reporter concluded that the ban had unleashed a backlash among Tibetans in exile. "Not only was Shugden worship forbidden by the Dalai Lama," the reporter wrote, "Shugden followers were subjected to a witch-hunt that has been well documented in the international media. The German television program 'Panorama' and the Swiss '10 Vor 10' have documented the human rights abuses by the Dalai Lama's administration—the violence and even death threats against the practitioners of this particular Buddhist tradition and their ostracism."[4]

Another prominent Gelugpa lama practicing Dorje Shugden, Geshe Kelsang Gyatso, moved to England in 1977 and started his own organization, the New Kadampa Tradition, which developed a significant following among Westerners. In 1996, when the Dalai Lama banned Shugden practice, the New Kadampa broke off from the Dalai Lama's leadership and began to protest against the ban. Since then, on at least one occasion, the group was able to muster a large crowd of Westerners in monk's robes to protest at Heathrow airport when the Dalai Lama flew into London.

The Karmapa Controversy

Unlike the dispute over Dorje Shugden, which has seen news articles examining both sides of the Dalai Lama's ban, few writers outside of India have seriously investigated the dispute over the identity of the current Karmapa. The four books published in 2003 and 2004 on the Karmapa have all supported the boy chosen by the Dalai Lama without questioning the basic assumption of the Tibetan leader's position—namely, that he has the authority to choose the Karmapa. This has prevented these writers from paying enough attention to the most dramatic events of the controversy, particularly the violent takeover of the Karmapa's Rumtek monastery in 1993.

The Karmapa story can be confusing, and it is difficult to find the facts buried in the mountains of rhetoric built by each side in the controversy. In general, Western journalists tend to rely on one main source for information and analysis about Tibetan Buddhism, the Dalai Lama himself. In the case of the Karmapa controversy, faced with the daunting task of understanding Tibetan religious politics and sectarian rivalries, it is understandable that writers would seek clarity from a trusted source. As a result, many have allowed themselves to be guided by the Dalai Lama's press office on the complex issue.

While this has simplified research for reporters, relying on the Dalai Lama's administration for information about the Karmapa has prevented writers from getting the full story, for one simple reason. In this particular case, the Dalai Lama is not an impartial arbiter of a dispute among two groups of Tibetan lamas. Instead, as in the ban on Dorje Shugden, the Tibetan leader is a party himself to the dispute, since he has given his official support to one of the candidates for the position of seventeenth Karmapa.

The Tibetan leader's word has been sufficient evidence for many writers outside of India to declare the controversy dead. If the Dalai Lama has recognized one boy as the Karmapa, then what need of further discussion? Surely, the lamas who persist in supporting the other boy, known as Trinley Thaye Dorje, must have little merit to their case.

Accordingly, hundreds of newspaper and magazine articles published in the West, along with the four recent books, have accepted Ogyen Trinley as the Karmapa. Though writers often cite other reasons, their primary rationale for accepting the one candidate over the other is usually that the Dalai Lama has recognized him.

Yet, in India, where most exiled Tibetans live, the controversy continues to rage. Interestingly, the Indian press has accorded credence to both Karmapa candidates. This book will examine press coverage of various events in the Karmapa story to highlight the contrast between Indian and Western reporting. This may encourage us to question the accuracy of the information that we in the West have received about Tibetan Buddhism in general.

To further highlight the difference between opinion in India and in the West on the Karmapa, the Indian government has shown suspicion of the Dalai Lama's candidate Ogyen Trinley, restricting his travels and limiting what his chief supporter in the Karma Kagyu, Tai Situ Rinpoche, can say about the controversy.

Meanwhile, the other Karmapa candidate Thaye Dorje has been able to travel freely in India and abroad. And after lamas involved in the dispute began to bring cases to the Indian court system, particularly in a property rights suit over Rumtek monastery filed by Thaye Dorje's supporters, judges have mostly ruled in favor of Thaye Dorje's party. If anything, opinion in India, both official and unofficial, appears to be running in favor of Thaye Dorje over the Dalai Lama's choice Ogyen Trinley. The important exception is Sikkim, where, as we will see, Rumtek monastery is located and where Ogyen Trinley enjoys significant support among leading families and in the local press.

The Dalai Lama's main rival on the Karmapa issue, Shamar Rinpoche, agrees with the followers of Dorje Shugden that there is a problem of religious freedom among exiled Tibetans. "The Dalai Lama asks that Tibetans have religious freedom in China," Shamar told me, "but unfortunately, His Holiness has not respected the religious freedom of Tibetans in exile to follow the traditions of their own religious lineages." Yet, Shamar has resisted allying himself with the advocates for Dorje Shugden, since he is uncomfortable with their high-profile and often acrimonious protests against the Dalai Lama. "I have always supported His Holiness Dalai Lama in every way, on freedom for Tibet, on spreading Buddhism around the world, and on human rights,"

Shamar said. "Only on one issue do I disagree with the Dalai Lama: choosing the reincarnation of the Karmapa."

Born in 1952, Shamar is the fourteenth incarnation in a line of tulkus going back to the thirteenth century. The first Shamarpa Drakpa Sengye (1283-1349) was a student of the third Karmapa Rangjung Dorje (1284-1339). For the next ten centuries, the Karmapa and Shamarpa worked as a team, one often recognizing the incarnations of the other. Their partnership was enshrined in parallel titles, based on the color of the identical ceremonial miters each lama wore: The Black Hat Karmapa (Karmapa) and the Red Hat Karmapa (Shamarpa).

The Shamarpas suffered an unusual setback to their line in the eighteenth century, when in the wake of a war between Tibet and Nepal, the Chinese emperor and the Dalai Lama's government blamed Shamar for the hostilities and imposed a bizarre punishment: an official ban on his future incarnations. This meant that Shamarpas could only reincarnate in secret until the ban expired with the demise of the government of Central Tibet in 1959.

The current Shamar is the nephew of the sixteenth Karmapa and was raised by the Karma Kagyu leader at Rumtek monastery in the sixties and seventies. He managed Rumtek until 1993, when supporters of Ogyen Trinley took over. Since then, Shamar has led the remaining officials of the sixteenth Karmapa's administration in court battles and publicity campaigns in India to try to regain the monastery.

Unlike Shugden advocates, Shamar has kept a low profile outside of the Himalayas. Though he is one of the highest reincarnate lamas of Tibet, most outsiders who follow Tibetan Buddhism probably would not recognize his name. However, journalists sympathetic to the Dalai Lama do know Shamar, and they have criticized him strongly. Three of the four books published about the Karmapa in 2003 and 2004 discuss the controversy (the other one is a biography of Ogyen Trinley), and all three books criticize Shamar for standing in the way of Ogyen Trinley taking his rightful place as seventeenth Karmapa.

Jeffery Paine, himself an author of a book on Tibetan Buddhism, summed up the perspective of this group of writers in the *Washington Post* in 2004. Paine noted that Shamar is the lama who all the recent books on the Karmapa portray as "doing the Tibetan cause harm in order to secure the profits from the Karmapa's holdings for himself."[5] This is a strong charge, and Paine said that he hoped it was not true. To see for ourselves, it is necessary to go beyond the books already published on the Karmapa issue. The Karmapa's property was actually held by a legal trust, not by Shamar personally. Indeed, this trust would later sue Tai Situ himself for illegally taking over the Karmapa's property, just the opposite of what the books mentioned by Paine claim.

Why Does Shamar Fight?

Does Shamar deserve this criticism? Has he acted improperly as his critics allege? Or, as he claims, has he defended the integrity of the office of the Karmapa and the purity of the Karma Kagyu lineage as was the duty of the Shamarpa, at risk to his reputation and even to his personal safety? Is he fit to recognize the seventeenth Karmapa? This book will examine his actions as well as his views as a way to understand the Karmapa controversy and corruption in Tibetan Buddhism. Without Shamar to oppose the Dalai Lama's candidate, there would be no Karmapa controversy, so understanding Shamar's motives is crucial. Therefore, we will hear from him many times throughout our investigation.

Here, let us begin with the basic issue of the Karmapa controversy: If the Dalai Lama has chosen the Karmapa already, why does Shamar insist on opposing him?

"I believe that the Karma Kagyu should be able to choose its own spiritual leader in the traditional way," Shamar told me. "Ogyen Trinley was not chosen the way the Karmapa should have been, but through political interference from the Tibetan exile government of the Dalai Lama, the government of China, and many others. All the other religious schools of Tibet are able to choose their leaders on their own. Why can't we choose ours? His Holiness Dalai Lama is putting politics before religion in this case.

"Because his devotees in foreign countries are not in the habit of questioning his actions, they support His Holiness Dalai Lama in this case. I call such followers 'package believers.' They follow the Dalai Lama because he is a Buddhist teacher and leader of Tibetans, so that is all they need to know. They just accept the whole package without investigating for themselves whether what His Holiness does is really right in this case. For example, if I had a house, and the Dalai Lama wanted to take it for himself, these package believers among his devotees would say that I am wrong to protect my property or even to complain, and that he is right to take it.

"I understand when Tibetans feel this way; their livelihood may depend on being on good terms with the Tibetan exile administration in India. Maybe they would lose their job if they questioned the Dalai Lama's right to choose the Karmapa. But for people around the world, this is an unhealthy development in Buddhism. If one man is so admired around the world that he can do anything he wants without fair scrutiny, then he is effectively a dictator. There is no oversight. And, if the Karma Kagyu school cannot choose its own leader, does this set a precedent for the other religious schools of Tibet? Will the Dalai Lama choose their leaders too?"

To outsiders, this may seem like strong language for a Tibetan lama to use to describe the man who is perhaps the world's most revered spiritual leader, the Dalai Lama. At this point, perhaps it is best to keep an open mind. Later, we will have the chance to place Shamar's criticism in context as we learn how he has acted in the course of the Karmapa dispute.

For now, let us consider Shamar's main premise, as he explains it: "Dharma is about thinking for yourself. It is not about automatically following a teacher in all things, no matter how respected that teacher may be. More than anyone else, Buddhists should respect other people's rights—their human rights and their religious freedom."

2 THE PLACE OF POWER

A Cloister of Ghosts

I had mixed feelings about going to Rumtek, the exile monastery of the
Karmapas, in October 2004. I knew that in the sixties and seventies,
Rumtek had been the functioning headquarters of the Karma Kagyu.
Then, the sixteenth Karmapa had set the tone. Some recent visitors have
reported that Rumtek remains a place of great activity. "That Rumtek is
an active, living monastery is immediately apparent," Australian novelist
Gaby Naher wrote after her visit in October 2003.[1]

According to the current Rumtek management, the monastery is
a bustling place of religious activity.[2] One hundred and fifty monks rise
at five o'clock in the morning daily to memorize Buddhist texts; study
Tibetan and English; learn to make ritual offerings known as *torma* or play
musical instruments; and perform tantric ritual ceremonies. Students at
the monk's college regularly study the *Kangyur* and *Tengyur*, respectively,
the scriptures and traditional commentaries of the Buddhist canon. At
special times in the year, the Rumtek monks celebrate festivals including
Losar, the Tibetan new year; the Buddha's birthday (when they recite
one hundred million mantras); and the Yarney, the summer rainy season
retreat. The monks also perform a ceremony on June 26 of each year—
Karmapa candidate Ogyen Trinley's birthday—beseeching him to live a
long life for the benefit of his students and all sentient beings.

But lamas who lived at Rumtèk before the monastery changed
hands in 1993 told me a different story. They said that after the takeover,
the school has operated only sporadically and that monks' discipline has
become lax. They claimed that many monks stayed on at Rumtek just for

free room and board. They warned me that the monastery had "lost its blessing" and had become desanctified due to the misdeeds of its new management.

For an outsider, if this were true, what would it feel like? Would the monastery seem like a government office where employees suffer their shifts in sullen silence, their eyes on the clock for quitting time? Or would it be more like a Sunday school run by a den of thieves, with clerical robes covering powerful physiques and a hint of back-room nastiness?

I thought that it was possible that the warnings I had received about Rumtek were exaggerated. I did not imagine that the monastery would be managed by local thugs running a floating mahjong game in a secret room behind the altar. Could a Tibetan monastery in India really be so bad? At least the monks there were safely out of Chinese control and could live free of government restrictions or influence. Surely, they would be engaged in the traditional activities of a Buddhist cloister in a free country. They would be performing ancient rituals, studying scripture, and teaching each other the sublime philosophy of Shakyamuni Buddha, the way to end all suffering for all beings for all time. Even if this was done amateurishly, or without much school spirit, I could not imagine how it would be bad.

Yet, the notion of "blessing" being present or absent nagged at me. I wondered how much of the grandeur of the late Karmapa's reign remained at the monastery he built. To find out, I made the trip into Sikkim with Harrison Pemberton, an American philosophy professor.

A Kingdom Disenchanted

We entered Sikkim through the town of Rangpo, coming up from West Bengal. Sikkim is India's second-smallest state, larger than Rhode Island but smaller than Connecticut and with a population of about half a million. At a couple of tourist offices just over the state line, we arranged for the permit that all foreigners need to enter the former Buddhist kingdom.

Only in 2005, a year after our visit and thirty years after India annexed Sikkim in 1975, did India's northern neighbor China officially recognize that the place was legally a state of India. To signify this, before 2005, Chinese maps continued to depict an independent Sikkim. China's attitude made the Indians nervous about who entered the state. Indeed, after fighting two border wars with China in the sixties, the Indians still consider all the states along the line of the Himalayas to be sensitive for national defense, and they like to monitor and limit foreign visitors, to keep out spies or agents provocateurs.

The Indians had good reason to be nervous. In the sixties, the Indian army clashed with the Chinese in the Chumbi Valley, just a few dozen miles from Rumtek. The military restricted access to the whole area and tourists could only visit Sikkim for a few days after obtaining a special permit. In the last few years, as tensions with China have decreased, the government has relaxed its restrictions. Today tourists can easily visit Sikkim for a couple of weeks with a free pass granted in a few minutes at the state line. But India still keeps a close eye on threats to its peaceful control of Sikkim, foreign and domestic.

Once inside Sikkim most travelers to Rumtek pass through the state capital Gangtok. Disappointingly for the visitor, the town's traditional mountain architecture has mostly given way to gimcrack concrete boxes built in the seventies and eighties. Yet, the otherwise charmless city of 50,000 at an elevation of 5,480 feet is notable not only for its spectacular views over the steep valley of the Rangit River, but also for its cleanliness.

In an attempt to win the hearts and minds of the Sikkimese after annexation, the Indian government has lavished subsidies on the local administration and tax breaks on businesses. This has given Sikkim, which competes with the neighboring kingdom of Bhutan for the tourist slogan "the Switzerland of the Himalayas," a prosperous feel missing in the areas of India and Nepal that also border it. Gangtok, like other towns in Sikkim, boasts newly paved streets with sidewalks, spacious shops, and a conspicuous absence of street-people and beggars.

From Gangtok, the drive to Rumtek takes about forty-five minutes on steep, winding roads in reasonably good repair by Indian standards. Like the main highway connecting Sikkim with the rest of India, most local roads in Sikkim also benefit from generous support by the Indian central government. This creates jobs and keeps Sikkimese drivers happy, perhaps buying some loyalty for India. But New Delhi also views good mountain roads as part of its military deterrent near the contested frontier with China. India makes it clear that it can speed troops and equipment into defensive positions along the Sikkimese-Tibetan border on a few hours' notice.

Approaching the Stronghold

Arriving from the capital, the tiny hamlet of Rumtek lay just outside the monastery. There we saw Tibetan restaurants offering *momos* (dumplings) and *thukpa* (thick meat and noodle soup) at low prices even for India, along with modest guest houses and gift shops selling film and curios. As in Gangtok, many shops sported oval window decals picturing Ogyen Trinley with the Dalai Lama, calling on the Indian government to let the Karmapa go to Rumtek. "To the locals," Gaby Naher wrote in her book on the Karmapa after seeing these stickers, "or so it seems, the Karmapa is the closest thing to a local hero cum Hollywood star they have."[3]

Yet, it was clear that not everyone was a member of the young lama's fan club. The decals were conspicuously absent from other shops, showing a continued schism in the village. Some of the houses had new tin roofs, while others had roofs covered in rust. We learned that the new roofs were purchased by supporters of Ogyen Trinley, with money they had received from the Rokpa Trust of Switzerland. Rokpa, a two-million-dollar charity, was founded in the 1980s by Akong Rinpoche and run by Akong's student Lea Weiler, a former actress in Switzerland. In late 1991, a year and a half before the takeover of Rumtek, Rokpa began distributing monthly payments to sponsor families in the village as well as monks in the monastery, according to monks living at Rumtek at the time.

The bringer of this largesse, Akong Rinpoche, was recognized as the second incarnation of a *ngakpa*, or lay tantric practitioner, from a small village temple in eastern Tibet. In the sixties, Akong worked at a school for Tibetan lamas in New Delhi set up by the Englishwoman Frieda Bedi, who would later become a nun at Rumtek under the name Gelongma Palmo. One of the students at the school was Chogyam Trungpa, with whom Akong developed a friendship. Later, Akong became Trungpa's attendant, and accompanied Trungpa to England when he received a scholarship to Oxford in 1963.

Afterwards, the two remained in the United Kingdom and founded the Samye Ling Tibetan Center in Scotland in 1967. After a falling out with Akong in the late sixties, Trungpa left for the United States in 1970, leaving Akong in charge at Samye Ling. In the seventies, Akong became close to Tai Situ, the third-ranking Karma Kagyu lama and a dynamic, ambitious leader. In the eighties, Akong served as Situ's representative in China.

The Rokpa payments were welcomed at Rumtek but they came with strings attached. Akong made it clear that the recipients were to be prepared to help Situ Rinpoche in the future. When the time came to take sides in the Karmapa controversy, families and monks who did not support Situ's Karmapa candidate Ogyen Trinley were cut off.

From the village, we entered the Rumtek complex. Like a medieval stronghold, the seventy-five-acre compound had two thick walls and two entrance gates. The inner wall surrounded the monastery proper, forming a courtyard around the main temple, topped by the residence of the sixteenth Karmapa. Behind was the shedra, or monk's college. Up the hill was an isolated building for monks to perform the traditional closed retreat of three years, three months, three weeks, and three days.

Polite guards, on loan from the Archeological Survey of India, patrolled the grounds and, at the end of the path, ran a metal detector at the entrance to the main courtyard. We noted a couple dozen guards in all parts of the monastery. Perhaps the security would not have met the standards of Washington Dulles or London Heathrow airports, and if a visitor wanted to smuggle in equipment for mischief he could probably do so without too much ingenuity.

But we were not used to seeing monasteries in India with metal-detectors or armed guards of any kind. We wondered who the guards were trying to protect from whom? "They were trying to stop the monks from burning down the monastery," Shamar Rinpoche later told us. Since Shamar and the late Karmapa's monks had been kicked out of the monastery eleven years earlier by some of those same monks we saw at Rumtek, we would have taken his opinion with a grain of salt, had we not seen for ourselves how the monks at Rumtek now appeared to live.

Near the front gate was the monastery's administrative office. It was locked and empty. Was this where Gyaltsab Rinpoche, the lama in charge of Rumtek for the past ten years, was supposed to work? Gyaltsab is one of the highest reincarnate lamas in the Karma Kagyu, and one of the major players in the Karmapa dispute. Two of his earlier incarnations who lived in the seventeenth century had official roles as regents of the Karmapa's monastery at Tsurphu near Lhasa, and gyaltsab means "regent" in Tibetan. But subsequent incarnations had no administrative role at the Karmapa's monastery until the current twelfth Gyaltsab, born in 1954, took over in 1993 from the administration that had run the monastery since the sixteenth Karmapa's death in 1981. When the sixteenth Karmapa moved his seat from Tsurphu in Tibet to Rumtek in Sikkim, he made an arrangement to manage the monastery after his death. In 1962, a group of families who accompanied the Karmapa from Tibet collected 2.5 million Indian rupees (about $525,000) as a donation for the Karmapa to apply towards construction of Rumtek and his other activities. On the advice of his disciples active in the Gangtok business community, to safeguard these funds, the Karmapa put them into a legal trust. In order to form the group under Indian law, the Karmapa signed the original title deed for the Karmapa Charitable Trust at New Delhi's diplomatic mission to the still independent kingdom of Sikkim.

Though not specifically written with Tibetan lamas in mind, Indian law contains a provision for "charitable trusts" that allows reincarnate lamas to safeguard their assets in the period between their death and the time when their reincarnation reaches age twenty-one. The sixteenth Karmapa established the registered office of his trust at the Calcutta residence of Ashok Chand Burman, an Indian industrialist and devotee. The Karmapa himself was the sole trustee, and he appointed seven laymen to the trust's board, including Burman and the two top Rumtek secretaries at the time, Damchoe Yongdu and the Karmapa's nineteen-year-old nephew Topga Rinpoche.

Originally the trust board consisted solely of laymen, but in the 1980s Shamar and two of the highest ranking Karma Kagyu lamas, Tai Situ and Jamgon Kongtrul, joined the group to replace members who had died or resigned. The Karmapa Trust ran Rumtek until the monastery changed management in 1993 and the Trust was evicted from its office on the monastery grounds.

After 1993, for a brief period Tai Situ Rinpoche ran the monastery together with Gyaltsab Rinpoche, until the Indian government banned Situ from reentering India on national security grounds in August 1994. The ban was the culmination of a decade-long Indian intelligence investigation of Tai Situ's activities in China, which I will discuss in more detail later in the book. With Situ gone, Gyaltsab took charge at Rumtek. In 1998, the Karmapa Trust launched a court battle to regain control of Rumtek. Gyaltsab represented Ogyen Trinley's followers in the case, and for several years claimed that he spoke for the Karmapa's *labrang*, or monastic administration.

Traditionally in Tibet, monastic labrangs were fiercely independent. The Karmapa, Shamar, Tai Situ, and Gyaltsab all had separate labrangs, run as their own monastic corporations (though Shamar's was disbanded in 1792 as punishment by the government of Central Tibet, as we will see in chapter 7). Each lama lived at his own monastery rather than at the monastery of the Karmapa. In exile, each lama kept his labrang. But, in a break with traditional practice, the sixteenth Karmapa invited several high lamas to live at Rumtek for a period as children instead of being raised by their own labrangs at their own monasteries. In exile, these child-lamas did not yet have their own monasteries, and the Karmapa hoped that raising them at Rumtek would provide them with the qualifications— tantric empowerments given by the Karmapa himself—and valuable personal contacts to help the young lamas succeed in the future.

Gyaltsab Rinpoche was one of these lamas, and he moved out of Rumtek in the 1980s to establish his own monastery. He paid occasional visits to Rumtek in the late eighties and early nineties, but he only returned to live at the monastery in 1993, after he and Situ took over the cloister. Recently, Gyaltsab has distanced himself from the monastery's management. Lawyers for the Karmapa Trust surmise that Gyaltsab may be worried that if valuables are found to be missing from Rumtek in the future, he could be held responsible in court. For whatever reason, recently he officially retracted an earlier claim that the Gyaltsabs were traditionally part of the Karmapa's labrang. But according to the monks living at Rumtek when we visited, Gyaltsab was still supposed to be in charge at the monastery.

We asked about Gyaltsab, but monks told us he wasn't living at Rumtek. They said he had his own monastery at Ralang, a four-hour jeep drive away. Did Gyaltsab Rinpoche come to Rumtek much? The monks said no, he has his own monastery, "Rumtek is for the Karmapa." Who was running Rumtek, then? The monks couldn't say, they just repeated that Rumtek was the Karmapa's monastery. But since neither Karmapa candidate has been allowed to take control of Rumtek or even visit the monastery (New Delhi has banned Orgyen Trinley from Sikkim; Thaye Dorje's status is unclear, but he has not tried to enter the state), we wondered if anyone was really in charge, or if the cloister was sailing aimlessly into perhaps dangerous waters, a ship without a captain?

Inside the front gate, we entered a large dusty courtyard. Monks' cells formed its perimeter, and many of their windows featured the oval decals seen in Gangtok and in the village featuring Ogyen Trinley with the Dalai Lama. We thought that the stickers indicated a politicization of the monastery that probably would not have sat well with the late sixteenth Karmapa, who took a dim view of lama politicking in general.

But when we visited Rumtek, sectarian politics seemed to be a higher priority than facilities maintenance. We did not have to look hard to see large patches of peeling paint and brown stains on the walls from water seepage and mold. Some of the window panes in the monks' rooms were cracked or shattered. We climbed up to the walkway on the roof of the monks' rooms, overlooking the courtyard. On the roof was a butter-lamp shed. It also had broken windows, and its corrugated iron roof was riddled with holes from rust. Next to the shed was a building listed on the map as a VIP Gallery. The dust on its half-built cinder-block walls indicated that it had been under construction for some time.

From the roof, we observed the courtyard at mid-morning. Dozens of monks loitered in the sun, and few appeared to be engaged in religious activity of any kind. At other monasteries, we were used to seeing young monks practicing debate. Tibetan monastic debate is an intellectual contest with an athletic component that makes it very photogenic. One monk stands while his opponent is seated. When the standing monk makes a point, offering, for example, a proof that "all beings have Buddha nature," he will slide his right hand over his left, almost taunting his opponent, as if to say "ha!" But there were no monks debating at Rumtek when we visited.

We were also used to monks poring over the long pages of *pechas*, loose-leaf books of rectangular pages printed on wooden blocks with scripture or ceremonies in Tibetan. But at Rumtek, there were no *pecha* books in evidence. The younger monks sat in small groups on the dusty concrete veranda in front of their rooms. The boys giggled and seemed to tease each other. The teenagers appeared more somber, quietly talking. Stern-faced adult monks leisurely crossed the courtyard, occasionally stopping to bark at a group of young monks, apparently not in any hurry to transact their daily business.

An ornate temple stood at the center of the courtyard. Unlike the other buildings in the courtyard, the temple exterior was freshly painted and scrubbed. Inside was a cavernous shrine room with seats for the monastic sangha, or monk's body, a giant golden Buddha in front, and ritual items all around. One thousand smaller Buddha statues occupied shelves near the altar. The shrine room was free of political decals, and appeared to be preserved well as a sacred space. An eight- or ten-year-old monk ushered us in to make a circuit clockwise around the room. Silk costumes for the "lama dances," ritual plays put on by the monks as part of the liturgical calendar, were draped over some thrones against the left wall.

A throne in the center of the room held a large framed photograph of Ogyen Trinley, dressed in the traditional silks of the Karmapa. Behind, on the altar, leaned two smaller portraits of the Dalai Lama. Until Ogyen Trinley's supporters gained control of Rumtek, portraits of the Dalai Lama, for centuries head of the government of Central Tibet but not a member of the Karma Kagyu school, had never been displayed at the Karmapa's monastery.

Above the shrine room sat the quarters of the sixteenth Karmapa, with a golden roof. It was not open to the public, but we could see from the ground, and from the roof on top of the monks' rooms, that it was a large suite of rooms offering a panoramic view of the monastery grounds. The exterior was plated liberally in gold and it shone brilliantly in the clear Himalayan sun. There, the sixteenth Karmapa lived until his death in 1981, though he traveled a great deal in his later years.

We then left the main monastery area, passing through a door manned by Indian guards, and out towards the Nalanda Institute, the monk's school. In a grassy area in front of the gate to the school, a couple of monks teased a young cowherd, kicking clods of dirt at him and laughing. The large modern building, perhaps five floors high, abutted a hillside. Though it was October, school was not in session, and the classrooms and offices were empty. The only monks in the area were three solidly-built men in their early twenties who sat on the school's front steps and glared at us in an unscholarly way.

Finally, we went to see the famous Golden Stupa, a traditional Tibetan pagoda holding the cremation relics of the sixteenth Karmapa. It took about an hour to find a monk in his fifties with the authority to ask the Indian guard at the entrance to the stupa-chamber to unlock the door. The monk ushered us into a dark hallway, and then, through another door, to the room with the stupa itself. A glass wall separated the stupa from a small area where another, younger monk sold maps and postcards. The older monk unlocked the glass door, and moved us into the stupa area. At his urging, we jogged once around the stupa, and then back out the glass door.

That was it. Twenty seconds and one athletic circumambulation were all that we were allowed with the Golden Stupa of the sixteenth Karmapa. We bought a map and some postcards and then made our way outside.

A City on a Hill

Apparently, it was not always like this at Rumtek. When the sixteenth Karmapa led the Karma Kagyu lamas out of Tibet in 1959, his first priority was to preserve the teachings of his school for future generations. He founded three main institutions at Rumtek, operating on a single campus, like other monasteries in the Tibetan tradition, but on a larger scale than at any other cloister established in exile at the time.

The first was the monastery proper, with a main temple for performing ceremonies and quarters for more than two hundred monks. Here the Karmapa gave the principal tantric empowerments—ceremonies preliminary to starting a Vajrayana ritual practice—of the Karma Kagyu to monks and lay people alike, and the monks' community regularly performed the *pujas*, or worship ceremonies of the Karma Kagyu liturgy. They invoked the wrathful deity Mahakala to protect the lineage, the bodhisattva Avalokiteshvara to help all beings live with compassion, and other figures of the mystical Vajrayana pantheon, each bringing a particular spiritual benefit to the local community of devotees and to all living beings.

Among Tibetan monasteries in exile, Rumtek had a reputation in the Karmapa's time for a high standard of discipline. Its monks were expected to adhere to their vows, particularly those relating to chastity, which were not well enforced at some other cloisters.

The second main facility at Rumtek was the *shedra*, or monks' school, known as the Nalanda Institute. There monks studied the traditional Eight Great Treatises that the eighth Karmapa Mikyo Dorje established in the sixteenth century as the Karma Kagyu philosophical curriculum. These treasured books covered the subjects of the Madhyamaka (philosophy of the "middle way" between realism and nihilism); the Prajnaparamita (the supreme wisdom of *shunyata* or openness); the Vinaya (rules for ethical living); the Abhidharma (higher logic), the Buddhist theory of perception; and the philosophy of Buddhist tantra expounded by ancient Indian pandits. The institute's day began at four o'clock in the morning and continued until about ten at night, six days a week for a challenging nine-year course of studies.

Khenpo Chodrak Tenphel Rinpoche was the head teacher at the school and the abbot of Rumtek from the mid-1970s until supporters of Ogyen Trinley took over the monastery in 1993. Now in his late fifties, Chodrak is one of the ranking scholars of the Karma Kagyu. He is also a distant relative of the late sixteenth Karmapa, and thus of Shamar Rinpoche as well. Ever since the takeover, Chodrak has been based in New Delhi, at the Karmapa International Buddhist Institute (KIBI), a school set up to help students mostly from Europe, the Americas, and eastern Asia study the classic texts of the Karma Kagyu tradition in translation. When he is not at KIBI, Chodrak travels to dharma centers around the world that are loyal to Shamar Rinpoche. He is usually accompanied by his interpreter of two decades, a Swedish devotee named Anne Ekselius.

Chodrak remembers the monk's school at Rumtek when he was in charge. "For all those years, until 1992, the Nalanda Institute functioned very well. Every year our students went for six weeks to three major Gelugpa institutes of learning reestablished in exile, Sera, Drepung, and Ganden, in order to debate and exchange views. The Nalanda Institute in Rumtek had a very good reputation as a center for higher Buddhist studies."[4] Among lamas, the educated logicians of the Dalai Lama's Gelug school, known as *geshes*, are considered some of the most formidable debaters of the Tibetan tradition.

From the early 1970s through 1993 a total of twenty-eight students grad-uated with the degree of *khenpo*, equivalent to a Ph.D. or doctor of divinity. Most of these students went on to teach Buddhist philosophy in India or abroad.

The last component of the Rumtek complex was the Samten Yi Wang Ling retreat center. Isolated from the other buildings at Rumtek, here monks performed the traditional long Tibetan meditation retreat. Retreatants would enter as a class of sixteen or seventeen monks and complete their days together, which were even longer than those of the shedra monks. Seven days a week the retreat center program began at three o'clock in the morning and concluded at eleven at night.

The program focused on realizing meditative power through a deep connection between body and mind, and sleep deprivation was a part of the training. Monks spent every night sitting up in wooden meditation boxes, yielding a light sleep considered ideal for the meditation practice of dream yoga, or lucid dreaming. The monks started their retreat with the Ngondro, four preliminary practices to prepare them for higher meditations. Then they learned various tantric visualization pujas—Dorje Phagmo, Khorlo Demchog, and Gyalwa Gyamtso—along with the Six Yogas of Naropa. After completing a retreat, monks would preach and perform pujas. Like the shedra graduates, retreat lamas worked both in India and abroad.

Foreigners at Rumtek

The three main components of Rumtek, the monastery, the shedra, and the retreat center, drew monks from all over the Himalayas and other parts of Asia to practice and study Buddhism under the sixteenth Karmapa. It was difficult for foreigners to visit during the seventies and eighties as a result of first Sikkimese and then Indian government security restrictions in Sikkim, but those who did get one of the coveted Sikkimese visas or Indian permits and managed to reach Rumtek express an abiding awe at the scale of activity under the Karmapa's benevolent dictatorship.

Ole and Hannah Nydahl were two of the first Westerners to visit Rumtek and become students of the sixteenth Karmapa. The Danish couple met the sixteenth Karmapa in Kathmandu in the late sixties. Beginning in the early 1970s with a single dharma center in Copenhagen, where they hosted the Dalai Lama on his first visit to Europe, the Nydahls have founded a network of more than four hundred Diamond Way Buddhist centers around the world.

A staunch partisan of Shamar, Ole Nydahl has been a lightning rod for controversy, criticized by followers of Ogyen Trinley for his flamboyant style of Buddhist preaching and for his unconventional personal life. Ole is a tall, fit man in his sixties with a blond buzz-cut that gives him the look of a Teutonic action hero. His energy comes out in his charismatic, vernacular teaching style, a frenetic schedule of world travel, and a fondness for extreme sports. It took him months to recover from a near fatal skydiving accident in 2003.

"His was an overpowering 'love bomb' approach," wrote Lea Terhune in *Karmapa: The Politics of Reincarnation*, "with whiff of the con artist about it, but his warm and friendly energy often neutralized negative perceptions of his character."[5]

Whatever Terhune and other Westerners who knew Ole Nydahl thought of him, it is clear that the sixteenth Karmapa placed great trust in the Nydahls and had a special, close relationship with Ole in particular. For his part, Ole Nydahl has credited the Karmapa with reforming him from a boxer and casual marijuana dealer into a devoted, if unconventional, student and teacher of Buddhism. In the late sixties, Ole Nydahl was a short-tempered street-fighter from Copenhagen who had gotten into buying hashish in Nepal and selling it back home in Denmark. Shamar told me the story of how the Nydahls, in Nepal on one of their supply expeditions, first met the sixteenth Karmapa in Kathmandu in 1969.

"Hippies from the West flooded into Kathmandu. Nepali traders brought all kinds of Tibetan goods from Lhasa and were selling them in Kathmandu, especially clothing. So we used to see hippie women wearing men's lama robes and hippie men wearing a Tibetan women's *chuba*. They were smoking a lot of marijuana. Among them one young man and young girl wearing jackets and strange-looking canteens from Afghanistan always came to the top of our monastery on Swayambhu hill, where many people were waiting. The woman did not talk much but the man was a big, smiling man who shook hands with everybody. He squeezed their hands hard and people screamed. This couple was Hannah and Ole, and they always came to Swayambhu at that time. Whenever His Holiness Karmapa came out and saw them there, he would joke with Ole, shake hands and then pull away and scream, as if Ole had broken his hand. He was always playing with him.

"After some weeks, a friendship developed between His Holiness Karmapa and the Danish man. Ole would help Gyalwa Karmapa walk down the long narrow staircases from the top of the hill, holding his hand. A very strong boy he was. Then it happened that this hippie boy was always there helping His Holiness, because he was a fat man and the stairs were all long and narrow and tricky. It naturally developed that Ole would be there to assist him.

"One day His Holiness did a very dangerous thing. On the east side of Swayambhu there is a long stone staircase, very steep. Karmapa and people started walking down. Gyalwa Karmapa was very naive. All of a sudden, he just jumped up on Ole's back. If Ole fell, both of them would start rolling down head over heels on the stone steps. When everybody saw this, they screamed. They were looking on very scared. But then, with His Holiness Karmapa on his back, Ole managed to keep his balance. His legs were shaking, but Ole started to carry Karmapa down the hundreds of steps carved into the hillside. The crowd started cheering the blond boy. After that, all the Nepali and Tibetan Buddhist people in Kathmandu started to like Ole."

The Nydahls first visited Rumtek in 1970 when they were in their early twenties. They spent the next few years shuttling back and forth between Rumtek and Europe. In the summer of 1973, Ole requested and received authorization from the sixteenth Karmapa to give the Buddhist refuge vow to his students in Europe, thus allowing them to officially become Buddhists. In 1974, the sixteenth Karmapa stayed at the Nydahls' Copenhagen center. During the seventies, Ole and Hannah returned to Rumtek with hundreds of European visitors to receive initiations from the Karmapa and study with his lamas. They brought donations of clothing and money.

In his characteristically ebullient style, Ole Nydahl has rhapsodized on his time at Rumtek during the time of the sixteenth Karmapa: "Actually, if anything was ever holy, it was Rumtek. I can tell you that on the way to Rumtek, you would often have two black birds flying in front of you the whole way; they would stop till you came closer and then they would fly on again. Your dreams would be prophetic, there would be a blessing there, there would be a power there that you cannot express in words. You would come in, you would see H.H. the sixteenth Karmapa. You would see a man who could laugh so that you could hear it five houses away. You'd see a house of power, something you'd never seen before."[6]

In 1983, in his capacity as regent of the Karmapa's administration and after consulting with Kalu Rinpoche, an elderly and venerated lama of the Karma Kagyu, Shamar gave Ole the title of "lama." By this time, the Nydahls had founded dozens of dharma centers and Ole was busy giving presentations to large audiences in his native Denmark and in neighboring West Germany. But Shamar was not close to Ole during this period, and he often criticized the Dane for his habit of giving "blessings" by touching the tops of students' heads, a practice traditionally reserved for only the highest lamas.

Meanwhile, Hannah Nydahl kept a much lower profile than her husband. A tall, slim woman in her fifties, Hannah speaks half a dozen languages, including Tibetan. For three decades, she has helped Ole open dharma centers. She has also served as an interpreter for prominent lamas on foreign teaching tours, including Shamar, Jamgon Kongtrul, and Gyaltsab. Hannah contrasted her visits to Rumtek in the early seventies to her last visit there in 1995, when she tried to visit the stupa housing the ashes of the sixteenth Karmapa.

"In the early days, as outsiders, Rumtek felt like a very powerful place and a very strong place because of the sixteenth Karmapa's presence. He had people visiting nonstop, Indian generals, Sikkimese politicians, and many others. They respected him a lot. They were also doing pujas inside of their huge shrine room. We learned many things; we practiced as much as we could. In the old days, the sixteenth Karmapa kept quite strict discipline. Compared to other exile monasteries, there was a high standard at Rumtek. He had the monastery, the shedra, and the retreat place. You could see that the people who were trained there when they came out were quite well educated. I think all that is gone now.

"I tried to visit again in 1995. I wanted to go to the sixteenth Karmapa's stupa. Rumtek had already changed a lot. It was terrible. Actually, there was one time when I came alone, it was a big story, and some monks didn't allow me to come up to the place where the stupa of the late Karmapa is. They tried to block me from going up there. How could they stop me from visiting the Karmapa's stupa? So I had to go to the office and get an escort. You couldn't recognize the place, the whole atmosphere was gone, and it was rather depressing.

"Back in the seventies, the Karmapa used his influence in Sikkim to extend our visas. We took the refuge to become Buddhists and a *genyen* vow to observe ethics for lay people; we took them both in a ceremony where he prepared everything just for the two of us. We even shaved our heads for it. That's how strong it was for us. We just gave ourselves to him without knowing what it really meant. It was very uncomfortable; we had to kneel for an hour because he did it in the old way, very slowly, without leaving anything out. After that, he let us come to see him again and again. He also sent different lamas to explain things to us.

"There were not many foreigners in the seventies. There was this British nun Gelongma Palmo. She used to be married to a Sikh, and was called Frieda Bedi. She ran the school for young Tibetan lamas in New Delhi where Chogyam Trungpa was a student, before he went to Oxford. She was very proper, very British, and very kind. She would translate sometimes for the Karmapa and the other lamas since she knew some Tibetan.[7]

"Ole and I started leading group trips to Rumtek after 1975. The lamas were all quite poor at that time. We were not rich either, we had a very small travel budget, but we got to know everybody. So later, we could do some good for the monks and others who lived at Rumtek. We used to come in big groups nearly every year, starting with 50 and going up to 108 people. We would bring a lot of second-hand clothes, all kinds of things they could use. We felt like we had become a part of Rumtek."

For the Nydahls and other outsiders who visited Rumtek in the seventies and eighties, the monastery was the center of their Buddhist world. Under the benevolent dictatorship of the sixteenth Karmapa, the Karma Kagyu lineage had been successfully replanted there into the soil of exile. But the ghosts of a turbulent past continued to haunt the cloister. Unknown to the Karmapa, lamas and lay officials alike inside Rumtek were starting to establish relations with outsiders that would bring violence and discord to the Karmapa's cloister. To understand the threats to Rumtek that loomed in the seventies, we must travel back a thousand years into the Tibetan past.

History lives in certain parts of the world more than in others. Forward-looking places like New York or Los Angeles may display a casual apathy for history and an impatience with those who nurse grievances from the past. But this cannot be said for the American South, for example. There, blacks and whites of all backgrounds mention the War Between the States as if it was fought last month. Southerners sometimes seem to speak of Robert E. Lee and Stonewall Jackson as if they had personally glimpsed them galloping down Main Street on the way to their armies. Icons like the Stars and Bars still inspire strong emotions as today's Southerners battle to reconcile their present with their past.

We have seen a stronger resurrection of feuds of centuries past in places like Bosnia, Chechnya, Afghanistan, and Iraq. In the Balkans, a battle between Serbs and Muslims in the fourteenth century becomes a battle cry for today. The writer Christopher Hitchens has even opined that Osama bin Laden planned the 9/11 terrorist attacks to commemorate the defeat of the Ottoman Turkish armies outside the gates of Vienna by combined Christian forces under Jan Sobieski and Charles, Duke of Lorraine, on September 11, 1683.[8] Of course, this date carried little resonance for office workers in the Twin Towers or the Pentagon, but was known to many in the Moslem world—thus showing that Al Qaeda's "message" in the attacks was meant perhaps more for the home audience than for its victims in the United States.

As we cannot understand the conflict between the West and extremists in the Moslem world without some knowledge of history as it is seen in the Middle East, so we cannot understand Tibetans today without understanding some of their history. In particular, the sectarian and regional rifts found in the Tibetan exile community today have deep roots in the past. They go back half a millennium or more to the age when lamas contended with each other through force of arms for political rule in Tibet.

3   AN ANCIENT RIVALRY

Religious Schools Compete to Rule

Religious conflict was commonplace in old Tibet. In a violent battle for supremacy, the original religion of Tibet, Bon, was replaced as the dominant faith in Tibet by Buddhism after its arrival from India in the eighth century.[1] Beginning in the eleventh century, Tibetan Buddhism developed four schools that shared many beliefs but ran their own monasteries and passed down their own lineages of oral teachings: the Nyingma, Sakya, Kagyu, and Gelug. Over the centuries, Bon continued to maintain followers and incorporated many Buddhist elements, effectively evolving into a fifth school of the Vajrayana. Devotees of each school respected the tenets and historic masters of the other schools and frequently took teachings from lamas of different schools. But it would be naive to believe that these schools coexisted peacefully under an official regime of religious tolerance.

Though Tibetan culture was imbued with Buddhism at every level, history belies the Shangri-La image of Tibetan lamas and their followers living together in mutual tolerance and non-violent goodwill. Indeed, the situation was quite different. Old Tibet was much more like Europe during the religious wars of the Counter Reformation than a neighborhood in Berkeley, California where synagogue, mosque, church, and dharma center make cozy neighbors. During the European religious wars of the sixteenth and seventeenth centuries, forces of Protestant kings and princes fought armies of Catholic rulers or troops of the Church itself. Likewise, for hundreds of years in Tibet, lay followers of each religious school sometimes clashed with each other for control of the government of Central Tibet or rule over provincial areas. Lamas often had to defend their monasteries and other landholdings from supporters of the other schools.

Tibet before the Chinese invasion was not a unified country under a single government. Instead, like medieval France or Italy, it was a large area inhabited by people loosely connected by language, customs, and religion but ruled by local aristocrats or religious leaders. For the last few centuries, until 1959, Tibet consisted of three main areas, Central Tibet, Amdo, and Kham. As we have seen, Central Tibet was governed since the seventeenth century by the Dalai Lamas from their capital at Lhasa, and it included the provinces of U and Tsang plus the dry areas of western Tibet. Aside from Lhasa, its major city was Shigatse, on the Tsangpo River. The Tibet Autonomous Region created by the Chinese in the 1960s corresponds approximately to the area claimed by the old Central Tibetan government.

Amdo occupied the borderlands with China in the northeast, and was a sparsely populated area of grassland and desert. Here, the current Dalai Lama was born in 1935 to a family of subsistence farmers, and his early childhood was rustic, as depicted in the film *Kundun*. Nomads thrived in Amdo's lonely expanses. Today, Amdo is divided between the Chinese provinces of Gansu and Qinghai.

Finally, Kham was sandwiched between Central Tibet in the west and both the nation of Burma and the Chinese province of Sichuan in the east. For centuries its dozens of small feudal principalities were ruled by local kings and nobles who fiercely guarded their independence from each other—and from the Dalai Lamas and the Chinese emperors as well. Three great rivers emerge from their high mountain sources and pass through the lush, tree-covered gorges of Kham to water the fertile plains of Southeast Asia: the Yangtse, the Mekong, and the Salween. Verdant valleys nestled between haughty peaks hosted a rich farming area that gave Tibet its greatest warriors, bandits, and saints. For centuries Kham was the stronghold of the Karma Kagyu, hundreds of miles and a world apart from the Dalai Lama's capital at Lhasa. In the 1950s and 60s the Chinese incorporated most of Kham into the provinces of Sichuan and Yunnan.

Much of Tibetan history is the story of how the rulers of Central Tibet tried to extend their rule into the border areas of Amdo and Kham, or how the different religious schools of the Tibetan plateau came to rule the central provinces of U and Tsang. After the Bon kings began to convert to Buddhism in the ninth century, each of the four Buddhist schools controlled the government of Central Tibet, one after the other in succession. The sects either ruled directly, with their chief lama sitting on the throne, or indirectly, serving as priests to secular kings. And while some schools proved to be kinder, more tolerant rulers than others, each school used its political influence against its religious rivals from time to time.

The oldest school of Tibetan Buddhism is the Nyingma, or "First Wave" school, deriving from the original Buddhism brought by the Indian missionary Padmasambhava in the eighth century. He opened Tibet's first Buddhist monastery, Samye, in 779 A.D. The Nyingma is known for its homeless ascetics and "crazy yogis" who perform advanced tantric practices in caves and wander the countryside giving blessings though the lineage also boasts significant monasteries. Modern lamas including Dilgo Khyentse Rinpoche, Sogyal Rinpoche, and the American Lama Surya Das have made the Nyingma teaching of Dzogchen, an advanced form of meditation, well known in the West.

The earliest Buddhist lamas of Tibet, whose lineages later became the Nyingma school, exercised strong influence on the dynastic families that produced the first royal patrons of Buddhism in Tibet, the three "Dharma Kings" Songsten Gampo, Trisong Detsen, and Ralpachen. These kings worked to spread Buddhism and, at times, to repress the native Bon religion on behalf of Buddhist lamas during the often turbulent period of early Tibetan Buddhism.

Three hundred years after Buddhism first came to Tibet, three Sarma, or "Second Wave" schools appeared. The first of these was the Sakya school. In 1073, Khon Konchog Gyalpo founded Sakya monastery and the Tibetan Buddhist school of the same name. Perhaps the least-known Tibetan Buddhist school in the West, the Sakyas are renowned among Tibetans for their advanced scholarship of Buddhist philosophy and formidable skill in dialectics and debate.

A non-celibate order, the Sakyas pass along their succession from father to son or uncle to nephew. The Sakyas were the first lamas to make fruitful contact with the Mongols, who would prove so important in Tibetan history. In 1247 Kunga Gyaltsen, known as the Sakya Pandita for his knowledge of Sanskrit, met with the Mongol Prince Godan at his camp north of Tibet in the region of Lake Koko Nor, located in the present-day province of Gansu in northwestern China. Godan summoned the Sakya lama to preach to his people and, since the lama was also the most powerful political leader in Tibet, to surrender his country to Mongol rule and thus save it from a devastating invasion. For this the Sakya Pandita went down in history as a wise statesman.

Despite his role in history, to Tibetans the Sakya Pandita is less famous as a shrewd political leader than as an accomplished spiritual master, scholar, and man of letters. He is the author of the *Sakya Lekshe*, a handbook of ethical behavior for lay people that became a perennial classic, held up as a model of elegant Tibetan prose style.[2] The Sakya Pandita became the spiritual advisor of the Mongol chieftain.

A few years later, in 1251, Prince Godan appointed the Sakya Pandita's seventeen-year-old nephew Phagpa as Mongol viceroy of Tibet. Standing out in the country's history, Phagpa came to be known for his religious tolerance. Later, when Kublai Khan became Great Khan, he asked Phagpa to create an alphabet for the vast Eurasian empire of the Mongols, then at its peak, stretching from Russia to southern China. He also urged Phagpa to merge the other schools of Tibetan Buddhism into the Sakya school. However, as Tibetan historian Tsepon W.D. Shakabpa has written, "Phagpa insisted that the other sects be allowed to practice Buddhism in their own way. This brought Phagpa the support of many of the Tibetan priest-chieftains; however, the presence of several different sects in Tibet was to weaken the power of the Sakya ruling family in the years that followed."[3] For more than a century the Sakya lamas ruled Tibet as agents of the Mongols until replaced by followers of the Kagyu school.

Meanwhile, back to the eleventh century—around the time Kon Konchog Gyalpo founded Sakya monastery and a century before the Sakyas would take over the Tibetan government—the Kagyu or Oral Transmission school began in Tibet. The founder of the school, a stoutly built householder named Marpa the Translator, brought the teachings of the famously unconventional Indian yogis Tilopa and Naropa over the Himalayas from India. Marpa's most gifted student, Milarepa, became the greatest yogi of Tibet. A murderer who later devoted himself to ascetic practice in caves, Milarepa authored hundreds of songs that became classics of Tibetan literature.

The largest of the so-called "four great and eight lesser" sub-schools of the Kagyu, the Karma Kagyu, began when the first Karmapa Dusum

Khyenpa founded Tsurphu monastery in 1185. The school became known for the inspirational power of its most advanced teachers, principally the Karmapas. The next chapter discusses the origin of the Karmapas, and their most famous ritual object, the Vajra Mukut or Black Crown of enlightened action.

The Gelug school was the last of the four major schools of Buddhism to appear in Tibet. A charismatic scholar and preacher named Tsongkhapa founded the Gelugpas in the early fifteenth century. His successors as head of the school became the Dalai Lamas, and they, in turn, with Mongol assistance, came to rule over the government of Central Tibet in the seventeenth century, just as the Sakya lama Phagpa had done three centuries earlier. The rise of the Gelugpas led to a political rivalry between them and the Karma Kagyu school of the Karmapas that would last five hundred years and continue after the lamas went into exile in 1959.

This rivalry forms the background for the current Karmapa controversy, so we will learn more about it later in this chapter. Now, let us return to the Middle Ages and see how the Kagyu school came to rule Central Tibet and how they set the country on the path towards becoming a modern nation-state.

The Kagyu Takes its Turn

While four reincarnations of Karmapas built up the Karma Kagyu school, the Sakyas continued to rule the government of Central Tibet. At the time of the fourth Karmapa Rolpe Dorje (1340-83), Sakya rule ended and secular kings under the tutelage of the Kagyu school seized power. When the Mongol Yuan dynasty began to wane in China, the Mongols were no longer able to support their surrogates, the Sakya lamas, in Tibet. Knowing that Mongol cavalry would not ride to the rescue if the Sakya Lama were attacked, various subordinates began to contend for the throne.

The last of these, Wangtson, came to power by murdering his predecessor in 1358. He was never able to consolidate his hold on power, and later the same year he was overthrown in turn by a regional governor named Jangchup Gyaltsen. In a vain attempt to preserve the appearance of imperial rule over Tibet, the last Yuan emperor Shundi hastily conferred approval on Jangchup's coup and awarded him the imperial title Tai Situ (He should not be confused with the Tai Situ Rinpoche of the Karma

Kagyu; "Tai Situ" was a common title in the imperial bureaucracy, equivalent to "chief secretary.") Jangchup Gyaltsen's line became the Pagmotru dynasty, the first of three royal dynasties to rule under the tutelage of the Kagyu school. The Pagmotru ruled until 1435. Afterwards, four kings of the Rinpung dynasty ruled in succession from 1435 to 1565, followed by three Tsangpa kings who ruled from 1565 until 1642. The Tsangpa kings were followers not only of the Kagyu school, but were personal devotees of the Karmapas. Playing a careful game of diplomacy with the deposed but still troublesome Mongols as well as with the new Ming dynasty (1368-1644) rulers in China, these kings governed Tibet relatively free from foreign control. Under the influence of the Kagyu school, Tibet enjoyed a three-hundred-year window of independence and peace between two periods of domination by the Mongols.

The Gelugpas Rise and Struggle for Power with the Kagyus

As we saw earlier, the last Buddhist school to appear in Tibet was the Gelug order of the Dalai Lamas. Tsongkhapa (1357-1419) was a skillful debater and charismatic preacher who lived at the same time as the fifth Karmapa Deshin Shegpa of the Kagyu school. Tsongkhapa founded the Gelug school when he established the Monlam Chemno, or Great Prayer Festival, in Lhasa in 1409. Known informally as the "Yellow Hats," the Gelugpas were famous for their skill at scholarship and debate, like the masters of the Sakya school.

But unlike the Sakyas, the Gelugpas placed great emphasis on celibate monastic life. Many writers have claimed that the Gelugpas were a reforming school of Buddhism, seeking to clean up the lax morality said to have infected the other schools. By analogy, the Gelug rise would be like the Protestant Reformation in Europe a century earlier, and Tsongkhapa would be Tibet's Martin Luther.[4] Other historians have disagreed, however, claiming that Tsongkhapa and the early Dalai Lamas placed no special emphasis on monastic discipline compared to the other religious schools. In any event, under Tsongkhapa's dynamic leadership, the Gelug school grew in political influence and established large monasteries in Central Tibet that began to rival those of the Karma Kagyu.

Tibetan historian Shakabpa has claimed that the popularity of Tsongkhapa, the first Dalai Lamas, and other Gelugpa teachers threatened the dominance of the Kagyu.[5] In response, the Tibetan royal governments who followed the Kagyu suppressed the rising Gelugpas to protect the Kagyu from spiritual competition.

The major traditional histories of Tibet, including the fifth Dalai Lama's own account of these years, contradict this claim.[6] During Tsongkhapa's lifetime, the Pagmotru dynasty of kings, patrons of the Kagyu school, ruled Central Tibet. The Pagmotru kings were succeeded by the Rinpung dynasty in 1435, whose kings followed the Kagyu school as their predecessors had, and in addition took the Karmapa as their personal spiritual advisor, as we have seen. The fourth Shamarpa Chokyi Drakpa Yeshe Pal Zangpo (1453-1524) even served a term of four years as regent during the minority of one of the Rinpung kings, and was known by the royal title Chen Nga initiated by the Pagmotru kings.

Near the end of the fifteenth century, monks from a nearby Gelugpa monastery sacked a temple that the seventh Karmapa Chodrag Gyatso (1454-1506) had begun in Lhasa. This angered the Rinpung king. In response, in 1498 the king forbade the Yellow Hats from participating in the annual Monlam prayer festival that their own founder had inaugurated ninety years earlier.

Meanwhile, a Gelugpa lama who was an energetic evangelist, Sonam Gyatso, attracted the attention of the Tumed Mongol chief Altan Khan. After the fall in 1368 of the Mongol Yuan dynasty, which controlled both China and Tibet, the Mongols split up into numerous warring bands. Their leaders competed with each other to seek influence among the nations of Inner Asia, including Tibet. There, Mongol leaders adopted prominent lamas as their spiritual advisors. In 1578 Altan invited Sonam to his camp to preach. There, he offered the lama the title Dalai, "Ocean" in Mongolian, and gave the patronage of his Mongols to Sonam Gyatso's Gelugpa order. Retroactively, the lama's two previous incarnations were recognized as Sonam's predecessors, making Sonam Gyatso (1543-1588) the third Dalai Lama.

When the grandson of Altan Khan was recognized as the fourth Dalai Lama Yonten Gyatso (1589-1617), the alliance between Altan's band of Mongols and the Gelugpas was complete. Altan's forces pledged to defend the Gelugpas against any enemies that might arise in Tibet. The first Dalai Lama had established a monastery near the royal capital of Shigatse, but later Dalai Lamas settled in Lhasa and established three monasteries in and around the city that became some of the largest and most powerful in the world: Drepung, Sera, and Ganden. These monasteries came to be known collectively as "The Three Seats." They would exert enormous political power over the government of Central Tibet in the coming centuries.

When the Dalai Lama settled in Lhasa, the Gelugpas became involved in regional politics, which escalated the tension between the Gelugpas and the Kagyus. While the Dalai Lama on the one hand, and the Karmapa and Shamarpa on the other, apparently tried to maintain cordial relations, their supporters—monks, regional rulers, and dueling bands of Mongols—found numerous occasions to clash. Under the rule of the three Tsangpa kings (1565-1642) this tension reached a boiling point.

The Dalai Lama Seizes Power

Under the previous dynasty, the Rinpung, the central government had become weak. This allowed regional rulers, particularly the *depas* or warlords of various states, to gain a high level of autonomy. Local leaders waged continuous low-grade warfare for decades with their neighbors for larger and larger holdings.

When he assumed the throne, the second Tsangpa king, Karma Phuntsok Namgyal (ruled 1611-21) sought to end this fighting by uniting the petty states of Central Tibet under a strong central government. He developed a plan for "Unification under One White [Benevolent] Law" that in many ways was ahead of its time.[7] The plan called for a federal system where cabinet departments at the national level would implement policy for defense, agriculture, education, and taxation. Numerous small states would be united for mutual defense and free trade.

King Phuntsok Namgyal upgraded his army and began a campaign, through force of arms and diplomacy, to unite the duchies of Central Tibet one by one into a single, larger Tsangpa state. He succeeded brilliantly and by the end of his campaign, only the city of Lhasa, under the rule of Kyichod Depa Apel, the Duke of Lhasa, resisted incorporation into the new unified Tibetan kingdom. The duke wanted to avoid paying taxes to the Tsangpa king and saw no benefit for himself to joining a larger Tibetan state.

To defend his autonomy, in 1616 Duke Kyichod Apel made an alliance with Drepung and Sera monasteries, which by this time had thousands of monks each. These included hundreds of specially trained *dopdops* or "fighting monks" who were skilled in Tibet's native martial arts and served as private armies for each cloister. By this alliance, the duke particularly hoped to gain the support of Mongol bands that patronized

Gelugpa lamas. According to the fifth Dalai Lama, Apel made a gift of a large statue of Avalokiteshvara to the Tumed Mongol chief Tai Gi.[8]

The statue was a national treasure of Tibet, brought from India centuries earlier by King Songsten Gampo for his personal devotional practice. Apel's family had acquired it earlier through questionable means from the Potala Palace. The Lhasa Duke presented it to the Mongol chief to forge an alliance with Tai Gi and enlist his band of Mongols for an attack on the Tsangpa king. Perhaps this would have been something like, for example, Confederate President Jefferson Davis capturing the Liberty Bell and giving it to the British to induce them to attack the North during the Civil War.

The treacherous duke was successful, and with his new Mongol allies, he and his successors in the Kyichod family fought the King of Tsang for the next two decades. This war of attrition took a hard toll on the Tsangpa kingdom as it did on the duke's own small realm.

Finally, after years of alternating victories and defeats, Duke Kyichod's successor Sonam Namgyal saw his chance to free himself of the Kyichod family's old foe by invading the heartland of Tsang itself. The duke gained ambitious advisors of the fifth Dalai Lama as his allies. He convinced them that the Tsangpa king was about to send a massive force against the main Gelug monasteries; if the monasteries did not act quickly, the Gelugpas would be wiped out. Tibetan historians say that the duke's claim was false, and that the Tsangpa king was not planning an attack on the Gelugpa monasteries. But the duke's word carried the day with Gelugpa leaders and their Mongol allies, who were eager to fight.

The Dalai Lama's minister Sonam Chopel was particularly eager for war and he invited the Qoshot Mongols under Gushri Khan to attack Tsangpa forces before getting the Dalai Lama's approval, as the Dalai Lama describes in his own *Autobiography*. Interestingly, the Dalai Lama seemed to take an exceptionally respectful and deferential tone with his minister, who effectively controlled the government of the young lama-king:

> At the time, there were many rumors that the king
> [Gushri Khan] had already left Tibet and returned to
> his homeland. Others said that he would soon arrive
> with new cavalry. Zhalngo [respectful title for minister
> Sonam Chopel] told me that "the Tsangpa lord and his

ministers have always distrusted the Gelugpa in the past
and have always tried to harm us. If we remain neutral
in this conflict, then Ganden Phodrang people [those of
the Dalai Lama's labrang] will say that we are siding with
the Tsangpa. Now, when we have the opportunity to do
so, if we do not take the chance to liberate ourselves from
the Tsangpa lord with the help of the king, then we will
never get free of oppressive Tsangpa rule. Therefore, I have
already sent a message to the king with the messenger
Gendun Thondup asking him to attack the Tsangpa lord."

"That was a rash act," I replied. "It would be better for
us if the Mongols just withdraw from Tibet. It would be
best to intercept the Mongols at Damjung [before reaching
Tsang] and stop the outbreak of war. If you yourself do not
find it convenient to do so, then I would be willing to go
myself. Stopping the king would be good in every way—for
our reputation and for our future success."

Then, Zhalngo asked me to do a *mo* [prediction]. I
threw the three dice of Palden Lhamo Dmagzorma [deity
of war]. The result was that war against the Tsangpa would
indeed bring us success in the short run, but that this war
would ultimately be harmful for the future of Tibet.

"Well, good," Zhalngo said. "There is really no
problem then. If we are successful now, that is enough.
What happens long after we are dead is not our concern."

In this way, Zhalngo would not allow me to stop the war.[9]

After the hasty action of his short-sighted minister, the Dalai Lama
appeared to have no choice. Since war with Tsang had begun, he had
to ask for Gushri Khan's help to win it, or else face retribution from
the Tsangpa king that may have threatened the future of the Gelugpa.
Thus, reluctantly, the fifth Dalai Lama sent his own plea to Gushri to
invade Central Tibet and drive all Tsangpa forces from the area around
Lhasa. The Mongol chief answered his lama's call and sent cavalry against
Tsangpa forces. In 1638, the Mongols routed the Tsangpa army and
secured Lhasa and the surrounding province of U. They placed the Dalai
Lama on the throne as Mongol viceroy.

Having gained control of Lhasa, the Dalai Lama was now ready to stop the war. But his Mongol allies were not. So, yet again against the Gelug leader's wishes but at the urging of his zealous prime minister, Sonam Chopel, the Mongol armies escalated the conflict.

In 1642, Mongols overthrew the Tsangpa ruler Karma Tenkyong Wangpo (heir to King Phuntsok Namgyal, who nearly united Tibet into one centralized nation-state, as we have seen) and went on to forcibly convert nearly a thousand Nyingma and Karma Kagyu monasteries throughout Central Tibet to the Gelugpa school. The Mongols killed seven thousand monks and beheaded many of their abbots.[10] Gushri Khan proclaimed himself king of all Central Tibet and, as before, he made the fifth Dalai Lama his viceroy. The new administration became known as the "Ganden Phodrang,"—named after the Dalai Lama's residence at Drepung monastery—thus signifying the identity of the government in Lhasa and the Gelugpa school.

Using the pretext of a revolt in Tsang later in the year, Gushri Khan executed the Tsangpa king, and forced the tenth Karmapa to flee to Yunnan province in China. The Karmapa's monastic seat at Tsurphu was not converted to the Gelugpa order, but the new government decreed that the monastery could ordain no more than three monks per year. As Tibetan historian Dawa Norbu put it, "When the Dalai Lamas came to power in the seventeenth century they began to expand their own sect, Gelugpa, using the state power at their disposal and often converting other sects, especially the Kagyupa monasteries, to their own sect."[11]

The Karmapa had the chance to retaliate, but he apparently decided against violence. The aged fifth Tai Situ Chokyi Gyaltsen Palsang (1586-1657) offered to bring about his own death so that he could be reborn as a prince of the newly installed Chinese Qing dynasty; then, he could grow up to lead a Chinese invasion of Tibet that would restore the power of the Karma Kagyu. The Karmapa rejected Situ's offer, saying that "everyone knows me as the man who won't even hurt a bug."

The king of nearby Li Jiang also offered his forces to aid the Karmapa, but he rejected the king's offer as well. "Now is the time of the Kali Yug, the age of darkness," the tenth Karmapa said. "In Tibet, the only dharma left is superficial teachings, so it is not worth your trouble to save it."

Later, historians, scholars, and even the fifth Dalai Lama himself would criticize Sonam Chopel and the other self-serving officials who stoked this avoidable conflict into flames of war. Yet, once he had ascended the throne in Lhasa, the Dalai Lama had to continue fighting to consolidate his rule.

The current Dalai Lama has made himself an internationally famous spokesman for nonviolence. But the example of the Great Fifth Dalai Lama shows that nonviolence was not always the policy of his predecessors. After a dozen years as ruler of Central Tibet, in 1660 the Dalai Lama was faced with a rebellion in Tsang province, not yet pacified and still the stronghold of the Karma Kagyu. The Gelugpa leader again called on his Mongol patron Gushri Khan, this time to put down the insurgency in Tsang. In a passage that may sound to modern ears more like that other Mongol Khan, Genghis, than an emanation of the Bodhisattva of Compassion, the Dalai Lama called for harsh retribution towards the rebels against his rule:

> [Of those in] the band of enemies who have despoiled the
> duties entrusted to them;
> Make the male lines like trees that have had their roots cut;
> Make the female lines like brooks that have dried up in
> winter;
> Make the children and grandchildren like eggs smashed
> against rocks;
> Make the servants and followers like heaps of grass
> consumed by fire;
> Make their dominion like a lamp whose oil has been
> exhausted;
> In short, annihilate any traces of them, even their names.[12]

In a few months, Gushri Khan quelled the unrest in Tsang and helped the Dalai Lama establish the Gelugpa as the undisputed spiritual and temporal rulers of Central Tibet. This marked the beginning of four hundred years of political rule by a religious leader, and the definitive end of the dream of the Tsangpa kings to transform Tibet into a unified secular state.

Until at least the early twentieth century, the Dalai Lama's government would hold an annual commemoration of its defeat of Tsang.

In the 1920s Sir Charles Bell, a British diplomat who spent nineteen years in Tibet and became close to the thirteenth Dalai Lama, witnessed this ceremony, where three men from Tsang province were compelled to climb to the roof of one of the buildings at the Dalai Lama's Potala Palace in Lhasa. Then, they slid down a rope two hundred and fifty feet long into a courtyard. "This annual event, provided and paid for the by Lhasan Government, refers to Gushri's defeat of the King of Tsang, and is intended to prevent the Tsang province from ever gaining power again."[13]

After the fall of Tsangpa rule, Karma Kagyu followers retreated to Kham in eastern Tibet, out of the control of the Dalai Lama's new hostile government. There, they reestablished their activities at such imposing monasteries as Palpung, the seat of the Tai Situs.

Meantime, after the Karmapa fled—eluding the Mongol forces, according to tradition, through miraculous means—the fifth Dalai Lama put his cousin, the fifth Gyaltsab Drakpa Choyang (1618-58), in charge of Tsurphu. Thus, the Dalai Lama signaled that he would not forcibly convert the Karmapa's seat into a Gelugpa monastery, as he had done with other Karma Kagyu cloisters. With Gyaltsab as regent, Tsurphu would remain in safe-keeping for the Karmapa's return.

The fifth Gyaltsab died in 1658. While in exile, the Karmapa, one of two who lived as a married householder, recognized the sixth Gyaltsab Norbu Zangpo (1659-98) and adopted him as his own son. When the Karmapa returned from thirty years of exile in the 1670s and resumed control at Tsurphu, he removed Gyaltsab from the Tsurphu labrang and gave him his own administration. Since that time, the Gyaltsabs have run their own labrang and have had no official responsibilities in the Karmapa's administration. A later Gyaltsab, in the nineteenth century, would even sue the Karmapa's labrang over a property rights dispute, a suit which would only end after the Chinese invasion of Tibet in the 1950s. Thus we see a historical precedent for high Karma Kagyu lamas taking each other to court over property, as they would in India in the case over Rumtek monastery in the 1990s.

The Karmapa's followers never regained the power they had lost to the Gelugpa in 1642. The two schools continued as rivals for centuries to come. In the following centuries there remained a close tie between the Dalai Lama's government and his own Buddhist sect. The new Lhasa government used its power to expand the Dalai Lama's school at the expense of the Kagyu and the other two Buddhist schools, the Nyingma and Sakya, as well as the Bon, the original pre-Buddhist religion of Tibet.

But some powerful Gelugpa lamas, especially the second-ranking master of the school, the Panchen Lamas, contended with the government as well. The ninth Panchen Lama Chokyi Nyima (1883-1937) quarreled with the thirteenth Dalai Lama over Lhasa's tax bite on the Panchen's monastery Tashilhunpo and its attached estates. The conflict led the Panchen to flee Tibet in 1923 and set up a "Field Headquarters" in eastern Tibet from which he feuded with the Dalai Lama and his government until his death in 1937.[14] At that point, Lhasa again quarreled with the Panchen's administration when each side supported a different candidate as the tenth Panchen Lama.

Sixty years later, finding the next Panchen (the eleventh) would create trouble for the current Dalai Lama as well. The tenth Panchen, overweight and stressed from a lifetime of persecution by the Chinese, died in January 1989 at his home in Shigatse, the old Tsang royal capital, at age fifty-three. Both the Dalai Lama and the Chinese government were eager to find his successor, since the next Panchen stood to become the highest-profile spiritual leader for Tibetans once the Dalai Lama would die. In addition, the next Panchen would probably recognize the next Dalai Lama, as many of his predecessors had done. The stakes to control the lama were thus very high and each side feared being sidelined by the other in announcing the reincarnation of the Panchen Lama.

In the early 1990s the Dalai Lama and the Panchen's administration— who were on the same side this time—carefully worked out a secret agreement with the Chinese to recognize the incarnation of the eleventh Panchen Lama together. Then, in 1995, the agreement collapsed. On May 14, the Dalai Lama announced his own choice, six-year-old Gendun Chokyi Nyima, without giving prior notice to Beijing or to officials of the Tibet Autonomous Region (TAR), the Chinese government of Tibet in Lhasa. The Chinese were furious. Within days, they whisked the boy off to house arrest in Beijing and started a crackdown on the Panchen's monastery. At the end of November of the same year, Beijing and TAR officials held a lot-draw in the Jokhang Temple in Lhasa to choose their own Panchen, Gyaltsen Norbu, the son of a Communist Party cadre.

The troubled history of the Panchen Lamas shows how the highest lamas contended with the Dalai Lamas for political power in old Tibet, and how in recent decades, lamas became pawns in the struggle between the Dalai Lama and the Chinese for control of hearts and minds in Tibet. We will encounter both of these themes in the rivalry between the Gelugpas and the Karma Kagyus that underpins our story. Later, we will see how this conflict played out in a contest between the Dalai Lama's government and the Shamarpa at the end of the eighteenth century. But first, we will return to the early days of the Karma Kagyu, before the dawn of the Gelug. There, we will find the origin of the Karmapas, the first tulkus of Tibet.

4   THE ORIGIN OF THE KARMAPAS

The First Reincarnate Lama of Tibet

Who was the lama whom the Great Fifth Dalai Lama and his massive monasteries so feared nearly four centuries ago? What was the source of his power?

The Dalai Lama may be the best known incarnate lama in Tibetan Buddhism, but as we have seen, the Dalai Lamas did not initiate the tulku system, the unique custom of lamas returning life after life to teach their students. Instead, it was the Karmapas. The first Karmapa Dusum Khyenpa appeared at the dawn of the twelfth century, in 1110, nearly three hundred years before the first Dalai Lama, Gendun Truppa, was born at the end of the fourteenth century, in 1391.

As the first of his line, Dusum Khyenpa (1110-94) set the example for all Karmapas to follow. Buddhism teaches that the highest bodhisattvas can choose their own rebirth, and Tibetan legend says that Dusum Khyenpa chose to be born in a family that could support his spiritual activity. He was born in the Male Iron Tiger Year of the Tibetan calendar (1110) in the small village of Ratag, located in the Treshod mountain range in Kham. His parents were not ordinary Khampas, but advanced spiritual practitioners.

His father Gompa Dorje Gon was a devotee of the fearsome tantric deity Yamantaka, the Lord of Death, and his mother Gangcham Mingdren was a "natural yogini"–a female adept who took up tantric practices without prior training. The boy received tantric initiations and instructions from both his mother and father. "Obtaining miraculous powers he made a clear imprint of his hand and foot on a rock," a classic sign of his spiritual attainment.[1]

Modern people can approach such stories simply as fairy tales, as revealing metaphors, or as occurrences that cannot be explained by the scientific laws of today but may reveal their truth to future investigations. Perhaps because they recognize a continuum between physical and ethereal phenomena, Tibetans have always found the existence of miracles uncontroversial, but still impressive. Apropos of the power of such stories, Picasso once said, "Art is the lie that tells the truth." Might myth or miracle work the same way?

Dusum Khyenpa was a remarkable and gifted child. At an early age he began studying with the greatest teachers of the day. Perhaps his most important teacher was Gampopa, the principal disciple of the cave yogi and poet Milarepa. After studying with dozens of teachers and mastering tantric rituals, at age thirty Dusum Khyenpa had an intuition that he should study with Gampopa, so he traveled to Gampopa's Dak Lha monastery to seek out the great master.

Originally a physician and a layman, Gampopa became a monk after his medical powers were unable to save the life of his wife and infant child. Gampopa took vows in the Kadampa school, the predecessor of the Gelug order of the Dalai Lamas (not to be confused with the New Kadampa Tradition of Geshe Kelsang Gyatso founded in England in 1977). There, Gampopa learned the graduated path to enlightenment, or Lam Rim, of the Kadampas. Later, Gampopa recorded the Kadampa approach in his book, The Jewel Ornament of Liberation, which became one of the most popular step-by-step guidebooks to the Buddhist path in Tibet.

At their first meeting, the new arrival presented his destined lama with a khata ceremonial scarf. In response, Gampopa jumped right into teachings on the graduated path to enlightenment. Thus began Dusum Khyenpa's training under Gampopa. Later, the lama gave his student tantric teachings and meditation instruction. For years, Dusum Khyenpa meditated under the guidance of Gampopa, and it soon became clear that, out of the master's hundreds of disciples, Dusum Khyenpa was the most accomplished.

Finally, after years of steady progress, Gampopa instructed his student to enter a period of intense meditation to push him along the last bit of the Buddhist path and into realization. For nine months he went into a shamatha, or mental-calming meditation, retreat. During his retreat, according to legend, "he never unfolded his hands long enough for the perspiration on them to dry."

Gampopa then recognized him as his most gifted student—out of hundreds of disciples—and started Dusum Khyenpa on his final stage to enlightenment, *vipashyana*, or insight meditation. After three years of insight meditation, Gampopa told him, "you have severed your bond with phenomenal existence. Now you will not return to samsara."[2] With his blessing, Gampopa sent his student to practice at Kampo Gangra in Kham and told him he would reach full enlightenment there.

But before he could carry out his lama's instructions, Dusum Khyenpa got involved in other projects, and was not able to return to Dak Lha monastery until he got news of his teacher's death years later. There, he met one of Gampopa's other main students, Pomdrakpa Sonam Dorje, from whom the eight "minor" lineages of the Kagyu school would derive. He begged Dusum Khyenpa not to go to Kham to meditate even though Gampopa had told him to do so, because it would shorten Dusum Khyenpa's life. The first Karmapa thanked Pomdrakpa for his advice, but replied that regardless of what he did, he would still live to age eighty-four, as a prophecy had foretold.

Accordingly, at age fifty, he made the trip to Kampo Gangra to practice Mahamudra—the highest meditation of the Kagyu lineage—and there he gained enlightenment. His liberation was celebrated by the *dakinis*, Buddhist angels, who made him a gift of a crown made from their hair. This Black Crown is said to always be present above the heads of all the Karmapas, though only visible to those with exceptional insight.

Dusum Khyenpa stayed at Kampo Gangra for eighteen years, and his reputation for spiritual realization spread around Tibet, earning him the title Knower of the Three Times for his ability to transcend time and grasp the reality behind events in the past, present, and future. The Kashmiri pandit Sakyasri, traveling in Tibet, declared that Dusum Khyenpa was the Man of Buddha Activity or Karmapa prophesied in the *Samadhi Raja Sutra*, said to have been pronounced by Shakyamuni Buddha sixteen hundred years earlier.

The first Karmapa began setting up the infrastructure for future Karmapas. He founded three monasteries that would become important Karma Kagyu centers, including the seat of the Karmapas at Tsurphu near Lhasa. The abbot of the monastery at Bodh Gaya in India, the site

of Shakyamuni Buddha's enlightenment, sent a conch shell to Tsurphu
as recognition of the Karmapa's spiritual attainment.

In addition, Dusum Khyenpa established the pattern for the future
activity of the Karmapas. He obtained the patronage of powerful regional
kings and rulers. He made peace between warring regions. He healed the
sick and helped the blind to see. He commissioned copies of Buddhist
scriptures to be published and distributed. He cultivated a group of
senior students to pass on the oral teachings he had received from his
own teachers—particularly the lineage of the Mahamudra, the highest
teaching of the Karma Kagyu school—and to find the next Karmapa.
Finally, Dusum Khyenpa even predicted his own death and rebirth.

On the morning of the third day of the new year, Dusum Khyenpa
gave his students his last sermon. Then, sitting up, he gazed into the
sky and entered into meditation. He died at noon. At his funeral,
good omens appeared in the local area and relics charged with spiritual
power emerged from his funeral pyre: his charred heart, representing his
compassion; his tongue, standing for his teaching; and pieces of bone
inscribed with letters of sacred syllables.

Like many high lamas, future Karmapas would also leave relics
after their deaths. In the twentieth century, the sixteenth Karmapa's
funeral pyre would yield up a charred-heart relic during his obsequies
at Rumtek in 1981. The ownership of this relic would create tension
between Tai Situ and the administration of the sixteenth Karmapa, as we
will see in chapter 8.

Almost ten years after Dusum Khyenpa's death, his main student
Pomdrakpa went on to recognize a boy prodigy born in 1204 at Chilay
Tsakto in eastern Tibet as the second Karmapa, Karma Pakshi. Thus
Pomdrakpa retroactively established Dusum Khyenpa as the first
incarnation of the Karmapa line by making Karma Pakshi the first
reincarnate master in Tibet. After this, tulkus followed in all four schools
of Tibetan Buddhism.

The Karmapa and the Emperor

Dusum Khyenpa was followed by the second Karmapa Karma Pakshi
(1204-83) and then by seven hundred years of Karmapas who lived in
Tibet. Each of these Karmapas is revered by Karma Kagyu devotees, but
a few of them particularly stand out in history. One of these is the fifth

Karmapa Deshin Shegpa (1384-1415), who became at age twenty-three the guru of a Chinese emperor.

To ensure peace on the frontiers of the Chinese empire, since the Later Han dynasty (25-220 A.D.) successive emperors encouraged or compelled chieftains of neighboring states—from Korea to Burma to Mongolia and Tibet—to undertake "tribute" missions to the imperial court. The historical significance of these missions has been a matter of dispute between Chinese and Tibetan historians ever since the 1950s.

To the Chinese, when a representative of a neighboring nation made a tribute mission to the imperial capital, it signaled that the envoy was placing his people in submission to the will of the Son of Heaven. Modern Chinese historians say that visits by lamas—powerful secular rulers of Central Tibet or other Tibetan states, in addition to their religious roles—effectively placed Tibet under the control of the emperors, and thus of their heirs, the Communist rulers of China. Tibetans reject this view. They say that visits by various lamas to the imperial court had no political significance. Instead, they were pilgrimages by a priest to his patron. In the Tibetan view, it was the lama, rather than the emperor, who was the superior.[3]

In any event, both Chinese and Tibetans agree that successive emperors hoped to gain political influence in Tibet and to take religious teachings from the most powerful lamas. After the fall of the Sakya rulers in Central Tibet in 1358 and of the Yuan dynasty in China ten years later, the Ming emperors (1368-1644) sought to establish relations with leading Tibetan lamas who might fill the power vacuum left by the Sakya Lamas. In particular, the emperors hoped the Tibetans would intercede with their patrons, the troublesome Mongols, to reduce their raids on Chinese imperial outposts in the northwest borderlands.

Hearing of the fifth Karmapa's great spiritual power and corresponding political influence in Central Tibet and in the kingdoms of the border areas in the east, in 1405 the third Ming ruler, Chengzu (1403-24, also known as Yongle) invited the fifth Karmapa to visit the imperial court. The twenty-one-year-old Karmapa accepted this invitation, and arrived at the Ming capital Nanjing after a two-year journey. At the gates of the city the emperor himself welcomed the Karmapa, and placed him on an elephant as a sign of respect. The Karmapa gave two weeks of teachings to Chengzu's court, and performed miracles that the emperor ordered to be recorded on large silk scrolls. When he returned to Tibet the Karmapa brought one of these scrolls back to Tsurphu, where it reportedly still remains, an invaluable resource for historians.

According to historical accounts, the emperor and his court developed great devotion for the Karmapa. Chengzu offered to make the Karmapa head of all Buddhists in Tibet—the same offer that Kublai Khan had made to the Sakya Pandita's nephew Phagpa 150 years earlier. The emperor was ready to send his armies all over Tibet to compel monasteries of other sects to join the Karmapa's school. He explained that cavalry was already mobilized in the west, ready to move at his command.

How sincere was the emperor? Perhaps he had already planned to invade Tibet merely to extend imperial influence there and had just offered this explanation to the Karmapa as a pretext. In any event, Deshin Shegpa was not tempted by Chengzu's offer. Just as the Sakya ruler Phagpa had refused to let Kublai Khan subdue the other sects of Buddhism in favor of the Sakyas in the thirteenth century, so the Karmapa politely declined the emperor's offer to make the Karma Kagyu supreme by force of Chinese arms.

In his refusal, given hundreds of years before the concept of religious freedom would appear, the Karmapa gave his imperial patron a lesson in the value of spiritual diversity. The Karmapa explained that he had no ambition to rule all sects because this would block the spread of Buddhism: "One sect cannot bring order to the lives of all types of people. It is not beneficial to think of converting all sects into one. Each individual sect is especially constituted so as to accomplish a particular aspect of good activity."[4] The emperor was disappointed, but he understood that the Karmapa would not accept his gift or fall into his trap, whichever this offer was. Later, despite pressure from a council of ministers eager for war, Chengzu gave the order to withdraw the troops massed at the Tibetan frontier.

The Black Crown of Enlightened Action

The legend behind the Black Crown, known as the Vajra Mukut, shows its importance for the Karmapas. The fifth Karmapa Deshin Shegpa remained in China and, according to legend, emperor Chengzu attended the religious rituals he conducted with great enthusiasm. At one ceremony held at the imperial court, Chengzu observed the ethereal Black Crown over Karmapa's head. He realized that he was only able to see the crown through the power of his devotion and his fortunate karma, but that to others less blessed the crown was invisible.

Shamar had heard this story many times as a child at Rumtek, and he explained that "this Ming emperor was not any kind of bodhisattva. He was not even one of the best rulers of China. But he had the potential for awareness, which was realized only when he met the Karmapa. He said to Karmapa, 'Whenever you perform a ceremony of blessing, you always appear to me in an unusual way. Your body seems to be in the form of Vajradhara and you are wearing a kind of black turban or crown on your head.'"[5]

Vajradhara is a meditational deity who is the source of the Mahamudra. As we have seen, from the time of the first Karmapa Dusum Khyenpa all his successors were said to have an ethereal Black Crown hovering over their heads, visible only to those of high spiritual attainment. The first four Karmapas manifested this Black Crown only to those who had the spiritual potential to see it.

The Karmapa responded that when a great bodhisattva is teaching in human, or *nirmanakaya* form, his body can also be simultaneously manifested in *sambhogakaya*, or ethereal form. Deshin Shegpa explained that the first Karmapa Dusum Khyenpa was such an emanation of that ethereal Buddha for our physical world. Many eons in the past, in a previous life as a cave-meditator he himself attained the eighth bodhisattva level, or *bhumi* (out of ten levels total). Traditionally, miracles and auspicious signs follow such a feat. On that occasion, a hundred thousand dakinis cut their black hair and offered it to the cave yogi as a prize. The dakinis wove their black hair into a crown that they placed on the future Karmapa's head, in a kind of enthronement ceremony that made him the king of their realm.

Pleased by this story, Chengzu offered the Karmapa another gift. To allow others to witness the ethereal Black Crown, the emperor offered to make a replica in physical form. Again, it is likely that the emperor's motives were a mixture of the spiritual and the political, and that if the Karmapa accepted a costly gift from the emperor it would be a sign of fealty from vassal to lord, and from Tibet to China.

The emperor asked, "If I make a similar crown and offer it to you, can you give the blessing of the Buddhas of the ethereal realms to all beings in our physical world?"

Deshin Shegpa responded, "Yes, the bodhisattva's blessing depends on his having attained the wish *paramita*—that whatever he wishes for the benefit of sentient beings will come true—so this can be."

Pleased that he had found a gift the Karmapa would accept, the same day the emperor commissioned skilled craftsmen to make a crown woven of black brocade and lavished with gold. The crown was studded with sapphires surmounted by a unique ruby the size of a human finger tip. The eight-inch-high Vajra Mukut would become one of the most famous material objects in Tibetan Buddhism. When it was completed, the emperor presented the crown to Deshin Shegpa. Using this imperial gift, Deshin Shegpa developed the Black Crown ceremony that ever since his time has become an integral part of the spiritual activity of the Karmapas.

In this ceremony, the Karmapa is seated on a throne in full lotus position. He begins to meditate and quickly enters a state of deep concentration or *samadhi*. An attendant hands him the Black Crown, and the Karmapa places it on his own head. Legend says that if the Karmapa does not hold the crown down with his hands, it will fly away, so great is its spiritual power. Once wearing the crown, the Karmapa then manifests as an emanation of the Buddha in ethereal, *sambhogakaya* form, while still remaining in his current physical body.

From the fifteenth century through the seventeenth century, the Karmapas used emperor Chengzu's crown for the Black Crown ceremony. Then, in the seventeenth century, after the fifth Dalai Lama took over the government of Central Tibet from the Tsangpa king, the Karmapa took refuge with the king of Li Jiang, a vassal state of China bordering on Burma, as we have seen.

Since the Karmapa had left the original crown behind when he fled Tsurphu, the Li Jiang king offered a duplicate Vajra Mukut. From then until 1959, the Karmapas traveled with this less valuable crown, leaving the original at Tsurphu for safekeeping. When the sixteenth Karmapa fled Tsurphu in 1959—unlike in the seventeenth century—he made sure to bring along the original crown, the one presented in the fifteenth century by Chengzu to the fifth Karmapa Deshin Shegpa. He had to leave the duplicate crown presented by the king of Li Jiang back at Tsurphu.

When Rumtek was completed in 1966, the Karmapa deposited Chengzu's crown, along with the other valuables he had brought from

Tibet, into the reliquary there. Later, after Tai Situ and Gyaltsab Rinpoches took over management of Rumtek in 1993, some would claim that there was confusion over whether the crown at Rumtek was the original or the later duplicate. "No one is certain today which Black Crown was brought out" of Tibet, since most of the Karmapa's valuables had to be left at Tsurphu, Lea Terhune wrote in her 2004 book *Karmapa: The Politics of Reincarnation*.[6] In his book *The Dance of 17 Lives* published later the same year, Mick Brown repeated much the same claim: "It is not known which crown the 16th Karmapa brought with him when he fled from Tibet into Sikkim in 1959."[7]

Despite doubts by Brown and Terhune, the Tsurphu officials who helped the Karmapa crate up his valuables for transport in 1959 say that they made sure to bring the older crown, given by the emperor Chengzu to Deshin Shegpa in the fifteenth century, leaving the newer one from the seventeenth century behind.

Lekshe Drayan was the younger brother of Rumtek's first general secretary, Damchoe Yongdu. Since their family had provided secretaries to the Karmapa's labrang for generations in Tibet, Lekshe and another brother followed Damchoe in entering the family business, and both served as assistant secretaries at Tsurphu. Lekshe related his experience with the Black Crown in an affidavit he planned to submit to the District Court in Sikkim in 2005. He provided me with an advance copy, written when he was seventy-eight years old.

> When the sixteenth Karmapa escaped from Tibet in 1959, along with my two brothers and other staff of the Karmapa, I helped pack his valuables at Tsurphu. This included the Vajra Crown as well as the most important movable statues, silks, paintings, and other ritual items of value that the sixteenth Karmapa wanted to take into exile. The newer crown was dark blue, while the older crown was much darker, a true black tone. The ruby on the older crown was much larger. Because he could not bring both crowns, and because the older crown was more precious, the sixteenth Karmapa decided to bring the older crown along in exile and leave the newer crown behind at Tsurphu.

The authenticity of the Black Crown at Rumtek has become another point of contention between followers of Ogyen Trinley, particularly Tai Situ and Gyaltsab Rinpoches, and Shamar. "I wonder where these writers Lea Terhune and Mick Brown could have heard that there is confusion about the crown," Shamar told me. "The Rumtek administration had no confusion; we knew for certain that the late Karmapa had brought the more valuable crown from Tibet. These writers' claims are suspicious. Maybe someone is spreading false rumors about the crown to confuse people. Did something happen to the Black Crown after Situ and Gyaltsab Rinpoches took over Rumtek in 1993?"

To determine the crown's status, Shamar has called on the Indian court system to conduct an inspection at Rumtek, over the objections of Situ, Gyaltsab, and their supporters. A later chapter deals with the dispute over the crown and the court battles to have it inspected.

Though the Vajra Mukut has been revered by Tibetans for six centuries, it was not known to the world until the sixteenth Karmapa began performing the Black Crown ceremony around Asia and in the West during the 1970s. We have seen how he packed the crown and left Tibet for exile in India, hoping to save the Karma Kagyu lineage from extinction at the hands of the Chinese Communists. We have also seen how Karma Kagyu supporters clashed with the government of Central Tibet for four hundred years before the Chinese invasion. Now, let us explore how sectarian politics followed the Karmapa into exile, posing a threat to the Karma Kagyu greater than any it had faced in the past, and even greater than the threat from Chinese Communism.

5 A Lull in Hostilities

Exiles Call a Truce: Temporary Allies

After the Chinese invasion of Tibet in 1950-51, the Tibetan leadership
did not flee the country, but remained in Lhasa after receiving Chinese
assurances of broad autonomy. During the 1950s, the Dalai Lama's
government and high lamas from all five religious schools tried to
cooperate with the Chinese leadership to govern Tibet as a part of China.
But pressures gradually mounted on the Tibetans to change their way of
life that created escalating tension with the Chinese.

Faced with a common threat in the form of Communism, the
historic rivalry between the Tibetan government and the Karmapa's
Karma Kagyu school abated for a time. In the fifties, the young Dalai
Lama formed a genuine, warm friendship with his elder, the sixteenth
Karmapa. This historic friendship began when the two lamas traveled
to Beijing together in September 1954. They were accompanied by the
Panchen Lama, the second-ranking master of the Gelugpa. In the Chinese
capital, the three lamas met with Mao Zedong and other Communist
leaders.

Together, the lamas tried to present a united front to their new
masters. They attempted to show that they were willing to cooperate
with the Chinese leadership as long as the Communists respected the
religious freedom of Buddhists in Tibet. There was much public talk
about the excellent relations between Beijing and the Tibetans and about
progress in economic development under the new regime. The Dalai and
Panchen Lamas were skeptical, but being young and idealistic, they held
out hope that Mao was genuinely concerned for Tibet's welfare and that

the Chinese would help bring their nation into the modern world. The thirty-year-old Karmapa, ten years their senior, was less optimistic.

The friendship between the Dalai Lama and the Karmapa continued when the lamas returned to Tibet. At the traditional seat of the Karmapas, Tsurphu monastery near Lhasa, the Karmapa supervised the construction of a residence for the Dalai Lama. Given the preceding five hundred years of rivalry between the two lamas, this was a revolutionary gesture of conciliation. It would have been comparable, say, to the United States president building a dacha for the Soviet leader at Camp David during the Cold War. But the Chinese occupation made Tibetan solidarity more urgent than ever and encouraged leaders of all the religious schools to put away their old sectarian and regional rivalries.

Afterwards, the Karmapa invited the Dalai Lama to visit Tsurphu and enjoy the house built for him there. Amidst lavish festivities, the Karmapa asked the Dalai Lama to give the empowerment of Avalokiteshvara, the bodhisattva who, Tibetans believe, emanates in both the Dalai Lamas and the Karmapas. The Tibetan leader gratefully obliged and, in turn, asked the Karmapa to perform the trademark ritual of his line, the Black Crown ceremony.

This friendship continued during the dark days that followed in Tibet as the turbulent era of the fifties drew to a close. The Dalai Lama and the Karmapa consulted each other on the best way to deal with rising pressure from the Chinese People's Liberation Army on one side and Tibetan rebels from the border areas of Kham and Amdo on the other. For the next few years, the Karmapa traveled widely in eastern Tibet as the ambassador of the Dalai Lama, working to defuse tensions between local people and occupying Chinese forces. Once the situation became untenable, the Dalai Lama and the Karmapa even conferred on when and how to leave Tibet in 1959. After arriving in India, the two leaders continued to consult each other in exile.

To many Tibetans, just deprived of their homeland, it seemed that the tragedy of military defeat, Chinese conquest, and exile had finally ended the ancient rivalry of the Tibetan government and the Karma Kagyu school.

Tensions Reemerge

But hundreds of years of habit would not die so easily, and after a few months in India, competition between the administrations of the Dalai Lama and the Karmapa resurfaced. The Dalai Lama and his ministers had just lost their country, Central Tibet. In exile, they wanted to create a unified Tibetan community that included not just their former subjects in Central Tibet and their allies in the Gelugpa, but also Tibetans from areas never governed by Lhasa and from all the religious schools. Thus exile leaders hoped to create a pan-Tibetan community that would be stronger to oppose the Chinese and perhaps speed the arrival of the day when the exiles could return home to a free Tibet. In the early days in exile, liberating their homeland was the shared dream of all Tibetans.

To realize this dream, exile government officials saw Tibetan unity as more urgent than preserving Tibet's regional or religious diversity. Indeed, the presence of a common enemy created a new Tibetan nationalism, a sense that Central Tibet, Kham, and Amdo were essentially one country though historically, they had been governed separately. Such pan-Tibetan nationalism had never existed before in Tibetan history. "In order to maintain the unity of the émigré community after the Dalai Lama's flight across the Himalayas in 1959, his exiled administration developed the idea of a giant, theoretical Tibet...Its focus was the idea of 'Po Cholkha Sum,' the unity of the three historic regions of ethnic Tibet: Amdo, Kham, and U-Tsang. People who had previously identified themselves with a particular region now became consciously Tibetan," Patrick French wrote in his book Tibet, Tibet.[1] The same went for Tibetan religion. No longer would Tibetans be followers of the Kagyu or Gelugpa schools; instead, they would be followers of Tibetan Buddhism.

In 1964 the Tibetan Government-in-Exile introduced reforms that it said would help the Tibetan community retain its coherence, with refugees scattered around India, Nepal, Bhutan, and Sikkim. The Dalai Lama's brother Gyalo Thondup led this initiative, and he formed an organization called the United Party to carry it out.[2] By pooling the resources of émigré Tibetans towards economic and social development, the United Party was intended to create a new political unity out of the diversity of the exile community, and strengthen the Dalai Lama's ability to face off the Communists. Tibetans abroad understood that the party had the full support of the exile government.

The United Party's platform was broad and ambitious. At the same time that the insane Cultural Revolution in Tibet was rooting out the "Four Olds" (old ideas, old culture, old customs, and old habits), the United Party proposed a much more rational-sounding platform of economic, social, and religious reforms for Tibetans in exile.

The unity initiative set up branch offices in Tibetan settlements throughout India and began to establish handicraft centers and even agricultural communes similar to the new collective farms in Communist China. But the most ambitious leg of the United Party's platform was religious reform that called for merging the administrations of the four Buddhist schools, along with the pre-Buddhist Bon religion, into one body under the new Department of Religion in Dharamsala, under direct control of exile government officials and the Dalai Lama.

It is unclear whether the initiative would have subordinated all the schools to the Dalai Lama's spiritual leadership, or whether the plan would have respected each school's traditional autonomy while increasing opportunities for cooperation. Gyalo Thondup was known as a modern thinker who believed that church and state should be separate. But others in the young Dalai Lama's exile administration thought that secularism was heresy and seemed to believe that Tibetans' only hope lay in reining in the religious schools outside of the Gelugpa, to which most exile ministers belonged.

In any event, when word of the United Party's religious reform got out in 1964, the exiled government was unprepared for the angry opposition that leaders of the religious schools expressed. To them, this unification plan appeared not as a benefit to Tibetans, but rather as a power-grab by the exile administration. Some critics charged that the plan was only a thinly disguised scheme to confiscate the monasteries that dozens of lamas had begun to reestablish in exile with funds they had raised themselves.

Though headed by the Dalai Lama, the exile administration's work was mainly secular in nature. It opened offices to start schools, to receive refugees, and to deal with foreigners, but it did not generally finance or build monasteries in exile. Instead, the dozens of transplanted monasteries built by the mid-1960s in India, Nepal, Sikkim, and Bhutan were the result of private initiative. "Lamas would go begging for donations to build monasteries," according to historian Dawa Norbu. "Rich Tibetans, out of piety and social prestige, made large donations towards the construction of monasteries. The same goes for the propagation of Tibetan Buddhism in the Western world. There is not a single meditation center abroad started by the Dalai Lama's exiled government."[3]

The United Party plan reminded some lamas outside the formerly ruling Gelugpa of harassment by the government back in Tibet before 1959. Even worse, the exile government's push for unity seemed uncomfortably similar to post-1959 Communist propaganda about uniting all Tibetans back home under the similarly named United Front in loyalty to the "socialist motherland" of China.

Accordingly, leaders of the Nyingma and Kagyu schools, along with lay families who followed each school living in thirteen refugee settlements around India and one in Nepal, banded together to protect their monasteries. To rally their supporters, they chose the most charismatic leader they could find—the sixteenth Karmapa. They formed a counter-party called the Tibetan Welfare Association which came to be known as the Fourteen Settlements group. The Karmapa agreed to serve as spiritual leader of this group, and its members elected a layman, Gungthang Tsultrim, as political leader. Dozens of other lamas, including Dilgo Khyentse Rinpoche, who later became one of the best known Tibetan Buddhist teachers worldwide, also joined the group. Dilgo Khyentse had been close to the Karmapa at Tsurphu, had fled Tibet with the Karmapa's party, and had spent much time at Rumtek after coming into exile.

The group went on to organize protests, write open letters, and publicize their arguments to preserve the historic rights of the five religious schools. They called on exiled Tibetans to reject Gyalo Thondup's plan. The Tibetan exile administration tried to meet this opposition with open debate, but also, reportedly, with behind-the-scenes maneuvering. In 1972 Gyalo Thondup asked the Indian Home Ministry to relocate twenty-eight prominent members of the Fourteen Settlements group to far-flung areas of India, based on unsupported charges that they posed threats to law and order.

Accordingly, the Indian government issued notices ordering the twenty-eight refugees to move. When two recipients of relocation orders, Sadhu Lobsang Nyandak and Gungthang Ngodrup, challenged their relocation orders in the Delhi High Court, these notices were withdrawn. This court victory marked the turning point in the campaign against the increasingly unpopular unity initiative. In 1973, the United Party closed down its branch offices, broke up its farming communes, and turned over its handicraft centers to the Home Department of the exiled Tibetan government.

All through this period, the imposing sixteenth Karmapa served as the highly visible rallying point for the Fourteen Settlements' opposition to the United Party. In the wake of the plan's defeat, the Tibetan exile community ended up deeply divided, just the opposite of what the Dalai Lama and Gyalo Thondup were trying to achieve. And against the Tibetan leader's pleas to forget old quarrels, apparently some officials in his exile administration in Dharamsala developed a resentment of the dissenting leaders.

On March 13, 1977, Fourteen Settlements political head Gungthang Tsultrim was shot several times at point-blank range while walking in his backyard in Clement Town, in the northwestern Indian state of Himachal Pradesh. Simultaneously, the electricity was cut to the local area, allowing the shooter to escape. When apprehended in Kathmandu, the murderer, Amdo Rekhang Tenzin, told the Royal Nepalese Police that the Tibetan exile government had paid him three hundred thousand rupees (about thirty-five thousand dollars) to assassinate Gungthang.[4]

Even more shocking, the hit man claimed that Dharamsala offered him a larger bounty to kill the sixteenth Karmapa. Nepali authorities handed the murderer over to India, and he repeated his story under interrogation there at a maximum-security prison in Lucknow.

When news of this assassination and the plot against the sixteenth Karmapa came out, large groups of angry demonstrators from the Fourteen Settlements group filled the streets of Dharamsala to protest against the exile administration's potential involvement. Meanwhile, back in the still quasi-independent kingdom of Sikkim, the location of the sixteenth Karmapa's seat at Rumtek monastery, the royal government provided the Karmapa with eleven armed bodyguards.

It is unclear what role the Dalai Lama himself played in the resurrection of the rivalry between his government and the Karma Kagyu school in India. Only twenty-four years old when the Tibetans fled to India in 1959, he relied heavily on the counsel of his advisors. The experienced ministers of his administration had their own views on how best to preserve Tibetan institutions in exile, and their counsel must have carried weight with the inexperienced lama-leader. Many of these ministers continued to see the religious schools outside their own Gelug as rivals, and sought ways to defend against them.

Perhaps as a peace offering to lamas of schools outside the Gelug, shortly after Gungthang's murder, the Dalai Lama invited Dilgo Khyentse Rinpoche, a leading lama in the Fourteen Settlements group, to become one of his teachers. After this, Dilgo Khyentse became closely associated with the Tibetan leader, and later went on to teach in Southeast Asia and in the West.

Tibetans who follow the Nyingma, Sakya, and Kagyu schools and the pre-Buddhist Bon religion have claimed that some exile government leaders still harbor dreams of expanding their influence at the religious schools' expense. For his part, the Dalai Lama has sought to restrain the enthusiasm of his ministers for partisan politics. Every few years the Tibetan exile leader has had to use his good name to put down the most fractious schemes of his administrators by threatening that unless all Tibetans could work together, this would be his final reincarnation.

Did the Previous Dalai Lama Choose the Sixteenth Karmapa?

Apparently discounting the long-standing enmity between the Central Tibetan government—before and after going into exile—and the Karma Kagyu school, Tai Situ Rinpoche, the main supporter of Karmapa contender Ogyen Trinley, has maintained that it has always been necessary for the Dalai Lama to approve Karmapa reincarnations. As evidence, he has cited the example of the sixteenth Karmapa: "Although the search for a new Karmapa is directed by the letter of prediction left by his predecessor, it has always been the tradition to seek final confirmation from the Dalai Lama. For instance, the 16th Karmapa was searched and found on the basis of the prediction letter left by the 15th Karmapa, but he was confirmed as the 16th Karmapa by the 13th Dalai Lama."[5]

This is another position that history contradicts. Khenpo Chodrak Tenphel, the abbot of Rumtek until the takeover in 1993 and the top authority on the history of the Karmapas, has told the story behind this incident.

"It is true that the thirteenth Dalai Lama's administration did attempt to participate in the recognition of the sixteenth Karmapa, but at that time the Karma Kagyu saw it as interference. After failing to install his candidate, the Dalai Lama eventually had to back down.[6]

"After the death of the fifteenth Karmapa in 1922, there was a period of eight years before the Tsurphu administration could find a suitable candidate as his reincarnation," Chodrak said. "In the meantime, government officials in Lhasa saw this as an opportunity to bring the border area of eastern Tibet under the control of the Dalai Lama's government as a buffer against China. Central Tibetan officials thought that if they controlled the Karmapa, then they could control Kham, where the Karma Kagyu was strong. Since nearly eight years had passed without Tsurphu finding a Karmapa, the Lhasa government figured that Tsurphu might never find one. Therefore, there would be no harm for the government to nominate its own boy to be the next Karmapa."

Accordingly, Tsepon Lungshar, the defense minister in the Dalai Lama's council of state, the Kashag, convinced the thirteenth Dalai Lama Thubten Gyatso (1876-1933) to proclaim Lungshar's son to be the next Karmapa.

There was no historical precedent for the Dalai Lama to appoint a Karmapa, and no Dalai Lama in the past had even helped to recognize a previous Karma Kagyu leader. Appendix A to this book includes a chart that lists each Karmapa along with the lamas who recognized him.[7] There are no Dalai Lamas on the list.

But the thirteenth Dalai Lama had his own political reasons to agree to the minister's request. After centuries as a satellite of the Celestial Empire, in 1913 Tibet was able to declare its independence and expel the small Chinese garrison in Lhasa. Weakened by internal fighting in the wake of the overthrow of the last Qing emperor "Henry" Puyi two years earlier, the new Nationalist Chinese government could not oppose Tibet's move by force. But the Nationalists never recognized Tibet's independence, and continued to claim the country as an integral part of China.

The Dalai Lama knew that China's weakness was a rare opportunity to establish Tibet's independence in the eyes of the world. Lungshar agreed, and with a group of progressives in Lhasa, he supported the Dalai Lama's efforts to modernize the Tibetan government against the opposition of strong conservative forces centered on the three large Gelug monasteries in Lhasa. The Three Seats of Drepung, Sera, and Ganden wielded considerable political clout through their armies of *dopdops* or "fighting monks" and their traditional influence over powerful noble families in Central Tibet. These huge monasteries used their power to block or delay reforms to modernize Tibet, claiming that such innovations as opening English-language schools, joining the League of Nations, or building a modern army would threaten the country's traditional Buddhist culture.

"The large monasteries were also concerned about losing power to a modern government under the Dalai Lama with a well-equipped army and centralized administration," Chodrak said.

Against the opposition of strong conservatives, the Dalai Lama attempted to push through reforms against the clock—before China would regain its strength and try to retake Tibet. In the early twenties, the government began an ambitious modernization program. In 1922, the same year that the fifteenth Karmapa died, the Dalai Lama established an army modeled on the British forces in India. His government then went on to introduce modern innovations such as passports, a postal service, and systemized national taxation, all to build Tibet's strength and show the outside world that the Land of Snows was a modern nation rather than a medieval vassal state of China. The thirteenth Dalai Lama thus hoped to gain international recognition of Tibet's independence.

The Lhasa government also hoped to unify the various regions where ethnic Tibetans traditionally lived into one modern nation. For its strategic importance, the Dalai Lama wanted more control over Kham, where the Karmapa was strong. Khenpo Chodrak provided his analysis.

"And so, perhaps against his better spiritual judgment, but for compelling political reasons, the Dalai Lama agreed to interfere in the Karmapa selection process and support Tsepon Lungshar's son as a candidate. In 1929 or 1930—Tsurphu records are not clear on the date—the Tibetan leader made a proclamation that his minister's son was the reincarnation of the Karmapa.

"Predictably, the Tsurphu labrang rejected this interference. The Karmapa's monastery said that the government had no role in choosing a Karmapa. As it turned out, at the same time, the Karmapa's administration had finally found its own candidate. In response to His Holiness the thirteenth Dalai Lama's proclamation about Lungshar's son, the Karmapa's administration politely informed the Tibetan leader that it had located a boy of its own, a son of a noble family known as Athub Tsang of the kingdom of Derge in Kham.

"At the time, the thirteenth Dalai Lama did not press the issue, perhaps recognizing that if the Karmapa's own labrang had found a boy at last, then it was better for everyone to have an authentic Karmapa than a politically appointed one.

"But before the Tsurphu administration could enthrone the Athub boy, out of respect for His Holiness the thirteenth Dalai Lama's

power as political ruler, Tsurphu officials had to formally request him
to reverse his action and allow them to proceed with the enthronement
of their own boy. In response, the thirteenth Dalai Lama did withdraw
Tsepon Lungshar's son as a candidate, thus showing that he recognized
the authority of the Karmapa's own school to choose its head lama's
reincarnation. This boy later became His Holiness the sixteenth Karmapa
Rangjung Rigpe Dorje." Sadly, Lunghsar's son, the failed Karmapa, soon
died after falling off a roof.

Lungshar suffered more hardship as well. In the thirties, facing
strong opposition by conservatives, the Dalai Lama had to back down
on his military and administrative reforms in Lhasa. After the thirteenth
Dalai Lama's death, conservative rivals pushed aside Lungshar's group
and arrested the defense minister. He was convicted of attempted murder
and plotting to overthrow the state. The government made an example of
the unfortunate minister, ordering his eyes to be put out and sentencing
him to life imprisonment. Tragically, the defeat of Lungshar's group
effectively ended reforms in Tibet, leaving the country isolated and
friendless in the world and defenseless against the Chinese invasion that
would come two decades later.

6 EXILE, DEATH, AND DISSENT

The Sixteenth Karmapa Goes into Exile

Fifteen Karmapas followed Dusum Khyenpa in Tibet, the last being the sixteenth Karmapa, Rangjung Rigpe Dorje (1924-81). All Karmapas became accomplished masters of meditation and tantric ritual, but each Karmapa also developed his own personal strengths and channeled his activity into a focus suiting his personality. Some Karmapas were known as accomplished scholars. Others founded monasteries. Still others, like the fifth Karmapa Deshin Shegpa, became the teachers of Chinese emperors or Tibetan kings.

His intimates knew the sixteenth Karmapa Rangjung Rigpe Dorje for the sheer strength of his personality. He was a likable autocrat who dominated every gathering he attended with the force of his will, the quickness of his mind, and the disarming effect of his booming laughter. He befriended children and animals and particularly liked birds, often finding them to be reincarnations of deceased followers.

Until the Chinese invasion, Rangjung Rigpe Dorje's life followed the pattern set by the first Karmapa Dusum Khyenpa. Though born in 1924, the same year Calvin Coolidge delivered the first presidential address on radio, the Karmapa's early life in Tibet was straight out of the Middle Ages. He was born into the powerful Athub family, hereditary ministers of the independent kingdom of Derge located in Kham. His childhood was said to be marked by precocious behavior and auspicious signs. As an adult, the sixteenth Karmapa managed and built monasteries, traveled around Tibet giving empowerments and the Black Crown ceremony, and, some would say, performed miracles.

The sixteenth Karmapa's life story begins to diverge from his predecessors when the Chinese invasion of 1950-51 dragged both Tibet and the institution of the Karmapas into the modern era. After nine years of uneasy peace with the occupying Communists, the revolt of Khampa fighters against the Chinese People's Liberation Army threatened to bring down massive repression from Beijing. As we have seen, by 1959, the ranking lamas, including the Karmapa, decided that it was time to flee Tibet for their own safety and to preserve their Buddhist lineages.

The Karmapa had to decide which movable assets to take into exile. Like other powerful lamas in Tibet, the Karmapas accumulated material wealth befitting their spiritual prestige. The economy of old Tibet was a feudal system much like that of medieval Europe. Wealth came from land planted in cash crops or used for grazing, and aristocrats and monasteries owned most of the land. The wealthiest cloisters owned hundreds of acres worked by peasants, serfs, or even slaves. For example, the richest monastery in Tibet, Drepung monastery in Lhasa, was one of the largest landholders in the world, with 185 estates, 20,000 serfs, 300 pastures and 16,000 nomads.[1] Other large cloisters, including the seat of the Karmapas at Tsurphu monastery with more than a thousand monks, controlled fewer assets but were still significant feudal landlords.

The landed riches accumulated over the eight-hundred-year history of Tsurphu all had to be left behind when the sixteenth Karmapa fled Tibet in 1959. However, the Karmapa was able to take along most of the movable religious and art treasures collected by past Karmapas. These included statues of Buddhist deities, important lamas in the history of the lineage, and the Buddha himself; relics and relic boxes made of gold and silver encrusted with jewels; and manuscripts of the Buddhist sutras and commentaries on them by great masters of the past.[2] But the most valuable of all the treasures that the sixteenth Karmapa brought from Tibet was the Black Crown, as we have seen.

With dozens of crates of valuables, the Karmapa's party made its way from Tsurphu into Bhutan. Once safely out of Tibet, the Karmapa started making plans to reestablish the activity of the Karma Kagyu school in exile. Bhutan was being overwhelmed by refugees, so the Karmapa decided to look elsewhere to settle. Sikkim was home to many Karma Kagyu devotees and already had a monastery founded by the ninth Karmapa Wangchuk Dorje four centuries earlier (now known as Old Rumtek monastery), located about fifteen miles outside the capital city of

Gangtok. In 1959 Chogyal Tashi Namgyal invited the Karmapa to settle in Sikkim, as he had done when the Karmapa paid a visit to the kingdom four years earlier. Now the Karmapa was ready to accept. But there were some in Sikkim who did not want the Karmapa to move in.

On his previous trip to Sikkim in 1956, the Karmapa had left behind in Gangtok, as an advisor to the Sikkimese royal family, a lama named Gyathon Tulku, who hailed from the seat of Situ Rinpoche at Palpung monastery. The Karmapa hoped that Gyathon would make friends for the Karma Kagyu in Sikkim in preparation for the day when the high lamas might have to flee Tibet. Gyathon was skilled in a cure from traditional Tibetan medicine in which the healer licks an iron ball and spits on a wound or affected area on the patient's body. This made him popular with the royal family and soon he became the personal guru to the Sikkimese queen mother.

Over the course of four years in Sikkim, Gyathon apparently began to take a proprietary attitude to the country, seeing it as his spiritual territory alone. He arranged with the queen mother that he should remain the chief Buddhist lama in the kingdom. After fleeing Tibet in 1959, Dudjom Rinpoche, the head of the Nyingma order, tried to settle in Sikkim, but the royal family asked him to leave, probably to protect the franchise of Gyathon.

After a few weeks as a guest of the Bhutanese royal family when he arrived from Tibet in 1959, the Karmapa decided to move on to India. At the border, he met a representative of the Sikkim Chogyal, who renewed the king's earlier invitation for the Karmapa to settle in Sikkim. The Karmapa accepted, and proceeded with his party to Gangtok.

The following year, the queen mother and Gyathon Tulku formed a private alliance to evict the Karmapa from the tiny kingdom. If the Karmapa could be expelled from Sikkim, then Gyathon could invite his traditional guru, Situ Rinpoche, a boy of six at the time, to settle in the kingdom. Once Situ came of age, he could then take over Gyathon's position as spiritual advisor to the royal family. To save Sikkim for Tai Situ, Gyathon opposed the Karmapa settling in Sikkim. He tried to influence the Chogyal to keep the Karmapa out. But the strong support of two of the Karmapa's followers in the Sikkim administration, Tashi Dundur Densapa and Tratin Sherab Gyaltshen Kazi, swayed the Chogyal towards the Karmapa.

Against his mother's wishes, in 1960, the Chogyal insisted on offering the Karmapa seventy-five acres to build his monastery in exile, thus killing Gyathon's plans. In recognition of the service of Densapa and Gyaltshen, in the following year the Karmapa invited the two Sikkimese administrators to join the board of the Karmapa Charitable Trust. Disgraced for opposing the well loved Karma Kagyu leader, in 1967 Gyathon was forced to announce that he would not reincarnate as a tulku in the future. The sixteenth Karmapa confirmed that there would be no further incarnations of Gyathon Tulku. Yet, even after his death soon afterwards, Gyathon's legacy continued to create contention between Tai Situ and the management of Rumtek, as we will see.

On land adjacent to the old Rumtek monastery, from 1962 to 1966, the sixteenth Karmapa constructed the new Rumtek Dharma Chakra Center. The Karmapa also obtained help from the Indian government of Jawaharlal Nehru, which made an immediate grant to build an assembly hall and living quarters for the monks. Rumtek would be the Karmapa's monastic seat in exile until his death in 1981.

Later, a lama who had fled Tsurphu in 1959 and settled in Ladakh, Drupon Dechen, suggested rebuilding Tsurphu if the Chinese government would allow it. The Karmapa was lukewarm to this plan. Even if the monastery had not been razed during the Cultural Revolution, it still would have lost all its "blessing"—had become desanctified—under Communist control. The Karmapa did not want to live in Tibet under the Chinese. He considered Rumtek his new seat and apparently did not look back. Nonetheless, after the Karmapa's death and the beginning of Chinese liberalization in Tibet in the early 1980s, Drupon Dechen would lead an effort to rebuild Tsurphu in the Karmapa's name, working with Tai Situ and his aide Akong Rinpoche. In 1992, Tai Situ would place his Karmapa candidate Ogyen Trinley at the rebuilt monastery.

At Rumtek, the sixteenth Karmapa received an endless stream of devotees, from Tibetan refugees to Indian generals and Bollywood movie stars. In the 1960s, he also met his first Westerners, including Ole and Hannah Nydahl. In 1974, at the invitation of the Nydahls and other European followers, Rangjung Rigpe Dorje became the first Karmapa to leave Asia and visit the West. He traveled to Europe, providing Westerners with their first experience of the Black Crown ceremony. On this trip, he astonished his new foreign students with many small miraculous acts of kindness. When presented with children for a blessing, the Karmapa would smile broadly and try to engage them in playful conversation with his few words of English.

He also showed kindness to animals, particularly towards birds. While driving around European cities he had never before visited, he would often ask to stop at a particular spot, which would just happen to contain the largest shop selling birds in town. Bounding out of the car, the Karmapa would stride into the store, and listen to the birds. "That one tells the finest stories, but this one over there only talks nonsense," he would say. When he put his hand in a cage, the bird he wanted would fly to him. Then he would say mantras and blow on the birds, explaining that he was teaching them to meditate.

Two years later, in 1976, Chogyam Trungpa Rinpoche, by then a popular spiritual figure in the West, invited the Karmapa to the United States. After leaving Scotland in 1970 Trungpa established himself in Vermont. Later, he founded dozens of Dharmadhatu centers (which later became Shambhala centers) around the United States. At Trungpa's centers, the Karmapa performed the Black Crown ceremony to large crowds. Visiting the Hopi Indians in Arizona, the Karmapa even brought rain to end a long drought.

The Karmapa paid his final visit to the United States in 1981 to get treatment for cancer at a hospital in Zion, Illinois, a suburb of Chicago.

Deathbed Tension

When the Karmapa was dying in 1981, a few of the highest Kagyu lamas came to the cancer hospital near Chicago. Shamar and Jamgon accompanied the Karmapa from Hong Kong, where he had undergone an operation. Gyaltsab stayed behind at Rumtek. In *Karmapa: The Politics of Reincarnation*, Lea Terhune wrote that he was fulfilling his traditional role there as the Karmapa's "regent."

Yet, although the title *gyaltsab* means "regent" in Tibetan, as we have seen, the Gyaltsab tulkus had not served as regents of the Karmapa since the seventeenth century. A more likely explanation for Gyaltsab's absence was that he could not afford the plane fare. Numerous Karma Kagyu lamas did not come to Chicago, because, at that time, before the days of large donations to Tibetan lamas from abroad, it was too expensive for them to fly from India to the United States. Situ was already in Scotland, so his ticket to Chicago was affordable, and he arrived there just after Shamar and Jamgon.

But according to Shamar, Situ Rinpoche came to Chicago only after urging from Jamgon. Two weeks earlier, Situ had visited the Karmapa in Hong Kong. Afterwards, Situ flew to Europe to preside over a conference for all his European centers that he had planned for months, and apparently he was not eager to leave the conference to see the Karmapa after so short an absence.

Jamgon Kongtrul called Situ from the Chicago hotel room he was sharing with Shamar, who heard Jamgon's side of the phone call. "Jamgon Rinpoche begged Situ to come and said His Holiness Karmapa's condition was serious, he was probably going to die soon," Shamar told me. "Situ Rinpoche still did not want to leave his conference. Then, Jamgon Rinpoche told him that he did not want to be responsible for Situ Rinpoche being away from His Holiness's passing, so Situ Rinpoche agreed to come to Chicago, but for two days only."

A few days later, Tai Situ arrived in Chicago. Shamar remembers that "he came with a changed attitude. Situ Rinpoche forgot his former important business, and now he was quite anxious to remain at His Holiness Karmapa's bedside until the end. I am not sure why he changed like this. Perhaps he wanted to show that he was the Karmapa's favorite disciple?"

Shortly after Tai Situ arrived in Chicago, he asked Shamar for a favor: to attend the conference in Brussels in his place. The event was due to start in a few days and last for a week. Situ told Shamar that if he himself went to Brussels as he had originally planned, then as the organizer of the meeting he would be bound by contract to remain for the duration of the conference. This would keep him away from Chicago for eight or nine days, and he would almost certainly miss the Karmapa's last moments.

However, if Shamar would attend the event in Situ's place, as a stand-in, he would be able to put in a cameo appearance and then excuse himself after a day or two to return to the Karmapa's bedside. Situ repeated this request several times and, according to Shamar, this wore down his own hesitation. "There were several witnesses to this conversation," Shamar said.[3]

"At that time, I was Situ's best friend," Shamar explains. "His family had been very kind to my mother after she escaped Tibet in 1959 and lived in Darjeeling. So I felt sorry for him and was willing to do him this favor if I could really get back before His Holiness would pass away."

Before agreeing to Situ's request, however, Shamar asked Situ to do a *mo* (prediction) to see if the Karmapa would live beyond the three or four days that he would be away from Chicago, including time in Brussels and round-trip travel.

In front of Shamar's brother Jigme (a lama who ran the Karmapa's monasteries in France beginning in the mid-seventies) as well as Topga Rinpoche, at the time the second-ranking administrator at Rumtek, Jamgon Kongtrul, and others, Situ cast the ritual dice, consulted his book of interpretation, and assured Shamar that the Karmapa would not die in his absence. The hospital staff also said that the Karmapa would probably live another twelve to fifteen days. So the next day Shamar left for Brussels.

When he arrived in Brussels, Shamar was surprised to hear from the conference organizers that there would have been no difficulty for Situ himself to have come for two or three days and then leave, especially under the circumstances. Later, Chogyam Trungpa, the lama who had become so prominent in the United States, reportedly would claim that his former attendant Akong Rinpoche, now Situ's confidant, had developed this plan as a pretext to get Shamar away from the Karmapa. According to Trungpa, Situ wanted Shamar out of the way so he could forge a prediction letter and then, after the Karmapa's death, Situ could present the forgery as a letter written by the Karmapa.

As it turned out, the Karmapa died on November 5, 1981 while Shamar Rinpoche was in transit from Europe back to the United States. Nonetheless, if Situ or any other lama had wanted to forge a letter at this time, the presence of Jamgon, Jigme, Topga, and others who saw that the Karmapa wrote no letter would have prevented it.

Situ and his sympathizers have claimed that it was the sixteenth Karmapa himself who sent Shamar to Brussels so that Tai Situ could remain at his bedside. Both Lea Terhune and Mick Brown have asserted this in their books on the Karmapa. As Brown put it, "There was a Buddhist conference going on in Belgium, to which Tai Situ had been invited as the Karmapa's representative. But the Karmapa said he wanted Tai Situ to stay with him, and that Shamar should go to Belgium instead." Brown concluded that for some observers, this decision represented the sixteenth Karmapa showing a preference for Situ over Shamar.[4] Other critics of Shamar have accused him of being amiss in absenting himself from the last moments of the late Karmapa's life while Tai Situ remained in Chicago, attending his guru as a good disciple.

However, this story does not accord with the facts. The conference in Brussels was not organized by the Karmapa, but by Tai Situ himself. And, it is unlikely that the Karmapa could have talked to either Shamar or Situ about the event: since his stay in Hong Kong, the cancer that had spread to his throat had destroyed the Karmapa's ability to speak, or even to swallow food and water. In Chicago, the ailing leader was fed intravenously.

"This seems to be a case of no good deed going unpunished," Shamar told me. "His Holiness Karmapa didn't even know that I had left and he was expecting me to return the next morning. After my departure Jamgon Rinpoche informed His Holiness that I had gone to Europe for Situ Rinpoche's conference. Gyalwa Karmapa did not say anything, since he couldn't talk. I heard later that he just smiled ironically.

"It was a painful lesson for me. I started to grow up at this time. I was too trusting and too inexperienced."

A Vulnerable Legacy

At the time of his death in 1981, the sixteenth Karmapa left a network of more than a hundred Karma Kagyu Buddhist centers with thousands of devotees around the world. This network had the potential to spread the teachings of Buddhism to millions of people and to help Karma Kagyu teachings take deep root on foreign soil. In the future, the network of dharma centers would also develop the potential to funnel millions of dollars in donations per year back to Rumtek for the activities of the next Karmapa.

But in the Karmapa's time, and just after his death, his administration operated on a strictly hand-to-mouth basis. "Back then, no Tibetan lamas had any money," Shamar told me. "Monasteries were very poor. Rumtek was actually better off, because of the reputation of the late Karmapa. Local Sikkimese would give him enough to pay the daily expenses. People would give ten or twenty rupees each. But money for building or growing, there was none. Tibetan lamas only started getting large donations in the mid-eighties. Then, Taiwan opened up to foreigners, and many lamas went there. Afterwards, money started coming from the West too."

During his lifetime, the sixteenth Karmapa followed a relaxed and seemingly idiosyncratic approach to fund-raising that sometimes baffled his staff. His personal painter of thangkas (religious icons) at Rumtek was

Karma Norbu. When I met him in France in 2003, he was a slim man in his sixties who told me a story about how the Karmapa liked to raise money for the monastery's support.

Norbu had long felt that there was a greater potential to reach out to wealthy followers and increase large donations to Rumtek. One day, he mentioned this to the sixteenth Karmapa. The Karmapa laughed, and then took Norbu to see the ledger where donations were recorded. What he saw there confirmed his thinking, but surprised him in its extent. There were few large donations from the wealthy. Instead, nearly every line item was a small offering from someone very poor: one or two rupees or even just a few *paise* from rickshaw pullers, rag pickers, cleaning women, or subsistence farmers with no more than a half dozen chickens to feed their families.

"Bodhisattvas like the Karmapa think differently than normal people," Norbu told me. "The Karmapa said that he actually preferred to receive small donations from the poor rather than large gifts from more comfortable people. This was shocking to me. Why take from the poor, who can so little afford to give? But that was exactly the Karmapa's point. When rich people give money, it is not much of a sacrifice for them and just increases their pride. But when the poor give, it is difficult. Their offering has much more value to them, and thus creates not pride but devotion in their minds, which is what they need to make spiritual progress."

When the Karmapa traveled, he did receive larger donations, but they were small compared to what high lamas would start to get in the eighties and nineties. Most of the money he received went to pay for his treatment at the cancer hospital in Chicago at the time of his death. He also received donations of land, principally a parcel in the Dordogne area of France, where he built the biggest Tibetan dharma center in Europe, Dhagpo Kagyu Ling. On a smaller parcel in Woodstock, New York, he began building his North American headquarters, Karma Triyana Dharmachakra.

While the sixteenth Karmapa lived, the international network of Karma Kagyu centers was firmly tied to Rumtek. His death left his fragile legacy vulnerable as it left control over the Karma Kagyu uncertain.

Never before had the transition from one Karmapa to the next occurred with the chief lamas of the Karma Kagyu so at odds over who had the authority to choose the Karmapa. To make things worse, a Karmapa had never been found and recognized in exile either. At Tsurphu, the Karmapa's labrang had the experience of choosing fifteen generations of Karmapas in the familiar social environment of Tibet. In exile, the sixteenth Karmapa's reconstituted administration at Rumtek was inexperienced in the ways of the modern world.

The old-style administrators of the Karmapa's labrang knew little about asserting property rights, gaining allies in local and national governments, and marshaling support from the new devotees of the Karma Kagyu around the world. In Tibet, though politics had usually played into tulku searches, the Karmapa's strong labrang had never needed to mount an active public outreach program to support a search for a new Karmapa. The previous Karmapa's chief disciples chose his successor quietly amongst themselves. In exile, by contrast, external alliances and legal cases would determine the future of the Karma Kagyu leader.

7 THE TRADITIONALIST

A Prediction of Troubles to Come

As he had made so many astonishing predictions throughout his life, near its end the sixteenth Karmapa Rangjung Rigpe Dorje also predicted the troubles to come. In January 1980 the Karmapa traveled to New Delhi to attend the ground-breaking ceremony for the new Karmapa International Buddhist Institute.

Early in the morning before the ceremony, the Karmapa started vomiting up blood. But he insisted on going through with the event, at which Indian President Neelam Sanjiva Reddy was due to preside. Through the power of his will, the Karmapa played his role in the ceremony. Government officials, devotees, and other guests saw little sign of the great pain the Karmapa must have been feeling and the ceremony was a success. Afterwards, in private, he collapsed. The Karmapa was taken to the All-India Medical Institute for immediate stomach surgery.

While recovering in Delhi, the Karmapa stayed at Sikkim House. There, twenty-two-year-old Drukchen Rinpoche, traditional leader of the Drukpa Kagyu school, paid a visit. The two lamas spent almost four hours talking together.

"I heard very sad news that Your Holiness was in bad health. But now I have come here and I see that you appear to have recovered very nicely," Drukchen Rinpoche reportedly said.

"No, no, no," the Karmapa replied, "in about a year I will die. So I have one request to make of you, Rinpoche. After I die, a major obstacle will appear for the future of the Karma Kagyu lineage. At that time, Shamar Rinpoche will be the only one to preserve the lineage from disaster. Please help and support him."

Then, the Karmapa took both of Drukchen Rinpoche's hands in his own and looked him in the eye. "You and Shamar Rinpoche should be to each other like the sun and the moon. Together, you will embody all my hopes for the future of the Kagyu school."[1]

The Most Famous Unknown Lama

Shamar is Tai Situ's chief rival in the battle to choose the seventeenth Karmapa. Without Shamar's opposition to Ogyen Trinley, the young tulku would probably be the undisputed head of the Karma Kagyu today. To his followers, Shamar is the last bulwark against the pollution of the Karmapa line. To his enemies, Shamar is the last obstacle to the return of the Karmapa.

To Tibetans of past centuries, the Shamarpa was one of the most venerated lamas of Buddhism. His name was often said in the same breath as that of the Karmapa. For seven hundred years, the close tie between the Shamarpas and the Karmapas served as the model of a student-teacher bond that transcended death and endured lifetime after lifetime.

Since the takeover of Rumtek in 1993, the current Shamar, now in his mid-fifties, has fought a lonely battle against the most powerful forces in the Tibetan Buddhist world. Stubbornly, for twenty years Shamar has refused to admit defeat in the face of imposing odds. He has also been accused of enriching himself at the expense of the Karma Kagyu, a charge with no merit.

In her book on the Karmapa, Australian novelist and Tibetan rights activist Gaby Naher has written that Shamar "received many gifts from his uncle, including a monastery in Mehrauli, India. Now a wealthy man in his own right, he owns property across India and Nepal, including the substantial Galinka House in Kalimpong."[2]

Unlike other high lamas, Shamar's alleged wealth is not apparent. When I asked Shamar if he owned a monastery in Mehrauli, India, he replied that Naher must have been referring to the Karmapa International Buddhist Institute in New Delhi, located in a development that used to be known as the Mehrauli Institutional Area, but was renamed the Qutab Institutional Area in honor of the nearby Mughal-era tower, the Qutab Minar. "We do not own the land, and the Karmapa's labrang, not me, holds it on a perpetual lease from the government of India," Shamar told me.

"At his death in 1981, His Holiness had very little, only about $160,000, and in the confusion of financial records then, the Rumtek administration could only get access to about $60,000 of that. Of course, my uncle left me nothing, he had no will and all his property went automatically to his labrang at Rumtek, under the control of the Karmapa Charitable Trust." Indeed, because it was difficult for the Rumtek administration to raise funds after the Karmapa's death, Shamar paid the day-to-day expenses of the monastery for a decade, raising the funds on his own primarily in Hong Kong and Singapore.

While his rivals Tai Situ and Gyaltsab Rinpoches have both built large, expensive monasteries for themselves in India, Shamar has been slow to start monasteries and Buddhist centers in his own name. His supporters say that Shamar has unselfishly sacrificed the chance to advance himself in order to serve the Karmapa.

Until recently, Shamar devoted himself to managing and building institutions for the Karmapa. Aside from running Rumtek until Situ and Gyaltsab took it over in 1993, Shamar completed the Karmapa International Buddhist Institute (KIBI) in New Delhi in the early eighties, raising 30 million rupees (about $3.5 million) for the project. In the mid-nineties, Shamar built a monk's school in Kalimpong, located in the northeastern Indian state of West Bengal, just three hours south of Rumtek in Sikkim. His Karmapa candidate Thaye Dorje was due to complete his education there in 2006, and the school is part of the Karmapa's labrang, not Shamar's.

Shamar's outreach in the West has also lagged behind dozens of other lamas. Only in the mid-nineties did Shamar start the first dharma center under his own management in the United States, the Bodhi Path center in Virginia's Shenandoah Valley. Back in Tibet, in 2003 he begin restoring Yangpachen monastery, the historic seat of the Shamarpas near Lhasa that was confiscated by the Central Tibetan government in the eighteenth century, as we will learn about, and then reduced to rubble in the Cultural Revolution of the 1960s. By contrast, Tai Situ had begun to restore the massive complex of the Situpas at Palpung in Kham twenty years earlier. Apparently, as Shamar was building institutions for the Karmapa, Tai Situ was doing the same thing for himself.

As to Shamar's residence in Kalimpong, Galinka House is a medium-sized bungalow built at the tail end of the British era that would not look out of place in a suburban development of Houston or Cleveland. But by American standards, its three bedrooms, dining room, sitting room, and office would each be considered cramped. Even in Kalimpong, it would be difficult to term substantial the house's two floors built on a single-acre lot, since some of his neighbors boast much grander houses than Shamar's. Yet, perched on a steep hillside facing the line of the Himalayas crowned by Kanchenjunga, the world's third-highest peak, the location is breathtaking. During the few weeks a year that he lives there, Shamar can enjoy a million-dollar view as he sips sweet Indian tea with milk from a small gazebo in his well groomed front yard.

The Red Hat Karmapa

It is his relationship with the Karmapa that defines the Shamarpa most strongly, as it defined his predecessors for the last seven centuries. As with the Karmapas, so a prophecy from the Buddha, found in the *Good Kalpa Sutra*, foretold the coming of the Shamarpas: "In the future, a maha-bodhisattva [a great saint] with a ruby-red crown will come to the suffering multitude, leading them out of their cyclic bewilderment and misery."

Nearly two thousand years later, the second Karmapa Karma Pakshi (1206-83) predicted the coming of the Shamarpas, saying they would alternate as student and teacher with future Karmapas and that the two lamas would support each other as the "Black Hat Karmapa" and the "Red Hat Karmapa." Tibetans traditionally compared the Karmapas and the Shamarpas to the sun and the moon. An early Shamarpa predicted that "At times the Black Hat Karmapas and the Red Hat Karmapas will act as spiritual masters of each other and at times they will be students of each other. In one instance, they will be related as father and son and in another instance they will be related as uncle and nephew."[3]

The third Karmapa Rangjung Dorje (1284-1339) selected the first Shamar Khedrup Drakpa Sengye (1283-1349) as his official deputy, a kind of permanent co-Karmapa, in recognition of the disciple's spiritual attainment. He became a popular preacher and evangelist, converting nonbelievers through his skill in logical argument and rhetorical presentation. The Shamarpa later went on to practice years of solitary meditation retreats in which he saw auspicious visions that helped guide him to found monasteries and locate the students who would become his leading disciples. The first Shamarpa spent the last twenty years of his life in an isolated cave perfecting tantric meditation practices and teaching students who took the trouble to seek him out.

Remembering the prediction of the second Karmapa a century earlier, the fourth Karmapa Rolpe Dorje (1340-83) presented the Shamarpa with an exact copy of his own mystical Black Crown in red and explained that future Karmapas would manifest in two human forms. "You are the one manifestation, while I am the other. Therefore the responsibility to uphold the Karma Kagyu teachings rests equally on me as it does on you."[4]

Later, Tai Situ, ·Goshir Gyaltsab, and other high lamas would appear, but for the next four centuries, the Shamarpas would shoulder most of the responsibility to recognize Karmapa reincarnations. The Shamarpas recognized six out of the nine Karmapas who came between the years 1384 and 1797, five working alone and one with another lama. In this same period, Tai Situs recognized one Karmapa alone and a second Karmapa with help from another lama, the fifth Sharmapa. The chart of Karmapas in appendix A of this book indicates which Karmapas were recognized by Shamar, Situ, and other lamas.

History Written by the Victors

Supporters of Ogyen Trinley and journalists sympathetic to them have tried to discredit the current Shamar Rinpoche by criticizing previous Shamarpas, particularly the tenth incarnation, who lived in the eighteenth century. Predictably, Tibetan Buddhism inspires this peculiar sort of critique. It would be difficult to imagine holding the current United States President responsible for the actions of Andrew Jackson or Rutherford B. Hayes, for example. But under the tulku system, the same mind-stream is said to inhabit generations of different individual lamas. Thus, it might stand to reason, at least for outsiders, that the current incarnation of a tulku would carry the praise and blame of his previous incarnations.

The current Shamarpa disagrees with this view: "Buddhist reincarnation does not work this way, that you are the same person in a different body lifetime after lifetime. It is merely a tendency of mind that continues from one life to the next. This carries over into accomplishments. For example, I cannot take credit for books written by earlier Shamarpas. I would have to write my own books. Political problems work the same way." Nonetheless, Shamar has found himself required to answer criticisms of his predecessor from two centuries earlier.

In the late eighteenth century, at the time of the tenth Shamarpa Mipham Chodrup Gyatso (1742-92), a tragedy befell the line of the Shamarpas that would remove them from Tibetan public life until the middle of the twentieth century. The role of the tenth Shamarpa has been hotly contested by historians and journalists. It has become a test of the current Shamar's fitness to recognize the seventeenth Karmapa—or to object to the recognition of Ogyen Trinley.

"Tibetan Buddhists believe that karma from one's past actions or deeds can cling to a person through many lifetimes," wrote British reporter Tim McGirk. "That is why many Tibetans explain the odd behavior of a lama named Shamar Rinpoche by referring to an event 202 years ago. In his incarnation then, Shamar Rinpoche was a monk so overcome by greed that he lured the Gurkha army into attacking a monastery for its treasure."[5]

Lea Terhune echoed this view in *Karmapa: The Politics of Reincarnation*: "The Gurkhas had been spoiling for a fight with Tibet. In this they were helped by the Shamarpa, who is credited by historians with instigating the Gurkha War with alluring descriptions of the riches at the Panchen Lama's monastery, Tashilhunpo, and egging on the Gurkha king."[6] Later, we will see how McGirk and Terhune worked as colleagues in New Delhi in the 1990s, so it would not be surprising that they shared the same interpretation of Tibetan history. In this case, their views appear to derive from the well-known history of Tibet by former Lhasa official Tsepon W.D. Shakabpa, whom we met in chapter 3, where we discussed his biased account of the fifth Dalai Lama's rise to temporal power in the seventeenth century.

In his book, Shakabpa blamed the tenth Shamarpa for starting the Tibet-Gorkha war. After the Dalai Lama's government intervened to prevent the Nepali Gorkhas from conquering Sikkim, Shakabpa wrote:

> The Gurkhas were annoyed at the Tibetan interference and
> were looking for an excuse to attack Tibet. An excuse was
> found in the controversy over the third Panchen Lama's

personal property, which was being claimed by the Panchen's
two brothers, Drungpa Trulku and Shamar Trulku; the
latter was the ninth [sic] Red Hat Kar-ma-pa Lama named
Chosdrup Gyatso. Shamar Trulku hoped to use Gurkha
backing for his claim to the Panchen Lama's property in the
Tashilhunpo monastery; while the Gurkhas wanted to use
his claim as a pretext for invading Tibet.[7]

Shakabpa's interpretation of the Shamarpa's role in the Tibet-Gorkha
War has been disseminated widely. Yet, as in the case of Shakabpa's account
of the rivalry between the Karma Kagyu and the Gelugpa that led to the
Dalai Lama's ascension to power in 1642, his story of the tenth Shamarpa
does not agree with standard Tibetan historical sources of the period.[8]
These sources show that Shakabpa is too easy on the Tibetan government
of the time and too hard on the tenth Shamarpa. This is not surprising,
considering that Shakabpa was a minister of the old Lhasa government,
since the seventeenth century the historic enemy of the Shamarpas.
    Tibetan chroniclers—especially a general named Dhoring who led
Tibetan forces in the Gorkha War and provided an eyewitness account
of the major players involved—are much more sympathetic to the tenth
Shamarpa. These historians explain that while trying to claim his portion
of a family inheritance, the tenth Shamarpa unwittingly became a pawn in
a conflict between Central Tibet and its overlord China on the one hand,
and Nepal and the British in India on the other. The outcome would have
disastrous effects for the future of the Shamarpa line.
    In the past, the Shamars and Karmapas sometimes appeared in the
same family, as the fifth Shamarpa had predicted. As we have seen, the
current Shamar is the nephew of the sixteenth Karmapa. However, in the
eighteenth century, the Shamarpa took birth in the family of the second
most powerful lama of the Dalai Lama's Gelug school, adding an unusual
political twist. The tenth Shamarpa Mipham Chodrup Gyatso was born
in 1742 in Tsang province as the half-brother of the third Panchen Lama
Lobsang Palden Yeshe (1737-80). The Shamarpa was thirty-eight years old
when his half-brother, age forty-three, died of smallpox while on a visit to
the Qianlong emperor in Beijing in 1780. The emperor gave a substantial
sum of silver coins as a condolence to one of the Panchen's brothers,
known as the Drungpa Hutogatu, to distribute to the Panchen's family.

The tenth Shamarpa and the Drungpa clashed about these funds. The Shamarpa argued that the bequest was intended for the Panchen Lama's family, and as a half-brother of the late Panchen Lama, the Shamarpa claimed a portion of the emperor's gift. But the Drungpa refused to share the Chinese funds, saying they were intended for the Panchen Lama's Gelugpa order. Perhaps fearing that this position would not stand up in court, the Drungpa, who like the Panchen was a lama of the Gelugpa order, enlisted allies in the Lhasa government. We have seen how the Gelugpas came to enjoy government patronage after the fifth Dalai Lama took power in Lhasa in the seventeenth century. By the 1780s, government preference for the Gelugpa over the other religious schools had become established practice.

The Drungpa found a willing ear in the regent Ngawang Tsultrim, who had refused to relinquish effective control over the government after the eighth Dalai Lama Jampal Gyatso (1758-1804) reached adulthood in the late 1770s. Regent Ngawang apparently saw in the dispute between the Drungpa and the Shamarpa a pretext to accomplish three long-cherished political goals: to extend the power of the Gelugpa school further over its old rival the Karma Kagyu; to settle a long-running trade dispute with Nepal, where Shamar had powerful supporters; and to assert Tibetan autonomy against Nepal's patrons, the British East India Company's administration of India, which had been trying to establish trading posts inside Tibet. The Tibetans and their Chinese overlords feared that trade relations with the East India Company would open Tibet to British interference and perhaps even colonization.

The Qianlong emperor was particularly nervous about European encroachment on his empire, of which he considered Tibet to be a part. Qianlong is known in the West as the Chinese ruler who rebuffed Britain's commercial overtures in 1793, only a year after the Gorkha War, arrogantly informing King George III's envoy Lord George Macartney that the British had nothing to sell that the Chinese wanted to buy. Fifty years later, Anglo-Chinese tension would explode into the Opium War of the 1840s. In the late eighteenth century, as this tension began to grow, Qianlong was as eager to exclude the British from Tibet as he was to keep them out of the port cities of southeastern China.

The Shamarpa had great influence in the kingdom of Nepal. In the early years of their partnership, the Karmapa and Shamarpa had divided Tibet into geographical spheres of responsibility. The Karmapa would teach Buddhism in eastern Tibet, while the Shamarpa would cover the south. Historically, this southern region included Tibet's neighbor Nepal. Over the centuries, the Shamarpas gained thousands of followers there, and the Shamarpas came to serve as spiritual advisors to prominent noble clans and even to the royal family. Shamarpa influence in Nepal continued even after the invading Hindu Gorkhas overthrew the Malla kings of the Kathmandu valley and consolidated their power over the formerly Buddhist kingdom in 1769.

In Lhasa in the early 1790s, Regent Ngawang convinced important Central Tibetan officials and, more importantly, the Chinese Amban, the de facto ruler of Tibet, that the tenth Shamarpa was about to betray Tibet to Nepal and to the Gorkhas' British allies. The regent claimed that the Shamarpa had invited Gorkha forces to cross into Tibet, first to help him claim the wealth of the Panchen Lama and then to go onto Lhasa to pillage the city and force on Tibet a trade agreement favorable to Nepal. The regent was able to make these charges stick at the Dalai Lama's court, and a warrant was put out for the Shamarpa's arrest. To escape capture and likely torture and execution without trial in Lhasa, as was Tibetan custom at the time, the tenth Shamarpa fled for safety to Nepal in 1791.

Nepal's King Prithi Narayanan Shah gave the Shamarpa political asylum—and, to preempt a Tibetan invasion, he sent an expeditionary force across his northern border and into Tibet. Meeting little resistance from the small, poorly trained Tibetan army, the Gorkhas advanced towards Lhasa and prepared to take the city. To avert the capture of their capital, the Tibetans were required to call on the Chinese for help. In response, the Qianlong emperor sent thirteen thousand troops to join a Tibetan force as large as ten thousand to halt the Gorkha advance. The imperial army arrived just in time to prevent a total Tibetan rout, and the Gorkhas were turned back and put on the defensive.

Meanwhile, Regent Ngawang Tsultrim died in Lhasa—Karma Kagyu lamas said that their school's protector deity, Mahakala, had punished the regent for his attack on the Shamarpa. The regent was succeeded by his deputy Tenpai Gonpo Kundeling, who continued to sideline the Dalai Lama as his predecessor had. On his own initiative, the new regent concluded the war, with terms to his own advantage.

With Lhasa no longer under threat of being sacked by Gorkha cavalry, and with the power of the Shamarpas broken in Tibet, the regent could make use of the property of the maligned Red Hat Karmapa.

Tenpai Gonpo confiscated the Shamarpa's monastic seat at Yangpachen and put it under the control of the large Gelugpa monastery Ganden, one of the powerful Three Seats. Dozens of other Shamarpa monasteries were forcibly converted to the Gelugpa order by official mandate. Regent Tenpai Gonpo personally took possession of the tenth Shamar Rinpoche's residence in Lhasa and turned it into a police court and lockup, where accused prisoners were subjected to physical mutilation and other tortures.[9] The regent then convinced the Qianlong emperor to issue a decree that forever after Shamar Rinpoche was prohibited from reincarnating in Tibet. The Lhasa government would enforce this distinctive punishment for the following two centuries.

The tenth Shamarpa died in 1792 in Nepal. Historians have speculated that he was poisoned by either the Nepalis or by Tibetan agents. But the current Shamar told me that his predecessor decided to transfer his consciousness out of his body through the practice of *phowa*—essentially bringing on his own death—to escape capture and torture by the Chinese. His body was cremated in Nepal, but this did not stop the victorious Qianlong emperor from demanding the the Nepalis hand over the ashes and charred pieces of bone, and taking them back to Beijing to undergo a ritual punishment as a warning for others, according to Qing dynasty custom.

Back in Tibet, the Shamar labrang was dissolved and the people and property attached to the Shamarpa under Tibet's feudal system were taken by the government or distributed to various Gelugpa and Karma Kagyu lamas. In light of the Lhasa government ban, no Karmapa could recognize or associate with a Shamarpa on an official basis. To avoid military reprisals against Karma Kagyu monasteries from the government of Central Tibet, the Karmapa observed the ban in public. In private, however, the Karmapas continued to recognize successive reincarnations of the Shamarpas for the next century and a half.[10]

The Shamarpa Returns

The Lhasa ban on the Shamarpas left a power vacuum in the Karma Kagyu hierarchy that was filled by the next highest ranking lamas. For this reason, Karmapa reincarnations for the next century and a half were recognized by other high Kagyu lamas, including the Tai Situs. Of this period, the sixteenth Karmapa commented that "merit was becoming smaller and smaller. There was much political interference. Black was becoming white. The real was becoming unreal. At that time it was not practicable to have any Shamarpas recognized or enthroned. Everything was kept secret. The incarnations appeared, but were not revealed."

In official records, the Shamarpa's spot in the hierarchy of Karma Kagyu lamas remained empty though it was not stricken from the rolls either in Lhasa or in the Karma Kagyu's own listing of lamas, the *Kagyu Gyalwa Yab Say* formalized under the Tsangpa kings in the seventeenth century. But in practice the Tai Situs moved up to the number two spot, the Gyaltsabs took the third spot, and each lama below them moved up one rung in status when Shamar and his administration disappeared. In the nineteenth century, Jamgon Kongtrul was inserted below Situ and above Gyaltsab.

In the absence of the Shamarpas, three incarnations of Situs and five incarnations of Gyaltsabs enjoyed their new higher status. Over a century and a half, their administrations settled into these positions and became accustomed to a Shamar-free Karma Kagyu and the additional privileges, spiritual and worldly, that they gained thereby.

This boon ended for them abruptly in the 1950s and 1960s with the official return of the Shamarpas to their spiritual and temporal leadership of the Karma Kagyu. First, in 1956 the sixteenth Karmapa publicly recognized the current Shamarpa at age four. The Karmapa felt he could make this move because the Chinese invasion of 1950-51 had softened the attitude of the Lhasa government towards the Karma Kagyu and reduced fears of intra-Buddhist rivalry. In addition, in the mid-fifties, the Karmapa had already obtained a promise from the Dalai Lama that he would lift the ban on the Shamarpa as soon as tensions with the Chinese lessened. But tensions only worsened, and the Dalai Lama was not able to officially lift the ban before he fled Tibet in 1959.

In exile, the situation became even more fluid. The defunct Central Tibetan government's ban on Shamarpa became toothless. In India, the Tibetan exile administration could not enforce the ban on Shamarpa. Thus, on his own and without any fear of reprisal, the sixteenth Karmapa could have restored Shamar to his predecessors' role as deputy Karmapa. Nonetheless, out of respect for the Dalai Lama's position as leader of Tibetan exiles, the Karmapa wanted to seek his blessing—in the form of an official end to the old ban—as a courtesy and to show his solidarity with the Dalai Lama's advocacy for Tibetan freedom.

I asked Khenpo Chodrak, the abbot of Rumtek before the takeover in 1993, if he thought that the sixteenth Karmapa's asking the Dalai Lama to lift the ban on the Shamarpas in 1964 was comparable to Tai Situ asking the Dalai Lama to recognize his Karmapa candidate in 1992.

"No, I do not think these are the same," Chodrak said. "Even though the Lhasa government ban had no legal power in exile in India, it was a gesture of friendship from the late Gyalwa Karmapa to His Holiness Dalai Lama to request a formal end to the ban. It was quite different in 1992. There had been no ban on the Karmapas, so there was no need for Situ Rinpoche to ask permission from the Dalai Lama. Instead, Situ's request was just a way for him to go around the traditional process for choosing a Karmapa within the Karma Kagyu by bringing in an outsider with great prestige, His Holiness Dalai Lama."

But in the mid-1960s, the Dalai Lama was grateful for the Karmapa's gesture towards Tibetan unity, and in 1964 he officially removed his government's old ban on Shamar incarnations. The Tibetan leader then offered his blessing to the twelve-year-old fourteenth Shamar Rinpoche.

"Many of the Karmapa's lamas and administrators had known Shamarpa from his early childhood," Chodrak said, "and they were happy to be able to openly train him to lead Rumtek in the future. But the administrations of all the other high lamas who were effectively taken down a notch in the Karma Kagyu hierarchy with the reinsertion of Shamar Rinpoche, particularly Situ and Gyaltsab Rinpoches, appeared to feel betrayed."

In exile, Situ and Gyaltsab had pledged their allegiance to the Karmapa as children, even though in Tibet their predecessors were proudly independent, and had often been rivals of the Karmapa, as we have seen in the case of Gyaltsab and will see with Situ in the next chapter. In fleeing Tibet in 1959, the once-rich labrangs of Situ and Gyaltsab had lost their imposing monasteries and massive landholdings. Now, so soon after that shock, the administrations of these exiled high lamas had to endure the humiliation of the return of Shamar as their superior. Monk-officials of Situ and Gyaltsab were particularly offended by the official return of Shamar.

"Every tulku in Tibet was surrounded and groomed from cradle to grave by a retinue of professional advisers and servants," wrote Indian journalist Anil Maheshwari. "Life after life, their families held the same functions around their lama. These groups grew in prominence and size until they became de facto courts, strait-jacketing their master...After 200 years of enjoying higher status, the protective families that surrounded Situ and Gyaltsab Rinpoches were unwilling to accept the latest declining twist in their fortunes."[11]

"At Rumtek, Situ and Gyaltsab Rinpoches were boyhood playmates of Shamarpa, as I was, and they seemed to care little for issues of hierarchy," Chodrak said. "But the officials of their respective labrangs never forgot how the sixteenth Karmapa had effectively downgraded them, and these men and their families—whose own power and prestige depended on the rank of their lamas—encouraged Situ and Gyaltsab to remember what they had lost in Tibet. As they grew up, the two rinpoches started to act more and more as if they felt they had been cheated out of their inheritance by Shamar Rinpoche."

When the Karmapa got Shamar's ban officially lifted by the Dalai Lama in 1964, he also decided again, as he had in Tibet, against reconstituting the old Shamarpa labrang. Instead, in the spirit of the historical identity between the "Black Hat" and "Red Hat" Karmapas, Shamar would share the Karmapa's administration. This would allow Shamar to be as close as possible to the Karmapa and put him in the best position to protect his legacy in the future. But this would also make Shamar vulnerable. Without his own loyal labrang, Shamar had relatively few allies in case of a conflict with lamas who had their own centuries-old administrations and retained, even in exile, ties of loyalty from hundreds of vassal lamas and regional families then living both inside and outside of Tibet.

8 THE MODERNIZER

Protocol, a Smile, and a Grammy Award

The current twelfth Tai Situ has done much to enhance the prestige of his office. He has built a sprawling modern monastery complex in northern India, Sherab Ling, housing more than six hundred monks and nuns. Some of these monks became the first Tibetans ever to win a Grammy Award.

In February 2004 *Sacred Tibetan Chants, the Monks of Palpung Sherab Ling Monastery* beat five contenders to win best album in the Traditional World Music category. Sherab Ling monks watched the ceremony from Los Angeles live on television with great anticipation, and they greeted news of their award with excitement. Today Situ Rinpoche proudly displays the award in his living quarters. Situ's attendant Lama Tenam Shastri explained to an Indian music reporter that "post-Grammy, Sherab Ling Monastery has made headlines across the world—there's been great curiosity about Sherab Ling and that's translated into more visitors."[1]

In addition Situ Rinpoche launched an international campaign for world peace in the late eighties, the Pilgrimage for Active Peace. Yet, his peace effort was short-lived and died out after the Dalai Lama won the Nobel Peace Prize in 1989. Tai Situ has made numerous teaching tours of Southeast and eastern Asia, Europe, and North America. He has also brought together lamas and Chinese politicians in an ambitious effort for the economic and religious development of eastern Tibet. Claiming the authority of the sixteenth Karmapa, he publicly recognized the nomad boy Ogyen Trinley in 1992 and has promoted him ever since as the seventeenth Karmapa. Until recently, Tai Situ was in charge of Ogyen Trinley's education.

Since Tai Situ did not respond to my offer to participate in this book, I have relied on published accounts of his recent life and views. Situ Rinpoche has been the subject of increasing press coverage in the English-speaking world in recent years. In particular, authors Lea Terhune, Mick Brown, and Gaby Naher have quoted him extensively and approvingly in their books on the Karmapa. Before writing her own book on the Karmapa, Terhune edited the Sherab Ling newsletter for a time and later helped Situ write two books of his own. In her book *Karmapa: The Politics of Reincarnation* Terhune wrote that Tai Situ was an "old, dear friend and teacher."[2]

On a visit to Sherab Ling Monastery, author Mick Brown found Situ to be genial and disarmingly casual, while still maintaining the dignity of his office. After describing how Situ met him—"He greeted me with a warm smile, but did not get up. Protocol."—Brown went on to relate their first conversation, a wide-ranging discussion about monastic life, the rarity of female rinpoches, and the existence of female Roman gladiators. Brown had heard that Situ "had a light humor, but this was positively surreal."[3]

Perhaps Shamar and Situ had fewer philosophical differences than they had differences of style, but their presentation could not have been more different. Situ balanced friendliness with formality. He was warm and open in casual meetings, while on special occasions he surrounded himself with ceremony and protocol, and enjoyed wearing the silk robes and elaborate headdresses of his office. Shamar, by contrast, was formal and often reserved when meeting new people or managing the monks at Rumtek, but he resisted official pomp and ceremony. When Shamar came of age in 1970, his uncle the sixteenth Karmapa offered to have a red crown made for him, as previous Karmapas had done for previous Shamarpas. But Shamar refused, saying he did not think performing crown ceremonies was useful for devotees.

Situ's upbeat style created a strong contrast with Shamar's approach to discipline at the monastery. "At Rumtek in the eighties, Situ Rinpoche would come to visit every few years, and he would bring gifts and money for everybody," Lunrig Gyaltso, one of the temple administrators expelled in 1993, told me. "Of course, this was tradition, for a visiting rinpoche to make gifts to the monastery. We liked Situ Rinpoche anyway. He was very pleasant and nice, smiling and saying kind words. But Shamar Rinpoche was in charge, and was at Rumtek everyday. He was paying for Rumtek to run, but he did not give people gifts. Also, he was always scolding the monks for not behaving properly. We were scared of him; we thought he was too strict. But after the troubles began the monks became afraid of Situ and thought that Shamar was the only one who could protect Rumtek."

In contrast to Shamar, it seems that Situ, whose family origins were more modest, has cultivated what used to be called the "common touch." And Situ has succeeded in making valuable friends in the West. At the end of her informative interview with Tai Situ at Sherab Ling, Gaby Naher enjoyed a casual conversation with the high lama, sharing photos of her dog and infant daughter. Afterwards, she felt that Situ had a "genuine concern for my well-being and the success of my book." Though she did not consider herself a Buddhist, Naher wrote that she felt blessed after meeting Tai Situ.[4]

Tai Situ has also accomplished the diplomatic coup of gaining valuable friends in Beijing and Lhasa while getting ever closer to Dharamsala. Yet, for all his likability, Situ also has been faced with as much controversy as any lama in Tibetan Buddhism. One of the first high lamas to travel to Tibet when China began opening up the country in the early 1980s, Situ established a working relationship with the Communist administration of the Tibet Autonomous Region and to a lesser extent, with officials in Beijing. This entente gave Tai Situ unprecedented freedom to operate inside Tibet and helped him to win official Chinese support for Ogyen Trinley as a "patriotic lama" and "Living Buddha."

Of course, all the time that Situ was getting close to China, he enjoyed refugee status as a guest of India. Yet, Situ apparently did not think that the Indian government would see anything wrong with his activities in China. This miscalculation has perhaps been his biggest tactical mistake. Starting in 1982, when Situ made his first trip back to Tibet, Indian intelligence began to follow his relations with China. The Indian government worried that Situ was making connections with Chinese officials who sought to gain influence in Sikkim.

In a 1997 report on the Karmapa controversy that became widely known in India, Sikkim Chief Secretary K. Sreedhar Rao summarized the government's suspicions. By joining Beijing in supporting the tulku Ogyen Trinley, Rao wrote, it appeared that "Tai Situ Rinpoche['s] group had wittingly or unwittingly played into the hands of the Chinese."[5] The full text of the Rao report is reprinted in appendix B of this book.

The next year, the Indian Ministry of Home Affairs came up with an even harsher indictment of Tai Situ's role: "He abuses his position as a high Lama of Tibetan Buddhism under the garb of which he indulges in nefarious activities."[6] Situ's followers have denied that their lama gave the Indian government any real reason to worry, and they have claimed that charges against him were instigated by Shamar.

Shamar confirmed to me that he has discussed the Karmapa controversy with intelligence officials in New Delhi, but he denied any wrongdoing. "The local government in Sikkim should have helped the Karmapa Trust regain control of Rumtek after Situ and Gyaltsab Rinpoches illegally took over the monastery in 1993," Shamar said. "When the Sikkim administration failed to uphold the law, we had no choice but to seek help in Delhi." Indian officials were willing to listen to Shamar because they saw events at Rumtek as a threat to their control over Sikkim.

The Lords of Palpung

After the Karmapa and Shamarpa, the Tai Situpas are the leading tulkus in the Karma Kagyu hierarchy. As we have seen, in practice, if not in Tibetan law or Karma Kagyu policy, the Situs were promoted from third- to second-ranking lamas during the 150-year-long Lhasa government ban on the Shamarpa. Before 1959, Tai Situ's labrang ran their lama's feudal lordship in eastern Tibet from the sprawling monastic complex at Palpung and dominated the Karma Kagyu monasteries of Kham.

Founded by the "Great Eighth" Tai Situ Chokyi Jungne in the eighteenth century, Palpung became the de facto headquarters of the Karma Kagyu in eastern Tibet, with more than a thousand monks. Palpung supervised one of two main publishers of religious books in Tibet, the active woodblock press in Derge. The Great Eighth Situ oversaw the printing of the Derge Canon, which remains the standard version of the Buddhist scriptures in Tibetan: the *Kangyur*, the teachings of the Buddha; and the *Tengyur*, traditional commentaries by later Indian and Tibetan masters. Palpung's library boasted more than 324,000 volumes, making it one of the largest in Tibet. Artists created more than 10,000 thangka paintings for use at the monastery. From their imposing monastic seat, the Tai Situs ruled 180 large monasteries and hundreds of smaller temples.

Previous Situs had been students and teachers of both the Karmapas and the Shamarpas. During the period of the Central Tibetan government's official ban on Shamarpa reincarnations (1792-1959), Tai Situs stepped in to take a leading role in the Karma Kagyu. But in the nineteenth century, tensions began to arise between Situ's Palpung labrang in Kham and the administration of the Karmapas at Tsurphu near Lhasa. Particularly during the childhood of the sixteenth Karmapa, the general secretary of Tsurphu at the time, Ngedon Gyatso, clashed with the Palpung administration on issues of protocol. Ngedon resisted what he perceived as efforts of Situ's labrang to assert their master's equality with the Karmapa.

On one occasion, when the young sixteenth Karmapa went to visit his guru the eleventh Situ Pema Wangchuk Gyalpo (1886-1952) at Palpung, the two were seated by Situ's attendants on similar thrones, denoting an equal rank. Situ's administration had even brought in a photographer to record the event in formal portraits, greatly irritating Ngedon and the other managers of the Tsurphu labrang. They later extracted revenge by failing to show the eleventh Situ the customary respect when he visited Tsurphu.

The current twelfth Tai Situ Pema Tonyo Nyinje was born in 1954 to a family of small farmers in Derge, the autonomous kingdom in Kham where the sixteenth Karmapa's Athub family provided government ministers for generations before the Chinese invasion. The sixteenth Karmapa enthroned Situ at Palpung at the tender age of eighteen months, and observers noted that the toddler recognized his former attendants and disciples. In 1959, when thousands of Tibetans escaped into exile, the six-year-old Tai Situ fled Tibet in the care of his tutors, leaving behind the mighty stronghold of Palpung and its wealth in buildings, lands, livestock, and religious treasures. Several chests of Chinese silver coins would pay for their upkeep in exile.

Just as the rivalry between the Tibetan government of the Dalai Lama and the Karmapa resurfaced in exile, so too did the rivalry between the administration of Tai Situ and the Karmapa.

As we saw in chapter 6, Situ's follower Gyathon Tulku tried to keep the Karmapa out of Sikkim in the early sixties. Despite the awkwardness Gyathon's plan caused between Situ's Palpung labrang and the Karmapa, Situ's caretakers initially settled in Sikkim along with the Karmapa.

The Karmapa invited the young Situ to live at Rumtek, along with two other guest boy-rinpoches, Jamgon Kongtrul and Gyaltsab. This was an arrangement without precedent. The first responsibility of any tulku's monk-administrators is to advance the reputation of their lama, because a famous lama brings wealth and power to his labrang. Back in Tibet, no Tai Situ had ever been raised by a Karmapa or had lived at the Karmapa's monastic seat at Tsurphu. Indeed, the two labrangs had often been rivals as we have seen. Since Palpung was one of the richest monasteries in Tibet, the Palpung labrang could afford to raise its own tulku in royal style.

Even in exile, Situ's labrang had enough wealth in silver coins to cover their lama's education. But given the immense prestige of the sixteenth Karmapa throughout the Himalayas and abroad, Situ's caretakers knew that their boy-lama would benefit from receiving the principal empowerments of the Karma Kagyu directly from the Karmapa. This would authorize Situ in the future to perform popular tantric ceremonies that would appeal to large numbers of devotees. In addition, the Karmapa could introduce Situ to powerful devotees whom Situ could gain as patrons for himself, such as the royal family of Bhutan.

For the advantages that an apprenticeship at Rumtek would give their tulku, Situ's labrang agreed to place him at Rumtek for several years. But Situ's caretakers remained suspicious that the Karmapa's administrators, particularly Rumtek General Secretary Damchoe Yongdu, had designs on their lama. "Now that these outsiders [Situ, Jamgon, and Gyaltsab] are under our control at Rumtek," Damchoe reportedly confided to a colleague in Rumtek's administration, "we can get them under our armpit and squeeze them."

Tai Situ's guardians had good reason to worry, and to protect their lama at Rumtek. Situ's labrang duelled with the Karmapa's administration on protocol. They complained that Situ did not receive the respect at Rumtek due to a tulku of his high station and they did what they could to bolster his position versus the other rinpoches at Rumtek.

But his labrang could not stop their boy-tulku from mixing with his classmates, especially the other high lamas under the sixteenth Karmapa's care. During their youth at Rumtek, Tai Situ told author Mick Brown, the four highest lamas were "like brothers" under the paternal supervision of their religious teacher, the sixteenth Karmapa. Situ was linked to Jamgon Kongtrul by a connection to Palpung back in Tibet. He was close to Gyaltsab because their previous incarnations were also friends. "'But Shamarpa,' he said, 'was the real friend of mine. He and I are from the same region in Tibet, Derge...We would spend hours together playing and sharing many things.'"7

Other high lamas at Rumtek, including Khenpo Chodrak Tenphel, the abbot of Rumtek until the takeover in 1993, were also Situ's playmates in the sixties. Chodrak said that Tai Situ was a lively, outgoing boy who always took the lead on elaborate make-believe games and practical jokes. He loved playing at sword fighting and gobbled up stories of adventure and derring-do. Later, like Tom Sawyer, Situ would lead his friends in dramatizing the stories he had read.

Situ practiced the determined application of religious protocol at an early age. "On entering or leaving Rumtek Situ Rinpoche would have his monks lined up in formation," Chodrak said. "The attendants would be dressed in golden brocades, wearing rosaries with large beads around their necks and holding their *gyalings*, Tibetan horns, ready to blast a salute to their lama. Whenever he sat on his throne during a ceremony, there would be two rows of monks in ceremonial robes. We thought they looked like ministers attending the emperor at court."

Situ's followers say that their lama's adherence to protocol gives him a gravitas appropriate to his high office, and inspires the devotion of his students.

A Declaration of Independence

Perhaps because his labrang had been powerful back in Tibet but was much less prestigious than the Karmapa's administration in exile, at Rumtek Situ showed an early interest in outreach to gain resources for missionary work. He was quick to connect with the foreign disciples who came in and out of Rumtek on short visits during the early seventies, but it was only after leaving the monastery that he made lasting relationships with Westerners and learned fluent English.

In 1974, at the age of twenty, with the encouragement of Rumtek's abbot or Khenchen, Thrangu Rinpoche, and the eager support of his own exiled labrang, Situ announced his intention to leave Rumtek to start his own monastery.

Back in Tibet, Thrangu was a mid-level tulku—among the "Fourth Ranking Religious Dignitaries of the Karma Kagyu School" according to the sixteenth Karmapa's roster of lamas—and several rungs down from the leading lamas like Shamar and Situ.[8] The current, ninth Thrangu Rinpoche, now in his early seventies, was born in 1933 in Kham. When Thrangu was five the sixteenth Karmapa and the eleventh Situ recognized him as an incarnate lama. In school, he excelled in philosophy and debate. In 1959, he fled Tibet with about twenty-five monks. In exile, the sixteenth Karmapa put Thrangu in charge of the monk's school at Rumtek, and later made him abbot of the monastery. Some of his monks joined him at Rumtek, but others would remain in a refugee camp for years.

By the mid-seventies, Thrangu Rinpoche had reached a ceiling in his career at Rumtek. While other lamas were striking out on their own to found monasteries in India or far-flung networks of dharma centers in the West, Thrangu found himself an employee of the Karmapa—for whom he had never worked back in Tibet—and without a monastery to house his own monks. He often talked with his brother-in-law Tenzin Namgyal, an assistant secretary at Rumtek, of moving on from the Karmapa's monastery. The monks at Rumtek heard Thrangu and Tenzin complain that the sixteenth Karmapa seemed to thwart their career ambitions and favor others less deserving for such boons as promotions, trips abroad, and financial support.

Thrangu taught Shamar and the other high lamas in his philosophy classes, but he became particularly close to Tai Situ. When Situ wanted to leave Rumtek in 1974, Thrangu supported his plan.

Tai Situ told writer Gaby Naher that by the time he was twelve, he had already received the full lineage transmission and that he was ready to graduate from the Karmapa's tutelage before he left Rumtek.[9] But Khenpo Chodrak has disputed this story.

"The sixteenth Karmapa opposed Situ Rinpoche's plan to leave prematurely, because Situ needed to receive more initiations to qualify as a full lineage holder of the Karma Kagyu," Chodrak said. "Abbot Thrangu and the officials of Situ Rinpoche's labrang had painted a bright picture of the young rinpoche's prospects on his own, and Situ was clearly determined not to further defer his dream to raise his administration in exile to the heights of Palpung back in Tibet. Later, after Situ's departure, His Holiness Karmapa would encourage Situ Rinpoche to return to Rumtek and receive the missing empowerments, but by that time Situ was too busy setting up his monastery and extending his work into the world outside of Sikkim."

Now that their standard-bearer was liberated from the control of the Karmapa, Situ's labrang apparently decided to get some distance from Rumtek and establish itself on the other side of northern India, far from Sikkim. Probably on the advice of Abbot Thrangu, Situ and his administration chose to locate in Bir in Himachal Pradesh, near the exiled Tibetan government at Dharamsala but a full thousand miles away from the Karmapa. Thrangu then helped Situ raise the money for a monastery by introducing him to a minister in the government of Taiwan, Chen Lu An. Chen was well connected in the ruling Guomindang party and exercised influence among wealthy devotees of Tibetan Buddhism in Taipei.

While his future rival Shamar was still living at Rumtek, Situ started building Sherab Ling monastery in Bir in 1975 and in 2005 was still completing parts of his ambitious plan. Set on forty-seven acres of wooded hillside, Situ's seat claims to host more than seven hundred monks and nuns, placing the exile cloister on a scale reminiscent of the complex at Palpung back in Tibet. The grounds feature a school for monks, multiple retreat centers, and more than a hundred stupas. The monastery also has a modern touch, with a clinic offering Tibetan, Ayurvedic, and Western medical treatments. A workshop and museum for traditional Tibetan handicrafts are in the works.

"With its efficient reception, outdoor café, and four-wheel-drive vehicles parked out front the establishment is a far cry from the dark, rat-infested chambers of Tibet's medieval monasteries," wrote reporter Julian Gearing.[10]

In the seventies and early eighties, the monastery grounds hosted a campground for Westerners to make extended stays to study Buddhism with Tai Situ and his lamas. The camp accommodated a couple hundred visitors at a time, and it became a popular destination for travelers who wanted to study with Karma Kagyu lamas but could not get permits for Sikkim to visit Rumtek. While Shamar was still living a protected existence at Rumtek under his domineering uncle the sixteenth Karmapa and learning Pidgin English from day visitors, Tai Situ made friends with some of the hippie-era devotees at his campground who taught him fluent, colloquial American English.

Was Situ the Sixteenth Karmapa's Chosen Disciple?

Tai Situ's supporters have told a story to bolster Situ's credentials for selecting the seventeenth Karmapa, a tale straight out of the Karma Kagyu's mystical past. After his death in Chicago in 1981, the Karmapa's body was flown to Sikkim in a coffin stuffed with salt. It was taken to Rumtek for the traditional funeral ceremony, consisting of forty-nine days of prayers followed by a ritual cremation of the Karmapa's sacred body, or *kudung*. At the funeral were thousands of lay devotees and hundreds of monks. Dozens of high lamas officiated at the pujas held in various parts of the large monastery, and a small number of these worked near the funeral pyre itself, built inside a specially constructed stupa made of clay.

Situ's supporters have said that an auspicious sign appeared to Tai Situ at the funeral pyre:

> During the cremation of H.H. XVI Karmapa, His heart
> flew from the fire and landed in front of His heart disciple,
> H.E. Tai Situ Rinpoche. This indicated that H.E. Tai Situ
> Rinpoche is the preeminent disciple of His Holiness. H.E.
> Tai Situ Rinpoche is considered by many people to be His
> Holiness' most gifted disciple. Therefore, H.H. Karmapa's
> closest disciples hoped that Tai Situ Rinpoche would be
> able to find the Karmapa's reincarnation.[11]

Situ himself has repeated this story, though more recently he has given a toned-down version. In *Karmapa: The Politics of Reincarnation* Lea Terhune wrote that the funeral was accompanied by miraculous signs, the first of which came when Situ came to perform a ritual walk around the burning stupa. "A large, black, burning mass rolled out of the opening in front of him, an event Tai Situpa describes: 'Someone nearby, I don't remember who, pointed to the opening in the cremation stupa and said something was falling out. I saw a black, burning mass drop down into the opening. I sent a monk to tell Kalu Rinpoche, who was the eldest there, to find out what we should do. Then I waited. He sent word back that it was the heart, eyes, and tongue. I used one of the offering bowls to take it up.'"[12]

Top officials of the sixteenth Karmapa's administration have disputed this story. One of these is Dronyer Ngodrup, who officiated at the burning stupa in 1981. One of the two brothers of Rumtek General Secretary Damchoe Yongdu who served in the Karmapa's administration at Tsurphu and then fled with him to Rumtek, Ngodrup is now in his early eighties. Reputed to be one of the strongest meditators in the Karmapa's labrang, Ngodrup has lost most of his eyesight but can still remember clearly what transpired at the sixteenth Karmapa's cremation in 1981.

His version does not place Tai Situ at the center of events. According to Ngodrup, along with Lopon Tsechu Rinpoche of Nepal, he served as one of two Chopons, or puja assistants, at the funeral pyre. Khenpo Chodrak worked the flames as well. While adding more sticks of sandalwood to the fire, Lopon Tsechu noticed a small round object, completely covered in flame, surfacing inside the funeral pyre. This object was visible through the main door of the funeral stupa, which faced the east. Tsechu Rinpoche then informed Ngodrup and Khenpo Chodrak. All three looked at the object, and agreed that it might be something special.

So using a long stick, the three worked together to carefully remove the ball from the flames. Since this ball was still aflame, they placed it in one of the many silver chalices that had been used for offerings. They covered the flaming ball with a second silver chalice. After a few minutes, they removed the second silver cup, and noticed that the flames had died, leaving a burnt sphere the size of a golf ball.

On examining the charred ball, the three attendants thought that perhaps this was the Karmapa's heart, because there were stories of such relics in the past, as in the case of the first Karmapa Dusum Khyenpa.

Later in the ceremony Shamar approached the funeral pyre to make offerings, and Ngodrup showed him the ball. Shamar told Ngodrup to keep the ball in the silver cup near the Karmapa's pyre. Still later in the ceremony, Situ and Beru Khyentse Rinpoches approached the burning stupa. Khenpo Chodrak pointed out the ball to Situ Rinpoche. In front of the four attendants as well as Beru Khyentse, and to their surprise, Situ silently picked up the cup and carried it away to his seat in the crowd, where he placed it under his own table.

The Rumtek officials were shocked. Traditionally, those responsible for the funeral pyre at a high lama's cremation have the responsibility to identify and safeguard any relics. In addition, it was well understood that funeral pyre relics are the property of a lama's own labrang, and not of visiting lamas from other administrations, such as Tai Situ. Thus, the Rumtek officials saw Situ's taking the silver chalice with the relic as a

breach of monastic protocol. But, to avoid disrupting the ceremony, none
of the funeral pyre attendants stopped Situ. They felt sure that they would
be able to retrieve the cup and the relic from Situ later.

After the funeral ceremony concluded, Situ took the relic to his
guest room, the same suite where he lived as a student at Rumtek before
leaving seven years earlier in 1974.

The following day, Damchoe Yongdu, Ngodrup's brother and
Rumtek's general secretary, arranged a conclave of Karma Kagyu lamas
and others. The meeting included members of the late Karmapa's own
administration such as the Shamarpa and Topga Rinpoche and lamas
from the administrations of lamas closely associated with Karmapa,
including Jamgon Kongtrul; Karma Kagyu lamas traditionally not closely
connected to the Karmapa including Situ and Gyaltsab; and lamas from
Kagyu schools outside the Karmapa's own Karma Kagyu, such as the
Drukpa and Drikung Kagyu.

General Secretary Damchoe opened the meeting and then turned
the floor over to Shamar Rinpoche, who gave a speech thanking the
guests, exhorting them to look to the future, and expressing gratitude to
the governments of India and Sikkim. Then Damchoe recognized Situ
Rinpoche, who spoke—to a largely Tibetan audience—in English.

In his speech, Situ spoke of the "heart sons," a term he often used
to refer to the six highest-ranking Karma Kagyu lamas. He said that "the
heart of Karmapa flew from the northern door of the cremation temple
and the heart is with them. This signifies that the heart transmission is
with the heart sons...I have talked to all of the rinpoches and the general
secretary and I want to tell all of you...I want a stupa to be made out of
solid gold. Big size. At least two or three meters high. When this is finished
I will offer and put in this heart for everybody. Until that, this heart came
in my hand. Because of that I will keep the heart with me."[13]

Rumtek General Secretary Damchoe, who did not understand
English and so could not know what Situ said, was about to recognize
another speaker when Shamar Rinpoche intervened. Intentionally, he
whispered loudly to Situ so that others nearby, including Jamgon and
Kalu Rinpoches could overhear: "Rinpoche, it would be better if you
repeat what you just said in English to the audience in Tibetan." At that
point, Situ stood up and repeated his remarks in Tibetan.

Situ's explanation in Tibetan elicited quite a different reaction
from his audience than his English speech. Once Situ sat down, Rumtek

General Secretary Damchoe took the floor. He was clearly angry and he challenged Situ in front of the whole crowd. "This is concerning His Holiness' heart," Damchoe said. "This is His Holiness' main seat and therefore must house his heart, and not only a two-foot high stupa, but if it needs a five-foot high stupa of solid gold, then I am going to take the responsibility that it will be made and kept here. I say this on behalf of all the people at Rumtek."

Observers report that it was embarrassing to see quarreling break out in public on such a solemn occasion. Situ smiled and replied, "Now I have the promise of the general secretary, and that wish is granted, with everybody here as witnesses." The meeting soon adjourned, leaving the Rumtek administration concerned for the future of the relic. Tai Situ remained in possession of the heart, and he kept it in his guest room.

Shamar told me his version of what happened next. The following day, at the request of General Secretary Damchoe Yongdu, Shamar went to talk to Situ in his guest room. "I told Situ Rinpoche that he should return the heart to the monastery," Shamar explained. "Situ Rinpoche said he would give back the heart, but he asked that first he would like to take the heart relic to his monastery, Sherab Ling, for a blessing and then bring it back. Afterwards, he would make a 'present' of the heart to Rumtek, because he said that the heart belonged to him. 'It is my property,' Situ told me, and he still was saying that he was the first to pick it up, even though many witnesses knew this was not true. Then, he made a suggestion that in the future, Rumtek should take the heart to Malaysia and Singapore to raise funds.

"I remembered how Situ Rinpoche had asked me to leave the late Karmapa's hospital room to take his place in Brussels, so I was suspicious of doing him more favors. Also, I was surprised and shocked that Situ Rinpoche would have the idea of taking such a holy relic abroad for fund raising. To me, this would have been quite disrespectful. But no matter, I tried to respond gently that any relics from His Holiness Karmapa's kudung belonged to the Karmapa's own monastery, no matter who claimed to have found them." In addition, the Karmapa's cremation was held on Rumtek land, which doubled the claim of the monastery on any funerary relics.

After this discussion, Shamar returned to General Secretary Damchoe Yongdu and reported his conversation with Situ, saying that Situ did promise to give back the heart. "The old general secretary just shook his head, not believing that it would really happen," Shamar told me. Throughout the day, the two consulted on how to prevent the heart-relic from leaving Rumtek with as little acrimony as possible. Towards this end, the general secretary and Shamar came up with a plan that the two of them executed the next morning.

At eight o'clock sharp, the general secretary posted monks as guards at each of the monastery's exits. Then, carrying a long stick of incense, Damchoe led a ritual procession complete with two *gyaling* trumpet players and two incense bearers. The procession wound its way first to Shamar Rinpoche's room. There, Damchoe asked Shamar to put on his ceremonial robes. Once this was done, Damchoe handed him a stick of incense, and the two led their small procession, solemnly, to Situ Rinpoche's guest room.

Arriving at Situ's closed door, Damchoe ordered the horns to blare. The door swung open, and Situ appeared in the doorway, a bit disheveled and apparently surprised. He then moved aside wordlessly, and Shamar and Damchoe entered the room. The general secretary announced that he and Shamar had come to return the heart-relic to its proper place in the main shrine room. Situ did not object. The silver chalice was sitting on top of a cupboard. Shamar picked up the cup, and in procession with another loud blast of horns, Shamar took the heart-relic in state to the Rumtek shrine room. There he presented it to Rumtek's relic master.

"I knew that Situ Rinpoche would be angry about losing the relic in this way, but I was relieved now that it was once more safe with monks of His Holiness Karmapa's own administration," Shamar said.

The Taiwan Connection

Soon after leaving Rumtek, Situ found that his ambition would take him far. Outside of the stuffy atmosphere of the Karmapa's cloister, Situ made friends easily. In the days when Tibetan lamas were still considered exotic by outsiders, Situ connected on a human level with spiritual seekers from both East and West. Former Rumtek Abbot Thrangu became Situ's mentor after the two left the Karmapa's monastery. Thrangu introduced his protégé to people such as Taiwanese minister Chen Lu An who would provide valuable support to Situ to achieve his vision for his own palatial monastery and later, for the Karma Kagyu.

During the 1980s, Thrangu made several visits to Taiwan, a Buddhist stronghold where interest in Tibetan teachers was growing as rapidly as this Asian Tiger's booming export economy. It was well known among Tibetan lamas that the best fund-raising was to be had in the overseas Chinese communities of East and Southeast Asia and North America.

"In 1984, Thrangu Rinpoche came up with an idea to get money in Taiwan," said Jigme Rinpoche, Shamar's brother, a lama in his own right and the director of two large monasteries in France since the mid-seventies. Like Shamar, Jigme lived at Rumtek in the sixties and seventies.. Now in his late fifties, the soft-spoken, baby-faced Jigme exudes an air of motherly care that seems ill-suited to controversy. Yet, he has been the most outspoken of Shamar's supporters in criticizing Thrangu's role.

"Thrangu Rinpoche chose a monk, he was called Tendar," Jigme said. "He left Rumtek with Thrangu Rinpoche in 1975 and followed him to his retreat place Namo Buddha in Kathmandu. Thrangu Rinpoche had the idea to present this Tendar as a high lama."

With specific instructions from Thrangu, the new "Tendar Tulku Rinpoche" went to Taipei with the credentials of a spiritual master, in order to teach and raise funds for Thrangu's work in Nepal and elsewhere. Jigme told me that "Thrangu Rinpoche asked his own monks in Taiwan, who knew that Tendar was merely an ordinary monk, to keep his secret and pretend that Tendar was a high lama." The monks in Taiwan went along with Tendar's masquerade until the following year when Tendar himself, apparently fearful of discovery, backed out of the scheme, but not before raising enough money to demonstrate the potential of this approach to his boss Thrangu Rinpoche.

Thrangu later elaborated on this strategy and reportedly went on to promote dozens of undistinguished lamas to rinpoches. "These lamas owed their new status and loyalty to Thrangu Rinpoche personally," Jigme explained. "Later, Situ Rinpoche followed his lead, recognizing more than two hundred tulkus in just four months during 1991, as we learned from our contacts in Tibet."

In 1988, while traveling in Taiwan, Thrangu met with Chen Lu An. "Mr. Chen approached Thrangu Rinpoche with a plan to raise millions of dollars for the Karma Kagyu in Taiwan," explained Jigme Rinpoche. In exchange for a percentage of donations, a kind of sales commission that would go to his own Guomindang party, Chen offered to conduct a large-scale fund-raising campaign. Chen asked Thrangu to convey his proposal to the four high lamas of the Karma Kagyu, Shamar, Situ, Jamgon, and Gyaltsab Rinpoches.

Together, according to Jigme—who said the Rumtek administration received reports from a dozen loyal monks in Taiwan who heard about this plan from their devotees and other Tibetans on the island—Thrangu and Chen worked out the details of a plan to raise as much as one hundred million dollars by finding a Karmapa and then touring him around Taiwan.

Beforehand, they would create interest with a publicity campaign announcing the imminent arrival of a "Living Buddha" and promising that whoever had the chance to see the Karmapa and offer him donations would be enlightened in one lifetime. On his arrival, the tulku would perform the Black Crown ceremony at dozens of Tibetan Buddhist centers and other venues on the island.

"With such a plan," Jigme said, "according to our monks on Taiwan, Mr. Chen assured Thrangu Rinpoche that he would be able to get between fifty and a hundred people to donate one million dollars each, along with hundreds of others who would give smaller amounts."

According to Jigme's sources, Thrangu asked Chen to keep the plan to himself. He promised Chen he would personally inform the Karma Kagyu rinpoches of their plan and Chen's offer to carry it out. However, when Thrangu returned to India, he did not share the plan with Shamar, Jamgon, or Gyaltsab, but only with Tai Situ. Situ was reportedly excited by the plan. "Soon after," Jigme explained, "Thrangu Rinpoche took Situ Rinpoche on a secret trip to Taiwan to meet with Mr. Chen."

"Together, the three worked out the details of a fund-raising tour for their future Karmapa. The plan was worked out at least four years before they announced Ogyen Trinley. Situ Rinpoche and Thrangu Rinpoche wanted to bring Gyaltsab Rinpoche into their plans, but they didn't think they could trust Jamgon Kongtrul Rinpoche." In any event, they were apparently certain that Shamar would not agree to participate and would spoil the plan, probably exposing it as he had exposed an earlier idea of Thrangu's, to take over the Karmapa's Kaolung Temple in Bhutan.

By 1973, the dozens of monks that Thrangu had brought into exile in 1959 still lingered at a refugee camp in northern India, in uncomfortable conditions. Thrangu had long sought his own cloister in which to house them. He set his eye on one of the Karmapa's monasteries in Bhutan for this purpose. Originally a gift of the grandmother of the current king, the Kaolung Temple was located within the campus of a large secondary school in eastern Bhutan.

Abbot Thrangu must have known that the sixteenth Karmapa would not willingly grant him control of the temple. But Thrangu apparently thought that if he offered his monks as "caretakers," that he could quietly place more and more monks there, eventually making control of the temple a fait accompli. Thrangu shared the whole scheme with Shamar, asking for his help. Thrangu must have thought that he could trust his former student. But he was wrong in this. Shamar immediately shared his former teacher's plan withwith Topga, who had not choice but to inform the sixteenth Karmapa, thus earning Thrangu a rebuke from the sixteenth Karmapa.

"Soon afterwards, the abbot resigned his duties at Rumtek," Jigme said. "Ever since that, Thrangu Rinpoche behaved coldly towards Shamar Rinpoche. Therefore, according to our monks in Taiwan, Thrangu told Mr. Chen that under no circumstances should Shamar Rinpoche hear of their dealings."

Khenpo Chodrak and other lamas who managed Rumtek before Situ and Gyaltsab took over the monastery in 1993 have confirmed that they received similar information from monks in Taiwan at the time. Of course, even if Chen and Thrangu were planning to tour the Karmapa around Taiwan as a fund-raiser, we cannot know what they would have done with the donations. It is possible that they would have subsidized expanded Buddhist missionary work. It is also possible, as Jigme has suggested, that the money would have been used to build support for Situ and his allies among local politicians in Sikkim and elsewhere.

9 A PRETENDER TO THE THRONE

Democratizing the Karmapa Search

It is unclear who came up with the novel plan to locate and recognize the reincarnation of the Karmapa by committee. Shamar told me it was his idea, "to keep any of the other rinpoches from recognizing a Karmapa on their own, without consulting me, the Rumtek administration, or the board of the Karmapa Charitable Trust." But Situ has claimed that the Karmapa search group flowed out of a "Council of Regents" that Rumtek's first General Secretary Damchoe Yongdu formed a year after the death of the sixteenth Karmapa in 1982. The Council of Regents was disbanded in 1984, but the three rinpoches outside of Shamar continued to refer to themselves as "regents" of the Karma Kagyu for years afterwards.

Whoever originated this approach to finding the Karmapa, in 1985, the four top rinpoches in the Karma Kagyu—Shamar, Situ, Jamgon Kongtrul, and Gyaltsab—formed the new Karmapa Search Committee at Rumtek. All four lamas had historical claims to recognize the Karmapa, as each lama's previous incarnations had found at least one Karmapa in the past. Shamar felt that he had the best case to recognize the Karmapa on his own, since his predecessors had found six Karmapas (five of these working alone). But Situ also clearly had a strong historical case: previous Situs had recognized two Karmapas alone and two more working with other lamas, giving them a total of four.

Back in Tibet, the reincarnation of the Karmapa had never been located by committee. It was a much more informal and private affair, with each high Karma Kagyu lama participating in the search based on his relationship with the deceased Karmapa. One or more of the lamas would interpret a prediction letter (if any was found) and give a reading of signs and portents gained through meditation, dreams, and divinations. Back in Tibet, finding the Karmapa was dignified and secret, the business of only a handful of high lamas conducted behind the thick stone walls of a half-dozen ancient monasteries. It was not democratic but hierarchical, and the mass of ordinary lamas and monks or lay devotees had no traditional role.

In exile, the Karmapa search would become more democratic and open, but also more chaotic. From the death of the sixteenth Karmapa in 1981, pressure mounted on Rumtek to find his successor. By the mid-eighties, it seemed to the lamas at Rumtek that everybody had an opinion about how to find the Karmapa, and everybody had a right to voice their opinion. People from all over the Himalayas proposed their infants or unborn children as candidates. The committee began by researching the merits of these claims, some of which were implausible to the point of ridicule. One Sikkimese boy was born three years before the sixteenth Karmapa's death, an obvious disqualification.[1]

Some of the pregnancies turned out to be girls, who, under pre-feminist Tibetan tradition, are not eligible to be Karmapa reincarnations. Two of these were prominent. The first was Achi Tutu, the wife of the sixteenth Karmapa's driver, Dala. The couple were friends of Rumtek's junior secretary Tenzin Namgyal and supporters of Situ Rinpoche, who reportedly indicated that Achi would have a son who would be the Karmapa. In 1982, when she was in her forties, Achi got pregnant for the first time, which was considered an auspicious sign—until her daughter was born.

The second was Bardor Tulku and his wife. During his wife's pregnancy in 1985, Bardor sent hundreds of letters to dharma centers around the world announcing that his son would be the next Karmapa. Recipients of these letters included the Dalai Lama, the King of Nepal, and Chogyam Trungpa in the United States. When the time came for Bardor's wife to deliver, a large crowd assembled at the maternity hospital in Kathmandu to witness the birth of a baby girl.

The Karmapa Search Committee continued its work at Rumtek, but it soon became a field of jousting as Shamar contended with Situ and Gyaltsab to control the search. The committee's biggest problem was that none of the rinpoches could locate a prediction letter written by the sixteenth Karmapa. A year after the committee was formed, Shamar began his own private search for suitable candidates. Separately, Situ probably began his own search at about the same time. After this, the search committee meetings degenerated into political theater, putting out announcements with little substance to beg the patience of devotees and keep up the appearance of cooperation among the rinpoches. In 1986, the group even put out a false announcement that they had found a preliminary or "outer" prediction letter written by the sixteenth Karmapa.

General Secretary Topga Rinpoche was taken in by this deception, and from Rumtek he called on Karma Kagyu devotees around the world to accumulate millions of mantra recitations to remove the "obstacles" to finding the final or "inner" prediction letter. The next year, when Topga announced that these rituals were completed, the rinpoches had to admit that there was no "inner" prediction letter, much to their embarrassment. All four rinpoches agreed to this ruse, which they saw as a white lie to buy their group more time to find an authentic letter. To outsiders, such behavior might seem to damage the credibility of all the rinpoches, including the two most active in the search for the seventeenth Karmapa, Shamar and Situ. But Tibetans tend to take a more charitable view of such well intentioned deceptions, seeing them as an occasional necessity to maintain faith in traditional institutions.

Shamar and Situ each conducted their own searches in private without informing the committee at Rumtek. But their style could not have been more different. The more conservative Shamar kept the details of his search to himself. He selectively and carefully enlisted individual lamas from time to time as he needed their help to find clues, follow leads, and report back. It was apparently frustrating to Shamar's followers that he shared information only on a need-to-know basis, and nobody had the full story of the Karmapa search except Shamar himself.

By contrast, Situ Rinpoche began widely sharing information among his allies, including Gyaltsab Rinpoche, Situ's own aide Akong Rinpoche, and former Rumtek Abbot Thrangu and his brother-in-law Tenzin Namgyal. In addition, Situ began recruiting outside allies as soon as he could. Clearly, Situ was less bound by tradition than Shamar. While Shamar continued to insist on the relationship between the Black Hat and Red Hat Karmapas from centuries past to justify his own authority, Situ quickly understood the value of alliances with powerful governments and the usefulness of mass popular support in the new world outside of Tibet.

In the late eighties, in his Karmapa search, Situ began working with the Chinese government and also, probably, with the Dalai Lama's administration. He also began to form political action committees of his supporters around the Himalayas. He helped organize families from Derge in Kham with traditional ties to the Tai Situs and their monastery at Palpung who had resettled in Kathmandu into the Derge Tibetan Buddhist Cultural Association. The group quickly began sending out open letters to the Karmapa Search Committee at Rumtek supporting Situ and calling for haste. Back in Tibet, lay people did not write to high lamas with their opinions about choosing the Karmapa. This was yet another innovation brought by the conditions of exile to the ancient process of finding the incarnation of the Karma Kagyu leader.

A typical letter from 1991 told the search committee that "We are very sad, that causes sadness, therefore, we run out of our patience and with great grief we sent [sic] our request...We request and urge you to have meeting, quickly, and according to Karmapa's written instruction, the incarnation should be found and there should be enthronement for every body's devotion, without any controversy, and purely."[2]

In 1992, Situ recruited local families in Sikkim into a second group of supporters, known as the Joint Action Committee. Prominent local leaders, who nursed hopes that their tiny state would someday regain its independence from India, ran the group to court the neighboring Chinese as a counterweight to the authority of New Delhi. The Joint Action Committee operated on the premise that religion should serve politics, and its members sought to increase their power in Sikkim by extending their influence into the Karma Kagyu through Situ Rinpoche. They would be valuable allies.

Situ Takes the Initiative

Tai Situ was the first lama on the search committee to nominate a boy as the seventeenth Karmapa. After years of searching for the late Karmapa's instructions about his rebirth, the search committee's progress was limited to releasing the fake announcement about "outer" and "inner" prediction letters. Then, Tai Situ Rinpoche asked for a meeting of the group. He said that he had important instructions from the late Karmapa that could not wait.

On March 19, 1992, the four members of the Karmapa Search Committee assembled at Rumtek. Hopes ran high among lamas and families in Situ's political action committees that their dynamic lama would present important news of the Karmapa.

On the morning of the search committee meeting, hundreds of Situ's followers were bussed into Rumtek. Prominent among them were excited young Khampa men from the Derge Association in Kathmandu. They were unfriendly to the monks at Rumtek, who they apparently saw as obstructing Tai Situ's Karmapa search. "Many lay people and monks from Nepal, Sikkim, and Bhutan, followers of Situ Rinpoche, came to Rumtek Monastery and started causing problems," said Omze Yeshe, one of the top officials of Rumtek at the time. "They said all kinds of things to us monks. Some were aggressive, others were very polite. We observed the situation, and we knew that what was going on wasn't good."[3]

As the rinpoches met in the sitting room used by the sixteenth Karmapa, the crowd waited outside in the large courtyard for hours, grumbling about delays and threatening problems if the rinpoches did not produce news soon.

All day the committee met with the crowd waiting impatiently in the courtyard outside. The morning began with Tai Situ taking control. He asked if any of the rinpoches had brought a tape recorder or other recording device. Jamgon Kongtrul produced a tape recorder and handed it to Situ. Situ placed it harmlessly in front of him on the table, power switched off. Then he turned and faced the seat of the late Karmapa. He performed three formal prostrations and solemnly placed a *khata* offering scarf on the chair. This ritual completed, Tai Situ turned back towards the rinpoches. "Do any of you have the prediction letter?" he asked. Each one said that he did not have a letter. Then Situ smiled and slowly removed a small, soiled pouch from his robe. "I have the letter," he said.

From the pouch, he extracted a crisp, white envelope. Situ told the other lamas that the Karmapa had given him the letter concealed within an amulet in 1981, on a visit to Calcutta just before his death later that year. Situ had worn the charm in a black silk brocade pouch around his neck ever since, and had only opened it recently. Then, he discovered the letter. Though thrilled by the discovery, he kept it to himself for a couple years, waiting for the right time and place to present it. This meeting at Rumtek was the right occasion.

Situ held the envelope up so the rinpoches could see the words written on its outside: "Open in the Year of the Iron Horse."

"I was stunned," Shamar told me. "I did not know what to say. I had expected something like this, a forged letter. But Situ Rinpoche showing us such a letter with this instruction, it seemed too sloppy or too careless." To be fair, as we have seen, Shamar and the other three lamas had all agreed to put out their own fake "outer" prediction letter in 1986. But to Shamar, perhaps it was less a problem that Situ's letter was probably forged than that it seemed to have been forged unskillfully.

In the Tibetan calendar, the Year of the Iron Horse had come two years earlier, in 1990. "Did Situ think that we could not count?" Shamar gestured to Situ for the letter, and Situ handed it to him. "The handwriting did not look like that of the late Karmapa. The letter was written in red ink, which His Holiness Karmapa never used, and the script was not clear. I had my doubts then. The part where the signature was, it also looked like it was washed, the signature was smudged. The envelope was clean and the letter itself looked so old and all the folds in the paper were old too." After examining the letter critically for a few minutes, Shamar told the group that he had doubts. He handed it over to Jamgon Kongtrul.[4]

Jamgon then studied the letter, apparently reading the text, noting the handwriting and signature, and comparing the envelope and the letter's paper for a few minutes as Shamar had. Then, according to Shamar, he looked up and told the group that he also had some questions about the letter. However, in Situ's account, Jamgon immediately showed his appreciation of the letter. All agree that from the other end of the table, Gyaltsab answered, with evident excitement, that he was sure the letter was authentic. Curiously, Gyaltsab had not even seen the letter yet; it was still in Jamgon's hands.

Jamgon looked around the room at the rinpoches and then sprang up from the table. He announced that he wanted to run over to his rooms and bring back some samples of the late Karmapa's correspondence that he had saved among his papers. The rinpoches waited in awkward silence the few minutes it took Jamgon to return. All eyes were upon Jamgon as he burst into the room with four or five letters clutched to his chest. He dropped them on the table, and he and Shamar spread them out so that they could compare them to Situ's letter. Shamar shook his head and looked at Jamgon, who gave him a quizzical look.

Shortly afterwards, Shamar explained his experience of the letter and the meeting:

> The signature is partly washed out, by water or sweat. The letter itself is very distinct, it gives precise information about the name of the father, the name of the mother and the name of the birthplace. It is very, very clear. Then Situ Rinpoche asked, "What do we do now? Do we all go there together to check out the information? What do we do?"
>
> I said, "I am sorry, but I cannot accept the letter right now. The handwriting is not similar to the handwriting of His Holiness. At first instance it might look like His Holiness' writing, but when you really look, it does not look like it at all. I have doubts. I cannot say it is not a true letter, but also I cannot accept it as being true."

"I was being diplomatic at that time," Shamar told me in retrospect. "I knew the letter must have been a forgery, but because so many of Situ's supporters were waiting outside, I thought it better to leave open some room for doubt." Shamar had seen hundreds of his uncle's letters, and this was unlike any of them. Instead, it looked more like the handwriting of Tai Situ himself.

Surprises Inside

In June 1992 Michelle Martin, an American devotee who would publish her biography of Ogyen Trinley *Music in the Sky* eleven years later in 2003 translated the letter:

> Emaho, self-awareness is always bliss;
> The dharmadhatu has no center nor edge.
>
> From here to the north [in] the east of [the Land of] Snow
> Is a country where divine thunder spontaneously blazes.
> [In] a beautiful nomad's place with the sign of a cow,
> The method is Dondrub and the wisdom is Lolaga.
> [Born in] the year of the one used for the earth
> [With] the miraculous, far-reaching sound of the white one:
> [This] is the one known as Karmapa.

He is sustained by Lord Donyo Drupa;
Being nonsectarian, he pervades all directions;
Not staying close to some and distant from others, he is
the protector of all beings:
The sun of the Buddha's Dharma that benefits others
always blazes.[5]

Tai Situ's supporters used the details in the letter to identify Ogyen
Trinley as the reincarnation of the seventeenth Karmapa: his birthplace
of Lhathok was northeast of Rumtek, located in Tibet, the Land of the
Snows; his parents were nomads; his father was named Dondrup and his
mother, Lolaga.[6]

Rumtek General Secretary Topga made his own observations on
the letter's style and grammar, as written in Tibetan.[7] Topga Rinpoche
was, like Shamar, a nephew of the sixteenth Karmapa. Perhaps no figure
has come under stronger attack from supporters of Ogyen Trinley than
Topga. Author Lea Terhune, who refers to him by his family name Yugyal
and refuses to accord him the title "rinpoche" by which he was generally
known during his lifetime, has written that "according to sources within
Rumtek, Topga Yugyal seemed to relish power. He systematically sidelined
any who dared to differ with him."[8]

Topga's most outspoken critic was a one-time subordinate at
Rumtek, Tenzin Namgyal. Before his death in 2005, Tenzin spoke to
author Mick Brown bitterly about his former boss: "In every individual,
human nature is for desire, to be a big man. But Topga had more ego,
more pride, more desire. He was always up to some mischief."[9] Tenzin
also accused the sixteenth Karmapa of nepotism in favoring Topga.

Tenzin had good reason to be bitter against Topga. Tenzin fled with
the sixteenth Karmapa from Tibet in 1959 and worked as an assistant
secretary at Rumtek. But in the seventies, Tenzin reportedly became the
first person in the Karmapa's administration to start working, secretly, as
an agent of the Dalai Lama's exile government.

He probably met with Juehen Thubten, Dharamsala's point-man
on Rumtek, numerous times in the late seventies and throughout the
eighties to update him on the Karmapa's doings and later, to help the
Dalai Lama's group gain influence at Rumtek. General Secretary Topga
suspected that Tenzin was working with the exile administration, because
Tenzin made numerous trips to the Tibet Hotel in Gangtok, the informal

office in Sikkim of the Dalai Lama's exile government. But only in 1988 did Topga have enough proof to confront Tenzin and then fire him from his post at Rumtek. Not surprisingly, soon afterwards Tenzin became a vocal supporter of Tai Situ.

Even his critics admit that Topga possessed great ability and drive. He became a monk at a young age and in his teens he showed an aptitude for study. Topga took diligently to his books and excelled in each subject of the traditional Tibetan Buddhist curriculum. In recognition of his learning, at age seventeen, the sixteenth Karmapa awarded Topga two titles usually bestowed on much older men: Dorje Lopon (Vajrayana ritual master) in recognition of his knowledge of Buddhism; and Garchen Tripa, an administrative title that enabled Topga to act as regent over Rumtek in the Karmapa's absence.

"Topga Rinpoche must have had the karma to be strongly criticized," Shamar told me. "Perhaps he was a target for his enemies because he stopped their plans. His loyalty to the Karmapa was the most important thing to him and he was willing to endure anger and hatred for his principles."

Topga was one of the top scholars of the Karma Kagyu, and was known as much for his learning as his dry wit. His skill as a writer was clear in the booklet he published on the Karmapa controversy in 1994, whose title can be translated as *Assorted Tales on the Art of Thinking*. There, Topga presented his analysis of Situ's prediction letter. His discussion is difficult to follow in English, but one of his points, on the opening of the letter, can help us grasp his approach and understand the doubts of Shamar, Jamgon, and Topga himself when Situ first presented the letter.

The first line of Situ's prediction letter is: "Emaho, self awareness is always bliss."

Emaho is an expression of joy like "Wonderful! Amazing!" or even "Wow!" used when someone experiences something extraordinary but has no words to express it. A great tantric master might use *emaho* in an exuberant tribute to the bliss of enlightenment, exhorting others to practice meditation to find the same boundless joy.

According to Topga, this is not the tone for a next-life prediction letter, which should instead be more somber and mournful. Anticipating his own death, a great lama or meditation master writes with sadness and compassion for the bad karma of humans that causes the suffering of earthly existence—birth, old age, sickness, and death. Topga cited the example of a letter written by the sixteenth Karmapa in 1944, at the age of twenty:

> I will not stay in Tibet
> I will wander to the ends of the earth
> Without destination to experience my karma.
>
> The cuckoo comes to Tibet in the springtime
> And sings its melancholy songs with six melodies.
> Isn't it sad, my followers?

We will see this letter again in our examination of Shamar's Karmapa candidate Thaye Dorje. For now, let us return to Topga's analysis of Situ's prediction letter.

In the Tibetan tradition, Topga continued, there is a set format for a letter that a high lama would write to predict his next life: he bemoans the negative activities that occupy most people's lives, and concludes that the time is appropriate for the bodhisattva to die—he or she cannot be of any further use in such a decadent world. He may even express disgust with monasteries and the practice of dharma in his day and age, and in his country. Then, he would provide details as to his parents and place of birth. *Emaho* would be out of place in such a letter, whose goal is to teach about death and the inevitable passing of all people and things.

"Now suddenly," Topga said of the prediction letter's first line, using the irony that was the trademark of his critical writing, "Karmapa acts like a Tibetan dancing clown, happy and amused with his death and happy that his followers are sad at his death."

After analyzing another dozen examples of such inconsistencies, Topga concluded that whoever wrote the letter had a poor understanding of the poetic conventions of prediction letters—literary rules that were well known to the sixteenth Karmapa. For Topga, the letter's language alone exposed it as a forgery. "Even if you finished the first grade of Tibetan philosophy," Topga chided the letter's author—presumably, Tai Situ—"you would know how to lie better than this."

In the weeks after Situ first presented the letter at Rumtek in March 1992, the monastery's administration analyzed it for authenticity. For the interested reader, appendix B contains a summary of the Rumtek administration's findings relating to the letter's signature, handwriting, and letterhead.

Secret and Confidential

Back at the Search Committee meeting at Rumtek in March, 1992, Shamar was not happy. "I strongly objected to revealing this letter," Shamar said. "The world now was not like Tibet in the old days. High lamas and normal people would analyze the letter and they would find it to be clearly false. Then after that they would also doubt the authenticity of all previous Karmapas as well. I told the group that it was better to say that there is no prediction letter."

Situ passed over Shamar's objections. Instead of answering them, he said that according to the letter it was necessary to send Rumtek General Secretary Topga to search for the boy. "Does that mean that you do not already know where the boy is?" Shamar asked. "I said again that we should not reveal this letter. But we could look for the boy anyway. In the meantime, we should send the letter for a forensic test. So later, if both the boy and the letter would prove true, we could reveal them.

"Situ Rinpoche objected that this would cost a lot of money and would take a lot of time resulting in delay finding the boy. I said that there was no problem; we could find a way to do it all quickly and without much cost. Anyway, Situ Rinpoche should not have had a veto on testing the letter. Whenever a prediction letter about the Karmapa was presented by anyone in the past, it has always become the property of the Karmapa's labrang. So the Rumtek administration should have decided whether to test it or not. But Situ just pushed ahead; there was no time for discussion.

"'Who should hold onto the letter for safekeeping?' Situ Rinpoche asked our group.

"'Well, you can't keep the letter because you have produced it and I can't keep it because I am opposing it', I said. Jamgon Kongtrul and Gyaltsab also did not want to keep the letter. So we decided to store it in a *gau* [a small silver relic box] and place the *gau* in a larger wooden box with a lock. All this time Situ Rinpoche looked nervous and Gyaltsab's face was red and angry-looking.

"Then Situ Rinpoche said that according to the letter, the direction to travel to find the Karmapa was east. He said it could either be Arunachal Pradesh state in India or somewhere in eastern Tibet. He then asked who should go to search for the boy," Shamar told me. Jamgon Kongtrul quickly said that he would volunteer. Though he had expressed his doubts about the letter, Jamgon seemed the least opinionated of all the rinpoches, so none of the others could object.

"We started talking about what to tell the people, especially all of Situ's followers visiting Rumtek that day. I asked Tai Situ, 'Tell me frankly, rinpoche, if you have found a remarkable boy through your own meditation whom you think could be Karmapa, and then if you forged this letter to try to convince us, please tell us. We can still look for the boy but we can just burn this letter here to protect the reputation of the Karmapa. Otherwise, we will have to show the letter to everyone. All the rinpoches today are very clever, and they will discover that the letter is fake. This will look very bad. Or, if you insist that the letter is genuine, then we must send it out for a forensic science test. Will you agree?' Situ looked at me, and he seemed about to say something. Then, he changed his face and just said 'No.'"

The meeting went on all day. By evening, Jamgon proposed that the rinpoches should not mention Situ's letter, but instead they should compose a public statement that the committee was beginning a search for a boy according to instructions in a vague prediction that the group had announced earlier. They thought this could buy them six or eight months more time to test Situ's letter and for Jamgon to find the boy. All the rinpoches agreed with Jamgon's proposal.

"I had already been doing a search for my candidate but had not said anything about it before and I did not mention it at this meeting either," Shamar told me. "I suspected earlier that Situ was involved in politics over choosing the Karmapa. This day it became evident that Gyaltsab was also involved."

Topga made photocopies of the letter and gave each rinpoche a copy. The four rinpoches agreed to keep the letter secret until Jamgon returned from his search. Then, they allowed the leaders of the groups waiting outside to enter the meeting room. "Lower lamas and politicians had never before gotten involved in a Karmapa search," Shamar told me. "But there was so much pressure on our committee; we could not keep these followers out. They thought they had a right to be part of the process." About a dozen guests came into the room, including Situ's aide Akong Rinpoche and Kunzang Sherab, a retired Sikkimese state government official who had just become the head of Situ's new political action committee in Gangtok, the Joint Action Committee.

"Akong and another man named Karge were the first to ask, 'Where was the prediction letter?' It sounded pre-arranged. Situ quickly showed the envelope and took out the letter and showed it from a distance. He just waved it in front of the group and people were not able to read it. But he should not have done this, it broke the agreement we had made just a few minutes earlier to keep the letter secret. Jamgon and I commented to each other on this behavior and we were both shocked. The visitors looked strangely at us whispering together.

"At that time, rumors were going around that Akong would deal with China as the 'foreign secretary' of Tai Situ and that Karge was his 'home secretary,' responsible for getting support in Sikkim. In the room, Karge said 'Don't tell us it will take more time to find the Karmapa, it has already taken so many years, and now again you say we have to wait eight more months. We cannot!' Then Akong announced that Karmapas had always been recognized in the past by Tai Situs and that Situ Rinpoche would make sure we found the Karmapa without delay. I quickly answered, 'Look at all the thangkas and books in this room. They show that different lamas have recognized past Karmapas. Look at history and don't say things that aren't true,'" Shamar said. The meeting then broke up.

Non-Partisan Monks

The ordinary monks who lived at Rumtek had no official role in the process of selecting the next Karmapa. But both Shamar and Situ Rinpoche tried to explain their respective positions to the monks, knowing that their opinion would influence the Rumtek administration and the board of the Karmapa Charitable Trust which controlled the property of the sixteenth Karmapa under Indian law.

Khenpo Ngawang Gelek was one of these monks. Now age 41, Khenpo Ngawang lives in the San Francisco area, where he teaches at one of Shamar Rinpoche's Bodhi Path centers. He first came to Rumtek in 1981, just after the death of the sixteenth Karmapa. He completed a ten-year course of study at the monk's school, the Nalanda Institute, earning the degree of khenpo. After graduation in 1991, Khenpo Ngawang was one of eight khenpos out of a graduating class of twenty chosen to remain at the school and teach. He began by teaching alternately at Rumtek and at the Karmapa International Buddhist Institute (KIBI) in New Delhi. He told me about his time at Rumtek.

He lived at the monastery through the turbulent years before Situ and Gyaltsab took over on August 2, 1993. That day, he fled Rumtek, leaving all his things behind. "The monks who stayed, I heard later, they broke open the door on my room and took all my things, such as black pills from the sixteenth Karmapa, a very old Kalachakra text with a lot of oil paintings, relics from Bodhanath in Kathmandu, and many holy pills I got from a Sakya lama. I also had some money, about 25,000 Indian rupees ($800).

"I don't mind losing the money but the texts and the pills are impossible to replace. The texts were more than a hundred years old, commentary on the Kalachakra, written by hand. Maybe they sold them or threw them out, I really don't know." After fleeing Rumtek, Khenpo Ngawang took refuge at Shamar Rinpoche's house nearby for a few days and then he moved to New Delhi to live at KIBI. In 1994, he left India to take up his teaching post in California.

Khenpo Ngawang then told me about how the problems began at Rumtek. "I think maybe they started back in the late eighties. We heard so many rumors from the outside but we didn't really know what to believe. Some said that Situ and Shamar Rinpoches were recognizing the next Karmapa. I heard these rumors in Nepal when I returned home to my family on vacation. But most of the monks ignored them because we believed in the four rinpoches as excellent."

Only when Situ presented his prediction letter at the search committee meeting in 1992 did the Rumtek monks start to get involved. "I was teaching at KIBI in New Delhi at that time and then I went back to Rumtek. We heard very good news before I got there, that the Karmapa had been found. But once I reached Rumtek I heard that it was not such good news, that Situ Rinpoche had brought lay people and his own monks from Nepal and Sikkim who were saying that we had to recognize Karmapa now.

"Some monks said it was great that Situ Rinpoche had found the Karmapa and they pressured the rest to agree with them, to sign papers saying this. We did not want to take sides between the rinpoches, and it was not our job to decide who would be the Karmapa. We just wanted to follow an authentic Karmapa. We were very confused."

Inquiring Minds Want to Know

The day after the Search Committee session, Sikkim Chief Minister Bhandari made the Karmapa search into official state government business. At his office in Gangtok, he organized a commission of four state government officials to "oversee" the search for the Karmapa conducted by the rinpoches at Rumtek. The four went straight to Rumtek and asked to speak to the rinpoches on the search committee. The officials began to inquire about the process for finding the Karmapa.

"We told them that Jamgon Rinpoche would go to look for the boy and that it would take about eight months to announce the result," Shamar told me. "But I asked them why state government people were showing interest in finding the Karmapa. These were lay people and should have been the last to know about a high religious matter like this. In Tibet, this never would have happened. Even in exile, the Constitution of India prohibited the government from interfering with religion. But in Mr. Bhandari's Sikkim, it seemed that his officials were among the first to get religious news from Rumtek. Things in exile had really gotten turned upside down."

Despite Shamar's protests and the doubts of Jamgon Kongtrul, the two other search committee members, Tai Situ and Gyaltsab, went ahead as if all the rinpoches agreed that their letter was authentic. They made dozens of copies of the letter and faxed them to their supporters around the Himalayas. Situ did not wait for Jamgon to go to Tibet. In April, on his own and without obtaining permission from or even notifying the search committee at Rumtek, Situ sent his aide Akong Rinpoche to inform the Chinese government about the nomad boy referred to in the letter, a child named Apo Gaga. Situ would rename him Ogyen Trinley when he recognized the child as Karmapa.

Over several years, Akong had developed a good relationship with the Chinese authorities and their Tibetan surrogates in Lhasa. The Chinese had even proclaimed Akong to be a "Living Buddha," a title the government used for Tibetan lamas who worked to create harmony between Buddhist devotees in Tibet and the Communist administration. Akong arranged permission from the authorities to bring the boy to the reconstructed Tsurphu monastery. To Shamar, the timing of Situ's actions after presenting the letter showed that sending Jamgon to Tibet was just a ruse, because Situ had apparently already arranged everything . necessary to bring a boy to Tsurphu and enthrone him there.

Whether his trip would have done any good or not, tragically, Jamgon Kongtrul never left for Tibet. On the morning of April 26, 1992, the affable rinpoche was killed when his new BMW, a gift from his brother in the United States, crashed into a tree on a rain-soaked road outside of the city of Siliguri. If Jamgon had lived, perhaps the worst of the Karmapa dispute could have been avoided. Many observers think that Jamgon could have made peace between Shamar and Situ and Gyaltsab. But with Jamgon gone, Shamar would be alone on the search committee in doubting Situ's letter. Immediately, the traditional extended funeral consisting of forty-nine days of ceremonies were organized at Rumtek.

At this point, with the help of Gyaltsab, Situ started to increase the pace of his activity. In May, at Situ's request, the government of the Tibet Autonomous Region issued a formal invitation for Orgyen Trinley and his family to come to Tsurphu. Situ's aide Akong and one of Gyaltsab's lamas headed a reception party that brought the boy and his parents in state to the monastery.

To Shamar and the Rumtek administration, it seemed clear from the timing of events that Situ had arranged to find the nomad boy even before he presented the prediction letter to the Karmapa Search Committee at Rumtek in March. They wondered how the boy could be found in the expanses of eastern Tibet in under a month, and who had found him? Indeed, though he said nothing about it at Rumtek, it later surfaced that Situ Rinpoche had already met the boy during a visit to the historic seat of the Situs, Palpung monastery, in the summer of 1991. Later, Situ sent him a rosary from Beijing. So the two already had a connection nearly a year before Situ presented his prediction letter at Rumtek in March 1992.

This meant that Tai Situ had chosen Ogyen Trinley without the help of his prediction letter.

Enter the Dalai Lama

On June 6, Situ and Gyaltsab disappeared from Rumtek. They rushed to Dharamsala to inform the Dalai Lama that they had found a boy who matched the clues in Situ's prediction letter.

As we have seen, Tibetan history gave the Dalai Lama no religious authority to confirm Karmapas, since the Tibetan leader was not a member of the Karma Kagyu school, but belonged instead to the Gelug order. Outsiders are used to hearing the Tibetan leader referred to as the "spiritual leader of Tibet." But such titles need to be seen in cultural context. In Tibet, both government officials and high lamas sported numerous honorific titles for formal occasions. Tibetans even addressed foreign rulers as "emanations" of various bodhisattvas: Genghis Khan and the Mongol chiefs were Vajrapani, Confucius and the Chinese Qing emperors were Manjushri, Queen Victoria was Palden Lhamo, and the Czars of Russia were Tara.[10] This was clearly diplomacy, not religion.

History tells us that the kings of Tibet were considered emanations of Avalokiteshvara and given the title "spiritual leader of Tibet." After the fifth Dalai Lama overthrew the Tsangpa kings in the seventeenth century, the Dalai Lamas inherited the "spiritual leader" title. Historically, the title did not confer on the Tibetan political leader any administrative authority over the monasteries of the four religious schools (three Buddhist, plus the pre-Buddhist Bon) outside of the Dalai Lama's own Gelugpa. In the same way, for example, during the Cold War, the United States President was known as the "Leader of the Free World," an honorific that did not give him administrative authority over the governments of France, Germany, or any other American allies.

"Since the Karmapas were the first series of recognized reincarnations," according to Tibet scholar Geoffrey Samuel, "there was initially no issue of their being recognized by the Dalai Lamas or the Lhasa Government, since neither existed at that time."[11]

Like Catholics and Protestants, the four main schools of Tibetan Buddhism, including the Gelug and the Karma Kagyu, had always been run independently of each other and of the Dalai Lama's government in Lhasa. Just as the Pope does not choose the Anglican Archbishop of Canterbury, so none of the previous sixteen Karmapas had ever been chosen by a Dalai Lama. Indeed, the Karmapas preceded the Dalai Lamas by nearly three centuries, so obviously they got their tradition started without help from the Gelugpa leaders.

Given how clear it is in the history of Tibet that the Dalai Lamas had no role in choosing Karmapas, this fact has been the subject of a surprising amount of contention. Shamar's supporters have tried to communicate this simple point of history for more than a decade, but many Western journalists in particular have dismissed historical fact as just Shamar's point of view. Many have gone on to accept uncritically the claim of Ogyen Trinley's supporters that the Dalai Lama's approval is needed to select a Karmapa. Clearly, only the prestige of the current

Dalai Lama has allowed this non-issue to become a point of argument.

But however much we might admire the Dalai Lama as a symbol of human rights, a spokesman for the Tibetan cause, or a Buddhist teacher, it is necessary to understand that the Dalai Lama's view is not a final judgment for the Karma Kagyu school but rather, it is merely his own position. And it is a position that Tibetan history contradicts.

"No Dalai Lama before this one has ever decided who should lead the Kagyupa school," explained a 2001 film investigating the Karmapa issue by *Japan Times* writer Yoichi Shimatsu. "Leadership issues have always been left to each of the four schools of Tibetan Buddhism to decide on their own. Yet, on the ninth of June 1992, the Dalai Lama took the unprecedented step of endorsing a candidate to succeed the sixteenth Karmapa."[12]

Though Situ and Gyaltsab knew that the Dalai Lama had no historical authority to choose the Karmapa, they recognized that the Tibetan leader's prestige and reputation carried great persuasive power in the world of exile. Thus, to trump Shamar and to brush aside his objections to Situ's prediction letter, it was necessary for Situ and Gyaltsab to get the Dalai Lama's public support.

But Situ may have had a darker purpose than just legitimizing his Karmapa choice. To many Karma Kagyu lamas, it appeared that Situ wanted to make the Dalai Lama the affective head of the Karmapa's school. In exchange for handing over control of the Karmapa to the Dalai Lama, Tai Situ would then gain control for himself of the wealth of the Karmapa at Rumtek. In the future, Situ could access the valuables at the monastery through a pliable figurehead Karmapa.

Whatever his motivation, Situ worked quickly and effectively to gain the Dalai Lama's support for his Karmapa candidate. After placing a couple of phone calls to the Earth Summit in Rio de Janeiro, where the Dalai Lama was speaking, the two lamas received a statement of his support for Ogyen Trinley on June 9. This would be the first of several statements that the Dalai Lama and his ministers would issue in favor of Ogyen Trinley.

The Dalai Lama's first statement was an informal confirmation of Ogyen Trinley, sent by fax from Brazil. On June 30, after separate meetings the previous day with Situ and Gyaltsab and with Shamar, the Dalai Lama issued a statement known as the Buktham Rinpoche, giving his formal seal of approval to Ogyen Trinley. As we have seen, with the confusing exception of the sixteenth Karmapa, never before in history had a Dalai Lama approved a Karmapa. Yet, for thousands of Tibetans and outsiders, as Mick Brown wrote in *The Dance of 17 Lives*, "the matter was settled."[13] But it was far from settled for Shamar and the monks of the sixteenth Karmapa at Rumtek.

Three days later, Tashi Wangdi, a minister of the Dalai Lama's exile administration, announced the Dalai Lama's approval of Ogyen Trinley, writing that "The Karmapas have the tradition of leaving behind a prediction letter detailing the whereabouts of their reincarnation. Aided by such prediction letters, the Dalai Lamas traditionally made the final confirmation of the reincarnation."[14] Again, as we have seen, history shows that this claim is incorrect. The Karmapas began reincarnating three centuries before the appearance of the Dalai Lamas, and afterwards they were often rivals. The Dalai Lama's group was clearly trying to justify its interference in the Karmapa recognition with a reference to history that was untrue.

Six weeks later, on July 23, the Department of Religion and Culture of the exiled Tibetan government issued yet another statement to clarify the Dalai Lama's position. Why so many statements? It was clear that the Dalai Lama's initial pronouncement on Ogyen Trinley did not in fact settle the issue. This statement said that based on a unanimous decision of the Karmapa Search Committee, the Dalai Lama was simply confirming Ogyen Trinley. The Dalai Lama used very precise wording. He did not give his own opinion on the boy, but deferred instead to the judgment of the Karma Kagyu lamas: "According to formal announcements issued from Rumtek, the Sacred Letter and its interpreted indications were approved by the four regents at their last Council Meeting held at Rumtek on March 19, 1992."[15]

Ever since, though the Tibetan leader has made statements in favor of Ogyen Trinley, it has been unclear how much initiative came from the Dalai Lama himself and how much came from his ministers and advisors such as Juchen Thubten, the point-man for Tibetan Government-in-Exile involvement at Rumtek.

As they had been watching Tai Situ ever since he started traveling to China in the early eighties, so Indian officials had been watching the Karmapa fight to see what effect it would have on their control of restive Sikkim. They were confused by the Dalai Lama's action. Why would he interfere in the Karma Kagyu? Why would he support a tulku candidate put forth by Communist China? In his fourteen-page report marked "secret" on every page and sent to the Indian cabinet in New Delhi (reproduced in full in appendix A), the chief secretary of Sikkim, K. Sreedhar Rao, opined that the Dalai Lama might have been influenced to make a hasty Karmapa recognition by his advisors, who in turn were influenced by Tai Situ. Rao went on to speculate on other reasons the Dalai Lama might have supported Ogyen Trinley:

> The second explanation could be that the Dalai Lama was
> at that point in time carrying on delicate negotiations with
> the Chinese in respect to Tibet and he was influenced
> to think that such a recognition may go in his favor
> during his further discussions with the Chinese. A third
> explanation put forth by the religiously inclined is that the
> Dalai Lama heads the Gelug sect which is not favorably
> inclined towards the Kagyu sect, particularly because
> of the growing influence of the Kagyu sect...The fourth
> explanation is that the recognition given by the Dalai
> Lama is not religious recognition but basically a temporal
> act placing the Karmapa in a hierarchy next to the Dalai
> Lama and the Panchen Lama. It is an act which need not
> be given any religious significance.[16]

Rao concluded that the affair needed more investigation, since it was the first time that the Chinese and the Dalai Lama had agreed on a tulku candidate.

10 ABORTIVE SKIRMISHES

The First Coup Attempt

In June 1992, the Dalai Lama's announcement for Ogyen Trinley had its intended impact and it lent great credence to Situ and Gyaltsab's efforts. They and their allies in Sikkim—in the state government and among powerful local families—would use the Dalai Lama's letter as a pretext to try to take over the administration of Rumtek from the control of the lamas and monks of the sixteenth Karmapa.

Why did Situ and Gyaltsab want to take over Rumtek? They knew they would not be able to convince the Rumtek administration—Shamar, Topga, and the board of the Karmapa Charitable Trust—to let them enthrone Ogyen Trinley at the monastery. But did the two rinpoches think that a Rumtek enthronement would be necessary to confer legitimacy on their candidate? We should keep this question in mind as we see how Ogyen Trinley's supporters first tried to make themselves the masters of Rumtek.

Shamar remained vigilant. After receiving word that Situ and Gyaltsab had started a search for the seventeenth Karmapa in Tibet, Shamar cut short a trip to the United States. He feared trouble at Rumtek and quickly returned to India. When he arrived at Bagdogra airport outside of Siliguri on his way back to Rumtek, by coincidence, he ran into Sikkim Chief Minister Bhandari. "I thanked Mr. Bhandari for having arranged for the prediction letter to be kept at Rumtek monastery," Shamar said. Earlier, at Shamar's request, Bhandari had been obliged to post guards outside the relic room at Rumtek where Situ's letter was stored. "Perhaps Mr. Bhandari would have liked Situ's prediction letter to disappear. But we made this request officially, and given the lively interest among Gangtok society in the Karmapa problems, he had to agree.

"I also informed him that I would need to borrow the letter to have a forensic test carried out. Mr. Bhandari just smiled and said that it wouldn't be possible, because he had already handed over responsibility for the 'prediction letter' to Mr. Karma Topden, a member of the Indian Parliament in New Delhi. This was a strong indication that Mr. Bhandari was himself involved. Why else would he turn down my request?"

Karma Topden had good reason not to cooperate with Shamar. A leading member of Situ's Joint Action Committee in Sikkim, Topden also nursed a family grudge against the sixteenth Karmapa and Topga Rinpoche, Rumtek's general secretary. As we have seen, before his death, in 1967 the disgraced Gyathon Tulku announced that he would not return as a tulku, and this was confirmed by the sixteenth Karmapa. Gyathon died soon afterwards, and was not expected to return. Yet, in the late eighties, acting on his own authority and at the request of Karma Topden, Situ Rinpoche recognized Topden's son as the new reincarnation of Gyathon Tulku.

The new would-be tulku's grandmother, an influential Gangtok matron, requested Topga Rinpoche to house the boy at Rumtek and offer him a high position in the monastery's administration when he came of age. But Topga saw no reason to contradict the decision of the sixteenth Karmapa, so he rejected Situ's action and refused the Topden family's request to elevate their child. The Topdens took Topga's lack of interest in their son as an affront to their family honor and were apparently interested in taking revenge against Topga and his Rumtek administration. They were ideally suited to help lead Tai Situ's Gangtok political action committee.

After hearing that Topden was in charge of the prediction letter, Shamar hurried back to Sikkim, fearing the worst at Rumtek. Meanwhile, unbeknownst to Shamar, Situ and Gyaltsab were planning a big meeting at Rumtek, in Shamar's absence, to announce that they had received the Dalai Lama's approval for Ogyen Trinley.

The same day the two rinpoches received the Tibetan leader's endorsement, hundreds of Sikkimese and Tibetan lay people from the two groups of Situ's lay followers, the Derge Association of Kathmandu and the Joint Action Committee of Sikkim, arrived at Rumtek in vans. A motorcade of regular Sikkim state police accompanied the vans that brought the guests. These joined eighty young monks who Situ had bussed in a few weeks earlier from his own monastery, Sherab Ling. These newcomers behaved aggressively to the resident monks. Without permission of the Rumtek administration, the new monks installed themselves in any vacant rooms they could find. They glowered and flashed German-made knives at the Rumtek monks, who thought that these young men must have arrived only to put pressure on the monastery.

Later in the day, a contingent of the elite paramilitary force founded by Sikkim Chief Minister Bhandari, the Sikkim Armed Police, joined the regular police at the monastery. Given India's constitutional separation of church and state, it was unusual to see dozens of local police and security forces in a monastery. But Chief Minister Bhandari said he expected a law-and-order problem, and he claimed the police and troops were needed to maintain peace at the cloister.

Over the protests of the Rumtek monks, Situ and Gyaltsab gathered their guests and the police in the monastery's courtyard for a public meeting. Its purpose: to demand that the Rumtek administration support Ogyen Trinley. The Rumtek monks were frightened by this development and they were unprepared to respond to this unauthorized gathering. Situ and Gyaltsab were visitors at Rumtek, with no administrative authority over the Karmapa's labrang or his monastery. But they did have the eighty tough new monks and hundreds of lay followers to back them up. Even more confusing, public meetings about choosing a Karmapa were never held back in Tibet.

By this time, Shamar had arrived at his house down the road from Rumtek, but he was not planning to be at Rumtek that day. When the meeting started, the monks in charge of the monastery phoned Shamar at his bungalow, ten minutes away. They begged him to come quickly. If he did not arrive, they told him they feared that Situ and Gyaltsab would take over the monastery, using their hundreds of followers as muscle. In response to the call, Shamar left immediately for the monastery. As it happened, about twenty troops of the Indian Army's Kumaon Regiment had arrived at his house the previous day. In response to reports from the Indian Central Bureau of Investigation that Situ and Gyaltsab had bussed hundreds of followers over the Sikkim state line, including illegal immigrants from China, Indian Army command in New Delhi had ordered the troops to deploy to Shamar's house and provide him a security escort. The problems at Rumtek had now become an open issue of Indian national security.

When he left for Rumtek, the ranking officer, a captain, insisted on accompanying Shamar with five or six of his men. After the threat to the sixteenth Karmapa's life was revealed in 1977, he often entered Rumtek with a similar security detail (as we saw in chapter 6), so Shamar's having a small escort was no surprise to the monks at Rumtek, especially since the atmosphere had gotten so tense at the cloister.

But Situ's supporters have claimed that Shamar entered the monastery with the escort to intimidate Situ and Gyaltsab. Indeed, once Shamar arrived and broke up Situ and Gyaltsab's unauthorized meeting, a violent confrontation resulted between supporters of each party that took nearly an hour to pacify. Lea Terhune wrote that "the incident was strongly denounced by then Chief Minister Nar Bahadur Bhandari, who pointed out that it was the state's prerogative to call in the army, and the central government must be involved."[1] Bhandari demanded an investigation of this alleged misuse of Indian troops in his jurisdiction.

In *The Dance of 17 Lives*, Mick Brown describes this episode dramatically.

> Inside the shrine room, Shamar jumped on to a wooden
> table and shouted, "Soldiers and rinpoches to stay.
> Everybody else, leave!" An alarmed Gyaltsab turned to
> Situ Rinpoche and whispered, "Do you suppose they
> intend to kill us?" Outside, scuffles had broken out, as
> monks attempted to prevent the armed soldiers entering
> the shrine room. "The old monks were saying, 'This is why
> we came out of Tibet,' remembers one onlooker, 'this is
> exactly what happened in 1959.'"[2]

"This story is a grain of sand that Situ Rinpoche's people have built into a mountain," Shamar told me. "Six Indian soldiers and I were no match for Situ and Gyaltsab with more than five hundred followers and maybe fifty soldiers and police officers of Chief Minister Bhandari." It turned out that the situation was indeed dangerous—but it was dangerous for Shamar, not for Situ and Gyaltsab. On his way to the monastery, Khampas and Sikkimese that Situ had bussed in to Rumtek assembled in front of the monastery and jeered at Shamar as he entered. The Indian captain feared a violent incident and ordered his troops to stand between the crowd and Shamar.

Shamar indignantly strode into the courtyard and saw Situ and Gyaltsab holding their meeting. "Nobody had told me about this meeting," Shamar explained. "It seemed that they were trying to do it without me." Shamar was followed by the security detail. When the two rinpoches caught sight of Shamar and his escort, they unceremoniously broke from their positions in front of the crowd. According to one observer, like commanders out of a Gilbert and Sullivan operetta, the two high rinpoches abandoned their followers in the courtyard, and beat a quick retreat to their guest rooms at the monastery. Once inside, they resolutely locked their doors and refused to come out and speak to Shamar.

"I didn't ask for the bodyguards," Shamar told me. "They insisted on following me into the monastery. I just wanted to talk with the two rinpoches. Why did they have a meeting without calling me? I was only a few minutes away. But when I arrived, they would not come out of their rooms. Did they think I was going to line them up against a wall in the courtyard and have them shot?

"I had no authority to order the Indian captain to make his troops kick the rinpoches out of Rumtek. This wasn't even in our plan. Though we feared trouble of some kind, we didn't know that Situ and Gyaltsab Rinpoches were trying to take over the monastery at that time. But looking back, perhaps it would have been better if I had requested the soldiers to remove the two rinpoches and their guests. It might have prevented worse trouble later on."

The Rumtek monks were relieved that Shamar had arrived when he did. They thought he had saved the monastery from a violent coup.

"After that, we Rumtek monks were stuck in the middle," Khenpo Ngawang, the teacher at Rumtek at the time, told me. "We were quite confused. We didn't belong to Shamar Rinpoche or Situ Rinpoche, but only to the sixteenth Karmapa. The three rinpoches were all recognized by the sixteenth Karmapa, and each was supposed to have served as head of Rumtek turn by turn. It was really confusing at that time. So we decided that we should only follow the Karmapa Charitable Trust founded by the sixteenth Karmapa.

"Then we requested Situ Rinpoche, please, because he kept trying to force us to sign a letter that Ogyen Trinley was the right Karmapa, and also another one that said if Shamar Rinpoche ever brings a Karmapa, you should not sign for him. We refused to sign these letters, we said that we didn't have the authority to decide who should be the Karmapa or not. We could not say yes or no. We only wanted to follow whichever Karmapa was the right one.

"We then asked Situ Rinpoche, since all the problems seemed to be coming from the prediction letter: Now the technology is quite good, if you put it to a forensic science test, then a hundred percent of us will all follow you. Situ Rinpoche said no. The reason was that never was a prediction done by a previous Karmapa treated like this. Also, he said that it was a very precious letter and that we could not expose it to electronic machines. He would not do the forensic science test.

"That made us more doubtful. Later, Situ Rinpoche then brought more unusual things into Rumtek—more signs of support from the Dalai Lama. Also, he and Gyaltsab Rinpoche started collecting a lot of signatures. We found it very doubtful. Whenever Situ Rinpoche came to Rumtek he always gave a speech. But each time, there would always be some bad signs, like rain, thunder, or the Karmapa's flag blowing down from its pole.

"We asked him to let us stay in the middle of the two groups disagreeing, but he said no, you have to support Ogyen Trinley, you have to choose. We then asked Shamar Rinpoche if we could stay in the middle. He said yes and told us, 'This is not your problem; this is mine and Situ's problem. One day, I will give you my evidence and then you'll have a choice whom to follow.' That was convincing to us, and helped us decide who was right and who was wrong. Shamar Rinpoche seemed more reasonable. He gave us the choice so we could analyze for ourselves."

Curiously, to the further relief of the monks who lived at Rumtek, the eighty monks from Himachal Pradesh vanished as quickly as they had arrived. "We later found out that these young men had illegally crossed into India from Tibet and that they were hiding at the refugee camp near Situ's monastery," Shamar said. If the Indian central government discovered that the Sikkim authorities had let eighty undocumented immigrants from China cross the tightly controlled state line into restricted Sikkim, then Chief Minister Bhandari might have faced sanctions from New Delhi. On local issues, Bhandari could usually do what he wanted, but when the Indian government feared that he was endangering Indian control over Sikkim, Bhandari faced tight scrutiny. "So he wouldn't get in trouble, Bhandari must have arranged for the eighty monks to leave Rumtek fast."

After this incident, Situ and Gyaltsab responded by increasing the external pressure on Shamar and the Rumtek administration to accept the prediction letter without testing and acquiesce in the enthronement of Ogyen Trinley.[3] They used the opportunity of Jamgon Kongtrul's funeral, whose forty-nine days of ritual were winding down, to demonstrate that they had the support of the majority of ranking lamas in the Karma Kagyu by mounting a signature drive. Like requesting confirmation from the Dalai Lama, or holding a public meeting in Rumtek's courtyard, asking lamas to sign petitions was not a traditional method to recognize a Karmapa. But in the new world of exile, the old traditions were under pressure from new ways of doing things. Situ and Gyaltsab were willing to innovate to push their case.

With all the most important lamas assembled in Rumtek for Jamgon's ongoing funeral, Situ and Gyaltsab typed up two petitions and presented them for signature by the lamas attending the ceremonies. After pujas on the evening of June 16—again while Shamar was away from the monastery—Situ and Gyaltsab asked all the high lamas who had come to the funeral ceremonies to sign two documents supporting Ogyen Trinley. The first petition said that Situ's prediction letter was authentic, and the second thanked the Dalai Lama for his confirmation of Ogyen Trinley as the seventeenth Karmapa. All the lamas signed these documents, though most had not seen Situ's prediction letter and did not know the Rumtek administration's reasons for thinking that it was a forgery.

By this time, Shamar's support among Karma Kagyu lamas had nearly evaporated. To all appearances, Situ had pulled off an unprecedented achievement: uniting the Karma Kagyu, the Dalai Lama, and the Chinese government in harmony on the choice of the seventeenth Karmapa. Seen in this light, Shamar appeared to be obstructing a historic détente for Tibetan Buddhism and the beleaguered Tibetan people. To many Tibetans, his motives seemed as questionable as his pretext seemed petty.

Did being the late Karmapa's nephew give Shamar a special right to choose his uncle's reincarnation? Discounting the Black Hat-Red Hat partnership of centuries past, Situ's followers contended that Shamar's claim was little more than nepotism. Perhaps Situ had played a bit loose with tradition by introducing a questionable letter and bringing outsiders like the Sikkim state government into the tulku recognition process. But of the two rinpoches, Situ was the leader who had brought forth a suitable boy. All Shamar could do was raise doubts and make objections.

Beru Khyentse Rinpoche was one of Shamar's few remaining allies at the time. Yet, he signed both of Situ's petitions. Later, Beru Khyentse claimed that Situ and Gyaltsab bullied him and the other lamas into signing the letters. "Two monks, moving at a slow pace, would go from one Rinpoche to the next and firmly deliver the paper into the lama's hands. Other more determined looking types would nicely position themselves behind the lama's back and observe, with an unflinching gaze, his progress. Their penetrating stare left little doubt as to what might actually happen if the lama in question would suddenly contemplate a little defiance and not sign the letters with sufficient fervor."[4] Beru Khyentse said that he had no choice but to sign.

Did Shamar Accept Ogyen Trinley?

Signatures in hand, Situ and Gyaltsab again increased the pressure on Shamar. Situ called in Shamar's own mentor, Tulku Urgyen, to ask Shamar to drop his opposition to the prediction letter and to Situ's boy. "Urgyen Rinpoche was afraid that the Karma Kagyu would split into two groups if I did not agree with the prediction letter," Shamar told me. "He asked me very strongly to stop questioning the letter and to come to agreement with Situ Rinpoche. Urgyen Rinpoche was my teacher from early times. He cried when he asked me. It was difficult for me to resist his insistent pleas. Also, Situ and his followers were putting a large amount of pressure on Rumtek. We were afraid of violence."

Accordingly, on June 17, 1992, Shamar held a meeting with Situ Rinpoche and the mediator Tulku Urgyen to negotiate a statement by which Shamar could formally withdraw his opposition to Ogyen Trinley. At that meeting, Shamar signed a letter appearing to accept Ogyen Trinley on the basis of the Dalai Lama's confirmation. This letter would itself become a subject of much contention between the two sides, and each side translated the letter into English differently.[5] Shamar saw the letter as a temporary suspension of his doubt about Situ's prediction letter; Situ and Gyaltsab saw it as Shamar's surrender, and they publicized it accordingly. The dispute comes down to fine points of textual interpretation that are difficult to adjudicate. But what was clear at this meeting was the involvement of the Dalai Lama's exile government at Rumtek.

Partway through the meeting, an unexpected visitor entered, Juchen Thubten Namgyal, a former minister of the Dalai Lama's Tibetan

Government-in-Exile. Juchen had officially resigned a year earlier from his duties in Dharamsala. But Rumtek officials suspected that Juchen was still acting on behalf of the exile administration, and that he had resigned only as a formality to give the Tibetan exile government plausible deniability concerning its role in the conflict at Rumtek. There was good reason to suspect that Juchen was trying to extend the Dalai Lama's influence to the Karmapa's monastery. In 1988, Topga Rinpoche had fired assistant secretary Tenzin Namgyal, as we have seen, for serving as Juchen's agent inside the cloister for several years.

At this meeting four years later, Juchen's presence disturbed Shamar. "He was behaving arrogantly," Shamar said. "He started lecturing me about not causing any more problems. I was shocked. I told him that he had no business interfering at Rumtek. He was not a Karma Kagyu lama, nor a lama of any kind, but simply a former lay official of the exiled Tibetan government. So I picked up the letter and said, 'If you do not think we should make peace, I can tear up this letter right now,' I said. Juchen became silent. Tai Situ and Tulku Urgyen then started pleading with me not to rip up the letter, but to sign it. So I signed. But Juchen's interference was very good proof to us that the Tibetan exile government had designs on Rumtek, maybe in revenge for the late Karmapa's spoiling their unification plan in the seventies."

Back in Tibet, the Chinese government gave the permissions necessary and provided assistance to help Situ and Gyaltsab plan the enthronement ceremony for Ogyen Trinley at Tsurphu monastery. On September 27, 1992, with a crowd reported at twenty thousand guests, Situ enthroned Ogyen Trinley as the seventeenth Karmapa. Neither Shamar Rinpoche, nor any representative of the Rumtek administration attended. Nonetheless, with sanction from the Chinese government and the Dalai Lama, the enthronement proceeded in two parts. In the morning, a ceremony was held for dozens of Communist officials to meet the boy and give him the government's approval. Having stamped their political authority on the tulku, the officials then left, and the religious enthronement ceremony began at noon. The events were broadcast nationwide on Chinese television.

Once enthroned, Ogyen Trinley would spend nearly a decade in Tibet. It galled Shamar and the Rumtek administration that Situ and Gyaltsab would presume to return the Karmapa from exile back to Tsurphu, where Thrangu Rinpoche, the ally of Tai Situ and former abbot

BUDDHA'S NOT SMILING

of Rumtek, was now in charge. "The sixteenth Karmapa left Tibet in 1959. His Holiness abandoned Tsurphu and established a new seat at Rumtek," Shamar told me. "The two rinpoches did not have any authority to install Gyalwa Karmapa back in Tibet, under Chinese control. They themselves had not decided to return to Tibet, but continued to live in India. Did they think that it would help the Karmapa to spread dharma more successfully if he was a political pawn of a Communist regime than if he lived in a free country as they themselves did?"

"Sign, there is no danger in it."

Since they came from separate labrangs than the Karmapa, the only legal way Situ and Gyaltsab could participate in managing the Karmapa's administration and Rumtek monastery after the Council of Regents was dissolved in 1984 was through Situ's seat on the board of the Karmapa Trust. But after Situ presented Ogyen Trinley in the spring of 1992, the other trustees refused to recognize the boy. Situ found himself increasingly a minority of one on the board and knew that the other members would never agree to have Ogyen Trinley enthroned at Rumtek. Situ's supporters have implied that this was because Shamar had stacked the board with his allies. Yet, records show that the majority of the eight trustees on the board in the early 1990s were still those appointed by the late sixteenth Karmapa himself in 1962.[6]

Nyepa Khardo was the official at Rumtek in charge of operations and accounting and a long-time student of Situ Rinpoche. His family came from Derge in Tibet, and lived for generations under the shadow of the monastic seat of the Tai Situs at Palpung, so Nyepa inherited an attachment to his family's lama. He told the story of an encounter with Situ shortly after he presented his prediction letter at Rumtek.[7]

> One evening around 8:30, I was summoned to Situ
> Rinpoche; I really considered Situ Rinpoche to be my
> main root-teacher. When Situ Rinpoche summoned me to
> see him, he first talked to me very kindly and stressed what
> close ties he had with my family and so on. Finally he said:
> 'I have a very important task for you.' The task he wanted
> me to take on was to sign a paper. I then asked him what
> the paper was about. Situ Rinpoche answered that in order
> to invite Ogyen Trinley to Rumtek he was setting up a

new trust and that I should sign on behalf of the Karmapa
Charitable Trust. I asked him, 'Since the trust formed
by the sixteenth Karmapa Rigpe Dorje in 1961 is still in
existence and active and since the trustees are all alive,
why do you need to set up a new trust?'

Situ then explained that he was going to change the Karmapa
Trust and set up a board with seven new members. He asked Nyepa to
sign on behalf of his father, who had been one of the original founders of
the trust, although he was not a board member. Situ assured Nyepa that
there was no risk involved in signing. "He added, 'The present trust isn't
doing anything, which is why we need the new trust for which you have
to sign,'" Nyepa said.

"I thought it wasn't right for me to turn down Situ Rinpoche's
request, but on the other hand, my faith in H.H. the sixteenth Karmapa
is so strong that I couldn't bring myself to sign a paper that is not the
original trust document" that the Karmapa had signed himself. So Nyepa
refused his lama's request, saying that years of devotion by his family and
himself prevented him from going against the intentions of the sixteenth
Karmapa. Situ assured Nyepa again that there was no danger, but Nyepa
replied that was not the point, he still would not sign.

Nyepa said that at this point Tai Situ got angry and threatened him.
"Situ Rinpoche said: 'Well, if you don't sign this, get out and let me never
set eyes on you again.' As I was told to go, I got up, but as I was about to
leave, Situ Rinpoche again said, 'Khardo, think about this carefully! Sign,
there is no danger in it!' In the meantime, Gyaltsab Rinpoche had come
in and said 'Sign, sign!' After Gyaltsab Rinpoche had told me to sign,
Situ Rinpoche again said, 'Reconsider it!' I said my decision was final, my
loyalty to H.H. the sixteenth Karmapa was total, so I wouldn't sign. Then
Situ Rinpoche said, 'In that case, your ties with me are severed for all our
lifetimes.' I said that was all right and went out."

Several weeks later while visiting Kathmandu, Shamar ran into
Tenzin Chony, now based in Woodstock, New York. In 1992 Tenzin lived
at Rumtek and supported Ogyen Trinley as Karmapa because he was close
to Tai Situ. When Shamar met him in Kathmandu, Tenzin was evasive
when asked what he was doing in town. Shamar became suspicious that
Situ had sent him there to make contact with the trustees living there. He
visited trustee Gyan Jyoti Kansakar to investigate.

"Sure enough," Shamar told me, "Tenzin had talked to Mr. Jyoti. Tenzin had brought a letter of resignation from the Karmapa Trust board and asked Mr. Jyoti to sign, claiming it was the wish of the other trustees. This of course was totally untrue, and just a plan by Situ Rinpoche on his own to remove the duly chosen board members so he could try to replace them with people of his own choosing." Later, Shamar discovered that Tenzin had already obtained a resignation letter from trustee Ashok Burman in Calcutta, but "we were able to keep the other trustees from being confused by this misrepresentation."

A Himalayan Party Boss

Without the help of Sikkim Chief Minister Bhandari, Situ and Gyaltsab Rinpoches would probably never have been able to take over Rumtek monastery. Bhandari provided the state police and special forces troops to back up Situ and Gyaltsab throughout 1992 and 1993 and also prevented Shamar from getting access to Situ's prediction letter for testing. Along with Bhandari, Sikkim Chief Secretary K. Sreedhar Rao faulted Tai Situ's allies: "It is due primarily to the Joint Action Committee that an ugly situation was created in the monastery itself, as a consequence of which two groups fought each other and the group of lamas owing allegiance to Shamar Rinpoche was physically thrown out of the Rumtek monastery."[8]

From 1979 until he was ousted amidst widespread charges of corruption in 1994, Nar Bahadur Bhandari served as chief minister of Sikkim. An ethnic Nepali, Bhandari was a product of the unique politics of India's second-smallest state.

Sikkim was settled by people ethnically related to the Tibetans and ruled since the thirteenth century by the Namgyal dynasty, kings descended from the noble Minyak clan of eastern Tibet. In the seventeenth century, the Namgyal kings upgraded themselves to Chogyals, or dharma-kings, of Sikkim. The British established a protectorate over the kingdom in 1890. Afterwards, British and Sikkimese landlords from the aristocratic Kazi caste began importing migrant laborers from Nepal to work their large tea estates. In the following decades, immigrants continued to pour in, and by the 1960s Nepalis had become the majority, outnumbering native Sikkimese.

Nepali leaders in Sikkim began to clamor for more representation in the government along with new rights to promote their culture.

Tensions between the Nepali and ethnic Sikkimese communities threatened to erupt into violence. Many in the Kazi ruling caste feared that within a generation native Sikkimese would become powerless in their own country unless they got help from India before then to protect their traditional culture.

For years, with covert support from New Delhi, Kazi Lhendup Dorje had led a movement of Sikkimese who wanted to join India. By the mid-seventies, Indian Prime Minister Indira Gandhi was ready to annex Sikkim. After a referendum where ninety-seven percent of voters favored union with India, Kazi Lhendup concluded an agreement with New Delhi to convert the kingdom into an Indian state. The last Chogyal, a tragic figure with an American socialite wife, abdicated. On July 23, 1975, Kazi Lhendup became the first elected chief executive of Sikkim, taking office as chief minister of the new state government.

Lhendup's deal with India reserved thirteen seats in the thirty-two-seat state legislature for ethnic Sikkimese including a couple seats representing the Buddhist sangha, but there were no seats reserved for Nepalis. This angered the Nepali majority, who denounced the agreement with India and called for Kazi Lhendup's ouster.

Nepalis revolted and Nar Bahadur Bhandari led them to power in Gangtok while also garnering the support of middle-class Sikkimese. These included the Topdens, whose resentment of the Rumtek administration that refused their son's claim to be the reincarnation of the disgraced Gyathon Tulku would lead them to back Situ's plan to take over Rumtek. To assert their rights against their traditional overlords the Kazis and in exchange for patronage from the new government, like many middle-class Sikkimese, the Topdens became strong supporters of N.B. Bhandari.

Born in 1940, Bhandari taught primary school before entering politics during the anti-Chogyal demonstrations of 1974 as a champion of Nepali rights. He formed his first government in 1977. In May 1984 Bhandari's government was dismissed amidst corruption charges. But in Sikkim, such charges usually did not mean the end of a political career, and Bhandari soon bounced back, stronger than ever. After only a year out of office, in 1985 his party won thirty out of thirty-two seats in the assembly, giving its leader unparalleled power in the state. In the next elections, held four years later in 1989, Bhandari won all thirty-two seats. Withsz no opposition to keep him honest, the chief minister began to run Sikkim like a Himalayan Tammany Hall. He openly steered government contracts and appointments to family members and allies, especially the Topdens and other families who would later form Situ's Joint Action Committee.

Bhandari also started to employ gangs of toughs—drawn from the unemployed youth of the Tibetan exile community who loitered around the Lal Bazaar market in the state capital Gangtok—as enforcers for his political machine. Despite his Nepali background, Bhandari became successful at delivering spoils to the leaders of both the ethnic Sikkimese and Nepali communities. This made him popular among ethnic leaders, who were willing to overlook the chief minister's growing reputation for corruption and violence, especially since Bhandari's dirty tricks often helped them. But Bhandari took no chances, and made sure to quickly silence any opposition.

Throughout Sikkim, stories of intimidation against those bold enough to risk Bhandari's wrath during this period abound. The head of an opposition party, Madan Tamang, circulated pamphlets accusing Bhandari of corruption and womanizing. In response, Madan was arrested and died in police custody. His body was later found in bushes alongside the Rongpo River.

Shortly after this R.K. Baid, a reporter in Siliguri, located in the state of West Bengal adjacent to Sikkim, published a story detailing recent examples of corruption in Bhandari's administration. In response, Bhandari sent undercover police into West Bengal—outside of their legal jurisdiction—to kidnap Baid and bring him secretly to Gangtok. Police held the reporter in prison and subjected him to beatings and threats. When Baid was released, Bhandari's party offered him a payment said to be as high as five million rupees (nearly three hundred thousand dollars) to sign a statement denying that he was kidnapped or mistreated. Baid later opened a hotel in Siliguri with these funds.

Hamelal Bhandari (no relation to the chief minister) was a young attorney in Gangtok who later filed the first case in 1998 for the Karmapa Charitable Trust to try to regain control of Rumtek monastery, as we will see in chapter 13. In the mid-eighties, attorney Bhandari circulated posters around town criticizing Chief Minister Bhandari for corruption. Afterwards, ruling party bullies abducted him and handed him over to the police, who threw him into prison. Jailers tortured the attorney and then threw him naked off a truck onto the main street of Gangtok. Observers in Gangtok at the time say he was lucky to escape with his life.

Stories of Chief Minister Bhandari's brutality helped silence potential critics of his rule. It was given that the police were his personal enforcers and that they or the Lal Bazaar toughs would punish anyone who criticized Bhandari in public. Yet, no matter how much control Bhandari had over the executive and legislative branches of the state government (along with law enforcement), in the best tradition of Indian jurisprudence the local courts remained independent. It was known that judges with integrity in Sikkim were ready to hear cases against Bhandari. However, no resident of the state dared file such a case, for it was equally well known that this would bring down the wrath of Bhandari's party bullies or the state police.

In her book on the Karmapa, Lea Terhune has written indulgently about Bhandari and brightly about his relationship with Rumtek. "Bhandari was a controversial figure in Sikkim," Terhune admitted, "often criticized for corruption. However, he respected the sixteenth Karmapa and frequently assisted Rumtek Monastery while he was in power."[9] Needless to say, since Bhandari was responsible for transferring possession of Rumtek from Shamar and General Secretary Topga (acting for the Karmapa Charitable Trust) to Situ and Gyaltsab, Shamar and his supporters view the former chief minister much more negatively.

Bhandari was skillful at running Sikkim as he liked without attracting too much attention from New Delhi. But more than once he risked sanctions for violating India's constitution. The remarkable Dr. B.R. Ambedkar, a former Dalit (Hindu "Untouchable") who converted to Buddhism weeks before his death and brought his new faith to millions of other Dalits, wrote much of India's 1949 constitution. This document guarantees freedom of worship to all and prohibits government from interfering in religious affairs. In particular, Part III lists Freedom of Religion as among the Fundamental Rights of Indians, and it strictly prohibits the national government or state administrations from interfering in religious matters.[10]

Bhandari treated the constitutional separation of church and state with contempt. Under his rule in the 1980s and 1990s, Sikkim's citizens were consistently denied the full protection of Indian law, whether freedom of religion or basic civil rights like freedom of speech. Many Gangtok officials, starting with Bhandari, were lukewarm about rule from New Delhi and not eager to enforce Indian law when it was inconvenient for their plans. It was said in Gangtok that the leading middle-class families of Sikkim such as the Topdens yearned to regain the state's independence and that Bhandari himself dreamed of becoming king of a new Sikkim free of Indian control. It was not surprising then that Bhandari's state government regularly overstepped its authority and trampled on the fundamental rights of those who were not under the chief minister's personal protection.

Indian intelligence suspected that Sikkim politicians were pursuing their own private diplomacy by trying to cultivate friendly relations with China, which did not recognize India's annexation of the kingdom until 2005. Representing Ogyen Trinley, a tulku sanctioned by the Chinese government and a Chinese citizen, it would have been easy for Situ and Gyaltsab to purchase the cooperation of Bhandari's government through substantial bribes in order to put pressure on Shamar and the administration of Rumtek. In 2002 the High Court in Gangtok decided that the state government was indeed bribed to interfere at Rumtek, but the amount of the payment and the individuals involved are still under investigation.

A Second Coup Attempt

By the fall of 1992, Situ and Gyaltsab, working with Bhandari, were ready to make their second attempt to take over Rumtek. Given all that they had accomplished, it is less clear why the two rinpoches were so eager to control the monastery at this point. They had already enthroned Ogyen Trinley at Tsurphu. With the support of the Chinese government and under the protection of Beijing's new liberal policy towards Tibetan religion, the boy was free to pursue his Buddhist studies (along with a mandatory Communist education). He could receive Buddhist teachings and Vajrayana empowerments from the two rinpoches, former Rumtek Abbot Thrangu, and others, all of whom shuttled freely between China and an increasingly notional "exile" in India.

More encouraging, the boy was already inspiring devotion among Tibetans, and with the Dalai Lama's approval, he seemed destined to become the biggest lama in Tibet. Even if Shamar would later find and enthrone his own candidate in exile, Ogyen Trinley had the advantage of being first, and being official. Ogyen Trinley could easily have thrived at Tsurphu as the Karmapa based in Tibet, dwarfing any future Karmapa based in India. As his stature grew over the years, it is likely that he would have been able to negotiate a settlement with the Rumtek administration that probably would have put him in charge.

But this would have taken years, and apparently the two rinpoches were not willing to wait. For some reason, they wanted the Rumtek administration to accept Ogyen Trinley quickly. Was it just because they wanted to control Rumtek for its own sake, and that Ogyen Trinley was merely an excuse to take the monastery? Shamar's supporters have suggested that Situ and Gyaltsab were more interested in the wealth of the sixteenth Karmapa at Rumtek than in establishing Ogyen Trinley as a legitimate Karmapa.

Whatever their interest in Rumtek, the rinpoches and their many supporters around the Himalayas appeared to be tiring of the obstinacy of the monastery's monks and their stubborn reluctance to accept Ogyen Trinley. "In my opinion, Situ Rinpoche expected the majority of the monks to support him in his attempt to prove that the boy in Tsurphu was the true Karmapa," said Khenpo Ngawang Gelek.

Just as Situ had brought in eighty young monks from his monastery, Sherab Ling, before his and Gyaltsab's abortive first attempt to take Rumtek in June 1992, five months later in the autumn he brought in thirty-two young men from Bhutan to make another attempt.

Ostensibly, these young men, also wearing monk's robes, came to enroll as students at the Nalanda Institute. But the school's administration found these young men to have little interest in study. The resident monks complained that the newcomers began to pressure them into switching their allegiance from the Rumtek administration to Situ and Gyaltsab and into accepting Ogyen Trinley as the seventeenth Karmapa. "The Rumtek monks were neutral on the Karmapa reincarnation at this time," Khenpo Ngawang told me. "It was the job of the high rinpoches to find the Karmapa, not us. It was our job to run the monastery. We tried to stay out of the arguments."

The new arrivals did not get along with the monks already living at Rumtek any better than the earlier monks from Situ's monastery did. "Some of the monks and individuals brought into the monastery from outside by Tai Situ Rinpoche and Gyaltsab Rinpoche tried virtually to take over the monastery administration by resorting to violence and strong-arm tactics," said Chultrimpa Lungtog Dawa, one of the top monk-officials at Rumtek during the tense months leading up to the takeover.

"The two rinpoches, it later became evident, were in fact inciting and abetting this handful of their supporters gradually to wrest power from our hands and thus to take over the entire administration of the monastery with all its precious relics," Chultrimpa Lungtog said. The resident monks, who deferred to the judgment of their spiritual superiors, the high rinpoches, tried to tolerate the newcomers as best they could and to avoid confrontation in the interest of unity at Rumtek. "We also decided that we would not become involved in the trouble and that we would support neither Situ Rinpoche nor Shamar Rinpoche."

Around this time, the Joint Action Committee, Situ's political action committee in Sikkim, commandeered the Kunga Delek Guest House across from the monastery in Rumtek village. Here they set up a kind of campaign office and free snack bar for the monks of Rumtek and the families in the village. They served meals and gave out literature supporting Situ and Gyaltsab. Handouts criticized the Rumtek administration of Shamar and Topga as corrupt and urged guest house visitors to support the effort to convince or pressure all leading Karma Kagyu lamas to accept Ogyen Trinley as the Karmapa.

Guest house visitors could also receive payments from Akong Rinpoche's Rokpa Trust, which, as we have seen, were given to those who pledged their support to Situ. The foundation was supported by hundreds of individual donors in Europe to provide food, clothing, and education to deserving Tibetan refugees. Donors in Zurich or Vienna probably would have been surprised to learn that frequent recipients of Rokpa largesse included the thirty-two new Nalanda Institute students that Situ had brought in from Bhutan.

"Even though we tried to do our best, the Institute wasn't running as successfully as before," said Khenpo Chodrak, abbot of Rumtek until August 1993. "One reason was that some of the students were receiving money from the other side, with the result that they didn't attend the classes any more, didn't keep proper discipline, and didn't listen when we tried to talk to them."

Worried by the rising tension at the monastery, in mid-November 1992, Shamar asked Chief Minister Bhandari for a meeting at his office in Gangtok. Accompanied by senior staff and monks from Rumtek, Shamar requested the state government's protection. He informed Bhandari that, according to talk around Gangtok, a large group supporting Tai Situ was planning to try to take over Rumtek. Shamar asked Bhandari for state police to protect the monks' community and requested a letter to the effect that the state government would uphold law and order at the monastery.

"I still hoped that the chief minister would enforce the law," Shamar said. "But there had been enough reasons to doubt his sincerity. So we also hoped that this meeting might force the issue of state interference in religious affairs." If Shamar was able to get hard evidence that Bhandari was planning to help overthrow the Rumtek administration, he could seek assistance from officials in New Delhi to prevent the coup. In any event, Bhandari avoided incriminating himself and did agree to protect the Rumtek monks, but he never put this commitment in writing.

After meeting Bhandari, Shamar left Rumtek for Bangkok, to visit the grandmother of the King of Bhutan who was hospitalized there. Since the first time that the sixteenth Karmapa had taken Shamar to Bhutan as a boy in the sixties, Shamar had maintained good relations with the royal family of the Himalayan kingdom.

Just as before, Situ saw Shamar's absence from Rumtek as an opportunity to take action and the dynamic rinpoche did not waste any time to use this chance to sideline Shamar. The day after Shamar's departure, Situ arrived at Rumtek accompanied by an official of the Sikkim state Department of Ecclesiastical Affairs, a police escort, and a crowd of a couple dozen Khampas from his political action committee in Kathmandu, the Derge Association. Situ had arrived to move into Rumtek. In addition, he wanted to hold a meeting of his followers there the next day, while Shamar would be away.

Rump Parliament

When Situ and his group arrived at Rumtek, they found the monastery office closed. The government official forced Lekshe Drayan, the assistant secretary at Rumtek who had helped the sixteenth Karmapa to pack the Black Crown before fleeing Tsurphu for exile in 1959, to open the office for him. The official demanded to know why the office and other rooms at the monastery were locked when Situ Rinpoche was planning to come to Rumtek. Lekshe asked what business this was of the official's, since Rumtek was a private religious institution. The official threatened Lekshe, saying he was sent by the Sikkim state government and the monk should obey or face jail time.

The Sikkim official insisted that Situ should have access to any room in the monastery. Lekshe replied that Situ already had a guest room there and was able to use it any time he visited Rumtek. The official became impatient, and lectured Lekshe. "No, Situ Rinpoche must be given Gyalwa Karmapa's own room next to where the Black Crown is," the official said, according to Lekshe. Then, to underline the importance of this order, the official added, "These are the direct orders of the chief minister of Sikkim, Nar Bahadur Bhandari."

The official told Lekshe that he had ten minutes to think about it or face the consequences. Lekshe decided that he had little choice but to comply. He led the official, followed by his police escort, up to the sixteenth Karmapa's suite above the main temple, opened the rooms and gave the keys to the official, who in turn passed them on to Situ, who moved in later the same day. For the next year Situ would make the Karmapa's private rooms his own.

The next day, November 27, Gyaltsab joined Situ at Rumtek, accompanied by more lay people from the Derge Association in Nepal and Situ's other political action groups. Without gaining permission from Topga Rinpoche or the Rumtek administration, the two rinpoches convened a six-day meeting of their supporters. "A large number of people from outside Sikkim were brought into the monastery by the two rinpoches, apparently to demonstrate their numerical strength," Rumtek monk-official Chultrimpa Lungtog said. "This meeting was organized without consulting us and against our wishes and consent, with the sole intention of illegally taking over the Dharma Chakra Center and the powers and privileges vested in the monastic community by H.H. the sixteenth Gyalwa Karmapa."

"When we learned that they were about to convene the so-called 'International Meeting' we, the original staff members and Rumtek monks, wrote a letter to those who were organizing this meeting," said Omze Yeshey, another monk-official at Rumtek before August 1993. "We made it clear that we, the Rumtek monks, were in charge of the monastery and that we would accept this meeting and its resolutions only if it was held in cooperation with the trustees of the Karmapa Charitable Trust." But Situ and Gyaltsab ignored this letter and proceeded with their gathering.

The rinpoches dubbed their group the "Kagyu International Assembly." In *The Dance of 17 Lives* Mick Brown wrote that in attendance were "representatives from KTD at Woodstock, from Samye Ling, Australia, Tibet, India, Nepal, and Bhutan. Also present were representatives of the five Kagyu monasteries, six Buddhist organizations and eight Tibetan organizations in Sikkim."[11]

But to the monks at Rumtek the group was little more than a lynch mob made up of followers of Situ, Gyaltsab, and their ally, former Rumtek Abbot Thrangu. "These people seemed excited, impatient, and angry. We were scared that they would take over the monastery," Khenpo Ngawang told me. The chairman of the meeting, Kunga Yonten, a Sakya lama—whose school, of course, had no connection to Rumtek—led the excited crowd in throaty support for one demand after another. These included a request to the Dalai Lama to restore the defunct Lhasa government's old ban on Shamar Rinpoche, as well a denunciation of Shamar and Topga for ordering, earlier in the year, that the valuables at Rumtek be locked away for safekeeping. This demand only made the monks more afraid that Situ and Gyaltsab's true interest in Rumtek was its valuables.

The day's main goal was to grant Situ and Gyaltsab legal control over Rumtek. And that meant trying again to take control of the Karmapa Charitable Trust. The meeting voted to dissolve the board of the trust and constitute a new board stacked with Situ's supporters. Then, this new would-be trust tried to dismiss Topga Rinpoche as general secretary and replace him with Tenzin Namgyal, the brother-in-law of former Abbot Thrangu. Both men were staunch allies of Tai Situ. Though the Rumtek administration did not recognize the authority of this meeting or its decisions, from November 1992 until his death in 2005, Tenzin claimed to be the general secretary of the Karmapa's labrang.

Halfway through the week of meetings, on November 30, Tai Situ submitted a request to the Sikkim Land Revenue Department, where the Karmapa Trust charter was filed, to change the membership of the board as his meeting had decided. On the following day, December 1, Land Revenue Commissioner T. W. Barphungpa Kazi released an official letter in response. He rejected Situ's request and ruled that his "delegates" had no right to make decisions concerning the Karmapa Trust; that the actions of the Kagyu International Assembly relating to the trust were illegal; and that, accordingly, the trustees would remain as before. Situ and Gyaltsab filed an appeal to this decision, but later withdrew their request.

Thus, after the conclusion of the Kagyu International Assembly, Situ and Gyaltsab had failed a second time to take over Rumtek. If they wanted to gain control of the cloister, they would have to try a different approach. Chultrimpa Lungtog said that soon after the meeting, Situ and Gyaltsab asked for help from Chief Minister Bhandari. They wanted him to expel Rumtek General Secretary Topga from Sikkim. Bhandari agreed, and in February 1993 the East District Magistrate issued an order banning Topga Rinpoche from entering the eastern part of Sikkim, where Rumtek was located.

With its general secretary prohibited from entering the state, Rumtek became more vulnerable than ever. According to Chultrimpa Lungtog, the monks at Rumtek learned through sources in Gangtok that Bhandari also told Situ and Gyaltsab that he was ready to help them take over Rumtek, but that he would need a pretext to send in police officers. Reportedly, the chief minister advised the two rinpoches to create a scuffle or fight inside the monastery that would require the police to intervene.

"By June or July 1993, the situation in the monastery had already become very tense," Chultrimpa Lungtog explained. "Supporters of Situ Rinpoche and Gyaltsab Rinpoche indulged in reckless violence within the monastery premises." In May 1993, Rumtek guests vandalized a jeep belonging to the cloister. The next month, a student named Trinley Dorje from Sonada Monastery stabbed Sonam Tsering, one of the teachers at the Nalanda Institute. Sonam and the Rumtek administration filed a criminal complaint with the police, who arrested the stabber. But he was soon out on bail provided by Kunzang Sherab, the president of the Joint Action Committee in Gangtok. The police took no further action against the stabber. Minor scuffles became commonplace at Rumtek, and with Topga unable to enter Sikkim to reassume the helm at the cloister, it was clear that management of the monastery was slipping out of the hands of the Karmapa's labrang.

Chultrimpa Lungtog said that the Rumtek monks "found it impossible to control the criminal elements brought into the monastery by the two rinpoches." As with the stabbing incident, when the Rumtek administration reported other problems with the new students to the police, nothing happened. "We never realized that Situ Rinpoche and Gyaltsab Rinpoche had successfully bribed the police officials and state government civil servants concerned in order to take over the monastery administration through acts of violence and criminal intimidation."

We have seen how Situ and Gyaltsab appeared to take advantage of any time that Shamar was absent from Rumtek to make a move. In June 1992, they announced the Dalai Lama's support for Ogyen Trinley when Shamar was off-site, at his residence near Rumtek village. Five months later, in November of that year, when Shamar was in Thailand, Situ and Gyaltsab held the so-called Kagyu International Assembly.

Following this pattern, on June 26, 1993, to celebrate Ogyen Trinley's birthday, Gyaltsab came to the shedra and organized a party. Shamar was also away from Rumtek at the time, again at his residence. According to Khenpo Chodrak, the school's head teacher, on this occasion Gyaltsab told the students that from now on it would be sufficient for them to just wear their monks' robes, they didn't have to attend classes or complete coursework. "From that point on, discipline at the Institute collapsed. Many of the students didn't study anymore and didn't abide by the rules," Chodrak said. In *The Dance of 17 Lives* Mick Brown wrote that a rainbow appeared over Rumtek on the day of this birthday party, an auspicious sign. But birthday parties, even for realized masters, were not prescribed in the Vinaya, the Buddha's rules for monks and nuns, and the Rumtek administration watched helplessly as discipline eroded at the school.

The next day, Shamar called the police and brought an officer with him to Rumtek to lecture the students. "I reminded them that they were only guests at Rumtek and should follow the rules and not try to interfere in the monastery's affairs. Otherwise, they were free to study and enjoy the facilities that we provided to them free of charge." Officer Sundar, the policeman who had accompanied Shamar, told the students to follow the school's rules in the future. Apparently, the officer had not received clear enough instructions from his superiors in Gangtok on how to behave at Rumtek. Soon after this incident, his superior lectured Officer Sundar, demoted him in rank, and then transferred Sundar away from the area.

At the end of this meeting, Shamar asked the monks to sign one of two lists. One list was for those who would obey the school rules, the other was for those who refused to do so. "Most of Situ's followers signed the second list, including the thirty-two monks Situ had brought in from Bhutan," Shamar told me. "This might sound like bold and shocking behavior for students who were Buddhist monks, but actually I was not surprised. I think that most of these young men had not taken monk's vows, but they simply pretended to be monks. They did not respect the Rumtek administration; they seemed to be loyal only to Situ Rinpoche."

A few days later, the Rumtek office forwarded the names of the monks on the "disobey" list to the minister of education in Bhutan with a request for information about their background. In response, the Bhutanese government confirmed that many had been convicted of theft or violent crimes, and some had even escaped from Bhutanese jails. But without the help of the Sikkim police, the Rumtek administration was powerless to expel these young men from the monastery or send them back to Bhutan.

Above: Rumtek monastery in Sikkim in 2004.

Above: The sixteenth Karmapa in 1962.
Below: The building on the grounds of Shamar's house near Rumtek where the expelled monks have taken refuge and built a make-shift shrine room at the top.

Above: The author in front of the main gate of Rumtek, with paint damage from humidity.

Above: The sixteenth Karmapa performing the Black Crown ceremony.

Right: The sixteenth Karmapa at the groundbreaking of the Karmapa Institute in New Delhi followed by Shamar Rinpoche in 1980. After the ceremony, the Karmapa collapsed from pain and Shamar rushed him to a hospital for immediate stomach surgery.

Left: The sixteenth Karmapa meeting with the Dalai Lama.

Left: Ole Nydahl and others carrying the Karmapa's body (kudung) at his funeral at Rumtek in 1981.

Above: The sixteenth Karmapa with Ole and Hannah Nydahl at their center in Copenhagen in the mid-seventies.

*Left: Shamar Rinpoche
in a simplified red
crown.
Center right: Tai Situ
Rinpoche.
Bottom: Shamar
meets with the Dalai
Lama at his residence
in Dharamsala in
December 1997 to
request a meeting for
Thaye Dorje and the
Dalai Lama. Initially,
the Tibetan leader
agreed, but then changed
his mind after protests
from Tai Situ.*

*Above: Gyaltsab
Rinpoche in
Copenhagen in 1989.*

*Left: Ogyen Trinley.
Below: Situ and
Gyaltsab Rinpoches
receive the Dalai Lama's
confirmation ("Buktham
Rinpoche") that
Ogyen Trinley is the
seventeenth Karmapa.*

*Left: Akong Rinpoche.
Below: The leaders of
the crowd of Tai Situ's
supporters demand
entrance to the main
shrine room at Rumtek
on August 2, 1993.*

*Left: Sikkim Home
Secretary Sonam
Wangdi prepares to open
the main shrine room
after compelling Rumtek
monks to surrender the
keys.
Center left: Rumtek
monks try to reenter the
monastery to perform
the Yarney retreat on the
third anniversary of their
expulsion.
Center right: Sikkim
elite security forces
prevent expelled monks
from re-entering Rumtek.
In protest, the monks
begin a hunger strike a
few days later.*

*Left: After he was voted
out of office in 1994,
former Sikkim Chief
Minister Nar Bahadur
Bhandari visits Shamar
to apologize for his role
at Rumtek.*

*Left: Shamar meets
with Rumtek monks
and hears stories of
their expulsion at the
International Karma
Kagyu Conference in
New Delhi, 1996.*

*Left: Thaye Dorje at
the Karmapa Institute
in 1994.
Below: Shamar
and Thaye Dorje in
Kalimpong, 1999.*

*Above: Sakya Trizin,
the leader of the Sakya
school, with Thaye
Dorje in Menlo Park,
California, 2003.*

*Above: Thaye Dorje's
mother, Dechen
Wangmo.
Right: Thaye Dorje's
father, Mipham
Rinpoche.*

Above: *Thaye Dorje
wearing the Gampopa
Hat.*
Right: *Shamar Rinpoche
giving a blessing.*

Right: Thaye Dorje
sailing off of California.
Below: Shamar
and Thaye Dorje at
Shamar's house in
Kalimpong.

Right: Thaye Dorje
traveling in Europe

11 THE YARNEY PUTSCH

Now or Never

By the late summer of 1993, Situ and Gyaltsab acted as if they were under pressure from their allies and supporters to launch their coup at Rumtek soon.

As we saw in the last chapter, control of Rumtek was not necessary to establish Ogyen Trinley's credibility as Karmapa. He already had the Dalai Lama on his side, which was enough for most Tibetans, who did not know that the Dalai Lamas had never chosen a Karmapa in the past. And it would certainly be enough to give Ogyen Trinley legitimacy with outsiders, for whom the Dalai Lama was a top celebrity.

Yet, for some reason, this was not enough for the two rinpoches and their supporters. After two failed attempts to take the cloister, they were more determined than ever to control Rumtek. Perhaps they had some other motive than supporting Ogyen Trinley? Shamar's supporters have made serious accusations—particularly that Situ wanted to sell off the priceless relics that the sixteenth Karmapa had brought from Tsurphu when he fled into exile, including the Black Crown. Situ's supporters have denied this charge, but as we will see, Situ's actions at Rumtek became increasingly suspicious.

"I had no objection to Situ proposing a boy to be Karmapa," Shamar told me. "Situs have recognized Karmapas in the past, though there was no need to bring in His Holiness Dalai Lama in this case; His Holiness has no authority over the Karmapa or the Karma Kagyu. But what I really object to is Situ's second agenda of taking over Rumtek by force, in collaboration with corrupt politicians and their hired thugs, for which there can be no justification.

"I am in favor of Tibetan and Buddhist unity, but not at the expense of integrity. Ultimately, different sects are not needed to spread dharma, and they can lead to fighting. The best would be to have one Buddhism, as long as believers are free to follow their traditional practices. This means that their teachers must be free to pass along the lineages of oral teachings that have been so carefully preserved from Shakyamuni Buddha down to the present day. Every Buddhist country has that, and it is unspeakably precious, it gives us confidence that the teaching is authentic. Once an oral lineage is lost, it is gone forever. We may still have the books of its teachings; but the torch of blessing, handed off from one generation to the next, has been snuffed out. Most important for me has been to preserve the purity of the Karma Kagyu lineage. That's my job as Shamarpa."

In 1993, Shamar said just this, protesting that he only wanted to preserve the unbroken lineage of the Karma Kagyu and the authenticity of the Karmapa. To the exasperation of Situ and his followers, Shamar continued to insist that the reincarnation of the Karmapa should be found by "traditional methods."

At Shamar's insistence, the Rumtek administration had stepped up its own efforts to get Situ's letter tested. "Though Chief Minister Bhandari's police and the young men working for his party kept a close watch on the locked room with Situ Rinpoche's prediction letter, we had plans to secretly get it out of Rumtek for a forensic test. We felt that we might succeed at this any day," Shamar told me. In the summer of 1993, time seemed to be running out for Situ and Gyaltsab. Yet, they still had the support of the Dalai Lama.

In June, the Dalai Lama attended a human rights conference in Vienna where he gave a stirring address.

Brute force, no matter how strongly applied, can never
subdue the basic human desire for freedom and dignity.
It is not enough, as communist systems have assumed,
merely to provide people with food, shelter, and clothing.
The deeper human nature needs to breathe the precious
air of liberty. However, some governments still consider
the fundamental human rights of their citizens an internal
matter of the state. They do not accept that the fate of
a people in any country is the legitimate concern of the

entire human family and that claims to sovereignty are not
a license to mistreat one's citizens. It is not only our right
as members of the global human family to protest when
our brothers and sisters are being treated brutally, but it is
also our duty to do whatever we can to help them.[1]

Though his audience in Vienna understood that the Dalai Lama
was criticizing China, Shamar and his followers found the Dalai Lama's
words ironic. They saw the Dalai Lama's intervention in the Karmapa
recognition as a violation of their religious freedom, a human-rights
abuse that Dharamsala leaders were trying to keep as an internal matter
of their informal Tibetan state-in-exile.

Back in Sikkim, Situ and Gyaltsab leveraged the Dalai Lama's
support to help put pressure on the monks and lamas at Rumtek. In July,
Shamar and the Rumtek administration feared that Situ and Gyaltsab
would try to take over the monastery at the upcoming Yarney retreat due
to begin August 2. "The Yarney summer retreat is supposed to be a very
peaceful period where the monks focus on studies and meditation," said
monk-official Omze Yeshey. "In fact, the responsibility is always with us,
the monks of the monastery." The Buddha himself began the tradition
of holding a retreat during the subcontinent's rainy season, a traditional
retreat that came to be known in Tibet as the Yarney. In all Buddhist
countries, nuns and monks continue to observe this retreat according to
the rules set down by the Buddha 2500 years ago in the Vinaya.

In the opening ceremony for the Yarney retreat, known in Tibetan
as the Sojong—which must be completed by noon—four monks at a time
take oaths from the abbot of the monastery. A time of introspection and
monastic renewal, according to the rules laid down in the Vinaya, the
ceremonies are held in closed sections of a monastery and lay people are
not permitted to be present.

The pressure at Rumtek had grown to such proportions that the
administration feared disruption during Yarney. They tried to prevent any
problems in advance. As principal of the Nalanda Institute, in mid-July
Shamar declared a school vacation, and instructed the monk-students
to leave Rumtek for their homes by August 1, 1993. Then, the Rumtek
monks decided not to perform the Yarney pujas that year. Having done
everything he could think of to prevent problems, Shamar reluctantly left
Rumtek to visit his ailing mother at a hospital in Germany on July 22.

As soon as Shamar was gone, following the pattern of the previous year, Situ and Gyaltsab went into action. First, they declared that they would proceed with the Sojong, despite the decision of Shamar and the Rumtek monks to cancel that year's retreat. Meanwhile, the shedra students ignored Shamar's instructions to go home, and remained at Rumtek, preparing to perform the Yarney pujas under the direction of Situ and Gyaltsab. The resident monks had to abide the decrees of the two high rinpoches because of their authority in the Karma Kagyu hierarchy, if not in the Karmapa labrang or at Rumtek itself. But perhaps even more compelling than protocol, the monks feared that the hundreds of followers that Situ and Gyaltsab had imported into Rumtek would support the two rinpoches' will with violence, if necessary.

The Rumtek monks still hoped to avoid conflict. The residents begged the visiting rinpoches, if they were determined to go through with the Sojong, at least to allow separate ceremonies for the shedra students and the resident monks. "We declared that if the Yarney were practiced together, that is to say if these shedra students participated, there would be bloodshed and the monastery's reputation would be damaged," said monk-official Omze Yeshe. But Situ and Gyaltsab disagreed, saying all the monks should practice together. "Situ Rinpoche insisted that the monastery monks and the shedra students should perform the Yarney together. He said that the Yarney was open to everybody and that we couldn't exclude the shedra students."

The monks tried to reason with the two rinpoches, whose motives they had good reason to doubt. Yet, the monks claimed that they still respected Situ and Gyaltsab as enlightened masters who could only have the wellbeing of Rumtek at heart. "Our discussions with Situ and Gyaltsab Rinpoche took place in the early morning of August 2, the day on which the Yarney was supposed to start," said Omze Yeshey. "We didn't contradict them but we just tried to make our point clear. While we were talking to them, many people and officials from Sikkim had gathered, and the atmosphere had become more and more tense."

After dozens of local lay people had arrived for the supposedly closed event, just as the monks had predicted, the tension at Rumtek threatened to break out into open violence. "Then these people started abusing us, saying that we were the ones who wouldn't accept the Karmapa. They kept calling us 'samaya breakers'," said Omze Yeshey. Samaya is a sacred oath taken by advanced Vajrayana practitioners to obey their teachers in their roles as tantric masters; a follower who breaks samaya risks rebirth in the Buddhist hell realms.

The resident monks now feared the worst. "While these two rinpoches and their supporters prepared themselves for the Yarney ceremonies, we, the legitimate and genuine monks of Karmapa, resolved to guard the monastery and to prevent the innumerable movable possessions of Karmapa from falling into the hands of outsiders and known smugglers," said Chultrimpa Lungtog. "We never dreamed that Situ Rinpoche and Gyaltsab Rinpoche had meticulously planned to take over the monastery illegally by joining forces with the local politicians." By nine o'clock in the morning, fifty young men employed by Chief Minister Bhandari as party workers from the Lal Bazaar in Gangtok had joined the crowd of shedra students and lay people from Situ's Derge Association.

Members of Situ's two political action committees—the Derge Association from Kathmandu and the local Joint Action Committee—were joined at Rumtek on this day by dozens of Sikkimese families. They had seen the posters that Situ had put up around Gangtok promising a big public initiation ceremony for the practice of White Tara. "Situ Rinpoche made a false announcement saying that he would give initiations on this particular day," Khenpo Tsering Samdrup, another teacher at the monk's school at Rumtek, told me. "There is no precedent for this in the history of Tibetan Buddhism—there is no tradition of giving any initiation on the first day of Yarney. He made this announcement purely in order to attract people. I think that there were many innocent people, but there were also people who knew that something was going to happen, who were aware of the plot."

"Karmapa Chenno"

By mid-morning, a total crowd of more than a thousand of Tai Situ's supporters had assembled in the monastery's courtyard. A tense standoff began outside the main temple. The Rumtek monks responsible for the shrine room locked the entrance and refused to hand over the keys. Situ and Gyaltsab led a crowd to the temple, and sat down in front of the locked doors. They held incense and chanted *Karmapa chenno* (Karmapa hear me), the mantra of the Karmapas. Their followers clamored for action from behind them.

The Rumtek monks began to lose control over the situation. Soon, officers sent by the Sikkim chief of police began to intervene on the side of the aggressors. "This was crossing the line between church and state, which broke India's constitution," Shamar said. "We can only guess that Mr. Bhandari must have had a very strong incentive to take such a risk." Bhandari knew that New Delhi could have taken strong measures against him for breaching the constitutional wall between church and state, up to dissolving his government and putting him in prison. As it turned out, after the Rumtek takeover, the central government did initiate an investigation into Bhandari's role to determine if his Sikkim administration had unlawfully interfered in religious affairs.

Shamar's supporters have claimed that Bhandari probably received a payment as high as one million dollars from Situ and Gyaltsab, to send state police and security forces into Rumtek in response to an incident that the two rinpoches would provoke. The money came, allegedly, from Situ's Taiwanese supporter, former government official Chen Lu An. But the only evidence for this payment, aside from hearsay, is inferential: Shamar's followers theorize that for Bhandari to openly defy India's constitution by invading a religious center, and thus risk punishment from New Delhi, the chief minister must have been well rewarded. However, both newspaper reports and government investigators have documented that Chen Lu An delivered a payment of $1.5 million to Bhandari a few weeks after the Rumtek takeover.

According to Indian journalist Anil Maheshwari, Chen visited India between November 28 and December 4, 1993 to attend a meeting organized by Karma Topden. As we have seen Topden was a leader of Situ's Joint Action Committee in Sikkim and the father of the would-be Gyathon Tulku, rejected by the Rumtek administration in the eighties. Situ Rinpoche was also present at this meeting, and Shamar's supporters claim that this meeting was connected to Bhandari receiving a second payment from Chen for the chief minister's role in the takeover of Rumtek four months earlier, in August.[2] The Indian government launched an investigation, and in January 1994, the Ministry of External Affairs in New Delhi banned Chen from re-entering India.[3]

Whether he was paid or not, Bhandari's intervention made the difference at Rumtek on the day of the Sojong. When the police arrived, the Rumtek monks finally lost control over the monastery. "Then tension mounted and we were completely helpless," said Omze Yeshey. "The people started to throw stones, and a number of monks were injured. The police also started to beat the monks of the monastery. They put a great deal of pressure on us, telling us for instance that we would be thrown in jail if we didn't cooperate and that what we were doing was illegal." As the lay people and the policemen beat the Rumtek monks, Situ and Gyaltsab remained seated facing the shrine room doors, serenely leading the seated crowd in the chanting of the mantra *Karmapa chenno*.

The monks still refused to hand over the keys to the shrine room. The crowd grew angry and the police again stepped in. "Finally, with the help of the police officers, a few state government officials and the public, we were forced to hand over the key to the main temple," said Omze Yeshey, the monk-official who was one of Rumtek's omzes, or chant-masters.

Another omze, Ngedon Tenzin, told the police officers that he could get the keys but would have to go through the crowd to do so, which he was hesitant to do, since several men had threatened to beat him. "But Suren Pradhan and the other policemen assured me it would be all right and that they would protect me," Omze Ngedon said. Suren Pradhan, well known in the local area as a bully with no respect for civil rights, was rumored to have several murders to his credit. "They insisted that I go. When I started walking towards the dining hall behind the monastery, some of the lay men and women began abusing me and beating me. They took my yellow dharma robe, tied it around my neck, threw me on the ground and dragged me along the whole way from the office outside, through the courtyard to the corner of the dining hall. While they were dragging me along, they continued to beat me."

This was humiliating for the whole monks' community, since Ngedon was one of the highest officials of Rumtek. Indeed, in recognition of his ability, the Karmapa Trust would appoint him general secretary of Thaye Dorje's labrang in 2004, making him the successor of Topga Rinpoche.

Back at Rumtek in August 1993, monks came out to rescue Ngedon, but the crowd started throwing stones and breaking windows. Finally the police put an end to the fighting. Then the Sikkim Home Secretary Sonam Wangdi ordered the monks to deliver the keys within five minutes or face arrest. The monks complied, and the government official unlocked the shrine room doors. The crowd erupted in cheers. Holding incense and chanting, with folded hands and teary eyes, Situ and Gyaltsab led their followers into the temple to pay obeisance to the sacred images of Buddhas and bodhisattvas within.

Then the police began to attend to the injured monks. "The police officers told the monks that they would take them to hospital for medical treatment, but instead they threw these monks into jail" in Ranipool, a suburb of Gangtok, said Omze Yeshey. Interestingly, many of the policemen were Buddhists, and these officers carried out their orders at Rumtek apologetically, approaching the monks with the respect normally due from lay people to members of the monastic sangha in Himalayan countries. That night, in the lockup at Ranipool, Officer Suren Pradhan, who was not a Buddhist, dragged two thieves out of their cells and started beating them savagely in front of the arrested monks, with no provocation but apparently as a warning. Yet the monks were not afraid. They knew that the Buddhist guards would not allow them to receive the same humiliating treatment.

Sign or Leave

During the next three days, the new Rumtek administration of Situ and Gyaltsab pressured the monks who had not fled or been arrested to sign a document affirming that they accepted Ogyen Trinley as the seventeenth Karmapa. On August 5, the police returned, again accompanied by Bhandari's party toughs from the Gangtok market. While the monks were assembled in the dining hall, the bullies and police entered. A group of the street toughs pulled the cook out of the kitchen and smeared chili powder over his face. They told him never to cook for the monks again. Then they put up a large framed photo of Ogyen Trinley and addressed the monks.

The leaders of the gang of toughs told the monks to perform prostrations in front of the photo as police looked on. "At gunpoint we were forced to accept Ogyen Trinley of Tibet as the one and only Karmapa," said Omze Yeshey. "We had to swear an oath on our acceptance. We were told that anybody who dared to say otherwise would face legal consequences." The intruders brought tape recorders to capture each oath. Then, the gang leaders drove the young monks into the kitchen and made them pick up the kitchen knives. They had to pose in menacing positions while the police snapped photographs, apparently to allege later that they were fighting. The police would create bogus criminal files for each monk.

Several of the street toughs carried knives and demanded keys to the monastery's prayer rooms and shrines. Just as they had refused to surrender the main temple keys three days before, so now the Rumtek monks would not yield the keys. This led to another stand-off. For six nerve-racking hours, the monks stood shoulder-to-shoulder in front of the door to the main shrine room, while Bhandari's bullies took up positions several feet opposite them, taunting the monks and periodically threatening to attack. The Sikkim police looked on without trying to stop the bullies or defuse the situation.

The stand-off was broken only by the appearance of more police officers at about five o'clock in the afternoon, this time elite security forces of the Sikkim Armed Police. With Situ and Gyaltsab leading the way, the soldiers chased the Rumtek monks to the back of the monastery. The monks locked themselves in a small storeroom. The soldiers and street toughs together broke down the locked door and began beating the monks, injuring twenty in the process.

Three Sikkim government officials—Police Inspector General Tenzing, the fearsome Officer Suren Pradhan, and another policeman known as Kharel—made a speech to the monks. They warned that unless all the keys were handed over, anything could happen. In response, the monks insisted that a monastery was a private religious institution protected by India's constitution from state interference. The government officials were not impressed with this argument, and they insisted on the keys. Finally, seeing that it was the only way to avoid further bloodshed, the monks handed over the keys to the police officers.

Officer Kharel then unlocked the main temple door and announced that from now on, Situ Rinpoche would control Rumtek. Later, the Sikkim home secretary handed over all the keys to Gyaltsab Rinpoche in exchange for a signed receipt.

Finally, the police arrested more monks. "A considerable number of our monks was illegally detained and locked up in police custody for several days," said Chultrimpa Lungtog. Monks who were not arrested fled the monastery to take refuge in the surrounding forest. After the week was out, about a hundred monks, or ninety percent of Rumtek's original monks before Situ started bringing in outsiders in 1992, left Rumtek rather than accept Ogyen Trinley as the seventeenth Karmapa.

"We were no longer allowed to enter the monastery, so we had to find somewhere else to stay," said Omze Yeshey. "This is why we had to seek refuge in Shamar Rinpoche's residence, where we could be close to the Dharma Chakra Center. He himself wasn't there. No preparations or earlier arrangements had been made. In fact it was very difficult. The house isn't that big, and we were a considerable number of monks. So we had to contend with numerous problems in terms of our accommodation."

"It is deemed strange," wrote the *Hindustan Times*, "that pro-China Situ Rinpoche, who has never in the past taken up any responsibilities at Rumtek has suddenly chosen to muster the Sikkim Chief Minister's support, to execute a coup d'état, while regent Shamar Rinpoche is abroad."[4]

Monks Exiled

With Rumtek in the hands of Situ and Gyaltsab, dozens of the sixteenth Karmapa's monks had lost their home. The two rinpoches appointed former Abbot Thrangu's brother-in-law Tenzin Namgyal as the new general secretary of the monastery. Tenzin then replaced the sixteenth Karmapa's ritual, chant, and discipline masters—most of whom had fled or been expelled—with loyal monks to take their places. He also appointed followers of Tai Situ to fill the other top offices of the monastery and the Nalanda Institute, the monk's school at Rumtek.

"Among the student body only those without the slightest interest in studying stayed at the school," said Khenpo Chodrak, ousted as head teacher at Nalanda in the Rumtek takéover. "As for the teachers, suddenly students who had been unable to reach the required standards and had failed and had to repeat classes were installed as teachers. They were simply given the title of teacher. It was just like a stage play. Evidently they are not qualified teachers."

The new monastery management under Tenzin asked lay people in Rumtek village to sign various documents: pledges of loyalty to Ogyen Trinley, petitions for the Indian government to allow him to come to Rumtek, and denunciations of Shamar and the ousted monks. "Those who tried to resist were blacklisted and harassed by the conniving police," according to Maheshwari. "Police saw it as their holy duty to re-educate the less enthusiastic supporters of the Chinese candidate. The families who stayed loyal to Shamar Rinpoche were persecuted."[5]

In the takeover, the Karmapa Charitable Trust had also lost its offices. The trustees appointed by the sixteenth Karmapa—or those who succeeded them, selected according to the bylaws of the group—were unable to enter the monastery and get access to the records and files of the Karmapa Trust. Yet, the absence of Karmapa Trust trustees did not stop Rumtek's new General Secretary Tenzin Namgyal from sending out correspondence on Karmapa Trust letterhead. Later, ordered to desist by the courts, Tenzin switched to letterhead of the Kagyu International Headquarters, an office set up by Topga Rinpoche under the control of the Trust to coordinate communication with dharma centers abroad. Tenzin would later claim in court that his control of this office's assets—basically a desk, the useful letterhead, and some rubber stamps with the office's name—made him the authorized secretary of the Karmapa's labrang. The court would reject this argument, as we will see in chapter 13.

Situ and Gyaltsab had triumphed. In August 1993 little seemed to stand in the way of the rinpoches' plan to enthrone Ogyen Trinley at Rumtek. To the delight of Situ's followers the Karma Kagyu would become closer to the Dalai Lama, though the independence of the Karmapa would be compromised. But there were more sinister implications as well. Through the boy-lama, the two rinpoches would gain control over the valuables at Rumtek, including the Black Crown. Would they try to sell off these priceless relics?

For Shamar, the Karmapa Trust board members, and the expelled monks—all acting in their own ways as the caretakers of the sixteenth Karmapa's legacy—it was intolerable to be excluded from the Karmapa's own monastery. They feared for the patrimony of the Karma Kagyu. After 1993 they would work together to regain control of Rumtek.

12 UNDER OCCUPATION

Shamar's Initial Response

After he heard by phone in Germany about the Rumtek takeover on August 2, Shamar Rinpoche left his mother's sickbed and returned to India on August 5. He knew his tasks would be to console the expelled monks, confer with Topga and the Karmapa Trust board, and plan what to do next. To Shamar, the situation looked grim.

Now, he knew that Chief Minister Bhandari had entered the conflict openly, as a partisan of Tai Situ and Gyaltsab. There would be no help for Shamar from the corrupt Sikkim state government, but instead, active opposition. Shamar began planning a response that would bypass Bhandari's administration.

Meanwhile lamas and lay supporters of Tai Situ celebrated their rinpoche's coup at Rumtek. For them, it was good riddance to the slow-moving, obstructionist administration of Shamar and Topga. It is difficult to gauge the true motivations of Situ and his followers. Many in his political action committees may have been motivated by little more than the cash payments they received. But surely others must have been more idealistic. They probably thought that Tai Situ was the chosen disciple of the sixteenth Karmapa and that Ogyen Trinley was the beloved Karmapa, finally returned.

But for Shamar's followers, the Rumtek coup was a poignant betrayal of everything the Karmapa stood for: non-violence, the purity of the Karma Kagyu lineage, and the sanctity of religion separate from politics. Rumtek under occupation represented a period of decline, a dark era.

Before his death in 1997, Topga Rinpoche talked about three periods of decline in the Karma Kagyu. The first occurred when the tenth Karmapa had to flee Tibet after the invasion of Gushri Khan in 1642 at the time the fifth Dalai Lama assumed temporal power. The second was when the tenth Shamarpa died in Nepal after the Gorkha War in 1792 and the Tibetan government put a ban on his future incarnations. We have examined both of these turbulent eras earlier in this book.

In both instances, Karma Kagyu monasteries were converted to the Gelug order and the Karmapa's school was weakened almost to the point of extinction. "However, both of these periods of decline were brought about by external circumstances—external because they weren't created by members of the Karma Kagyu school," Topga said. "The current period of decline is not the result of external circumstances; it has been created from within by individuals who claim they are holders of the doctrine of the Karma Kagyu school," namely, Situ and Gyaltsab, respectively the third- and fifth-ranking lamas of the school.

"The reason for all the trouble at Rumtek," said Karma Chochok, another monk who had to flee the cloister in August 1993, "is not that we, the monks, took Shamar Rinpoche's side against Situ Rinpoche's side. We never declared that we were against Ogyen Trinley. The actual root of the problem lies in a conflict between H.H. the sixteenth Karmapa and the nominated Ogyen Trinley. Why? We, the Rumtek monks in the administration had been appointed to our functions by H.H. Karmapa himself. He asked us to take care of the monastery with all its sacred objects. When Ogyen Trinley was installed as the seventeenth Karmapa the process involved a great deal of politics, and his followers tried to gain control of Rumtek. We simply tried to protect the monastery."

The whole Rumtek coup happened while Shamar was abroad and General Secretary Topga was banned from entering the district of Sikkim where Rumtek was located. "We were devastated," Shamar told me. "We had feared some violence, so we had taken every precaution we could think of. But we had never imagined something on this scale. It was incomprehensible."

Shamar had ambitious plans to continue the work of the sixteenth Karmapa and spread Karma Kagyu Buddhism around the world. "I had wanted to study in America and then start dharma centers, schools, and monasteries in many countries. But now I had to put my plans aside and dedicate myself to one task—getting back Rumtek so we could enthrone an authentic seventeenth Karmapa there some day."

A month after the takeover, Shamar sent an open letter to Situ, Gyaltsab and their chief supporters listing the many actions that Situ, as a board member of the Karmapa Trust, had taken without the Trust's approval. First, Situ had tried to set up an illegal trust in order to get around the legitimate one and gain control of the assets of the sixteenth Karmapa. Second, he took over Rumtek by force, sending hired thugs and calling in police to attack the resident monks, sending some to jail, and expelling the rest. Third, Situ had stirred up trouble for the government of India, which had hosted both Situ and Shamar as refuges.

Shamar said that Situ had brought negative attention in India down on the Karma Kagyu and laid the school open to international intrigue. Then, he called on the members of the Karmapa Trust to join him "to reverse by legal means all the latest changes that Situ had made to the status and peace of the Rumtek monastery." He added that he would never accept the use of force to assume control over a monastery in the name of religion. He pledged to initiate proceedings in court to regain Rumtek for the Karmapa Trust.

Situ and Gyaltsab Rinpoches denied that they had usurped power at Rumtek. On the contrary, they launched an energetic publicity campaign claiming that they were merely trying to protect the Karmapa's legacy and that while doing so, their supporters became the victims of aggression by the Rumtek monks. They continued to send out open letters to this effect to Shamar. Situ's group of local families, the Joint Action Committee, sent a letter signed by numerous prominent Sikkimese to Shamar denouncing his lack of cooperation with Situ and failure to recognize Ogyen Trinley, saying that by so doing he had disgraced his Buddhist robes and the dharma he claimed to follow.

Another open letter put out by the Joint Action Committee claimed that a "handful of monks" in a "sabotage of religious functions" had prevented "a large number of devotees" from participating in public ceremonies at Rumtek on August 2. The document went on to add that police discovered a large cache of weapons at Rumtek stored by these monks in order to use later against the devotees—a bald-faced lie. The outraged local leaders condemned such actions as "mischievous, unwarranted, and with ulterior motive," probably inspired by "foreign elements with vested interests." They called on the state government to confiscate the property of all foreigners involved, clearly referring to Topga Rinpoche, who held a Bhutanese passport after his marriage in the seventies to a Bhutanese

princess, Ashyi Chokyi. Apparently, these activists did not remember that
many Tibetan rinpoches—including Shamar, Situ, and Gyaltsab—also
had Bhutanese passports, which the Himalayan kingdom provided as a
courtesy extended to leading exiled lamas.

Situ and Gyaltsab also mobilized their allies—and Chief Minister
Bhandari's friends—in the local press to tell their side of the story. A
Gangtok paper's headline was typical of the coverage the takeover received:
"Cops Quell Querulous Clergy." But Situ and Gyaltsab found that while
their alliance with Bhandari could help them in Sikkim, it did little good
in New Delhi. There, one of India's national newspapers, the *Hindustan
Times*, ran its story headlined "Pro-China Coup in Gangtok Monastery."

In response, another of Situ's allies, the Tibetan exile government
in Dharamsala, tried to help. Kunga Tamotsang, an official of the Tibetan
Government-in-Exile, complained to Indian External Affairs Minister
Salman Khurshid that there was an Indian government campaign against
Situ and a smear campaign in the New Delhi press.[1] This complaint
apparently had little effect, and the *Hindustan Times* and other large Indian
papers continued to print stories critical of Situ.

The original Rumtek monks have claimed that Situ and Gyaltsab
were not satisfied with making their own criticisms of the monks, but that
they resorted to covert "dirty tricks" reminiscent of Watergate to embarrass
the monks. "On one occasion," monk-official Omze Yeshey said, "some
people wrote a letter to the Dalai Lama claiming that we openly oppose
him. The letter was written in our names and bore the forged signatures
of five of our monastery staff. We tried to clarify the matter." The Rumtek
monks claimed that they did not oppose the Dalai Lama and did not
even want to take sides against Situ and Gyaltsab—they just wanted to get
back into Rumtek. But they lacked a forum to express their views at the
time. Meanwhile, Tenzin Namgyal's new Rumtek administration lodged
various criminal complaints with the Gangtok police, leading to criminal
investigations of forty-five monks. The monks have claimed that these
charges were fabricated.

Nuns under Threat

After expelling the monks from Rumtek, the new Rumtek administration
next took aim at the sixteenth Karmapa's nuns. Ani Chotso, who
established a convent near Rumtek on the instructions of the sixteenth
Karmapa, said that her thirty nuns had practiced at Rumtek for many

years until the takeover. Then, "after Situ Rinpoche caused all these problems, some of the nuns were beaten up very badly by his people, and they were forced to follow Situpa and his party."[2]

Citing decorum, the abbess declined to provide detail, but she implied that Situ's followers sexually harassed, assaulted, and even raped the nuns. "Furthermore, some nuns were bribed, some gave up their vows and got married." When Ani Chotso would not accept Ogyen Trinley as the reincarnation of the Karmapa, Situ sent hired toughs to pressure her and her nuns to proclaim their support. "The people from the other side came to the convent and made all kinds of accusations. They said that in my function as a teacher I had beaten up the young nuns, that I had torn off their clothes and kicked them out of the windows naked. I never did this."

Situ's followers then leveled charges of "samaya-breaking" against the abbess and her nuns. As we have seen, to break a samaya is considered a cardinal sin in Vajrayana Buddhism and a charge of samaya-breaking is not supposed to be made lightly. Yet, such charges became increasingly common after the Rumtek takeover in 1993. "It seems that in their view those people who maintain unbroken loyalty to H.H. the sixteenth Karmapa are all samaya-breakers," Ani Chotso said.

She then related the story of her own teacher on the serious subject of samaya. An extraordinary woman, Khandro Chemno was the tantric consort of the fifteenth Karmapa, one of the two Karmapas who did not take monks' vows but remained as householder yogis. "Khandro Chemno used to tell us that we should never even use the words 'samaya-breaker,' but these people used the words just as often as we recite the mantra 'Om mani padme hung.' I sincerely asked myself whether I had broken my samayas or not, but I came to the conclusion that I hadn't broken my samayas. So I can only think that they call people with faith in the Karmapa 'samaya-breakers.'"

Continuing to visit Rumtek even after the takeover for more than a year, the nuns eventually found their visits to the cloister too awkward and dangerous. The nuns filed a criminal complaint against twenty of the new Rumtek monks for threatening the nuns with beatings if they ever returned to Rumtek. The complaint also alleged that one of the leaders, a monk named Dorji, had beaten one of the nuns with a bat and that only the intervention of onlookers from the village had prevented the monks from molesting and raping the nuns. To the nuns' frustration, the police never acted on their complaint, and they made no arrests, even against the group leaders that the nuns named. After this incident, the nuns stopped their visits to Rumtek.

Other acts of violence occurred at Rumtek after the takeover, probably perpetrated by Situ and Gyaltsab's monks. According to witnesses, on May 4, 1994, a group including students at the Nalanda Institute began digging up the private garden originally planted for the sixteenth Karmapa and tended since his death by the caretaker of his residence, Benza Guru. A man in his seventies, Benza remained at Rumtek even after the takeover and quietly went about his gardening. But when he saw the young men destroying his work, he sharply scolded the group and ordered them away. The angry students left, but promised revenge.

That night, a young tough employed by Gyaltsab, Tashi Wangdi, appeared at Benza's room with a larger group of angry young men, ready to thrash the old caretaker. This time, a sympathetic senior monk prevented the assault. But early the next morning, monks discovered the mangled body of Benza Guru on one of the pathways that led to the Karmapa's residence.

Gyaltsab said that Benza must have fallen from the roof, even though the old caretaker's body was found ninety feet from the building. The police did not open an investigation of this incident and the new Rumtek monks refused to perform the customary funeral ceremony for the old man, an attendant to the sixteenth Karmapa for twenty-five years. Ten days later, six young toughs working for Gyaltsab led by a bully named Batruk surrounded Benza Guru's grand nephew, Sherab Namgyal, at the main gate of the monastery. The gang beat him severely. Shortly afterwards, bullies beat up another elderly man, Apa Tsewang, a former attendant of Rumtek's first General Secretary Damchoe Yongdu.

Barriers to the Courthouse

Shamar's first idea was to file a civil case to regain possession of Rumtek. "Chief Minister Bhandari had interfered in monastic affairs in violation of India's constitution," Shamar told me. "We could have tried to make a case in Delhi against him. But we thought it would be less complicated just to file a property rights case on behalf of the Karmapa Charitable Trust." The judiciary in Sikkim was answerable to New Delhi and not to Bhandari, so it retained its independence. "But if anyone tried to file a case against him or one of his allies in local courts, Bhandari tried to intimidate them." Under Bhandari's protection, Situ and Gyaltsab enjoyed a de facto protection from prosecution.

As an example, according to Khenpo Ngawang Gelek, one of the teachers at Rumtek before the takeover in August 1993, Karma Gunbo, a former member of the Sikkim parliament and a devotee of the sixteenth Karmapa, filed a case in Gangtok District Court in 1993 against Situ Rinpoche charging that he had forged his Karmapa prediction letter. Once Chief Minister Bhandari was informed of this, he arrested Karma Gunbo's family, including wife and children, and held them in prison for two weeks during which guards taunted, threatened, and administered numerous beatings to Karma Gunbo and his wife.

Meanwhile, perhaps to ensure that they would not make trouble for Situ and Gyaltsab Rinpoches, Bhandari initiated an intimidation campaign against the board members of the Karmapa Charitable Trust. He had already expelled Topga Rinpoche, so he added a ban on Shamar entering Sikkim. And against the two trustees who were residents of Sikkim, T.S. Gyaltshen and J.D. Densapa, both formerly high officials in the state government, Bhandari sent his party bullies to stone their houses and cars.

Bhandari's threats against the trustees were successful. J.D. Densapa in particular became so afraid to file a case to regain Rumtek in Gangtok that he attempted instead to file in the High Court in New Delhi in early 1994. The High Court responded that since this was a civil case, it should be submitted in the local state court, in Sikkim. Later, Situ's supporters would say that the Delhi court dismissed this case because it lacked merit. In fact, the court simply ruled that it was not the venue for a case that should be heard in Sikkim. But filing in Sikkim was out of the question while Chief Minister Bhandari remained in office.

The Fall of Bhandari

For the hundred monks who were evicted from Rumtek, things never looked bleaker than during the ten months in 1993 and 1994 that Situ and Gyaltsab ruled the monastery under the protection of Chief Minister Bhandari. Under his strong-arm rule, open opposition to Situ and Gyaltsab was impossible. Through kickbacks to his allies and intimidation of his rivals and critics, Bhandari appeared to have a grip on power strong enough to last for years.

But behind the scenes, Bhandari was in trouble. Even before the Rumtek takeover, the chief minister's position started to weaken. Word got out in Sikkim that the Government of India had expanded its ongoing investigation of Bhandari for corruption. Heartened by increased scrutiny of Sikkim's boss from New Delhi, Bhandari's opponents started to actively work against him. In June 1992 Pawan Kumar Chamling, one of Bhandari's ministers, began to plan a campaign to replace the chief minister. He publicly accused Bhandari of corruption and began to refer to him as a "dictator." In response, Bhandari arrested Chamling's assistants and tortured them in prison. Chamling himself escaped and went into hiding until the situation cooled down.

Like Bhandari, Chamling was part of Sikkim's new Nepali majority. Born in 1950 in a village in southern Sikkim, Chamling came from a family of small farmers. He entered politics at age twenty-three, and later joined the Sikkim Sangram Parishad, allying himself with its rising star N.B. Bhandari. In the eighties, Chamling's popularity threatened to surpass the chief minister's own, and Bhandari started to fear that Chamling might challenge his position as party leader. So he found an excuse to fire Chamling from the cabinet and then expel him from the party. Undeterred from his political ambitions, Chamling has said that Bhandari's dismissal letter was the "redeeming touch" for his future.

It was clear that Chamling would run against Bhandari at the next opportunity. In June 1992, while Chamling was beginning to openly criticize Bhandari, Shamar's secretary, Khedrub Gyatso, met with the candidate to offer his support. Khedrub offered a loan to assist with Chamling's election campaign, and asked for Chamling's future assistance in regaining Rumtek for the Karmapa Charitable Trust, a typically open Himalayan quid pro quo.

Chamling, however, had a different approach to political ethics than Bhandari. Presenting himself as a reformer, Chamling said that he wanted to come to office free of promises to campaign supporters. He also said he wanted to return the rule of law to Sikkim, and pledged to respect the Indian constitution's separation of church and state. Therefore, the candidate agreed to accept the campaign loan, but only on condition that he would owe nothing more than to repay the sum loaned with reasonable interest. "Mr. Chamling would not make a deal to get the money," explained Shamar.

Still holding his seat in the legislature despite his falling out with Bhandari, in September 1992 Chamling pulled a publicity stunt that turned out to be a dangerous act of defiance against Bhandari. During an open session of the state legislature, he entered the State Assembly hall in Gangtok carrying a lighted candle, and announced that he was "searching for Democracy." He then stopped in front of the podium, where Bhandari was speaking, and posed a sardonic question, "Is not Democracy inside the chief minister's pocket?" After this, the threats on Chamling's life increased.

In March 1993 Chamling formed a new party, the Sikkim Democratic Front, to contest Bhandari's rule. This move brought down the wrath of Bhandari's political machine and Chamling became a target of intimidation by party bullies and harassment by the state police. In June 1993, after numerous threats to his life, Chamling went into hiding again. For three months, he waged a war of words with Bhandari from underground in Sikkim, an act of boldness that earned him the admiration of much of the electorate.

When Chamling emerged from hiding in September, he rode a wave of popularity that Bhandari could not resist. Still confident, Bhandari predicted that he would win the November 1994 general elections. After the polls closed, perhaps ironically, he told a press conference "that he would rule like Adolf Hitler if he was returned to power," and keep better control over his potential opposition.[3] Nonetheless, Sikkim voters brought in Chamling by an overwhelming margin. The fifteen-year rule of Bhandari in Sikkim was over and an anxious calm settled over the tiny Indian state.

Situ Rinpoche under Investigation

Meanwhile, the central government's investigation of Tai Situ had also advanced. Officials in New Delhi were convinced that Situ's dealings with the Chinese government and his attempt to hand over Rumtek to Beijing's choice for Karmapa all represented a threat to Indian control over the state of Sikkim. China would not recognize the state as part of India until 2005, and in the mid-1990s officials in New Delhi remained nervous that the Chinese were using Tibetan lamas in the state to increase their influence in Sikkim.

The Indians did not want a Chinese-supported tulku to gain control over Rumtek and its movable valuables since they were afraid that this would open the door to Chinese claims on Sikkim itself. "Given the fact that Sikkim occupies a strategic position," Sikkim Chief Secretary K. Sreedhar Rao advised the government in New Delhi, "it would be most undesirable to have a situation where a Tibetan reincarnation, who is basically a Chinese National recognized by the Chinese, formally occupies a position in a monastery in Sikkim."[4]

Situ made further trips to China that may have been unauthorized— he held a Tibetan Refugee Certificate which required him to seek permission from the Indian government for all foreign travel. Then, the government also suspected the rinpoche of smuggling people and goods from Tibet into India. In August 1994, while he was away on an international teaching tour, the Indian Ministry of Home Affairs banned Situ from returning to the country.

Supporters of Tai Situ dispute the validity of this ban. In *Karmapa: The Politics of Reincarnation* Lea Terhune has written that Shamar may have bribed officials in New Delhi to ban Situ from returning to the country. She paraphrased "members of Sikkim's Joint Action Committee," who "feel that the ban order against Tai Situpa came from greasing the palms of susceptible bureaucrats and agents in the intelligence bureau," though she has admitted that "hard evidence of this kind of activity is difficult to come by, of course, especially if the recipients of the largesse are in Indian intelligence, where Shamarpa is said to have his strongest allies."[5]

The Indian government had other charges against Tai Situ. New Delhi was investigating Situ's followers for organizing smuggling rings throughout India, Nepal, and China. Indian intelligence was particularly interested in a group of Khampa businessmen in Lhasa associated with Situ and headed by Bhu Chung Chung, a member of the Chinese Bureau of Public Security. New Delhi police found that Chung and his associate Ogyen smuggled $2.5 million worth of shahtoosh wool into India for sale in the city. The endangered Tibetan antelope must be killed to yield the wool. Therefore an international treaty banned all trade in shahtoosh in the 1970s. Possession of shahtoosh is a crime in India, China, and other countries, and those who try to move it across international frontiers to meet the demand of unscrupulous dealers face stiff penalties. Police arrested Ogyen, but Bhu Chung Chung escaped.[6]

With Situ gone and Bhandari forced to resign both in the space of a couple months, Gyaltsab became increasingly isolated at Rumtek. No longer enjoying the active protection of the Sikkim state government, he had to rely on the support of the Joint Action Committee and its powerful local families.

A Gandhian Response

After Bhandari left office, the ousted monks took a chance to try to reenter Rumtek. Allied with the nuns from Ani Chotso's convent as well as a group of local lay supporters, the monks planned to try to enter Rumtek peacefully to perform the annual Yarney retreat in August 1995. "I advised them not to do this," Shamar told me. "Such a confrontation would not help. But the leaders of the monks were impatient."

The monks said that they wanted to be able to perform the ceremonies for this important monastic observance in the temple built by the sixteenth Karmapa, but the timing was also symbolic. It represented the second anniversary of Situ and Gyaltsab's takeover of Rumtek at the opening of the Yarney retreat in 1993. Now, after twenty-four months of performing ceremonies in a makeshift shrine room housed in a concrete and corrugated iron shed on the property of Shamar Rinpoche's residence outside Rumtek village, the monks wanted to get back into the temple they considered to be theirs.

Gyaltsab has said that the monks attacked Rumtek that day. In his version of events, Topga Rinpoche, who could now reenter Sikkim after Bhandari's ouster, led a convoy of eight trucks carrying two hundred men to take the monastery by force. Before their attack, the intruders cut off the monastery's phone lines so that the Rumtek administration could not call for help. When Topga's men passed the monastery's outer gate and got about five hundred yards into the compound, Rumtek residents started to realize that there was a hostile invasion. In response, they lined both sides of the road and placed themselves in front of the attackers, presenting hands folded in *namaste*, the Asian gesture of peaceful greeting, and chanting prayers. Only the timely arrival of the police prevented a fight.

The original monks and their supporters in the lay community of Rumtek have contradicted Gyaltsab's account, claiming that the monks who came to Rumtek were peaceful. Tsewang Chorden led the families who supported the exiled monks. "When we heard that the monks were planning to go up to the monastery on August 1, 1995, we lit a fire as a sign of welcome," Tsewang said. "But then the police prevented the monks from entering the monastery."

Even though Bhandari was no longer in office, Sikkim state government officials still supported Gyaltsab for their own reasons. Many of them were allied with Situ's Joint Action Committee, and were probably still receiving payments from Situ and Gyaltsab. The new chief minister, Chamling, could not publicly take sides against them, because he needed Joint Action Committee support to remain in office. In addition, since his government could be held liable for the actions of his predecessor, in his role as chief minister Chamling had to defend Bhandari-era officials who remained in government service.

Despite taunts from the crowd, witnesses say that the procession of ousted monks remained peaceful. Denied entry to the monastery, the monks decided to execute the second part of their plan: to conduct a hunger strike in protest at their exclusion from Rumtek. They began the strike after midnight on August 8 in seventy-two-hour relays, with teams fasting for three days each while living in tents they had pitched by the road outside the monastery's main gate.

The monsoon had begun, the tents leaked, and some of the weakened monks came down with fevers. "It was a very sad situation," local supporter Tsewang said. "All of us, the lay people and the nuns, spontaneously joined the hunger strike. I myself, for example, even though I am sixty-eight years old, took part in the hunger strike for twenty-four hours without drinking a single drop of water. During daytime it was the women who participated in the hunger strike, at night the men."

The hunger strike went on for more than a month, during which Gyaltsab's supporters threatened and sometimes attacked the hunger-striking monks. Gangtok market bullies beat four monks badly enough to send them into the hospital. They also targeted the monks' lay supporters, and reportedly tried to burn down the house of a seventy-year-old woman at night while she was asleep. Because of his role supporting the strikers, Tsewang became a target of aggression.

One evening at about eight o'clock in the evening, three of the new monks at Rumtek attacked him. "I recognized one of them, Patru. Then I fainted," Tsewang said. "When I regained consciousness, I found myself lying in the ditch next to the road, my whole body bleeding. First I thought it was water, but then I realized it was all blood. Luckily my arms and legs weren't broken, so I managed to get home. Then I went to the people who were on hunger strike, and they saw to it that I was taken to hospital, where I had to stay for a fortnight."

To respond to the hunger strike, Gyaltsab called in help from the Joint Action Committee, which sent Bhandari-era local politicians to lead demonstrations of hundreds of local supporters against the hunger strikers. Reportedly, Gyaltsab spent several hundred thousand rupees (tens of thousands of dollars) bussing in and feeding people who came to join the demonstrations.

Topga Rinpoche witnessed the hunger strike, and he commented on the monks' probable motivation. "The monks who participated in the hunger strike did not want to suffer," Topga said. "They hoped to be able to return to their monastery. A hunger-strike entails physical and mental hardship. There was no other option, the monks had no choice. In the course of the hunger strike, the monks became physically weak and dejected. They would burst into tears from time to time. Their mouths dried up, they abstained from eating, and they were tormented by pangs of hunger.

"The monastic body is made up of individuals of different ages," Topga explained. "Some are only eight years old. If the situation persisted, their lives would be in ruins because they were denied the traditional training in the monastic way of life. Rather than being able to develop towards attaining enlightenment, being able to develop compassion and other good qualities, negative states of resentment and anger would come to the fore. Kunzig Shamar Rinpoche has provided for their needs at this difficult and distressing time. But it would be next to impossible to alleviate the distress and torment which each of the monks is going through."

The hunger strike apparently embarrassed the Dalai Lama's exile government, which continued to support Ogyen Trinley, and thus, Gyaltsab Rinpoche. "Officers from the Dalai Lama's government in exile came to visit us, and they were really very diplomatic," according to a statement by the monks made after the conclusion of the strike in 1994. "They advised us not to do what we were doing, not to fight. When we explained that we weren't fighting, that we had been kicked out of our monastery, they just remained silent."[7] The Dalai Lama's representatives did not help the exiled monks to get back into Rumtek.

Topga explained that Gyaltsab's attitude in particular was painful for the monks, who were used to thinking of him as one of their spiritual leaders. So Topga decided to write Gyaltsab a letter. "As if their hardships were not enough, Gyaltsab Rinpoche announced that the people who took part in the hunger strike had broken their allegiance to their lama and to the dharma. This comment caused me great anguish. My intention was not to offend Gyaltsab Rinpoche. I wrote the letter because of the distress I felt. The monks wished to study the Buddhist scriptures, but they had no opportunity to do so. They wished to practice meditation, but they had no opportunity to meditate. Greater harm could not have been done."

In his letter, Topga accused Gyaltsab of breaking samaya—the fearsome bond between a teacher and students who have received tantric vows from that teacher—with the late sixteenth Karmapa by persecuting his monks. Topga admitted that Gyaltsab had also accused the monks and Topga himself of breaking samaya.

You are aware that there is no court of law in existence
to adjudicate such contentious and complex issues...
Therefore, there is no alternative at all but to keep the
Dharma Protectors as the judges to decide on whom the
actual "Damnyam" (samaya breakers) are. In order to do
so, I for one am ready and ever willing to sit in fast, in
front of the Mahakala statue in the monastery or in front
of the late Karmapa's "Kudung Stupa" or whichever place
you choose for this purpose. In fact, all of us are willing
to sit in fast in any of the aforesaid places, without food or
water and without any medical aid or assistance, until we
breathe our last. I have made a firm decision to undertake
the aforesaid solemn fast and am confident that you will
be also ready and willing to sit in fast, in the same manner
in the same place.[8]

Topga sent the letter with a sub-inspector of the Sikkim police department. The next day, the police officer returned the envelope unopened with a note saying "Gyaltsab Rinpoche refused to accept the letter; and hence, it is returned to you."

The hunger strike ended on September 16, when state government officials finally promised to look into the monks' grievances. But in reality new Chief Minister Chamling had little to offer. He invited forty senior lamas to his residence for a conference, but there he merely told them that there was "no point in sleeping on the road" and continuing their protest. The government could not legally remove the monks of Situ and Gyaltsab Rinpoches from Rumtek. Instead, the monks' only remedy was to request a court order to return them to their monastery.

Frustrated at the ongoing occupation of Rumtek and exclusion of the sixteenth Karmapa's monks, in November 1995 nearly two thousand business leaders, students, and monks from around Sikkim held a rally outside Rumtek. "The leaders of the rally tried to initiate a peaceful dialogue with Gyaltsab Rinpoche," former Rumtek monk-official Chultrimpa Lungtog Dawa said. But Gyaltsab would not talk. "Instead, Gyaltsab Rinpoche told his supporters to chase the participants in the rally out of the monastery gate." Some of the rougher young men at Rumtek threw bricks and stones at police officers on hand, "which led to utter chaos and a very tense situation at the gate. Eventually, the police force resorted to *lathi*-charges [attacks with Billy clubs] and the use of tear gas, injuring several innocent citizens who had joined the peace rally to demonstrate their support of our just cause."

Gyaltsab was not inclined to surrender Rumtek. As Sikkim Chief Secretary K. Sreedhar Rao put it in his report to New Delhi:

> The presence of Gyaltsab Rinpoche and the fact that the group owing allegiance to Tai Situ Rinpoche is in physical possession of the monastery has enabled them to claim that the monastery already belongs to the seventeenth Gyalwa Karmapa reincarnate from Tibet and he should be brought from Tibet and be enthroned in Rumtek. The Joint Action Committee keeps issuing pamphlets, monograms, cassettes all calculated to establish that the Tibetan reincarnation is the only correct reincarnation. This propaganda has no doubt had an impact on the local population. It needs also to be highlighted that the local bureaucracy and the police have also been heavily influenced by this strong propaganda. Attempts by the

Shamar Rinpoche's followers to enter the monastery even
for the purpose of worship have been beaten back by use of
force by the group in occupation of the monastery.[9]

Despite the apparent indifference that Situ and Gyaltsab showed
to the plight of the monks expelled from Rumtek in August 1993, or the
hostility of the young men left at the monastery after the takeover, almost
incredibly the original Rumtek monks claimed that they still did not
want to take sides in the dispute over the Karmapa. "We had consistently
been branded as 'Shamar Rinpoche's monks,' and false information
had been circulated all over Sikkim and beyond with the intention of
sullying our reputation," said Chultrimpa Lungtog. "We therefore left
the residence of Shamar Rinpoche and camped outdoors in temporary
tents and dilapidated shacks which are barely adequate to protect us from
the torrential monsoon and the harsh conditions of the winter season."

"We have suffered a great deal—to such an extent that I cannot find
suitable words to describe our anguish and pain," Chultrimpa Lungtog
said. "We have, however, not deviated from the path of dharma and
truth. We are committed to proceeding in accordance with our tradition
and the dharma, and we hope that truth will eventually triumph."

13 Lamas on Trial

Clear to the Courthouse

With Chamling in power as chief minister in Gangtok, the Karmapa Trust no longer had to worry that Bhandari's party bullies or state police would harass them if they filed a legal case in Sikkim. "I started to talk with Karmapa Trust board members. I recommended that we start a court case against Gyaltsab and the Sikkim government to get back Rumtek," Shamar told me. All of the trustees except one agreed with Shamar's recommendation. J.D. Densapa, who had been personally targeted by Bhandari for harassment, was afraid that Bhandari's party would return to power and exact revenge. Densapa refused to support filing a case. "We would only file a case if we could all agree. We said we would wait until Mr. Densapa was not afraid to start a case."

In early 1996, word came that Densapa was ready to go forward with a case, finally convinced that Bhandari would not return to power in Gangtok. Shamar convened a meeting of the trustees at the Sinclair Hotel in Siliguri, four hours south of the Sikkimese capital. "The others were elderly or else they had to take care of sick relatives. And, as laymen, they were uncomfortable directly confronting Situ and Gyaltsab, two high rinpoches. So I offered to be the one to file the case, on behalf of the whole Karmapa Charitable Trust," Shamar said. "They all agreed, and we passed a motion to start with the lawyers." Shamar began working with attorneys in Gangtok and Calcutta to prepare the documents required.

It might seem shocking that Tibetan lamas would sue each other. Many outsiders believe that these lamas are beyond worldly disputes. But this is just another of the romantic, Shangri-La stereotypes that

Westerners in particular too often harbor about Tibetans and their
Buddhist teachers. Back in Tibet, many lamas were large property owners.
Consequently, they could not avoid going to court occasionally. As we
have seen, the eleventh Gyaltsab Drakpa Gyatso (1902-52), for example,
had a long-running dispute in the courts of the Tibetan capital Lhasa
against the Karmapa's labrang over a parcel of land. The case continued
even after the eleventh Gyaltsab's death and was only halted when the
Chinese People's Liberation Army occupied the city.

"In my opinion, if someone sues another person only for revenge
or to realize some financial gain, then this is wrong action according to
Buddhist ethics or any ethics that I am familiar with," Shamar said in a
statement on his court efforts.[1] "By contrast, if it will prevent some harm,
then it is proper to defend oneself. And in a civilized society, the way to
defend oneself is through legal channels rather than to pursue violence."

Situ's supporters have accused Shamar of being litigious—and of
being unsuccessful in court. In her book, Lea Terhune wrote that Shamar
continued to file legal actions in Sikkim and other places, and that some
of them even accused the Dalai Lama of collaborating with the Chinese
government. "Most of the cases, which amount to harassment, were
dismissed." Terhune claimed that other cases continue or have been filed
again in other venues, such as Bihar state, where corruption runs rampant
and judges will hear cases that have been thrown out elsewhere.[2]

Terhune appears to be confused here. Since the 1980s, numerous
cases have been filed or threatened by both sides in the controversy.
Some cases were even filed by people unconnected to the events, but
who sympathized with one of the parties. This was the situation with the
case Terhune mentions concerning the Dalai Lama. It was filed by an
Indian, Sri Narayan Singh, who had been a monk at Rumtek in the early
seventies, and, after returning his vows, then moved back to his family's
home in the state of Bihar. Singh filed his case on his own and without
consulting Shamar or the Karmapa Charitable Trust. Shamar Rinpoche
has said that he has no connection to Singh, and the Dalai Lama's office
has acknowledged this.

Perhaps Terhune is most confused when she seems to get lost in
the number of minor court actions but ignores the one case that really
matters: the case for Rumtek. And on that litigation, the Karmapa Trust
has prevailed at three levels of the Indian court system, while Ogyen
Trinley's supporters have lost each time.

On July 31, 1998 another of Shamar's Gangtok devotees, Dugo Bhotia—with the help of attorney Hamelal Bhandari mentioned earlier as a target of Chief Minister Bhandari's wrath—filed Civil Suit No. 40 of 1998 in the Court of the District Judge, East and North Sikkim in Gangtok. In the case of Karmapa Charitable Trust vs. the State of Sikkim and Gyaltsab Rinpoche, the plaintiffs asked the court to restore the status-quo ante of Rumtek in the Trust's favor as it existed on August 2, 1993. The Karmapa Trust also asked the court to order an inventory of the valuables held at Rumtek to determine if any of the sixteenth Karmapa's properties had been stolen since the 1993 takeover. The suit listed three primary defendants: two Sikkim government officials—the Sikkim chief secretary, and the secretary of ecclesiastical affairs—and Gyaltsab Rinpoche. Since Situ was still banned from re-entering India and Gyaltsab was residing at Rumtek in Situ's place, the suit named only Gyaltsab of the two rinpoches as a defendant.

Gyaltsab and the two state government defendants raised preliminary issues that delayed the case for three years. Then, in October of 2001, the court ruled that the case should proceed. In his decision, District Judge S.W. Lepcha based his ruling on an admission by Gyaltsab and the Sikkim government themselves: "It is seen that the defendants 1, 2, and 3 do not dispute that possession of the suit properties were with the plaintiffs till 2.8.1993."[3] That is, Gyaltsab and the state government admitted that the Karmapa Charitable Trust ran Rumtek until August 2, 1993. Thus, the judge was ready to hear the case for Rumtek.

Meanwhile, the Indian government lifted the ban on Situ reentering the country thanks to Situ's attorney Ram Jethmalani, then a minister in the new right-wing Bharatiya Janata government. "The Home Ministry revoked the order in early August 1998 and the Rinpoche returned to the country soon after," according to a September 1998 report in the Asian Age, an Indian newspaper. "This was done despite advice from intelligence agencies like the Research and Analysis Wing [of Indian intelligence] that it would not be in India's interest to allow the monk to return."[4]

In the fall of 1998, Shamar's follower Dugo Bhotia challenged the lifting of Situ's ban. He was not able to get the all-India ban re-imposed, but he was able to get a permanent order banning Situ from nine northern states of India, including Sikkim, again for "anti-India activities." Indian intelligence was still worried about Situ, and the central government soon

sent out a Lookout Circular warning immigration authorities throughout
the country about Situ Rinpoche:

> He is strongly suspected to be an agent for Chinese
> intelligence. Besides clandestine activities in conjunction
> with Chinese authorities including facilitating furtive
> movements of unauthorized persons from China to India,
> smuggling of antiques and remains of killed animals
> including tiger skins [and] rhino horns from India he has
> also come to notice for fomenting disturbances in the
> sensitive regions including Sikkim, Darjeeling Hills, and
> Himachal Pradesh.[5]

This regional ban prevented Situ from returning to Rumtek. But
it did not stop him from visiting the rest of India, including New Delhi
and his own monastic seat, Sherab Ling. From there he continued to
advocate for Ogyen Trinley and advise Gyaltsab by phone on Rumtek
matters and especially the case filed by the Karmapa Trust.

Ogyen Trinley's Publicity Coup

We have spent much time with Shamar, Situ and Gyaltsab, and the
Rumtek monks. Now, it is time to return to the young man at the center
of the Karmapa dispute. While the case for Rumtek was progressing, in
January 2000, Ogyen Trinley suddenly appeared in India, having fled
Tibet. His surprise arrival elevated him to instant celebrity status, and
hundreds of articles were published in the international press saying that
his departure from Tibet, allegedly against the wishes of the Chinese
government, struck a heroic blow for Tibetan freedom comparable to the
Dalai Lama's own escape into exile four decades earlier in 1959.

The four books on the Karmapa published in 2003 and 2004—by
authors Michelle Martin, Lea Terhune, Mick Brown, and Gaby Naher,
respectively—all retell the story of the lama's flight from his point of view,
so there is no need to repeat it in detail here. But to summarize, after his
enthronement in June 1992 at the former monastery of the Karmapas,
Tsurphu, in Chinese Tibet, Ogyen Trinley reportedly began the
traditional training of a Karmapa, under the direction of Situ Rinpoche.
The Chinese government allowed him to pursue a religious education,
but they also used him for propaganda. Officials in Lhasa and Beijing

regularly corralled the young reincarnate into photo ops and publicity events to show his loyalty to China.

Later, in a news conference he gave in April 2001, a year after he arrived in India, Ogyen Trinley would claim that the Chinese began to restrict his access to Tai Situ and his other teachers during the late nineties. For the young tulku, it became increasingly difficult to be a Karmapa in China. Finally, he realized that if he stayed he could not perform his religious duties. So he made a secret plan to escape from Tsurphu for exile in India. In late December 1999, under cover of night and dressed as a layman, the fourteen-year-old lama left Tsurphu with half a dozen attendants. A week later, passing Chinese checkpoints undetected and crossing mountain passes successfully, Ogyen Trinley arrived safely in Dharamsala in India, the headquarters of the Tibetan Government-in-Exile. There, he was welcomed warmly by the Dalai Lama.

On his arrival in India in the early days of January 2000, Ogyen Trinley did not talk directly to the press. He would not do so until his press conference in April 2001. But in the meantime, officials of the Tibetan Government-in-Exile told reporters that the young tulku had walked most of the way from Tsurphu near Lhasa in Tibet, over the Himalayas, and into freedom in Nepal and India.

Western journalists widely reported this story at face value. "He completed the last week on foot, crossing mountain passes in heavy snow, before arriving at Dharamsala at 10:30 am on Wednesday," reported the London Telegraph in a typical report.[6] Arthur Max wrote in the San Francisco Examiner that "The arrival of the 17th Karmapa, leader of the Karma Kagyu sect, has given exiled Tibetans a new and tangible leader they can embrace alongside the 64-year-old Dalai Lama, spiritual leader of all Tibetans. They wonder whether the tall 14-year-old with the engaging smile and mature demeanor will go beyond his spiritual role and join the Dalai Lama in the struggle against China's harsh rule of their homeland."[7]

The Indian media was less willing to accept the young lama's story that he had covered nine hundred miles on foot in eight days, all in the middle of the harsh Tibetan winter. This would have meant walking an average of 112 miles per day in temperatures well below freezing and crossing Himalayan passes higher than 15,000 feet covered in snow and ice 8 feet deep or more. In particular, once he reached Nepal, the tulku would have had to cross the Thorang-La pass. At an elevation of 17,599 feet, the pass is higher than the tallest peak in the Continental United States or in the whole range of the Alps. Few trained porters attempt to cross the treacherous pass in winter for risk of losing a limb or suffering death from frostbite.

After Indian journalists began raising doubts, Ogyen Trinley's spokespeople changed their story, admitting that the young tulku traveled most of the way from Tsurphu by jeep. But the Indian press remained skeptical that Ogyen Trinley escaped from Tibet without the Chinese government knowing or even helping. "Did China's 14-year-old Karmapa Lama flee repression in Tibet, or did Beijing stage a defection as part of larger designs?" asked the Hindustan Times. "Preliminary official investigations do not show that the boy-lama and his entourage slipped through the heavy Chinese security cover. On the contrary, the investigations suggest that they had a fairly smooth passage out of their Chinese-occupied homeland, indicating that Beijing may at least have acquiesced in the departure." According to the paper, Indian Home Minister Lal Krishna Advani said that the boy had arrived in India in "mysterious" circumstances and he doubted that the young lama could have evaded the elaborate security arrangements made by the Chinese authorities to prevent his escape.[8]

Indications of a Fake Escape

Strong evidence that Ogyen Trinley's escape was staged with the help of the Chinese government came in 2001, with the release of a film called Flight of A Karmapa. The film was made by a team of four journalists from Japan, Hong Kong, Taiwan, and Nepal to investigate whether Ogyen Trinley's escape was staged with the assent of the Chinese government. "We discovered a far different story than the one reported by the media," said director Yoichi Shimatsu in the film's narration. "We learned that Ogyen Trinley Dorje's journey was not an escape to freedom. His real intention was to gain possession of the mystical Black Crown in Sikkim and bring it back to Tibet as the undisputed Karmapa. When his plan failed, he went to the Dalai Lama, because he had nowhere else to turn."

Shimatsu, a writer for the Japan Times based in Hong Kong at the time he made the film, told me he began his investigation because "the Karmapa news was a huge story in China and Hong Kong, obviously, since the Chinese government had invited journalists to meet 'their' Living

Buddha, the term the press even in Hong Kong used to describe him." An avid hiker, Shimatsu was also stunned by Ogyen Trinley's original story.

"In college in the United States, I had studied science for three years and always in my journalism I look at the scientific basis for news reports, by habit. I noticed that Ogyen claimed to walk from Tsurphu to Dharamsala in eight days. Not knowing where Tsurphu was, I looked on a map and noticed the vast distance of nearly a thousand miles. Since I do a lot of trekking as a hobby, I realized the impossibility of this claim, which was repeated uncritically by BBC, CNN, etc." So he assembled his reporting team and "went with a digital video camera, which was pretty new then, still using hi-8 tape, to Jomson and Manang [in Nepal], the first of a half dozen journeys. And the adventure began."

To investigate Ogyen Trinley's story on his escape route, Shimatsu recruited Susanna Cheung, a Hong-Kong based radio reporter for BBC radio and writer for the *Hong Kong Economic Times*; Prakash Khanal, a Nepali environmental writer who was a former editor with the prestigious Royal Nepal Academy of Science and Technology and contributor to the *Economist* and other European magazines; and Makalu Gau, a Taiwan-based photographer and mountaineer who survived the expedition that attempted to summit Mt. Everest in 1996. Gau escaped the disaster with his life but lost his fingers and toes.

In Nepal, the crew shot interviews with Ogyen Trinley's main guide as well as people who met the lama during his travel through Tibet, Nepal, and India. Situ, the Dalai Lama, and Ogyen Trinley himself have all claimed that the young man left Tibet to escape religious persecution by the government and to study Buddhism and receive tantric empowerments: "These I could only receive from the main disciples of the previous Karmapa, Situ Rinpoche and Gyaltsab Rinpoche, who were predicted to be my teachers and who reside in India," Ogyen Trinley told his press conference in April 2001. Yet, the guide, a lama from Tsurphu called Gyaltshen who was known as the "Tall Managi," explained that Ogyen Trinley's true motivation for leaving Tibet was not religious persecution or lack of opportunities to study with his teachers. When asked if the young tulku was unhappy in China, the Tall Managi said, "No, he was OK in China."

So what was his motivation? After completing their research, the reporters concluded that the young lama intended to enter Sikkim, collect the Vajra Mukut—the Black Crown of the Karmapas—and return to Tsurphu. He would have to cross into India secretly, because he knew that the Indian government would not welcome a Chinese-supported tulku in the disputed state of Sikkim:

> The plan was to fly Ogyen Trinley from Kathmandu to
> Durang and then smuggle him in a jeep into Sikkim.
> Then, flush with new wealth and with the mystic Black
> Crown he would return to China as a national hero. But
> that didn't happen. Before Tai Situ and the nun Ngodrup
> [Ogyen Trinley's sister] could enter Sikkim, lamas from
> Tibet got into an argument with Tai Situ's monks over
> who was in charge of the crowning. A fight broke out and
> one monk was fatally stabbed. When the Indian police
> had arrived, Tai Situpa had fled back to his Sherab Ling
> monastery and Ngodrup went into hiding. The Indian
> security forces now knew that Ogyen Trinley was on his
> way from Tibet. The Black Crown was now out of his
> reach. His journey to Rumtek was over. Instead, he was
> bound for the headquarters of his old foes, the Gelugpa
> order of the Dalai Lama.[9]

Though he wrote a letter on his departure from Tsurphu saying that he was just leaving for a short visit to India to collect the Vajra Mukut, after arriving in India, Ogyen Trinley claimed that the letter was intended only to deceive his Chinese handlers. He has consistently denied that he intended to return to China with the Black Crown, saying that would only mean putting it "on Jiang Zemin's head."

"Tai Situpa's camp was trying to follow our every move, and revised their story as we discovered one fact after the next in the interviews," Shimatsu told me. "Dalai Lama camp, ditto. Representatives of Chinese President Jiang Zemin were eager to get the video and were overjoyed at the fact that they could get the real story. They admitted the episode was mysterious, that the Tibet Autonomous Region was blocking the President's inquiries about the affair. But they also said that the video was much too explosive for broadcast in China." Many journalists requested copies and television stations in Hong Kong, Taiwan, and elsewhere in Asia aired excerpts from the film.

Shimatsu's team discovered that a helicopter that picked up Ogyen Trinley in Nepal was owned by a company that had previously done work for the United States CIA, Fishtail Air. Even more suspicious, the Fishtail Air office had lost all flight records for the day of Ogyen Trinley's pickup. "When Susanna Chung and Prakash Khanal broke the story of the Mustang escape route and the Fishtail Air helicopter pickup at Thorang-La, I rushed the story and video to the *South China Morning Post* in Hong Kong Internet news department," Shimatsu told me. "Their news producers were very excited and promised me five thousand dollars."

"Then we had to clear the story through editors of the print version of the newspaper. We were greeted by three editors. They were female, and I suspect two of them were MI-6 (British intelligence) agents. They killed the story with totally bogus questions, all of which were proven on tape and in notes. They wanted to know who our key contact was in Mustang (a businessman) but I refused to disclose his identity, since he could easily be killed by the Manang smugglers involved with the Karmapa escape." So the *South China Morning Post* killed Shimatsu's story.

Outside of East Asia, Shimatsu's film got little attention, and he attributes some of that to government influence and some to media bias. He claims that the United States government had an interest in Ogyen Trinley, perhaps because of lobbying by Tibetan rights groups in Washington who support the Dalai Lama. Shimatsu singled out the American Himalayan Foundation in particular, funded by San Francisco real-estate billionaire Richard Blum, husband of Senator Dianne Feinstein from California.

"Plus, most Western journalists, including Chinese journalists in Hong Kong, are pretty brainwashed by the 'human rights' non-governmental organizations (NGOs), since they wrongly assume that these NGOs are honest little guys fighting for truth and justice," rather than groups with their own biases—often in favor of Western governments—that cause them to paint a one-sided picture of alleged rights abuses. Shimatsu felt that by making his film, he was striking a blow for press freedom. "This media monopoly made it all the more important to produce an independent documentary using portable DV mini-cameras, so *Flight of A Karmapa* was one of the first documentaries using this new media."

Two Ogyen Trinleys?

Shimatsu's team went on to make a further claim in a short video released at the same time as *Flight of A Karmapa* in 2001. In *Lost Child* the reporters claim that not merely was Ogyen Trinley's escape staged, but that the boy who arrived in India in 2000 was a different boy from the one who had been enthroned at Tsurphu monastery in 1992. To outsiders, this story may sound too ridiculous to have any merit. However, after hearing the evidence that Shimatsu's team has presented, the theory of two Ogyen Trinleys is much more compelling. In the film, Shimatsu narrates:

> While pursuing the story of the two Karmapas, our
> reporting team discovered to our great surprise that there
> could also be two Ogyen Trinleys. One of them was a
> fourteen-year-old boy at the time of the escape and the
> other is an impostor, a full grown adult of at least twenty-
> four years of age when he was welcomed by the Dalai
> Lama. The mysterious ten-year difference in age came
> to light during a medical check-up at one of India's most
> reputable hospitals [The Postgraduate Institute of Medical
> Education and Research at Chandigarh].

An Indian medical reporter, Ravi Sharma, told Shimatsu's colleague Prakash Khanal that x-ray and chemical tests showed that the young man was older than the fourteen years he claimed. According to reporter Sharma, the hospital's trustee Dr. Surendra Kumar Sharma (no relation) "said that he could not term [Ogyen Trinley] as a child, he's crossed the age that he can be termed a child. He could not confirm that he is twenty-one or twenty-seven but surely he has crossed the age of fourteen." But Dr. Sharma would only speak to the reporter off the record. The Indian Ministry of Home Affairs had given instructions that the story should not get out, since the Karmapa had become a contentious issue in India after Ogyen Trinley's arrival the previous year.

In his book on the Karmapa, Mick Brown wrote that he interviewed a hospital official at Chandigarh who denied the story. "I had checked with the Chief Administrator of the hospital in Chandigarh and had been told that the story was completely untrue."[10] In turn, Gaby Naher mentioned Brown's research in her book as proof that the theory about Ogyen Trinley's age must be false. To Naher, this demonstrated that attempts to discredit Ogyen Trinley as·Karmapa seemed to have "become more shrill and less credible."[11]

Shimatsu replied to me that he was not surprised that an administrator at the hospital (was it Dr. Sharma? Brown did not say) would refuse to speak on the record now, since Dr. Sharma had spoken only privately when the film was made in 2000 and 2001. "Also Prakash met another younger doctor who was directly involved in the medical examination of Ogyen, who said that the definitive (unmistakable) medical evidence was in the x-rays of Ogyen's bone structure. At the joints of the arm and legs, teenagers have soft-bone growth areas but 'Ogyen' was fully developed. The examining doctor estimated his age as between twenty-four and twenty-seven years old. By saying he was a 'grown man,' the doctor implied that Ogyen's genitals were fully developed as well."

Based on interviews with Ogyen Trinley's attendants who had come from Tsurphu, Shimatsu's team put together a theory about the switch:

> The identity switch took place in 1997 when this eleven-
> year old went into a retreat for several months. He went in
> as a small boy of only four feet in height. Yet in a space of
> just a few months a six-foot tall adult emerged claiming to
> be the same Ogyen Trinley. There were some similarities in
> appearance, yes, but his nose was wider and his chin more
> prominent and he had the facial hair of a grown-up. All
> of the personnel at Tsurphu monastery were transferred
> during this retreat and replaced by new people. Adding to
> the mystery, the two lamas of Tsurphu most familiar with
> Ogyen Trinley died untimely deaths in the same year.
>
> Why did the switch take place? Sources from inside
> Tsurphu monastery told us that the young Karmapa was
> suffering from frequent blackouts and had a learning
> disorder that prevented him from memorizing the sutras.
> In other words, he had to be kept away from public view.
>
> Where is the little boy now? Perhaps hiding with his
> sister Ngodrup? Or maybe receiving therapy in a foreign
> psychiatric institution? That is, if he's still alive. The
> whereabouts of the real Ogyen Trinley Dorje is the deepest

darkest mystery that will haunt Tsurphu monastery and
the Tibetan exile government for years to come.

Perhaps no amount of evidence can make such a story sound
credible to an outsider. In the West, we usually assume that secret plans
and covert operations are well-planned and convincingly executed, the
work of clever strategists. This story, by contrast, may sound less like
a plot by Ian Fleming or John Le Carré than an episode out of Peter
Sellers' *Pink Panther* spy-satires. Shimatsu told me that Ogyen Trinley's
escape story has not convinced many in the Tibetan exile community
or the Indian press, but that Westerners believe it because they are most
vulnerable to the Shangri-La stereotype of Tibetans. And, Westerners
generally do not question the Dalai Lama. "Foreigners are gullible and
will believe anything, since Tibet is a place where all rules of logic and
science are suspended, levitated," Shimatsu said.

Lest we dismiss Shimatsu's claim as exaggeration, we should review
some of the bizarre beliefs and airy stereotypes that Westerners have held
about Tibetans for the last four hundred years. Martin Brauen's book
Dreamworld Tibet catalogs many of these, complete with illustrations. Let
us take a quick sample: The first Jesuit missionaries, Father Antonio
de Andrade and Father Manuel Marques, traveled to Tibet in the
seventeenth century, as they believed, to reestablish contact with an
isolated pocket of Nestorian Christians who had been brought into the
fold by the mythical Prester John and place them under the umbrella of
Rome. In the nineteenth century, the Theosophists of Madame Blavatsky
claimed to have received secret teachings on Occult Science, delivered on
an astral level by a Brotherhood of Masters living in Tibet.

More to Shimatsu's point, a Frenchwoman named Alexandra
David-Neel went to Tibet in the 1910s and 1920s and claimed to have seen
flying monks there. In 1925 the surrealist poet Antonin Artaud, who like
many outsiders writing about Tibet never bothered to visit, nonetheless
addressed an impassioned plea to the thirteenth Dalai Lama:

We are your most faithful servants, O Grand Lama.
Grant us, grace us with your wisdom in a language our
contaminated European minds can understand. And, if
necessary, transform our minds, make our minds wholly
oriented towards those perfect summits where the Human

Mind no longer suffers...Teach us physical levitation of
the body, O Lama, and how we may no longer remain
earthbound![12]

James Hilton's 1936 *Lost Horizon* (which introduced the term
Shangri-La to English readers) and the bestselling books of Cyril Henry
Hoskins, a British plumber who wrote such titles as *The Third Eye* (1956)
and *Doctor from Lhasa* (1959) under the name of T. Lobsang Rampa,
brought twentieth-century readers the ideas that Tibet was a place where
one could live forever or where fantastic special powers, such as the power
of flight, could be gained by spiritual adepts.

Western Tibet-worship had its dark side too. Before World War
II, the Nazis set up an office called the Abnenerbe (Ancestral Heritage)
within the personal staff of Reichsfuhrer-SS Heinrich Himmler that was
fascinated with Tibet, sending several expeditions there in the thirties to
establish a racial connection between the two "Aryan races" of Tibetans
and Germans. Some of these expeditions were said to be searching for
esoteric knowledge to "place the Luciferic and Ahrimanic powers [of the
Tibetans] at the service of National Socialism and to support the planned
mutation that should signal the birth of the new race of supermen."[13]

Neo-Nazism followed Nazism into the eccentric when Chilean
Fascist Miguel Serrano pronounced that Hitler was a bodhisattva or
tulku who was able to duplicate himself during his own lifetime and take
incarnation in several people, including Benito Mussolini and the pro-
Japanese Indian revolutionary Subhash Chandra Bose.

This quick survey shows that it would be difficult to exaggerate just
how receptive Westerners have always been to bizarre notions about Tibet.
It would not be surprising if many outsiders who heard of Ogyen Trinley's
escape believed that he evaded the Chinese through miraculous means—
as a security officer of the Tibetan exile government actually suggests in
Flight of A Karmapa. "But he is different than a human being," according
to the officer, Tenzin Donyo. "So I think that while he was walking from
the Himalayas, though there are many Chinese soldiers in the Himalayas,
because of his religious practice and because he's different, higher than a
human being, I think they didn't notice him."

Shamar Rinpoche has on occasion called for a bone-marrow test
of the young tulku to determine his true age. Not surprisingly, Ogyen
Trinley's supporters have balked at this, as they have balked at Shamar's

calls to test Situ's Karmapa prediction letter. But the evidence collected by Shimatsu's team of reporters, combined with Ogyen Trinley's own changes in his escape story make the nomad boy—or young man—look suspicious. To date, neither he nor his followers have addressed the doubts raised about his revised escape story by the Asian press and the Indian government. Needless to say, they have not addressed the issue about his age either. Meanwhile, the Indian government has continued to restrict Ogyen Trinley's movement, despite pleas from many supporters and allies, especially the Dalai Lama, to let him move freely, and especially to let him go to Rumtek.

An Unpopular Inspection

Back in Sikkim, in response to a filing by Shamar and the Karmapa Trust, in October 2001 District Judge S.W. Lepcha ordered the office of the Reserve Bank of India in Calcutta to conduct an inventory of the assets on site at Rumtek. The court chose the bank for this task because of its experience assessing the value of disputed property. The inspection would determine if Situ and Gyaltsab had removed any valuable items and would be conducted in the presence of representatives of both parties to the lawsuit.

Ogyen Trinley's followers occupying Rumtek monastery at the time challenged the inventory in court. But first, they tried to convince Karmapa Trust board members to drop the inventory request. In January 2002, Tenzin Namgyal, acting as secretary for the Rumtek administration of Gyaltsab, paid a visit to board member T.S. Gyaltshen at his house in Gangtok. Since Gyaltshen died in 2003, his son Jigme Dorje Gyaltshen told me the story of Tenzin's visit to his father. "Tenzin Namgyal and Gyashab Nerpa along with two others from Rumtek came to meet my late father T.S. Gyaltshen at his residence about two months before the date of the inventory.

"The main purpose of their meeting with my father was to approach him personally and to request him to stop the inventory at Rumtek monastery. Their strong reason not to conduct the inventory was because Tenzin Namgyal said that His Holiness Gyalwa Karmapa had earlier kept a pistol in one of his cupboards. So if found during the inventory, this could cause much embarrassment to the followers and devotees of His Holiness.

"My father told them that the inventory of Rumtek came about from a court order. So, therefore, he had no authority to stop the order. Nor could anyone else do it. About the pistol, my late father told Tenzin Namgyal that there was no reason to worry, as the pistol formed part of the kit for religious ceremonies," Jigme Gyaltshen said. The previous King of Bhutan, Singye Dorje Wangchuk, had offered it as a gift to the sixteenth Karmapa before his death in 1981. The king was a hunter, but also a Buddhist, and giving the gun to the Karmapa was a way for the king to purify his own karma and also that of the animals he had killed. The gift came with a certificate attesting to its religious function.

"Similarly several members of the Joint Action Committee of Situ Rinpoche's supporters in Gangtok came to meet my late father after the visit of Tenzin Namgyal with a request to stop the inventory," Jigme Gyaltshen told me. "To them also my father expressed his inability to interfere with the order of the court as no one could stop the course of law."

Gyaltsab Rinpoche's reaction to the court order for the inventory at Rumtek indicated that it made him uneasy as well. Perhaps Gyaltsab knew some valuable objects were taken from Rumtek while he was in charge. One of Shamar's lawyers told me he thought that Gyaltsab may have feared prosecution on a criminal charge for theft. For whatever reason, on March 11, 2002 Gyaltsab challenged the order to begin the inventory in the High Court of Sikkim on the grounds that it would create a "law-and-order problem" in Sikkim and cause sacrilege to be committed. Of course, the so-called law-and-order problem may have been just a kind of threat from Gyaltsab himself—a threat of protests and possibly violence from his and Situ's supporters in the Joint Action Committee.

The High Court denied Gyaltsab's challenge and ordered a full hearing on the question for May. Meanwhile, on March 15, Gyaltsab organized a meeting of his supporters at the Guards' Grounds, a large meeting venue outside of Gangtok. Hearkening back to the days of Bhandari, Chief Minister Chamling and the Sikkim state advocate general put in an appearance. As many as three thousand people attended this meeting, reportedly after receiving promises of various boons from state politicians still tied to the Joint Action Committee.

The meeting passed two resolutions. The first called on the Indian central government to allow Ogyen Trinley to come to Rumtek by the end of May. The second called on Chamling's government to oppose the court-ordered inventory. In response, because two officials of the Sikkim state government were named as defendants in the suit seeking the inventory at Rumtek, Chamling agreed to ask the Sikkim state advocate general to challenge the court order as well.

On March 25, more of Gyaltsab's allies came to his support. An official of the Dalai Lama's administration in Dharamsala, Tashi Wangdi, told the *Times of India* that "Our rules are clear. The last Dalai Lama too left certain invaluable items before his departure. These items can only be touched by His Holiness. Similar is the case for the Karmapa." Kunzang Sherab, president of Situ's Joint Action Committee in Sikkim, said that "The court order has to keep in mind religious sentiments of Buddhists. A stranger touching any item here violates the millennium-old Karmapa Kagyu protocol."[14]

Shamar has always given the same response to these claims. "This is just not true." As the second-highest reincarnate lama in the Karma Kagyu, Shamar has a traditional authority that an official of the Tibetan exiled government or a lay person from Sikkim lack. "There is nothing in Karma Kagyu history that requires holy relics to be handled exclusively by the Karmapa. On a regular basis, relics are touched by monks and lay people. Before and after ceremonies, the Karmapa's attendants pack and unpack his ritual implements and they hand them to him during the event. In between use, officials of the Karmapa's labrang inspect, clean, and repair all religious items on a regular schedule. The Karmapa need not be present and he is usually not, as this is the routine activity of a monastery.

"I think Tibetan lamas are being spoiled by foreign disciples. When talking to Tibetans, no one would make this claim about not being able to touch 'holy objects.' One can say this sort of thing in English, because outsiders do not know any better. Situ Rinpoche's people have said that this prediction letter is holy and that it cannot be tested. But Tibetans would ask, for example, if a letter perhaps written by the late Karmapa is holy, then wouldn't his own body have been holier? If so, then why were doctors in Chicago allowed to perform a blood test on him when he was sick before he died in 1981? To us, it's just common sense that such claims are silly. Dharma has always been about investigating for oneself and not taking things on faith. If we have the karma to live in a world with modern science, we should take advantage of that to find the truth."

In April 2002 Gyaltsab again asked the High Court to postpone the inventory, as he said, to prevent violence, but the court denied his request. The judge ruled that the inventory should proceed as scheduled. Gyaltsab appealed this decision to the Indian Supreme Court in Delhi but was again disappointed when the court rejected his plea on April 22, 2002. On April 29 he then went back to the Sikkim High Court in Gangtok, for a third try, but was again refused.

Finally, on May 17, the High Court in New Delhi held a hearing to consider Gyaltsab's requests to postpone the inventory in depth. Shamar's attorneys felt that the court was about to dismiss the challenge, when Gyaltsab's lawyer raised still further issues, gaining an adjournment for a month.

Eventually, from July 8 to July 13, an inventory did take place under Commissioner V.K. Sharma. As expected, his team from the Reserve Bank of India found valuable items missing. "At least four items have been found to be missing so far—and one of them given away to Ugyen Trinley Dorje—from the articles of faith belonging to the Karmapa at the Rumtek Dharma Chakra's enthronement room," said a news report.[15] The highlight of the inventory was to have been an inspection of the Black Crown, stored in the main treasure room at Rumtek. But when the inspectors found that the seal placed on the lock on the crate containing the crown was probably a fake, Commissioner Sharma cut short the inventory to seek advice from the court on whether to break the lock.

On the last day of the inventory, Tenzin Namgyal requested that the locks that had been broken be closed again with the seal of the Tibetan Government-in-Exile to "unite Buddhists under one umbrella."

To Shamar and the Karmapa Trust board members, this was a strong indication that Tenzin and his allies were not loyal to the institution of the Karmapa, but instead were trying to hand over Rumtek to the Dalai Lama's exile government. The Trust's representative objected to Tenzin's proposal, since the Dalai Lama's administration had no authority over Rumtek. The inspector instead applied the seal of the Sikkim District Court to the locks and concluded the inventory for the time being. Since that time, Shamar and his supporters have been trying to get the inventory restarted. "We are especially worried that the Black Crown may be damaged or missing," Shamar said.

Confusion about Lamas and Labrangs

While his representatives tried to postpone or stop the inventory, Gyaltsab Rinpoche submitted a new application to the court, asking that he be excused from the case. In the new filing, Gyaltsab claimed that he had r.o rights to manage Rumtek and that the Gyaltsabs were historically part of a separate labrang, a different monastic administration, from the Karmapas back in Tibet.

This filing was a stark departure from Gyaltsab's earlier claims of authority over Rumtek. In an apparent attempt to shift any blame away from Gyaltsab Rinpoche for items potentially missing from Rumtek, he and Tenzin Namgyal created a new entity called the "Tsurphu Labrang." They hoped to include this pseudo-group—with the real name of the Karmapa's administration—as a party in the case for possession of Rumtek. This would enable them to replace Gyaltsab as defendant number three in the case while continuing to defend their claim to Rumtek from Shamar's court challenge.

The attorneys of Shamar and the Karmapa Trust took this as a move intended to confuse the court. In Tibet, the Tsurphu labrang controlled the Karmapa's property from the time the first Karmapa Karma Pakshi founded Tsurphu monastery in the twelfth century up until the Chinese invaded and the sixteenth Karmapa fled Tibet in 1959. But the Tsurphu labrang was never recognized as a legal entity under the laws of Tibet.

In any event, after the loss of Tibetan sovereignty, Tibetan laws ceased to have force. When the sixteenth Karmapa transferred his monastic seat to Rumtek, he did not establish the Tsurphu labrang as a legal entity in Sikkim, though he continued to refer to his administration informally by this traditional name. Instead, as we saw in chapter 2, he created a new entity under Indian law, the Karmapa Charitable Trust, to manage the assets of the Karmapas after his death. Since Rumtek is located in India, the Trust is the only legally authorized owner of the Karmapa's assets under Indian law. This makes the Trust the inheritor of the rights and privileges of the old Tsurphu labrang.

Apparently, Gyaltsab hoped that the court would see things differently and would recognize his Tsurphu Labrang ("Labrang" spelled with a capital "L" as a proper title) group as the legal continuation of the sixteenth Karmapa's administration. As we have seen, this would allow him to withdraw himself as a defendant in the case without abandoning a claim to Rumtek altogether. The new group was headed by Tenzin Namgyal, listed as general secretary to the Karmapa. In a surprise to Shamar, Tenzin submitted a letter written by Shamar himself in 1989 as evidence in the case. "They translated my letter from Tibetan quite well and sent it to the court," Shamar told me. "At that time, in the early nineties, I wrote a letter asking to be excused from political activities at Rumtek. I wanted to get away from Sikkim and start teaching at other monasteries and dharma centers. Maybe also do a retreat."

If Situ's supporters have been trying to assert for years that Shamar was trying to gain more power over the institution of the Karmapa, why would they present a letter where Shamar tried to resign his role at Rumtek? "In my letter, I stated that I was ceding my authority to the 'Tsurphu labrang,' as we called the Karmapa's administration. Tenzin must have thought it was worth it for them to contradict their old views to try to bring this group into the case." Tenzin filed Shamar's letter to support his claim that the group he was trying to create, with the "Tsurphu Labrang" name, was the legal owner of Rumtek.

After the Sikkim District Court agreed to hear the case in October 2001, it became clear that Tenzin's Tsurphu Labrang group had no documentation to prove its stewardship of Rumtek, because no group by that name ever officially ran the monastery. By contrast, the Karmapa Charitable Trust could produce dozens of documents, including minutes of meetings dating back to the mid-1980s, concerning its administration of Rumtek monastery after the death of the late sixteenth Karmapa.

Accordingly, the District Court ruled that Gyaltsab and Tenzin's group had no standing as administrator of Rumtek, and that the Karmapa Trust was the only group with *locus standi* to bring a case for possession of Rumtek. Nonetheless, Situ, Gyaltsab, and Tenzin Namgyal appealed this decision in the name of this same group to the Sikkim High Court in Gangtok. The High Court denied the appeal in a decision announced on March 19, 2003. This meant that Gyaltsab remained a defendant in the case.

Having failed to excuse himself from the civil case over Rumtek, Gyaltsab was again in a position that would leave him open to criminal prosecution in the future for potential thefts of religious valuables from Rumtek. Perhaps worried about his exposure, Gyaltsab began to show interest in settling the case out of court. He sent word to the Karmapa Charitable Trust that he wanted to negotiate.

In response, Shamar proposed a seven-point settlement requiring that the inventory of valuable items at Rumtek should be completed; Gyaltsab should account for any items found missing; all monks that Situ and Gyaltsab installed at Rumtek should leave; each legitimate Rumtek monk ousted by Situ and Gyaltsab should receive compensation; Gyaltsab should cover the legal costs of the Karmapa Trust in this case; Situ, Gyaltsab, and their followers should pledge not to interfere in Rumtek's affairs or to visit there in the future; and Situ and Gyaltsab should make a public apology for their roles in the violence at Rumtek and retract all the allegations they had made against Shamar, the ousted Rumtek monks, or the Karmapa Trust board members.

Gyaltsab reviewed the terms, consulted with his attorney, and signaled Shamar that he was ready to accept all points of the settlement except paying financial compensation to the monks or covering the legal fees of the Karmapa Trust. Shamar consulted with the Trust, and the trustees all agreed that this would be acceptable. They drew up a revised agreement and sent it to Gyaltsab.

Meanwhile, when he heard that Gyaltsab was about to sign the settlement with the Karmapa Trust, Situ reportedly summoned Gyaltsab to New Delhi. There, Situ apparently convinced Gyaltsab that the settlement's terms would be just as bad for their cause as losing a third time in court, and therefore, that they had nothing to risk by mounting a final appeal. Thus, Situ and Gyaltsab's invented group, the Tsurphu Labrang, took its appeal to the Supreme Court of India in New Delhi.

In July 2004, the Supreme Court rejected the Tsurphu Labrang's appeal, refusing to overturn two earlier court decisions ruling that the group had no standing in the case. The text of this decision can be found in appendix B of this book. Effectively, the decision left the Karmapa Charitable Trust as the only recognized legal entity with authority over Rumtek. This was the best piece of news that Shamar, the Karmapa Trustees, and the exiled Rumtek monks had heard in years. Shamar's lawyers quickly began proceedings in the local Sikkim court to remove Situ and Gyaltsab's monks from Rumtek and return the monastery to the stewardship of the Karmapa Trust.

Partisans of both Karmapa candidates eagerly followed the progress of the case in India, but abroad, the impact was little felt. "Karmapa Ogyen Trinley's close circle reportedly is demoralized," journalist Julian Gearing wrote in the *Asia Times*, "The few followers of the young lama worldwide who even know of the court decision are said to be struggling to come to terms with this dramatic setback." Gearing quoted an official of the Tibet Information Office in London as saying that if the Karmapa Charitable Trust gains Rumtek it "would be a bitter defeat" for Ogyen Trinley.[16]

The War for the West

In the wake of Shamar's court victories, it is arguable whether Himalayan Buddhists continue to support Situ and his Karmapa candidate Ogyen Trinley, or whether they have started to come around to Shamar. By 2004, Shamar's support had increased from its low point in the mid-1990s, according to Khenpo Chodrak, abbot of Tsurphu until the takeover. "When the seventeenth Karmapa Thaye Dorje [Shamar's candidate and Ogyen Trinley's rival] arrived in New Delhi in 1994, there were approximately ten tulkus who agreed with this." By the time of a 2002 ceremony in Bodh Gaya, there were "approximately fifty tulkus. It seems quite a few have changed their minds so far."

But in exile, winning Himalayan opinion has not been sufficient. "Back in Tibet, sixteen Karmapas were chosen and enthroned," Chodrak said. "There was a problem in only one instance, choosing the sixteenth Karmapa. That was resolved in a few months. Only in exile did this problem happen that we have an argument about who is the Karmapa for more than ten years."

The role of outsiders has been crucial to stoking the conflict. Foreign support, particularly from wealthy American admirers and Free Tibet groups, has greatly increased the power of the Dalai Lama relative to the leaders of the four religious schools outside of the Gelug, including Shamar. Back in Tibet, the Karma Kagyu and the other schools had significant sources of financial support and political power. In exile, money and prestige provided by foreign sympathizers has tipped the balance decidedly in favor of the Dalai Lama, who had become perhaps the most respected religious leader alive by the time the Karmapa dispute began in the early nineties.

Yet, while international sympathy for the Dalai Lama has grown in tandem with international conversions to Tibetan Buddhism, it has not generally translated into support of the Dalai Lama's scholarly Gelug school. Instead, the Karma Kagyu, with its emphasis on meditation, has become the most popular type of Tibetan Buddhism embraced by

Westerners. The prevalence of Karma Kagyu centers in the West made control of the school more attractive and thus, more contentious.

"Some people have said that controlling the Karma Kagyu is to make money," Shamar said. "*Time* magazine wrote in 1994 just after we welcomed Thaye Dorje in the ceremony at the Karmapa International Buddhist Institute in New Delhi, that the assets of the Karma Kagyu are worth $1.2 billion and that the lamas all want to take that and get more donations from abroad.[17]

"Other writers have repeated this figure over and over. I have always objected to these discussions. The Karma Kagyu school has very few assets of any financial value, perhaps some real estate, little more. But you cannot sell a monastery, or a dharma center, or a monk's school. And the Karma Kagyu school would never sell the Black Crown or any of the religious relics that His Holiness the late Karmapa brought with him from Tibet. These are for spreading Buddhism, not for making a fortune. I hope that Situ and Gyaltsab Rinpoches feel the same way, but I have my doubts. I want to make sure that the religious relics of our school kept at Rumtek are safe."

After the split in the Karma Kagyu became definite in 1993, the school's devotees around the world started to divide into followers of Shamar—and after 1994, his Karmapa choice Thaye Dorje—on the one hand and followers of Situ, Gyaltsab, and Ogyen Trinley on the other. The lama or group of lay people in charge of a dharma center would decide which party to follow, and members who did not agree would be encouraged to leave the group. In some cases they would be expelled.

In 1990 Ole and Hannah Nydahl, the Danish couple who became some of the first Western followers of the sixteenth Karmapa in the late sixties, came to India to meet with Shamar, who was in the city for a meeting of the Karmapa Charitable Trust. By that year, the Nydahls had founded more than a hundred Buddhist centers around Europe and in North and South America. In New Delhi, Ole met Shamar, Jamgon, Topga, and Jigdral Densapa, all trustees. Ole brought a list of the addresses of all the Buddhist centers he and Hannah had founded in Europe and the Americas. He was now prepared to sign them over, legally, to the Karmapa Trust. The Nydahls began the paperwork to transfer their centers to the Karmapa Trust. "All the trustees were touched by the purity of this man's motivation," Shamar said.

Then, two years later, in 1992, when unrest began at Rumtek, the Nydahls stopped the transfer of their centers to the Trust. "Up until the problems started, Hannah and Ole said they had faith in the ethics of high lamas," Shamar said. "Now, they told me that they did not trust Tibetan rinpoches to control their dharma centers in the West, so they would not finish the work to give their centers to the Karmapa Trust. I was not surprised by this. They now saw the real color of some lamas, with ego and ambitiousness worse than normal politicians in Europe who had ethical principles." To organize their expanding network of centers, the Nydahls founded a group they called the Diamond Way as an umbrella, but they still pledged their support to Shamar and Thaye Dorje.

Following their founders' lead, the Nydahls' centers in Europe and North America generally stuck with Shamar, as did a smattering of the sixteenth Karmapa's centers in Hong Kong, Singapore, and Taiwan. Shamar seemed to do well in continental Europe, perhaps due to the influence of Lama Gendun at the sixteenth Karmapa's European seat, Dhagpo Kagyu Ling in the Dordogne region of France. But most Karma Kagyu centers in the English-speaking world went to Situ, including Karma Triyana Dharmachakra, the sixteenth Karmapa's North American headquarters, in Woodstock, New York. The dozens of centers founded in England and America by Kalu Rinpoche generally supported Situ as well. Only the Shambhala centers founded by Chogyam Trungpa and his successors in the United States managed to maintain a neutral stance.

Beginning in 2001, Shamar and the Karmapa Trust started winning the court cases they had filed to regain control of Rumtek. By their second victory in 2003, it was not just open letters, reports from the Indian press and homegrown publications that validated Shamar's position, as in the past. Instead, two levels of the Indian court system had accepted many of the major points of his argument, particularly that the ad-hoc group formed by Situ and Gyaltsab had no legal claim on Rumtek, but that the Karmapa Trust did.

The courts have been careful to limit their decisions to the issues specifically listed in the cases, and judges have refused to be drawn into the dispute about the identity of the Karmapa. Nonetheless, their verdicts had the effect of implying that Shamar and the Karmapa Trust were authorized to make decisions about the sixteenth Karmapa's legacy, while Situ and Gyaltsab were not. "A court can say who should manage

Rumtek, but no law court can decide who the real seventeenth Karmapa is," Shamar said. "Soon the arguments should finish. The Karmapa will make himself known by the power of his presence and the benevolent force of his actions."

14 THE SECRET BOY

A Boy Waits in Lhasa

Back before Shamar filed his legal case, and even before Situ and Gyaltsab took over Rumtek in August 1993, a boy was waiting for Shamar in Tibet. Shamar would give him the name Trinley Thaye Dorje. But this would come later. First, he was called Tenzin Khyentse. And when he was a boy, before he met Shamar Rinpoche, Tenzin Khyentse was glad that he did not have to be a big lama.

The boy was eight years old and lived in Tibet's capital city. His family rented a one-room apartment in the medieval market district, the Barkhor. Here, Tenzin Khyentse lived with his father, a lama of the Nyingma school, his mother, and his six-year-old brother. Tenzin Khyentse was slim and fair-skinned. Recently, a doctor had given him eyeglasses. He spent most of his time inside the apartment with his small family. While his parents were talking with each other or entertaining one of his father's many guests, and his brother was napping, Tenzin Khyentse entertained himself.

He would sit on the floor and collect pieces of broken toys. As punishment for losing their novelty, his little brother would dismember these toys and scatter their appendages around the apartment. Tenzin Khyentse had observed this behavior in his brother many times, and so, he would pay special attention when the boy received a new toy. Cars, trucks, planes, people, animals, all would ultimately meet the same doom. Old toys were not allowed to fade away, but faced swift judgment. Once he had sufficiently chastened a toy that had ceased to please, the boy's sense of justice was satisfied, and he moved on to the next toy.

Then, Tenzin Khyentse would begin work. He carefully searched the apartment and collected the parts he could find. He put them in a pile and then laid them out on the floor as if he was assembling all the pieces of a model kit. He could usually figure out how to reunite the pieces with glue, tape, and string. Sometimes he had to improvise for parts that were shattered, crushed, or chipped beyond repair. Once he had put the pieces back together, he would place the rehabilitated toy on his shelf. Now it was his toy.

Tenzin Khyentse never had a sense that he was different than other boys. For him it was normal to feel the way he did. He didn't give it much thought. When he was young, he used to tell people that he was the Karmapa. He would recognize lamas who came to visit even though he had never met them before. The boy would call them by their names. Later, his parents would say that these lamas had known the previous Karmapa, who had died two years before Tenzin Khyentse was born in 1983.

As he got older, rumors spread around the Barkhor that Mipham Rinpoche's son could be the Karmapa. From the market district, news of the boy spread around Lhasa. The Miphams' little apartment had always been a favorite stop for visitors to the busy Barkhor, since the Nyingma lama had a reputation for clairvoyance. Pilgrims from the countryside especially liked to consult Mipham when they visited the holy city. They wanted him to advise them where to continue their pilgrimages for the most auspicious effect.

Now, lamas started to visit the family just to investigate the elder Mipham boy. Tenzin Khyentse was quiet and alert. He was suspicious of the lamas who visited his father. The boy did not want to be a special lama with a lot of responsibility. He had heard his parents whispering about the government. The boy knew that the Communists took a dark interest in special lamas. He was afraid they would take him away from his family. Maybe he would have to go to prison. Tenzin Khyentse wanted to stay with his parents and his brother.

The boy also liked to read. His parents had started him on Buddhist texts early on. After that, Tenzin Khyentse would read whatever he could find. One day in June 1992, he came upon a Lhasa newspaper that his father had finished reading. Tenzin Khyentse picked up the paper and started looking over the page that his father had folded open. A story about a nomad boy from eastern Tibet caught his eye. The boy was named

Ogyen Trinley and the article said that the government had just appointed him as the Karmapa Lama and enthroned him at Tsurphu monastery south of Lhasa. The new Karmapa would be a patriotic Living Buddha who would help spread Buddhism and serve the Chinese motherland.

Tenzin Khyentse was shocked and then he was relieved. If this other boy was the Karmapa, then Tenzin Khyentse had nothing to worry about. He didn't have to start acting like a big lama or spend his time meeting people from all over, like his father did. He would not have to leave his parents and his brother and he would not have to go to prison. He was glad that the government had found another boy. Now he was free.

At the end of the day Tenzin Khyentse went to sleep happy. But that night he dreamt that he was the Karmapa. In the morning, he told his mother about the dream. He said that he was sitting on a throne and surrounded by a crowd of followers. His mother smiled indulgently. She told her son that Ogyen Trinley was the Karmapa now and that he shouldn't speak like this any more. She didn't want him to go around the Barkhor with his little brother, the two of them telling people that Tenzin Khyentse was the Karmapa and "other such nonsense." She did not tell her son that this kind of talk would attract unwelcome attention from the authorities. But Tenzin Khyentse knew that he had to keep his secret.

The Other Karmapa

Compared to Ogyen Trinley, Thaye Dorje—the young man who was born and raised in Lhasa as Tenzin Khyentse—has received little publicity in the West, though he has made personal contact with devotees, government officials, business people, and interested journalists in more than a dozen countries.

The boy who would become Thaye Dorje was born in the Tibetan Year of the Water Pig, 1983. Given the name Tenzin (Holder of the Dharma Lineage) Khyentse (Union of Wisdom and Compassion), he was the first of two sons born to a Tibetan couple joined by an interest in Buddhist practice and scholarship. His father was a prominent tulku of the Nyingma school, the third Mipham Rinpoche, and his mother was an unconventional young woman from an aristocratic family named Dechen Wangmo.

The first Ju Mipham Rinpoche (1846-1912) ran dozens of monasteries in Kham and was the spiritual leader of the Jumo Hor monastery. He was counted among the most extraordinary masters of his time because of his extensive knowledge and deep realization. He authored more than three hundred treatises and served with the nineteenth-century master Jamgon Kongtrul the Great as one of the leading teachers of the Ri-me movement. Sometimes incorrectly translated as the "Nonsectarian" Movement, Ri-me was a spiritual revival in the late 1800s that revitalized the Nyingma, Sakya, and Kagyu schools of Tibetan Buddhism after years of decline under dominance by the Gelugpas in Lhasa.

The current Mipham incarnation was born in 1949 and descends from a family of physicians of traditional Tibetan medicine. As a youth, poor health prevented the ten-year-old Mipham from following most of the principal lamas, including Dudjom Rinpoche, the leader of his own Nyingma school, out of Tibet and into exile in 1959. But his condition also worked to his advantage and it helped convince the Chinese authorities to allow Mipham to remain at his monastery, Junyung Gompa, when they started evicting monks and lamas later on. Along with his own teacher, Mipham found a retreat in the mountains where he was able to practice rituals and pore over Buddhist texts safe from army patrols or the angry gangs of students and peasants who roamed the countryside during the Cultural Revolution of 1966-76.

For two decades, Mipham lived a precarious life in Kham, shuttling back and forth between Junyung Gompa and his mountain redoubt, successfully remaining just beneath the notice of Communist officials while pursuing the traditional training of a tantric yogi. Thirteen years of this period Mipham spent in retreat, performing body-mind practices including two thousand cycles of the rigorous Nyungne fasting ritual.

Signs, Omens, and Portents

In 1982, after a general relaxation of government restrictions on religious activities, Mipham felt that it was safe to come out into the open with his practice. A connection with the Panchen Lama, who had just been rehabilitated by the Chinese during this period, allowed Mipham to start rebuilding his monastery, destroyed like so many others during the Cultural Revolution. Later, he was able to obtain permission to travel to Lhasa. He took up residence in the city and joined the revitalization of Buddhism enabled by the authorities' new tolerance. In the early 1980s, during a tantric visualization practice, Mipham's personal yidam deity predicted to him that if he got married he would produce sons who would become great bodhisattvas.

The next day a group of pilgrims from Kham arrived to see Mipham; among them was a pretty woman in her early twenties named Dechen Wangmo, daughter of a noble family from Derge in Kham that traced its descent back to the legendary Gesar of Ling, the King Arthur of Tibet.

Dechen was an independent-minded young woman. At age twenty, she and a friend made an unaccompanied pilgrimage from Kham to Lhasa. They fell in love with the city and decided to try to stay. It was difficult for a young Tibetan woman to make a living in the Chinese-occupied city, but an uncle helped Dechen find housekeeping work. When Mipham met her at the home of a friend, he thought that she might be a suitable wife for a tantric practitioner. After talking with her for several hours, Mipham learned that Dechen was an accomplished meditator in her own right, a practitioner of the visualization practice of Chakrasamvara. He also thought that she was clever but not conceited about her abilities. When he proposed marriage, she immediately accepted.

As man and wife, Mipham and Dechen settled in an apartment rented from an elderly woman in the crowded central market district of Lhasa's medieval old city. "Our house was actually just one big room," remembers Thaye Dorje. "It was in old Lhasa, near the Barkhor. Now I hear that it's been demolished and another building put on the site."

On the night that she believes that her son was conceived, Dechen dreamt that she was standing in front of a gathering of women. The most beautiful among them left the group and walked over to Dechen, presenting her with a bowl that was decorated with the Eight Auspicious Symbols of Buddhism, a traditional harbinger of good tidings. Inside the bowl was a druma root, a small tuber eaten as a delicacy in Tibet. Then, the woman placed a *khata* offering scarf around Dechen's neck.

During the pregnancy she had several recurring dreams, including one of a large, swarthy man with a white beard. Mipham told his wife not to worry, that the figure was a dharma protector watching over her. Later, during her delivery, at the most intense points of pain, this figure from the dreams reappeared to her in a vision and the pain disappeared.

Her husband also suspected that there was something special about the pregnancy. Four months in, Mipham Rinpoche had to travel to his monastery in Kham and leave Dechen behind in Lhasa. Before departing, he gave his wife traditional instructions from Tibetan medicine for the pregnant mother of a high tulku. Though there had been no medical examination to determine the child's sex, Mipham told his wife she would have a son. He advised her to pay special attention to hygiene for herself and the baby. He also counseled her not to eat meat during the pregnancy. Finally, he gave her a special undergarment as spiritual protection to wear until the birth.

In the early morning hours of May 6, 1983 Tenzin Khyentse was born in the family home. People in the Barkhor area reported that a rainbow appeared in the clear sky directly above the house on this day. During the birth there was little or no blood, but instead a white milk-like fluid, considered a particularly auspicious sign during a birth.

While Tibetans believe that all tulkus can be identified and recognized by qualified students or lamas, the Karmapas are unique in the history of Tibetan Buddhism for always recognizing themselves first. According to his mother, Tenzin Khyentse told many people in Lhasa that he was the Karmapa, even before the age when children normally begin to speak. Dechen Wangmo has told one such story. When the boy was six months old, the mother and child were at home when a visitor arrived. Ama Dorje Khandro was a close relative of the sixteenth Karmapa. Dechen welcomed the visitor, and the two women sat down facing each other to enjoy a visit together.

The mother held her baby on her lap. Just when Dorje Khandro was seated, the six-month old stretched out his arms and began to speak. Quite clearly he said, "I am the Karmapa." The visitor was astonished to see a baby speak and even more shocked to hear these words. Dechen was surprised as well, and confirmed that the baby did not know how to speak yet, but normally just mumbled like other infants his age. The next day, the Ama returned with gifts for mother and child. "Having seen His Holiness, I can now die in peace," she said on this occasion, apparently predicting her own death of a few weeks later.

Boyhood in the City

The Barkhor area surrounds the famous Jokhang Temple, sometimes called the cathedral of Lhasa for its imposing scale and its thousand-year-old towering statue of the Jowo Buddha. Legend says that the Chinese Princess Weng Cheng brought the huge statue as a gift when she was sent to marry King Songsten Gampo and form an alliance between Tibet and the Celestial Empire in the year 641 A.D.

Considered the holiest site in Tibetan Buddhism, the Jokhang was begun by King Songsten Gampo in the middle of the seventh century. The temple underwent a long series of additions and reconstructions in the centuries that followed, but the present temple is largely the product of the construction by the fifth Dalai Lama, who greatly enlarged the building in the seventeenth century. During the Cultural Revolution, Red Guards sacked the Jokhang, sparing only the Jowo Buddha and one other of the temple's hundreds of religious statues. The shrine was rebuilt in the 1980s when the authorities relaxed restrictions on religious practice and began to encourage foreign tourism.

Today, the Jokhang is one of the two top tourist sights in Lhasa, the other being the imposing Potala Palace of the Dalai Lamas. While the Potala retains all the somber dignity of the abandoned palace of an exiled king, the Jokhang is immersed in lively activity. Tibetans wander the market in the square and stroll along the Barkhor pilgrims' route that encircles the Jokhang. Dozens of pilgrims are usually seen prostrating outside the front entrance, over which a golden eight-spoked Dharma Wheel flanked by two deer stands guard.

When I spoke with him at the Sri Diwakar Institute for Higher Buddhist Studies in Kalimpong in 2004, Thaye Dorje, who received his new name in 1996, was an athletic young man of twenty-one. His fair skin, rimless glasses and sedate manner gave him a scholarly air. But his square-cut jaw, broad shoulders, and confident movements suggested the physical fitness of a young man who took his weekly cricket match seriously. In easy idiomatic English with the trace of an accent less Tibetan than mid-Atlantic, Thaye Dorje told me about his youth in Lhasa.

Growing up in this milieu, Thaye Dorje found the lively Barkhor market fascinating, but "the best moments were visiting the Jokhang," he told me. He fondly remembers his visits to the famous shrine in the company of a family friend. "My uncle would take me. He was not a blood relative, but a friend of my father. The caretaker of the temple would let me climb up next to the big Buddha statue and sit up there, looking down on the people coming and going. We went there almost every morning. We never attended the pujas or services but simply went there to do a circumambulation, buy some bread in the market, and then come home. I did like to listen to the monks chanting. I didn't meet many monks or lamas, but did meet those who came to see my father."

As a boy, Tenzin Khyentse also encountered one lama at the Jokhang who would play an important role at Rumtek. While walking around the temple, the boy and Mipham's friend noticed that a crowd had formed. Curious, they followed the group inside the temple. There, a stocky lama was applying gold paint to the face of the temple's old Buddha statue. The visitors asked about the identity of the lama, and were told that he was a high rinpoche who had come from India. Mipham's friend set Tenzin Khyentse down so the boy could walk around the temple and climb up to take his usual post beside the Buddha statue.

Instead, the boy ran up to the portly lama and put a question to him: "Do you remember me?" The lama from India turned his head and looked back on the boy, answering "no." Tenzin Khyentse then ran back to Mipham's friend, and the two went home. Mipham's friend told the story to the boy's parents, who became curious. They took the boy back to the Jokhang. Making inquiries there, they discovered that the lama from India was Gyaltsab Rinpoche, and they decided that they would introduce themselves to him. But as they were going to meet Gyaltsab, the boy said, "I don't want to meet him, because he does not recognize me. There's no point in seeing him."

Such stories appear as more than coincidence for Tibetans. The childhoods of high tulkus are rigorously scrutinized for signs of unusual behavior. And for his supporters, much of the evidence for his claim to be the Karmapa derives from portents and mystical signs reported by those who knew Tenzin Khyentse as a child. Apparently, the unusual events in his life are not the dramatic miracles reported in the chronicles of Karmapas past—the appearance of twin sons in the sky, earth tremors in the local area, springs bubbling up from dry rocks to end a drought. Instead, the serendipities around the young lama seem to come from the human reactions of sensitive people who report that the boy exerted a power over them that acted as a sudden challenge to the assumptions of everyday life or even a kind of warp in the space-time continuum.

Khenpo Ngawang Gelek, one of the teachers at the monk's school at Rumtek before the 1993 takeover, explained to me his approach to such signs. "These things may seem silly to outsiders, but Buddhists consider them meaningful," the khenpo said. "The first I ever heard of Thaye Dorje was in 1992, from Lama Sherab Gyaltsen who came to Rumtek after visiting the boy's family in Lhasa. He told us the story of how strongly he was affected by meeting the child. He showed us a photo of the boy. At that time we didn't know that he was Shamar Rinpoche's Karmapa. There were rumors that Shamarpa was choosing a Karmapa as one of the children of the Bhutan royal family. But hearing Lama Sherab Gyaltsen's story helped me to believe.

"Four years later, when the Rumtek monks put on the first Karma Kagyu Monlam (prayer festival) at Bodh Gaya in 1996 we invited His Holiness Karmapa. I flew on the plane with him from New Delhi to Patna, the nearest big city. We didn't know beforehand, but that day was also the opening day of the Patna airport. There was a ceremony prepared for the prime minister of India to arrive, so there was already a special welcome gate put up in front of the terminal. Since our flight arrived first, Karmapa Thaye Dorje essentially received the first welcome when he went through this gate.

"Something similar happened when we arrived at Bodh Gaya. Just when His Holiness Karmapa arrived, it was time to beat the loud gong at the Japanese temple. We call this 'dharma melody,' the sound of Buddhist teaching. Later, when we finished the ceremony at the end of the day, there was a lot of milk in big cans left over from the kitchen, just sitting out where we had done our puja. Buddhism also considers this special—a lot of milk, water, or butter, left accidentally, is auspicious."

Were these just coincidences? "Coincidences coming together without planning are considered auspicious signs that are very good in Buddhism. It's quite difficult to explain so many coincidences as just accident, but that's just my belief," the khenpo said. "For me what was impressive was that Karmapa seemed to have such compassion, so much respect to the teachers of dharma who he met in India. That's not normal in an eleven-year old boy, even from Tibet. And since the Karmapa is considered such a high lama, he could act arrogantly. But he doesn't act proud at all."

In Lhasa in the eighties, as Tenzin Khyentse grew up, word continued to spread that Mipham Rinpoche's son was special, perhaps even the next Karmapa. At the age of two and a half, the toddler had begun to speak and still liked to tell people that he was the Karmapa. When he was three years old, he recited the entire Madhyamaka Avatara, without ever having seen this text running to hundreds of pages. In another coincidence, the Miphams' landlady in the Barkhor was a distant relative of the late sixteenth Karmapa. Before the Karmapa escaped from Tibet in 1959, the landlady had met him, and at that time she received a prophecy: "Before you die, you will meet me again."

She felt that this prophecy was fulfilled in Mipham Rinpoche's son. Out of a sense of devotion, she offered the use of her apartment to the ·family rent-free. Mipham suspected that his son was someone special, but was skeptical about indications that the boy was the Karmapa. Mipham held out hope that his son might turn out to be the reincarnation of a great Nyingma master instead.

One day in early 1985, Ngorpa Lagen, an elderly lama of the Sakya school, was circumambulating the Jokhang temple. He noticed fair-skinned, three-year old Tenzin Khyentse peering out of the window of an old house nearby. Drawn by curiosity, he walked up to the window. Gazing at the old lama with a severe look on his gentle features, the boy said, "Don't you know that I am the Karmapa?" As if in a game, Ngorpa Lagen replied, "If you are, then give me a blessing." The boy stretched out his arm and touched the lama. "At that moment," Ngorpa Lagen said, "I felt the calm and mental expansiveness that I had previously only known during deep *samadhi*."

Later in 1985, Ngorpa Lagen went to Kathmandu, and joined a large annual prayer and recitation gathering led by Sherab Gyaltsen Rinpoche, the disciple of the sixteenth Karmapa who would later show Thaye Dorje's photo to Khenpo Ngawang and other monks at Rumtek. The two soon became acquainted, and Ngorpa Lagen began telling Sherab about his encounter with the little boy in the Barkhor. After this, Sherab Gyaltsen and his attendant left for a visit to Tibet. Their destination was Tsurphu monastery, and on the way they stopped off in Lhasa to visit Mipham. The boy was not in the room when they arrived, so Sherab Gyaltsen asked if he could meet the boy. When Tenzin Khyentse was brought in, he sat next to his father quietly, but from time to time he would eye the guests and smile with obvious amusement.

During the course of the conversation, Sherab apparently went into a trance. He started to tremble and was unable to stop himself from shaking, a condition he had never experienced before. When he looked at Tenzin Khyentse, he saw a vision of the late sixteenth Karmapa. Sherab offered a *khata* and some money, but later Sherab could not remember how much. At one point, he found himself off his chair and sitting on the floor, which he also could not explain. As soon as Sherab and his attendant left, the attendant asked his lama if he was feeling well. The attendant had noticed that Sherab had been shaking and trembling.

Thaye Dorje's earliest memory was of seeing his brother born—also in the family home—in 1985, when he himself was two years old. "It was fun growing up in Lhasa," he told me. "My brother was my main playmate. From time to time mom and dad would take us out, but we spent most of our time in the house." Later, after the family arrived in India, the Dalai Lama would personally recognize Tenzin Khyentse's brother as the reincarnation of the Gelugpa lama Sonam Tsemo Rinpoche.

Because Mipham wanted to give his two boys a Buddhist education, he home schooled them both. "We didn't go to school, to avoid Communist brain-washing. My father didn't want us to have that. We learned to read and write from my father and mother." When they first got married, Mipham had spent hours each week reading Buddhist texts with Dechen. He helped her to commit the texts to memory and learn to analyze them using traditional rules of logic.

Later, both husband and wife tutored Tenzin Khyentse and his brother in the key texts of Buddhist philosophy, including the *Way of the Bodhisattva* by Shantideva and *Verses on the Middle Way* by Chandrakirti. "Actually, we didn't study separate subjects," as students did in Lhasa public schools, Thaye Dorje explained. "We studied in the traditional Tibetan way, which was to memorize a lot of writings. Once I memorized a text, I would then recite it in front of my parents. We would have all the topics in our head after that, and then once we got a chance to go to the monastery, we would learn the commentaries on each text.

"My father was very jolly. He loved to talk about anything. He was a very good writer of texts in the Tibetan way. He would hand-copy texts, or even rewrite them, or write commentaries on them. He wasn't very strict but he was very just. When my brother or I did something wrong, he would correct us as we needed. Also my mother was quite well educated, very curious and good at explaining things to me and my brother."

When he was not studying, Tenzin Khyentse enjoyed making figures out of paper, pretending that they were monks in their monastery. He would then describe in detail what the monks were doing in different parts of the paper monastery. This was his favorite game, according to his mother Dechen Wangmo.

During the seven years that Tenzin Khyentse lived in Lhasa, the family traveled to various monasteries to visit lamas of their acquaintance. On one occasion, the family made a journey to Reting Gompa in Amdo in northeastern Tibet, now part of the Chinese province of Qinghai. In the company of Reting Rinpoche, several other high lamas, and a renowned yogi, Mipham and his son were watching a horse race, a popular game of skill among the nomads of the plains.

Interestingly, Reting was the reincarnation of the Dalai Lama's famous regent in the thirties and forties. The earlier Reting was a charmer, attractive to men and women alike. He became embroiled in controversy and was executed by his successor in a power struggle in 1947. Reting's next incarnation was born far from the intrigues of court in Lhasa and was apparently more sedate. In addition, even though he was a prominent Gelugpa lama, he became close to Tenzin Khyentse in Lhasa and was eager for him to visit Amdo and spend time there. Considering this, and also that Tenzin Khyentse's younger brother would be recognized as a Gelugpa tulku, we might conclude that the old sectarian rivalry of the Gelugpa and Karma Kagyu was not clear-cut. Clearly it did not prevent lamas from cooperating across sectarian lines.

Sitting on a large flat rock near Reting's monastery, the party had a view of the hermitage on the opposite mountainside. Reting Rinpoche said to the boy, "You know we have a very good retreat place up there. You should go there and meditate one day, and then I can serve you."

To this, the child replied, "No, I will not do that. My monastery is Tsurphu." Of course, Tenzin Khyentse had never visited Tsurphu monastery.

The Search Begins in Earnest

Meanwhile, word of Tenzin Khyentse reached Shamar in India. In October 1986, the renowned Sakya lama Chobje Tri Rinpoche came to visit Shamar at the Karmapa Institute in New Delhi. He told him about Mipham Rinpoche's son and showed him a photograph of the young boy. A relative had given him the photo the day after he himself had a dream about the sixteenth Karmapa that he interpreted as prophetic. The Sakya lama felt that it was urgent to inform Shamar about the boy, so he came to the city as soon as he could.

"In 1988 I undertook my own independent investigations to determine the authenticity of the Mipham Rinpoche's son as the Karmapa," Shamar said. "First I asked Lopon Tsechu Rinpoche, who visited Tibet as part of a Nepalese government delegation, to obtain more information about the young boy during his visit. Next I sent a lama to go to Lhasa to investigate the boy more directly. Immediately upon their first meeting, the boy recognized that this lama had been sent to investigate him. The results of all these reports and investigations prompted me in July 1988 to go into a long retreat when I confirmed to my satisfaction that the boy was the reincarnated seventeenth Karmapa."

During the late eighties, Shamar made a very important acquaintance, a lama whom he has so far declined to name. Shamar first encountered this unnamed lama, "a person who was very devoted to His Holiness the late Karmapa," as Shamar explained, at a conference in Varanasi in the late eighties of representatives of the four schools of Tibetan Buddhism. This lama told Shamar he had received instructions from the sixteenth Karmapa. Was it possible that the Karmapa had indeed left a genuine letter and that Shamar would now find it?

Shamar has so far refused to reveal the instructions that the sixteenth Karmapa gave to this unnamed lama. But he did say that over the years this lama has given him advice on how to proceed in locating the right boy and in parrying the moves of Situ and Gyaltsab. Situ's supporters have challenged Shamar to reveal both the source and the content of these secret instructions, but so far he has refused to do so. "I know that people are curious, but this person was very specific that the late Karmapa told him what to say and when to say it. When the time comes, I will make everything clear." Needless to say, such secrecy has not helped the credibility of Shamar's search for the Karmapa for many observers, but Shamar has insisted that it is necessary.

Shamar decided to go to Tibet to see the boy. "I became very excited and booked a trip to Lhasa, traveling incognito." Dressed in a business suit, Shamar flew from Hong Kong through Chengdu in China's Sichuan province and arrived in Lhasa on a tourist visa. Just like the three agents whom Shamar had sent already, his plan was to mix with the crowds in the Barkhor and then pay the Mipham family a casual visit on the pretext of seeking spiritual advice from the well known Nyingma lama.

Shamar's investigators had managed to make contact with Tenzin Khyentse, though the final agent had to beat a quick retreat because the boy recognized the purpose of his visit. Shamar was eager to avoid word getting out that he was interested in Tenzin Khyentse, because then the Chinese authorities would want to be involved.

Even though he had never been to Lhasa, Shamar had a much higher profile among Tibetans there than his scouts did. "As this was my

first time in the city, I did not know what to expect. I never thought that
the Barkhor was so compact. But it turned out to be quite a small area
filled with people, just like the shops and stalls around a monastery. It
was clear that I couldn't mingle with the crowd unnoticed. There were
many Tibetan traders from India and Nepal who would easily recognize
me. To enter the Mipham family's house to observe the young child
could have undesirable consequences. I had learned that the authorities
knew that I was in the country and that they were probably watching my
movements."

Shamar had to scuttle his plan to meet the Miphams. He cut short
his visit to Lhasa and decided to forego a planned trip to the White
Lake of Tsari, a traditional spot for the Karmapas and the Shamarpas to
meditate and seek help on finding each others' reincarnations. Shamar
had planned to perform a seven-day retreat at the lake to clarify his course
of action. Fearing detection, he changed his plans. "In order to divert the
authorities' attention from my real purpose, I went off to the northern
part of the country, to a tourist area called Namtso. When I got back to
Lhasa, I took the next flight to Kathmandu."

After he returned to Rumtek, Shamar kept quiet about his trip
to Tibet and his research into Tenzin Khyentse. He also continued to
contact the unnamed lama who claimed to have the instructions of the
sixteenth Karmapa. "Each time I obtained certain information, and
when I became convinced that the child in Lhasa was the authentic
reincarnation I contacted this person to ask if he had any objections. He
always answered that he didn't but that he couldn't reveal the information
he'd been given until the time he was instructed to do so had come."
Shamar's search was mysterious to outsiders and apparently it had an
element of mystery for Shamar himself as well.

In spite of his personal conviction about the identity of the Karmapa,
Shamar did not yet feel that it was safe to make a formal announcement
about Tenzin Khyentse. He did not want to draw Chinese government
attention to the boy. Even before the Communists had recognized Ogyen
Trinley, Shamar knew that they would create an obstacle if they discovered
that Shamar had a candidate and that the boy was in Tibet.

To solidify their rule in Tibet, in the late eighties the Chinese were
planning to resurrect the old policy of the Qing emperors that required
Beijing to approve all choices of high Tibetan tulkus. In 1995, as we have
seen, the collision of this policy with the Dalai Lama's authority led to

the installation of two Panchen Lamas. Years before the Panchen affair, the Chinese government had wanted to gain Shamar's cooperation in installing a "Patriotic Karmapa." They sought out Shamar since their sources told them that Shamar's claim to the authority to recognize a Karmapa was stronger than Situ's. The Chinese embassy in New Delhi had approached Shamar half a dozen times to offer its cooperation to him if he would only agree to submit his candidate for government approval. But Shamar had always refused. Now, if the authorities found out about Tenzin Khyentse, at the very least the Chinese would demand Shamar's cooperation with their propaganda efforts. "The Chinese were friendly, but I did not want any government help," Shamar told me. "The Karmapa had always been chosen by the Karma Kagyu school alone, and there was no need to establish a precedent for outsiders to be involved now."

Shamar Shows his Hand

Despite the danger, Shamar knew he had to release some basic information about his search to maintain his credibility at Rumtek, since he feared that Situ would soon come out with an announcement of his own. So, at the 1991 inauguration of a monastery built by Shangpa Rinpoche at Pokhara in Nepal attended by more than four thousand Karma Kagyu devotees, Shamar made a general announcement. He said that the next Karmapa would probably be born in Tibet.

He instructed monastic ritual leaders to replace the prayers their monks had been chanting for the sixteenth Karmapa to take an early rebirth with prayers for the long life of the seventeenth Karmapa. Finally, he said that he had decided on "Thaye Dorje" as the name for the next Karmapa. "The obvious conclusion to be drawn from this announcement was that I had in effect confirmed the reincarnation of the seventeenth Karmapa," Shamar says. "My announcement at Pokhara provoked many comments."

While secretly completing his own investigation, at Rumtek Shamar waited out the events of 1992, responding defensively when Situ and Gyaltsab announced Ogyen Trinley, enthroned him in Tibet, and tried to build support for him. Though Shamar was unsuccessful at keeping the two rinpoches from dominating the official Karmapa search process and then taking over Rumtek itself, he did gain the time necessary to make contact with Mipham and get his family safely out of Tibet.

Mipham was in danger in Tibet. In 1988 and 1989, encouraged by
the Dalai Lama in Dharamsala, Tibetans held demonstrations in Lhasa
in favor of independence. Lay people and lamas alike gathered in groups
in public and demanded freedom for Tibet. Predictably, the Communist
administration in Lhasa efficiently repressed the demonstrations
and jailed the most outspoken protestors. Mipham Rinpoche did not
participate in these demonstrations but he sympathized with them and
the lama did not hide his opinion of Chinese rule. The government put
Mipham under surveillance but allowed him and his family to remain in
Lhasa for the time being.

Life soon became more dangerous for the Miphams. "We heard
that Situ Rinpoche informed the Chinese about the Miphams' boy
in Lhasa," Shamar claimed, citing sources loyal to him in the Tibetan
capital. Earlier, the government invited Shamar to work with them to
install an officially sanctioned Karmapa, as we have seen. But now that
they had their own Karmapa, through Situ and Gyaltsab, the Chinese
did not want competition from another candidate and they took action
against Thaye Dorje's parents.

"When Ogyen Trinley was enthroned at Tsurphu in 1992, the
government kicked out the Miphams from Lhasa," Shamar said. "The
family was relocated to Mipham Rinpoche's monastery in Kham and put
under house arrest there. Now their movement was restricted to the local
area. The parents knew that their son was perhaps in some danger."

As a result of the stress of being observed by the Chinese and put
under house arrest, Mipham Rinpoche, whose health was always poor,
suffered a stroke in 1993. He became paralyzed from the waist down and
was confined to a wheelchair. He lost the ability to speak, but his mind
apparently remained clear. He was still able to write, and with help from
Dechen he could continue his scholarship and teaching. Nonetheless, the
family used the illness as a pretext to apply for permission to leave Kham
so that Mipham could receive medical treatment elsewhere in China. The
government granted Mipham, Dechen, and their two sons permits for
internal travel in China. In early 1994, the family used the opportunity to
travel to leave China altogether and flee into exile. Tenzin Khyentse left
first, and traveled separately from his parents and his brother by a route
that Shamar arranged. Mipham, Dechen, and their other son followed,
by land to Nepal and then into India.

Thaye Dorje remembers that he was not sad to leave Tibet and that before their trip, he and his brother shared the excitement of many Tibetan children traveling to India for the first time. "I didn't know about it until just before we left. A year before, my family left Lhasa and stayed at my father's place in Kham. I was actually quite excited once I found out we were traveling abroad. Until I was really away from my parents, it would be fine. I did have some butterflies in my stomach, but my nervousness was only about leaving mom and dad. Otherwise, I was quite excited to get out to a country with a lot of things happening. It was wonderful, beautiful, and very healthy and quiet living in Tibet. But we just wanted to see tall buildings."

To protect the identity of people still living in China who helped Tenzin Khyentse and his family flee Tibet, Shamar has declined to release the details of their flight. However, he did provide me a broad sketch of how the boy-lama left Tibet. A European man came to Kham to pick up the boy. The man had two sons, both with valid passports and visas for China. The man and his sons resembled Tenzin Khyentse in appearance, since the Miphams' boy had light skin and almost Caucasian features.

The European had only brought one of his sons along, so he was able to pass off Tenzin Khyentse as his other son, thus allowing him to travel on the absent son's passport. Together, the three left China as a family and reached Bangkok. From there, they flew to New Delhi. Tenzin Khyentse entered India on the European boy's passport, but after he was safely in the country, Shamar informed the Indian immigration authorities of the ruse. He applied for and obtained permission for Tenzin Khyentse to remain in India legally.

Thaye Dorje told me that "When I met Shamar Rinpoche in India the first time after my trip in early 1994, he touched his head to mine in blessing and it was very tender. He asked me about the trip and how I was doing. He was very sweet and caring."

Another Prediction Letter

Shamar cites a prediction to confirm his selection of Thaye Dorje, in a letter written by the sixteenth Karmapa when he was twenty. We saw this letter earlier, and noticed how its mournful tone contrasted with the upbeat feeling of Tai Situ's prediction letter. Here, the Karmapa mentions Rigdrol, a name he often used to refer to himself:

I will not stay in Tibet
I will wander to the ends of the earth
Without destination to experience my karma.

The cuckoo comes to Tibet in the springtime
And sings its melancholy songs with six melodies.
Isn't it sad, my followers?
Mournfully, you will wonder what happened
To the man called Rigdrol.

The year which belongs to the bird catching the victory
At that time my followers and I
Will gather together again with happiness and joy.
I pray for this.[1]

"This passage comes from a letter written by His Holiness the late Karmapa in 1944," Shamar told me. "In the first two stanzas he talks about his own death. Then, in the last stanza, he predicts his rebirth." Though he has never presented this document as an answer to Situ's prediction letter, Shamar finds the timing mentioned in the letter to be prophetic for Thaye Dorje.

He focuses on the stanza "The year which belongs to the bird catching the victory." When Tenzin Khyentse met all his disciples at the Karmapa International Buddhist Institute (KIBI) in New Delhi in March 1994, it was at the end of the Year of the Water Bird. "According to the Tibetan calendar, in this particular year the twelfth month was the so-called month of victory. Since we smuggled Karmapa illegally out of China, we did not know exactly when he would arrive, and of course we could not have planned the timing of his welcome ceremony until he was out of Tibet. As it turned out, it was in the right month and year predicted in the late Karmapa's letter from exactly fifty years earlier. To us, this is a very auspicious sign."

Of course, such signs, if they favor their own candidate, are convincing to each side in the Karmapa controversy. But no signs, it seems, are enough to decide the issue for both sides.

In the end, is the evidence for Thaye Dorje any better than that for Ogyen Trinley? Like Shamar and other supporters of Thaye Dorje, Tai Situ and those who follow Ogyen Trinley claim that their Karmapa was recognized on the basis of a prediction from the sixteenth Karmapa, auspicious signs and omens, and the meditation of a qualified high lama whose predecessors have recognized past Karmapas. Even if we are willing to discount the Dalai Lama's support for Ogyen Trinley—because the Tibetan leader lacks historical authority to recognize the Karmapa—if we compare evidence, it may appear that this is no more than a case of Shamar vs. Situ. The monks at Rumtek felt that they were not qualified to judge which candidate was the genuine Karmapa. How, then, can outsiders do so?

The conclusion to this book will take up this question in greater detail. For now, we might consider the behavior of the respective followers of Shamar and Situ. Situ's followers tried to take over Rumtek from the management set up by the sixteenth Karmapa himself twice during 1992 and 1993. They finally succeeded with the help of the corrupt administration of Sikkim state in August, 1993. If we believe the testimony of dozens of monks who were involved, this takeover was brutal, violent, and in contradiction to the basic tenets of Buddhist ethics. We might further consider the behavior of Tai Situ's followers at the welcome ceremony that Shamar held for Tenzin Khyentse in March 1994, the subject of the next chapter.

15 THE RETURN OF THE KING

An Angry Welcome

On March 16, 1994, at about 9:30 in the morning, a car delivered eleven-year-old Tenzin Khyentse to the gate of the Karmapa International Buddhist Institute (KIBI) in New Delhi. Like Rumtek but smaller, the school is constructed on the plan of a Tibetan monastery, with a wall of student rooms forming a courtyard around a temple in the center.

Quietly, attendants took the youngster through the main courtyard, and then led him upstairs to a room on the third floor of the main temple building. There, the boy rested for a few hours, received instructions about the events of the next day and met with various lamas. Khenpo Ngawang Gelek, one of the teachers at the monk's school at Rumtek before the takeover in 1993, was one of these lamas. "I went to see His Holiness Karmapa to drop off a damaru (a ritual drum), and a bell, with Khenpo Chodrak's brother, Tashi. We entered his room and we bowed. Tashi then said we had brought very special toys today. But the Karmapa replied 'No, they are not toys.' That was the first time I met him."

Then, the boy was put to bed. None of the nearly one hundred students and staff of the school knew that the child who would be officially welcomed the next day as the seventeenth Karmapa was already on the premises.

Around seven o'clock the next morning, a large crowd assembled in front of the institute's main gate awaiting entrance to the festive event. Security guards frisked arrivals and searched their bags before allowing them inside. About five hundred guests were seated in the main temple for the ceremony. Most were monks and lay people from Rumtek and around the Himalayan area, but nearly two hundred Westerners, including about eighty students at KIBI, were in attendance as well.

Lea Terhune, who would write her book *Karmapa: The Politics of Reincarnation* ten years later, also came to attend the ceremony, in her capacity as a freelance correspondent for the Voice of America. Interestingly, Terhune had worked at KIBI several years earlier, during the eighties, before leaving to work exclusively with Tai Situ. On the morning of Tenzin Khyentse's welcome ceremony, Terhune arrived at KIBI with Tim McGirk, the writer for the *London Independent* who accused the tenth Shamarpa of starting the Tibet-Gorkha War of the eighteenth century, as we saw in chapter 7. Flashing press credentials, Terhune and McGirk managed to make it past the guards at the gate. But a KIBI staff member recognized Terhune as Situ's secretary, and asked her and McGirk to leave the premises. They were ushered past the main gate, and waited outside.

Inside the main temple, the guests were seated and the puja was ready to begin. At about eight o'clock in the morning, Shamar gave the word for the welcome ceremony to proceed. In procession under a traditional yellow umbrella, Shamar led Tenzin Khyentse into the temple, giving his eager followers their first glimpse of the boy they believed to be the seventeenth Karmapa. The boy wore glasses and walked between the two halves of the crowd as if he was used to appearing before hundreds of people on a regular basis. To the blare of *gyaling* horns and the rattling of cymbals Tenzin Khyentse walked slowly into the shrine room, moving with quiet confidence towards the oversized Buddha statue in the back of the room.

Under the gaze of the eyes of devotees who had come from around the Himalayas and around the world to welcome the new Karma Kagyu leader, the child stopped in front of the Buddha statue and performed three prostrations. Then, he mounted the throne reserved for the Karmapa, a seat that had sat empty from the day it was installed a decade earlier. The ritual master of the shrine, Nendo Tulku, handed the boy a replica of the Vajra Mukut, the Black Crown of the Karmapas, and placed a brocade robe around his shoulders. Horns, drums, and cymbals sounded. In a state of meditative concentration, the new Karmapa placed the Black Crown on his head and the puja began.

Barbarians at the Gate

The ceremony continued for more than an hour. Inside the temple, there were monks and devotees chanting, musical instruments playing, and sticks of incense and butter lamps burning. At about 9:30 a.m., the ceremony drew to a close.

Meanwhile, outside the shrine room and across the street from KIBI, seven vans pulled up, bringing more than a hundred monks from Tai Situ's monastery Sherab Ling and dozens of lay people from Sikkim to begin a protest demonstration. A total of about two hundred protesters massed in front of the institute's gate and unfurled cloth banners with slogans written in English including "The Dalai Lama's word is our word," "Topga Yugyal [general secretary at Rumtek before the 1993 takeover] don't hide behind Shamarpa," "Joint Action Committee, All Buddhist Organizations of Sikkim," and "Stop using the boy." The demonstrators chanted slogans denouncing Shamar and Topga and promising to expose their "fake Karmapa." The KIBI management identified some of the monks as the same shedra students who had overwhelmed the sixteenth Karmapa's monks at Rumtek and had helped expel them when Situ and Gyaltsab took over the monastery in August 1993.

According to Indian journalist Anil Maheshwari, "Shamar Rinpoche was aware that the following day Situ's men would try, at all costs, to stage a demonstration in front of KIBI."[1] But Khenpo Chodrak Tenphel, the abbot of Rumtek before August 1993 and the director of KIBI at the time of Tenzin Khyentse's welcome ceremony, denies any advance knowledge about or planning to respond to a protest.

"We did not expect any kind of demonstration and certainly not the attack that did happen," Khenpo Chodrak said. "That's why we did not try to keep the welcome ceremony a secret, but we announced it a month in advance, so that our guests could attend. KIBI is located in a development in New Delhi with business schools, a hospital, and a Hindu ashram, but no other Tibetan centers of any kind, so we thought there would be no trouble from our neighbors. Also, there are more observers in a city like New Delhi. We had invited journalists from the *Times of India* and the *Indian Express*. Troublemakers can't get away with so much in a big city. The situation was different than at Rumtek, which is in Sikkim, a far-off state that could be dominated by a corrupt little regime like Bhandari's. If we had expected a problem at KIBI, we would have simply asked the New Delhi police for protection."

Writer Terhune witnessed the fight from outside the gates of KIBI: "Outside, a contingent of monks from Delhi and Himachal Pradesh were assembled to demonstrate against Shamarpa and what they saw as a sacrilegious introduction of a fake Karmapa. It was meant to be a silent protest. It was unclear who cast the first stone."[2] But for the five hundred guests at the ceremony and the KIBI staff, it was clear that Tai Situ's supporters launched an unprovoked attack on KIBI to disrupt the welcome ceremony for Shamar's Karmapa candidate. This version of events is backed up by dozens of eyewitness accounts and fourteen minutes of video footage shot by an Austrian filmmaker who had come to New Delhi to record the ceremony.[3]

The protesters were apparently disappointed to find that they had missed nearly the whole welcome ceremony. Just as the puja was concluding inside the temple, outside the monks started picking up stones and bricks from the street. Then, they charged the institute's locked gate. The three or four private security guards inside panicked and then fled. Though a couple of KIBI monks tried to hold the gate, a surge of protesting monks pushed through and flooded into the courtyard. Once inside the KIBI gates, the protesters began throwing their stones and bricks at the main temple, aiming at any windows they could reach.

As glass started to shatter, the monks and guests in the temple exchanged looks and then sprang to their feet. Bricks and stones began to crash through the windows onto the heads of the crowd inside. The puja finished just at this point. A KIBI official signaled the ritual master to conclude the ceremony. Then, he asked the crowd to remain calm and urged everyone to take cover, assuring visitors that the police had already been called and would arrive soon. KIBI monks and staff ran outside and tried to push back the invaders.

"One journalist who wasn't thrown out reported that projectiles such as coke bottles and bricks were stockpiled on the roof of the monastery, apparently for just such an eventuality," Lea Terhune wrote.[4] But KIBI staff members tell a different story. According to Khenpo Ngawang Gelek, after the protesters began to throw stones and bricks at the temple windows, on their own initiative, the mostly-Nepali kitchen staff began collecting bottles that they normally saved to return for a deposit. They ran the racks of bottles upstairs to the roof. From there, they rained down bottles on the courtyard to try to scare off the attackers. They had no bricks. Dropping bottles helped to contain the fighting, and later the KIBI management paid each kitchen staff member a bonus for his or her role in the institute's defense.

Meanwhile, attendants brought Tenzin Khyentse down from the throne and waited with him on the stage at the back of the main shrine room for ten minutes until the fighting subsided. Thaye Dorje described his own impressions of the attack to me. "I simply didn't know what was going on. I just thought there were so many visitors that they were trying to crowd in to see me. It's like that in Tibet. People see a rinpoche once or twice in their lifetimes and they just have to push their way in to get a blessing, it's their only chance. So there are many crowds like this at special ceremonies, people just barge in. Later, when the lamas put me behind the throne, I didn't really understand why."

Once it was safe to leave the shrine room, his attendants took Tenzin Khyentse upstairs to his room on the third floor. From his window there the boy looked down at the fight below as it was winding down. He said that he still wasn't scared for himself, but that he was concerned that others might get hurt. "When we went upstairs and looked out the window, I suggested that we bring out big water hoses to push the crowd away without hurting them," Thaye Dorje told me.

Khenpo Ngawang Gelek was with the young lama. "The protesters came into the courtyard, just at the end of the ceremony," he said. "They kept shouting and throwing stones. Karmapa went to his room and was watching from a window to see what they were doing. He wasn't scared at all."

During the melee, a young Polish student of the Danish Lama Ole Nydahl managed to close the main gates but was badly injured in the process by monks from Situ's group. Blood from a head wound that the young man had sustained splattered onto the shirt of Tim McGirk, the London Independent reporter who came with Lea Terhune. During the fighting, the KIBI monks invited McGirk into the facility to make sure he was not injured. They washed his shirt. This gave him a chance to ask questions of Shamar Rinpoche. McGirk told Shamar that he had somehow gotten the idea that Shamar's monks were the aggressors, and that they were trying to take over the monastery.

"I think the reporter got things backwards," Shamar said. "As the fighting went on outside, I talked with Mr. McGirk. When he saw that the stones were actually coming from outside the gates, he asked me 'Shouldn't you be throwing the stones?' Then, I said to him 'Why would I want to injure my own monks?' He looked puzzled. Then he said 'But you're supposed to be taking over the monastery.' I explained that KIBI was already under my management and that it was Situ Rinpoche's monks who had come to disrupt the ceremony. The reporter looked at me again and then he looked down at the ground. He obviously thought that Situ's monks were already inside KIBI and that our monks were attacking. Maybe it was too big a change from what he had come to expect and he couldn't understand the true situation."

Despite what he must have seen for himself, McGirk later published his article blaming the fight on Shamar and his monks. Though he admitted that the protesters threw the bricks, McGirk implied that they had good reason to do so. "The tale took a more sinister twist when, in Delhi yesterday, Shamar Rinpoche unveiled his candidate for 17th Karmapa, a shy, rather scared 11-year-old Tibetan. Three coach loads of Tibetan monks and students arrived and waged a fierce battle with Shamar's renegade followers. 'Shamar's manipulating this boy for money and power,' shouted one protesting monk as he threw a brick."[5]

The Indian press would have less trouble understanding the situation at KIBI. One national paper in New Delhi wrote: "A ceremony to crown a 10-year-old [sic] Tibetan boy as the one chosen to be Karmapa, head of the prestigious Rumtek monastery in Sikkim, ended on a violent note Thursday morning when members of a rival Buddhist group, who plan to install another boy living in Tibet as Rumtek chief, reached the scene and indulged in heavy brickbatting."[6]

While Shamar was talking to McGirk at KIBI, the battle in the courtyard went on for about five more minutes, until the New Delhi police arrived. Once on the scene, police officers arrested nine protesters for inciting violence and committing assault. About twenty people were injured, including monks who had been violently expelled from Rumtek just seven months earlier. The institute sustained several thousand dollars in property damage. While the main shrine room had largely been spared, nearly every window on the premises was broken, a walkway had been ripped up, the rails and posts of a protective fence had been torn out, and the guardhouse at the front gate had been sacked. "The KIBI courtyard was covered with bricks, stones, and broken glass and stained with spots of blood. It looked like the scene of a big riot," Khenpo Ngawang Gelek told me.

First as Tragedy, then as Farce

In the *Eighteenth Brumaire of Louis Napoleon*, Karl Marx wrote: "Hegel remarks somewhere that all great world-historic facts and personages appear, so to speak, twice. He forgot to add: the first time as tragedy, the second time as farce." To Shamar and his followers, the takeover of Rumtek by Situ and Gyaltsab in 1993 was a tragedy that deprived many of them of their home and put the monastic seat of the Karmapas under the influence of their historic rivals in the Tibetan administration of the Dalai Lama. By contrast, the attack on KIBI the following year turned out to be little more than an annoyance for supporters of the new Karmapa.

On the same day as the welcome ceremony for Tenzin Khyentse, the Dalai Lama was addressing a human rights conference. After his speech, word of the attack at KIBI got out. Two facts, that the protester-attackers were supporters of the Dalai Lama's Karmapa candidate, and that they carried banners invoking the Dalai Lama's authority, reached attendees at the conference. In response, a group of foreign delegates sent a memo to the Tibetan exile leader asking him how he could criticize Chinese human rights violations while he himself was involved in this incident that threatened freedom of religion for his own Tibetans in exile. I was not able to discover what answer, if any, the Dalai Lama gave.

A few days later, Tai Situ held a news conference in New Delhi to give his opinion of the events at KIBI. Standing in front of a large photo of the Dalai Lama, smiling, and with hands in prayer position, Situ answered questions from a podium. When a reporter asked Situ if his monks had attacked KIBI, according to witnesses, the rinpoche replied mendaciously that he did not know who the attackers were, but that he heard they might have been Nyingma monks. Situ did not add that many of the protesting monks came from his own monastery, Sherab Ling.

He then spoke about the need for world peace and cooperation, hearkening back to his aborted Pilgrimage for Active Peace of five years earlier. "The peace and harmony of the sacred order, which has been laid down by the Karma Kagyu tradition of Tibetan Buddhism has been disturbed."[7] Finally, when a reporter from an Indian magazine asked him what would happen if Shamar tried to enthrone his Karmapa candidate at Rumtek, Situ replied "I'm afraid that may lead to a bloodbath in Sikkim."[8] This was taken by the monks who had been thrown out of Rumtek in August 1993 as a threat.

Three months later, in June 1994, Tai Situ's attorney Ram Jethmalani brought a suit against Shamar for control of KIBI in the High Court of New Delhi. Jethmalani argued that since Ogyen Trinley had been recognized as the seventeenth Karmapa, his "regents" Tai Situ and Gyaltsab had the legal right to control the Karmapa's school, KIBI. Jethmalani was a formidable opponent, a charismatic courtroom presence, and one of the best known lawyers in India. We have already seen how Jethmalani got the ban on Situ entering India lifted. However, this time, Shamar's attorney, a young unknown lawyer named P.K. Ganguli, produced arguments that convinced the court to dismiss the case at its first hearing.

An Education Ancient and Modern

Tenzin Khyentse was uninjured by the attack on KIBI, and this rough welcome did little to reduce his joy at being united with Shamar and having the opportunity to study under the teachers at the Karmapa Institute. "My traditional monastic education continued. But now I met with more teachers, especially Topga Rinpoche. Also Khenpo Chodrak. I was able to properly start on Tibetan grammar. I started English at this time too, studying with a Russian man who then lived in America. Later I had teachers from Australia and other countries, so my accent should be a bit mixed. I also got a smattering of math, science, and world affairs."

In November 1996, in the Mahabodhi Temple at Bodh Gaya, where Shakyamuni Buddha had gotten enlightened twenty-five hundred years earlier, Tenzin Khyentse had his hair-cutting ceremony and took monks' vows. He officially took the name Trinley (Buddha Activity) Thaye (Limitless) Dorje (Unchanging). In 1998 Khenpo Sempa Dorje, one of the most prominent scholars of the Tibetan monastic tradition and a professor at Banaras Hindu University in Varanasi—which claims to be one of the three largest residential universities in the world, with 128 teaching departments—began to tutor the Karmapa on Buddhist philosophy. Interestingly, Sempa Dorje was trained as a Gelugpa geshe, again showing that some individual lamas of the Dalai Lama's school are not scared off by the Karmapa controversy.

In 1997, Shamar was able to arrange a meeting for Thaye Dorje with the Dalai Lama in Dharamsala. Shamar has insisted that he did not want to obtain the Tibetan leader's approval, and he has continued to assert that the Dalai Lamas had never had any authority to choose or recognize a Karmapa. But Shamar wanted the meeting to demonstrate that the Tibetan leader was not implacably opposed to Thaye Dorje. The Dalai Lama signaled that he was ready to meet Thaye Dorje, and a time was set. Then, the meeting was just as quickly cancelled. "Beforehand, Situ's supporters found out about our meeting with His Holiness Dalai Lama," Shamar said. "They threatened to make the streets of Dharamsala run with blood if the meeting took place. Therefore, His Holiness had no choice but to postpone this meeting."

In November 1999, Thaye Dorje accepted an invitation to make a tour of Southeast Asia. This would be his first trip abroad. He met with thousands of devotees at dharma centers in Singapore and Malaysia. But he almost did not make it into Taiwan, according to Ngedon Tenzin. Earlier, we encountered him as the senior monk-official at Rumtek who had his monk's robe wrapped around his neck by angry local supporters of Situ when he and Gyaltsab took over the Karmapa's cloister in August 1993. Since 2004, as we have seen, Ngedon has served as the general secretary of Thaye Dorje's labrang, the post held by Topga Rinpoche until his death from cancer in 1997.

"Our staff obtained a Taiwanese visa for Gyalwa Karmapa Thaye Dorje weeks before he was supposed to enter Taiwan. We used the diplomatic passport issued to him by the Bhutanese government," Ngedon said. "But the day before he was due to fly into Taipei airport, officials in the Foreign Ministry tried to stop His Holiness Karmapa from coming in because of a technicality."

Immigration officials noticed that his passport said that Thaye Dorje was born in Tibet. As a result of its strained relations with Beijing, the Taiwanese government required travelers born in China to obtain a special permit to enter the island nation. Only the timely intervention of one of Thaye Dorje's supporters in Taipei saved the trip. This devotee used his influence in the Foreign Ministry to convince the manager of the relevant office to remain open after normal closing time at five o'clock to process an emergency permit for Thaye Dorje. The tulku was able to obtain clearance and fly into Taipei the next day.

Ngedon suspects that Chen Lu An, who by this time was a former government official but one who still enjoyed influence in the tight-knit administration of the island nation, tried to block Thaye Dorje's entry into Taiwan. "Through our devotees in Taiwan, we heard that Mr. Chen had already lined up perhaps fifty people willing to pay one million dollars each to carry the box for the Black Crown and hand it to Ogyen Trinley during the Black Crown ceremony," Ngedon said.

Here we might recall that Jigme Rinpoche accused former Rumtek Abbot Thrangu of planning with Chen to tour the next Karmapa around the island to raise funds, as we saw in chapter 8. Now, it appeared that Chen had started to put a similar plan into action with Tai Situ.

According to Ngedon, Chen had even more Taiwanese pledged to pay five hundred thousand dollars each to hand Ogyen Trinley the so-called Body, Speech, and Mind Objects during the ceremony—a stupa or sacred pagoda, a statue of the Buddha, and a text of Buddhist scriptures. "Mr. Chen had made commitments to Karma Kagyu lamas in Taiwan, as well as monasteries around the world, from Kathmandu to New York, to distribute these funds. If His Holiness Thaye Dorje came to Taiwan, Mr. Chen's plan would be spoiled. We heard that he was practically sleeping in front of the Foreign Ministry office to stop Karmapa Thaye Dorje from getting into Taiwan."

As it turned out, Thaye Dorje received a royal welcome on the island. The Karmapa controversy led coverage on the local television news for a couple of days. Meanwhile, Thaye Dorje gave empowerment ceremonies around Taiwan and toured the Taiwanese legislature and the studios of a major television station. "In the city of Tainan, more than ten thousand devotees attended one of his ceremonies. The line of people waiting for blessings was endless," Ngedon said. "At some point, we had to stop, or it could have gone on forever. About two hundred lamas who supported Ogyen Trinley attended Thaye Dorje's empowerments just to get donations themselves from the generous devotees."

In January 2000, Thaye Dorje went on to Europe, giving teachings to and performing ceremonies for thousands more students. He concluded his European visit with a retreat at the Dhagpo Kagyu Ling center in France, under the management of Shamar's elder brother Jigme Rinpoche.

At that time, when he was sixteen years old, Thaye Dorje explained that traveling was an important part of his education. "There are many new things that I have never experienced before, both good and bad, but my main discovery was the differences in culture. In each country, they have their own way of talking or relating to each other. In every aspect of life, there's something different, so that has been quite interesting to see.

Otherwise, what I really like the most is that people are genuinely devoted to dharma. Since I'm a teacher, that's what I am looking for. There are many people who are really interested and who do their practice from the heart, and that's been the experience I have liked the most."[9]

When he travels, particularly around Asia, Thaye Dorje is often met with Byzantine protocol and extravagant displays of devotion and respect. During his first visit to Europe, he said that "it is totally wrong to see a lama as some kind of supernatural being. A lama is someone who shows the path to enlightenment, and that's it. He's simply a teacher. It is similar with the Three Jewels: you can rely on the Buddha and the Sangha because they've been through this saṁsara, know what it is and how to overcome all this suffering; the dharma is the path for this aim. This kind of special treatment, I really don't expect it and I don't want it. It is not important for me. All I want is to help people find real happiness. What I mean is the real happiness that is achieved in the state of liberation. I myself go through my spiritual practices in order to become able to guide others on this path. It is for this reason that I am getting the teachings from all the high lamas, teachers and professors."[10]

The young lama has divided the last few years between studying at the monk's school in Kalimpong and traveling. In December 2003 he went through his Vidyadhara ceremony, a kind of graduation held at the Karmapa Institute in New Delhi to signify the completion of his formal monastic education. However, at Shamar's urging, Thaye Dorje has continued to study Buddhist philosophy at the monk's school in Kalimpong as graduate-level study. Shamar, who is in charge of Thaye Dorje's education, said that, "I want His Holiness Karmapa to receive the broadest schooling possible in Tibetan Buddhist studies and also to gain a basic knowledge of Western science, culture, and thought, for the modern world."

In the summer of 2004, to introduce Thaye Dorje to Western philosophy, Shamar invited Harrison Pemberton, the philosophy professor who accompanied me to Rumtek, to teach Thaye Dorje in Kalimpong. Pemberton had just retired from forty years in the philosophy department at Washington and Lee University in Lexington, Virginia. Pemberton accepted Shamar's invitation, and he began teaching in Kalimpong in October 2004. For five weeks, Pemberton tutored the young tulku and five other young lamas on his specialty, the dialogues of Plato. Pemberton ran his class solely in English with no Tibetan translator present and he taught in the style of an American seminar course, with the emphasis on discussion over lecture. "In the tradition of Socratic dialogue, I really wanted class to be an interactive encounter," Pemberton said.

Along with Plato, Pemberton also introduced the leading philosophers of the European tradition including Descartes, Kant, Hegel, and Heidegger. "This will be the first Karmapa who can bring together East and West on an intellectual level," said Pemberton. "He was particularly interested in the role of Socrates as a guru, prodding students towards knowledge and wisdom. I don't know if I'm a Buddhist or not, but I can say that the Karmapa displayed one of the sharpest analytic minds I have ever encountered."

Tantra in California

Thaye Dorje made his first trip to the United States in June, 2003. On this low-key visit, he remained in California. He spent two months studying in the Menlo Park home of Sandy Yen, a sponsor from Silicon Valley's thriving Chinese-American community. The young lama used the relative isolation of Yen's residence from his normal responsibilities as an opportunity to fulfill a long-held dream of the sixteenth Karmapa. In the eleventh century, the legendary Tibetan founder of the Kagyu lineage, Marpa the Translator, brought fifty tantric ritual texts from India to Tibet. He passed on the empowerments for these texts to his students, and these texts became valued lore of the Kagyu linage until the death of the last teacher who could pass them on in the nineteenth century.

Fortunately, the nineteenth-century scholar Jamgon Kongtrul the Great had preserved these texts and passed them on to lamas of the Sakya school. The Sakyas in turn passed along the oral teachings surrounding these texts up to the present day within their own school. The sixteenth Karmapa had wanted to receive these Tantras from the Sakya lama Chobgye Trichen Rinpoche in the mid-1960s in Sikkim. But, since Sikkim had not yet joined India, permission of its traditional ruler, the Chogyal, was necessary for Chobgye Trichen to enter the small kingdom. This permission could not be obtained. The sixteenth Karmapa never had another chance to receive the empowerments for these texts, and he died without realizing the dream of returning them to the Karma Kagyu.

Thaye Dorje decided to fulfill this dream. Originally, he wanted to receive the Marpa Tantras from the Chobgye Trichen himself, but the elderly lama's health did not permit him to travel. Another high-ranking Sakya lama, Ludhing Khenchen Rinpoche, agreed to present the empowerments to Thaye Dorje and to Shamar as well. After more than a century, these fifty tantric texts from Marpa and their oral teachings returned to the Kagyu lineage in a series of sessions held in a ranch house in northern California.

After receiving these empowerments, Thaye Dorje then went on to give more general teachings and empowerments to his students in California. He said he liked the United States, "in America everything is very big...I see big roads, big cars, even big people (laughter). But generally, people have open minds, which is very important for Buddhism."[11]

In the summer of 2004 Thaye Dorje made a two-month tour of Europe, giving teachings at dharma centers and holding empowerments in auditoriums in nine countries. At the beginning of the tour, Thaye Dorje consecrated the new Kalachakra stupa at Ole Nydahl's center in Malaga, Spain. This forty-foot-high stupa is one of the largest in the Western world. In Hamburg, the young lama attended a twenty-fifth anniversary celebration for Nydahl's center. Also present were Nydahl himself, the mayor, members of the city's senate, and the Lutheran Bishop of Hamburg.

In Braunschweig, Thaye Dorje blessed an abandoned factory that Nydahl's students were turning into a dharma center. In Copenhagen, he gave a forty-minute interview to Denmark's largest TV station. In Perpignan, France, the young lama attended an inter-faith conference with Christian, Jewish, and Muslim representatives. In Kuchary, Poland, he gave interviews to TV stations and to Poland's largest weekly magazine, Przekroj. In the same city Thaye Dorje also gave the empowerment of Amitabha Buddha and the Bodhisattva Vow to three thousand devotees from Poland, Russia, the Ukraine, Lithuania, and other eastern European countries.

On his plans for the future, Thaye Dorje told me that he will finish his formal education in 2006 and then devote himself to travel and teaching worldwide. "There are already many dharma centers started around the world. Maybe fifty new centers a year are started. There are a lot of eager people, a lot of intelligent people. They keep me going and give me inspiration to study and practice well so to really be able to help others."

Thaye Dorje has already become the most cosmopolitan lama in the history of the Karmapas, but his philosophy of life remains that of the first Karmapa Dusum Khyenpa or for that matter, Shakyamuni Buddha. His favorite movies are *The Lord of the Rings* series. He edits Tibetan texts on his laptop and thinks that the Internet can be a powerful tool for his teaching. "Certainly, for our Buddhist activity, I think it's quite important," he said. "What we do is we teach, so all the teachings can be written down and put on the Internet. Thanks to the Internet, our teaching can reach a wider audience. One good thing there is to see is that for youngsters, the Internet is their life. They really enjoy it, you know? If we use the net to give more information about dharma, youngsters can have better contact with the teachings."

Thaye Dorje recognizes that because of the Internet and mass media people today may suffer from data overload. But he does not think the confusion caused by too much information is a new one. "I think that's quite normal. It's not just because of the Internet, it has always been like that. To think that it's happening only now is like saying that things were perfect in the past, and that's not true."[12]

In line with the Buddhist view that time and history are cyclical—good eras alternate with unfortunate ones in an endless cycle—he considers other problems of the contemporary world as nothing new. Perhaps this is why Thaye Dorje does not propose political reforms such as programs for world peace or environmental cleanup, but instead, like his predecessors, he offers what Buddhism would consider a more fundamental approach. He thinks that international terrorism, for example, is a sign of a deep malaise of our era, a malaise that was foretold in Buddhist prophecy. "Now as it says in the Buddha's teachings, is a time of degeneration," Thaye Dorje told me. "More and more problems will arise in the future. We should take that as a reason to practice dharma and make an effort to save ourselves and all sentient beings. We should practice diligently."

Thaye Dorje's approach to practice and its final goal is rigorous but practical. He realizes that many Westerners may think that enlightenment is an impossible goal but he counsels them not to give up on it. "It's really far to reach the full enlightenment of the Buddha. We don't really have to reach that stage now though. We can reach the first Bodhisattva *bhumi* or level. We can also keep the Bodhisattva Promise and be virtuous in our thoughts and actions."

16 CONCLUSION

Thaye Dorje's View

However modestly he may express himself, Thaye Dorje has no doubt that he is the Karmapa. "The main holders of the Karma Kagyu lineage are the so-called Black Hat Karmapas and the Red Hat Karmapas. The first refers to my own line of reincarnations. The latter refers to the line of reincarnations of the Kunzig Shamarpas. In many cases the Karmapas have recognized the respective next Shamarpa and the Shamarpas in turn the next Karmapa. This is also what has occurred with my recognition.

"Of course, the whole principle of reincarnation is not easy to understand, in particular if one is not familiar with Buddhism. Normally, samsaric beings are reborn through the power of their karma and their emotions. In the case of the successive lines of the Karmapas reincarnations this is different. Taking rebirth happens due to the wish to be reborn to help sentient beings. In this way I took rebirth as the 17th Karmapa."[1]

Thaye Dorje said that he had proclaimed himself to be the Karmapa at an early age and that he had "a strong feeling that I could do something good, simply put, that I could perform the activity of the dharma and take up the challenge to teach. I had very strong confidence." He went on to say that he still had this confidence and had augmented it since he arrived in India with confidence in the way he was recognized as the Karmapa. "Just saying 'I am Karmapa' is not enough. To recognize the Karmapa, one needs proof. It takes a lot of work and intense meditation on the part of the person who is responsible for recognizing him," in this case, Shamar Rinpoche.

Is it important for the Karmapa to be recognized by the Dalai Lama? "The Dalai Lama is certainly a great man. The Karma Kagyu school, however, is an independent lineage and according to our tradition, the Karmapas have to be confirmed in this Karma Kagyu lineage and not by the Dalai Lama. There is no need for that."

Of the split in the Karma Kagyu school, he said that it is not important in the long run: "Whether there are one or two groups doesn't really matter. What matters is that people benefit and for that it is essential that the teachings transmitted in the Kagyu tradition remain intact. In fact, there is no division. Many people talk about it, yes, however, what matters is the dharma as such and the dharma is not divided. People who don't really understand the dharma think there is a division. They think about institutions. For an authentic dharma practitioner, however, there is no split. For this kind of person there is only the dharma."

Even though he has been winning in court, Shamar has been careful not to place too much importance on placing Thaye Dorje at Rumtek. "His Holiness Karmapa can perform his activity from anywhere in the world. All previous Karmapas were based in Tibet, but the sixteenth Karmapa left that behind. He established a new seat at Rumtek and did not think it was important to return to Tibet. It is not necessary to return to Rumtek now either. Yes, it would have symbolic value for devotees, but the Karmapa can have another monastery. It is the young man who is special, not the building."

Likewise, Thaye Dorje has said that he does not need to live at Rumtek or claim the symbols of the Karmapa such as the Black Crown. He has said that these objects do not have any intrinsic power, but that they gain their force from the faith of devotees:

> It was important. It was a tradition kept until the sixteenth
> Karmapa, but still only a tradition, no more than that.
> For me it is not so important. We can have it, but if we
> don't, it will not make a big difference. We say that the
> Black Crown is a symbol of Karmapa's activity, and it was
> true for that time. Now, given the right moment, even a
> baseball cap could open someone's mind. It's like a door
> handle that opens a door.[2]

Thaye Dorje has no objection to meeting his rival: "Yes, I would like to meet Ogyen Trinley if we could talk things out, why not?" He hoped that Ogyen Trinley would be able to help people by teaching Buddhism but said that "within the lineage, there can be, of course, only one Karmapa. I personally hope the issue will soon be resolved."

Whom to Believe?

It is now time to take up the question posed at the end of chapter 14: After our journey over the landscape of the controversy over the Karmapa and Rumtek monastery, do we have any more certainty than when we started?

We have traveled back in time to the early days of sectarian conflict in Tibet and we have seen how this conflict followed the lamas into exile in 1959. We have seen how the rivalry between the Dalai Lama's Gelug school and the Karmapa's Karma Kagyu spread into the Karmapa's school itself and helped split the lamas he had raised to carry on his lineage. We have seen how Tai Situ and Gyaltsab Rinpoches clashed with Shamar at Rumtek, leading to their proclamation of Ogyen Trinley, with the backing of both the Dalai Lama and his arch-enemy China.

Then, we have seen how Situ and Gyaltsab took over Rumtek monastery with the help of the corrupt state administration of Sikkim. We have heard the stories of the monks who were expelled from Rumtek on August 2, 1993 and in the days that followed. We have also learned the views of supporters of both young men who aspire to the role of seventeenth Karmapa, Ogyen Trinley and Thaye Dorje. In particular, we have heard much from Shamar Rinpoche, whose story has been little told outside of the Himalayas.

Throughout the tangled story of the problems at Rumtek, we have sought answers to the biggest questions of the Karmapa issue: Why are Buddhist lamas fighting each other over two young men and a monastery? And which side in the dispute has a better claim to truth? Tibetans spend much effort interpreting good and bad omens, but to outsiders this may seem little more than a kind of mystical "he says, she says"—his prediction letter says this, her dream-vision says that.

Perhaps more convincing to us are the methods each side has used to make its case. In some ways Situ might seem more in tune with today's world, because he embraced what are essentially tactics from contemporary electoral and issue campaigning, such as forming political action committees and forging outside alliances. By comparison, Shamar may seem old-fashioned for insisting that the reincarnation of the Karmapa must be located and confirmed using "traditional means."

However, this has not prevented Shamar from adopting what is useful in modern technology and conflict resolution to make his case for Thaye Dorje and thus, as he sees it, to preserve the tradition of an unbroken lineage of genuine Karmapas. Notably, Shamar has embraced ideas of accountability and transparency, calling for verification and testing on major issues in the Karmapa dispute by mutually acceptable, neutral authorities. He has asked that Situ's prediction letter be tested by a graphologist for authenticity; he has asked that the valuables at Rumtek be inventoried and inspected to make sure that they have not been removed or damaged; and most importantly, he has asked the Indian court system to decide who has a right to manage Rumtek monastery. Perhaps quixotically, Shamar has also, on occasion, called for Ogyen Trinley to have a bone-marrow test to determine his age, and thus to verify the charges leveled by Yoichi Shimatsu's international team of investigative journalists in 2001 that the original boy was switched with an older child back in Tibet.

While Shamar has called for openness and accountability, Tai Situ and other supporters of Ogyen Trinley have resisted calls to verify their claims in a neutral, rational setting. Ironically, for a lama who has been an innovator and modernizer in waging a wide-ranging campaign for his Karmapa candidate, when it comes to his own most significant claims, Tai Situ has fallen back on the most traditional of attitudes—blind devotion to the sacred. Throughout the controversy, Situ has asserted that all the most contentious issues of the controversy are hands-off: the authenticity of his prediction letter, the identity of the boy, the safety of the valuables at Rumtek, and the ownership of the monastery itself. His main argument has been that to verify these things would constitute sacrilege. Thus, Situ seems to offer little more than an empty reassurance to the effect: "These things are holy. Trust me."

Modern people are correct to find this rationale unconvincing. And we should know that, for centuries, Tibetans themselves have also rejected blind faith in religious leaders. It seems that when it comes to a healthy skepticism, East and West may not be so far apart.

Lessons of the Tulku System

Choosing leading lamas through reincarnation may have taken the politics out of monastic succession when the Karmapas began this practice in the Middle Ages, but some Tibetans and outside observers think that, for the last few centuries, the tulku system has created more problems than it has solved. Rarely has it functioned as in the movie *Kundun*, where as we saw at the beginning of our investigation, the Dalai Lama's incarnation was found strictly on the basis of whether the child could pass various tests to prove his authenticity as a tulku. Many lamas admit that even in old Tibet, it was the rule rather than the exception that tulkus were chosen for political reasons.

Over the centuries, more and more creative stories arose to justify questionable tulku choices. If there was a dispute, a compromise solution would be to say that there could be more than one reincarnation of a great master—"body, speech, and mind" emanations—as in the 1993 film *Little Buddha*, where two boys and a girl are all recognized as incarnations of the recently deceased Lama Dorje. Or, if a lama did not trust his disciples to choose his successor, he could choose his own reincarnation himself before his death, a so-called *ma-dey* tulku.

Two parallel lines of tulkus (with two competing incarnations) could even be "absorbed" back into one lama in the following generation. The Tibetan scholar Gene Smith has documented this in the case of the Khyentse incarnations, a line of tulkus that expanded from one original founder in the nineteenth century to several lamas living simultaneously a century later, all claiming to be Khyentse tulkus.[3] These included many respected lamas, including two prominent contemporary tulkus, Dilgo Khyentse Rinpoche and Dzongsar Khyentse Rinpoche, a young lama-filmmaker who directed the highly acclaimed 1996 film *The Cup*.

Such tulku tall-tales made the whole system of finding reincarnates look spotty to many in Tibet in the old days. Some reincarnates were known to be authentic Buddhist masters; others were simply tulkus of convenience. But after the Chinese invasion of 1950-51, and particularly in the last twenty years, things have gotten much worse, and tulkus have begun to multiply rapidly both inside China and in exile. Now, there are thousands more reincarnates than before, including such questionable cases as Stephen Seagal and Catherine Burroughs, the "Buddha from Brooklyn," both recognized as reincarnate lamas by a major Tibetan lama.

Surprisingly, considering that Tibetans believe him to be a high tulku himself, Shamar is one of the loudest critics of filling leadership positions in Tibetan Buddhism with reincarnate lamas. "I have criticized Tibetan monastery administration since I was a boy at Rumtek," Shamar told me. "Choosing tulkus has always been political. Now, this is becoming painfully clear to all. Tulkus are just bodhisattvas. They can reincarnate as humans, but also as fish or birds, for example. They do not need to be recognized officially to do their work to help sentient beings. I pray that bodhisattvas will continue to help our world. But we do not need to make them our administrative leaders. This just leads to too many fake tulkus and cheapens both religion and politics. We should slowly work to abandon this system and begin choosing leading lamas on the basis of their merit."

Shamar believes that lamas who serve as leaders of Buddhist schools or powerful monasteries should be elected by their peers, as in the case of the head lama of Bhutan, known as the Je Khenpo, or the Ganden Tripa of the Gelugpas. Both of these positions are filled by older, experienced lamas who serve a term as leader after being selected by a qualified group of other high lamas. "They are not treated like gods, but merely respected as experienced elders," Shamar said.

What about Thaye Dorje, the tulku that Shamar recognized as the reincarnation of the sixteenth Karmapa? "I know he would agree that tulkus need to be taken into the modern world and out of their environment of magic and ceremony. He's a young man. I'm sure he doesn't want to live the old kind of life, wrapped in cloth inside and locked away from the world outside."

We have seen that Thaye Dorje has said that he would like to meet Ogyen Trinley and work out the Karmapa situation together with him. Shamar supports this solution as well, and he told me that Ogyen Trinley had even contacted him in the last year to arrange a meeting. "I told the young lama that we should wait some time, and then meet in the future, once he has gained some life experience and has had a chance to look at the records of the Karmapa controversy himself. I believe that he is quite intelligent. Once he is more mature, I hope he can work for the benefit of the Karma Kagyu."

As to the future, perhaps the two young men can come up with a solution to choose the eighteenth Karmapa as well. "My responsibility as Shamarpa was to protect the Karma Kagyu lineage," Shamar told me, "to find a boy through traditional means, and to hand over the sixteenth Karmapa's property to him. Once I give Rumtek to Thaye Dorje, then my job will be finished. Rumtek may not be necessary for a Karmapa, but it is my duty to protect his legacy. After that, if he likes, he can meet with Ogyen Trinley, and the two of them can decide what to do."

Obviously, no human institution has yet come up with a perfect system of choosing its leaders. United States presidents are chosen by an unrepresentative Electoral College, and in 2000, the election was bedeviled by disputed ballots (with their famous "hanging chads") and decided by the Supreme Court in a contested process leading to years of acrimony. Corporate CEOs, school principals, union leaders, baseball team managers—all are chosen in processes subject to dispute, dissension, and discord. Perhaps we should look to the Catholic Church's selection of the popes for a model of orderly succession of wise leaders? Well, only if we are willing to ignore a past that included some sinners along with the saintly and, in the fourteenth century, dueling popes in Rome and Avignon. Today, many Catholics complain that the Pope does not represent their approach to faith and is not responsive to their views on Church reform. They call for a different way to choose their leader.

So, on balance, is the tulku system any worse than many other ways of choosing people to lead large groups? I believe that we should leave that question to the Tibetan lamas themselves. As outside observers, admirers, or followers, our role should be to get beyond the tulku mystique, and learn to judge for ourselves which Tibetan lamas or spiritual leaders anywhere are worth our full faith and trust. Some are, and some are not. Our responsibility is to learn to tell the difference.

The bodhisattva Avalokiteshvara is the patron saint of Tibet, where he is known as Chenrezig. His mantra is Om mani padme hung, and Tibetan children drink in its soothing melody with their mother's milk. The old kings of Tibet were considered to be emanations of Chenrezig, and both the Dalai Lama and the Karmapa are still seen as embodiments of Tibet's beloved bodhisattva, as we saw in chapter 5.

Legend says that when he was an eager but inexperienced bodhisattva, Chenrezig promised to help all beings reach enlightenment, a commitment he sealed with an oath: "If I ever waver from this sacred mission, may my head explode into ten pieces!" Chenrezig went to work diligently helping all beings he encountered. But after several eons, he began to realize that no matter how many beings he saved from suffering, there would be innumerable more who still suffered. He began to despair of fulfilling his vow, and wondered if he should stop trying to save others and just focus on his own enlightenment. At that point, his head split into ten pieces. Shakyamuni Buddha, looking down from the celestial realms, took pity on Chenrezig, and put him back together, but with a difference. He gave the bodhisattva ten heads, to better see and hear the suffering of all beings, along with a thousand arms to better relieve their plight.

As we investigate Tibetan lamas, other spiritual leaders, or any leader or teacher that we might choose for ourselves, we should be ready to take Chenrezig's journey. At first, we may be enthusiastic and energetic. Then, sooner or later, if our eyes are open, we will certainly become disillusioned, and our faith may break into pieces. Then comes the most crucial point. What will we do with our disillusionment? Will we take refuge in denial, and proclaim our faith loud enough to drown out our own doubt? Will we descend into cynicism, saluting our former idol with a knowing smile and a wink as we walk away? Or will we find a middle path, a way to balance skepticism and faith?

"Only a truly compassionate religious teacher is worth following," Shamar told me. "People today need to decide for themselves whether a teacher is compassionate or not. A selfish teacher might tell his students that 'west is east and if you want to follow me then you have to accept this without question. Otherwise, you will be breaking samaya.' But a compassionate teacher, like His Holiness Dalai Lama for example, will not do this."

Surprisingly, even after more than a decade of opposing the Dalai Lama's attempts to choose the Karmapa, Shamar still admires the Tibetan exile leader. "I have seen that often students ask His Holiness to tell them, from his great wisdom, something hidden, such as predicting the future. A charlatan teacher might indulge this request, or at least imply through dramatic behavior that he has some special knowledge and powers that he cannot reveal. But His Holiness Dalai Lama never does this. He sets an example for honesty in his spiritual teachings. That is why I respect him, even if we have differences when it comes to religious politics.

"His Holiness made a mistake getting involved with the Karmapa. He may have been misled at the beginning by Situ Rinpoche and his supporters that all members of the Karmapa Search Committee agreed with his boy. Later, even when the dispute began, and it became clear that I opposed Situ's choice, His Holiness persisted in supporting Situ and Ogyen Trinley, and strongly implied that the Karmapa needed to be approved by him. This was wrong. History shows that Dalai Lamas have never selected or confirmed Karmapas, and we will not accept a change now. We must have a genuine Karmapa chosen according to Karma Kagyu tradition—not for political reasons. I oppose any attempts to subvert the Karmapa for the purposes of Tibetan politics. Even so, I still support His Holiness Dalai Lama in helping the Tibetan people, as long as he follows his own Buddhist principles. He should stay out of sectarian politics, and just work purely for Tibetan freedom while teaching Buddhism around the world. That would be a noble role for him."

Shameful Means and Questionable Ends

Earlier, we speculated on 'the motives of Situ's followers. Did they campaign for him just because they were paid, or did they believe that their ambitious rinpoche was involved in something exciting and heroic? I think that it was a bit of both. Now, we should consider Situ's own probable motives. Outsiders, who are used to thinking of the highest Tibetan lamas as international paragons of non-violence, compassion, and wisdom, may be tempted to search for an altruistic motivation behind Tai Situ's actions. How could a respected lama with a 700-year history knowingly promote a Karmapa candidate on evidence he knew to be false, employing pressure tactics that obviously contradicted Buddhist ethics?

Situ has maintained that he was a devoted disciple of the sixteenth Karmapa and that his goal in selecting and promoting Ogyen Trinley, and even in taking over Rumtek, was to protect the Karma Kagyu lineage and to ensure a genuine seventeenth Karmapa. If Situ really had this view, then judging by his actions he must have believed that lofty ends would justify unethical means. How else could he justify such dirty tricks as forging a Karmapa prediction letter, bribing politicians in Sikkim, putting street toughs in monks' robes, and either encouraging—or at least failing to stop—his supporters from violently attacking not one, but two monasteries of his own order?

Taking over Rumtek seems to be the hardest to reconcile with any altruistic motivation that Situ and his supporters might have had. It seems to me that if Situ Rinpoche had only wanted to enthrone and support Ogyen Trinley as Karmapa, then he could have stopped short of taking over Rumtek. It was not necessary for the young lama to wear the Black Crown or to take over the sixteenth Karmapa's monastery to gain legitimacy. In the eyes of many Tibetans and most outsiders, Ogyen Trinley already derived all the legitimacy he needed from the Dalai Lama's support. As we have seen, in 1992 Shamar himself even wrote a letter accepting the boy on the basis of assurances from both Situ and the Dalai Lama.

Ogyen Trinley did not need to control Rumtek in order to play the role of Karmapa. He could have remained on the throne of the previous sixteen Karmapas at Tsurphu monastery and inspired growing devotion from Karma Kagyu followers inside Tibet and in exile without ever leaving there.

Later, in 2000, as we have seen, Ogyen Trinley's supporters would make the unconvincing claim that the Chinese interfered with the boy's Buddhist education and that he had to flee Tibet in order to gain his religious freedom. In 2001, the boy himself repeated this claim. Perhaps only a Cold War mindset whose first impulse is to see China as a godless totalitarian state bent on destroying all religion could induce outsiders to believe that the boy was repressed by the Chinese in light of strong evidence to the contrary. We have seen how Gyaltsen Lama, the boy's own guide across the Himalayas in his staged escape of 1999-2000, said that Ogyen Trinley was not unhappy in China. Indeed, he seems to have been quite happy under the Chinese. Reports from Tsurphu in the nineties indicated that, in an effort to win Tibetan hearts and minds, religious authorities of the Tibet Autonomous Region in Lhasa treated Ogyen Trinley like a king.

Further, at the time Situ took over Rumtek in 1993, Situ and his supporters had not yet started to criticize the Chinese. On the contrary, at the time Situ and Gyaltsab were collaborating closely with Beijing and Lhasa to install and promote their Karmapa candidate. Ogyen Trinley had been enthroned at Tsurphu the year before with Chinese help, and Situ and Gyaltsab, along with other lamas who supported Ogyen Trinley, were able to freely travel to China to see the boy for extended visits. Ogyen Trinley had everything he needed at Tsurphu because his teachers had good relations with the Chinese government.

Yet, for some reason, at the height of Situ's friendship with China and of Ogyen Trinley's glory there, Situ decided to incur the trouble and expense to stage a putsch at Rumtek in Ogyen Trinley's name. Was Ogyen

Trinley merely a pretext for Situ to take the cloister? Legally, strategically, and of course, morally, taking over the sixteenth Karmapa's monastery from the sixteenth Karmapa's own legacy administration appears to have been a grave error on Situ's part. As a result of his coup, Situ has faced years of litigation and stands to face years more, perhaps even criminal charges. The fight for Rumtek has cost Situ the goodwill of the Indian government and has handicapped Ogyen Trinley, who remains under virtual house arrest in India, unable to travel the world as Thaye Dorje has already begun to do. And Situ himself remains a target of Indian suspicion, banned from returning to Rumtek or entering the state of Sikkim. Under such restrictions, it would be difficult for either lama to preach Buddhism or spread the teachings of the Karma Kagyu school in an effective way.

Finally, how can taking a monastery by force from monks of your own lineage appointed by the master you claim to venerate, the sixteenth Karmapa, ever be a way to advance the teachings of the Buddha?

Not surprisingly, Shamar has a strong opinion about the takeover of Rumtek. "Buddhism teaches that there are Four Acts of Limitless Consequence or limitless karma," Shamar told me. "If you knowingly perform any of these acts, you do so much harm to living beings that the suffering you create cannot be calculated. One of these acts is known as Splitting the Sangha, that is, creating a division in the community of ordained practitioners—monks, nuns, and lamas. By taking over Rumtek, Situ split the Karma Kagyu sangha, turning spiritual brothers against each other, making spiritual fathers and sons into enemies. How much suffering this has created! I fear that it will take a long time to heal the deep wounds of this rash and selfish act."

If taking Rumtek was not necessary to support Ogyen Trinley as Karmapa, and if it exposed Situ to so much trouble, then why did he do it? He must have had some other motivation. We have already seen that Shamar's supporters think that it was larceny. Given that several valuable items were found to be missing from Rumtek on Situ and Gyaltsab's watch, as we have seen, I can find no other motive that appears more likely.

Yet, despite the history of his abuses well documented in the Indian press, Situ continues to claim that he has done nothing wrong, and that Ogyen Trinley is the real Karmapa. Of course, Shamar makes the same claim for Thaye Dorje. One of these two lamas must be wrong, since by tradition there should only be one Karmapa. A compromise allowing two Karmapas would seem to further undermine any credibility that the tulku system has left. We have seen strong evidence that Situ's candidate was chosen in a corrupt process marred by unnecessary haste and interference by outsiders including the governments of China and Sikkim. Given the crimes and misdemeanors committed to bolster Ogyen Trinley's candidacy, I do not see how an observer with the facts could honestly embrace the young man as the reincarnation of a high Buddhist lama.

Let us now consider the evidence for Thaye Dorje. On the plus side, he does not have the black marks on his record that Ogyen Trinley does. Yet, logically speaking, the misdeeds of Tai Situ and his party are merely evidence *against* Ogyen Trinley and not evidence *for* Thaye Dorje. Neither investigative reporting nor modern science can prove that one boy is the genuine reincarnate. And outsiders cannot be expected to find the mystical signs and portents that both candidates' supporters cite to be very convincing. So what else do we have to go on?

For now, the case for Thaye Dorje appears to rest on the strength of the assurances of Shamar and his party, and the ethical standards that they have maintained in promoting their candidate. They have not broken the law, incited violence, or colluded with outsiders as Tai Situ has.

In addition, Thaye Dorje has already shown signs of much promise as a religious leader worthy of trust and a teacher skilled enough to present the ancient and arcane tradition of Tibetan Buddhism to modern people. Interestingly, like Shamar, Thaye Dorje seems most comfortable when sharing the teachings of the Kagyu masters with an audience that does not insist on too much flash or spectacle, a strong contrast to Tai Situ's animated style. In another contrast with Situ, neither Thaye Dorje nor Shamar has shown much interest in promoting ambitious programs to solve world problems, as Tai Situ did in his short-lived Pilgrimage for Active Peace in the late 1980s. Instead, both lamas have called and continue to call on their students to meditate earnestly in order to get themselves out of the cycle of cyclic existence and suffering Buddhists call samsara.

This may be a different way of thinking than we are used to, but I believe this approach harmonizes better with Buddhism's bottom-up path to happiness, to change the world by helping people change themselves.

Ever since the European Enlightenment, the world has been treated to one system after another to reform society en masse—humanism, secularism, Marxism, popular revolution, environmentalism, and post-colonialism, to name only a few. Indeed, up until now there has been no shortage of political and social philosophies to change the behavior of large groups of people and thus improve our world. I am willing to bet that the supply of reform movements will probably not run out anytime soon either.

While the past century has brought much progress in solving human problems, it has also brought human suffering on a level unparalleled in history: two world wars; two atomic bombs; the Holocaust; massive deaths under Stalin and Mao; the nuclear brinksmanship of the Cold War; continued war, famine, and disease in Africa; and the spread of AIDS around the world. Now, we face the twin apocalyptic threats of international terrorism and global environmental collapse. If all our reform movements were unable to prevent such tragedies, can we say that they have made humans happier as a whole?

Many today believe that Buddhism should spur social reform. But Buddhism teaches something else than this. Though its ethics can be used to create better governments or organizations, improving today's world is not the primary purpose of Buddhism.

Shakyamuni Buddha taught that life is suffering, or more subtly, that life is unsatisfactory. Did he say that with a little bit more altruism or creativity applied to good works and well-designed social programs we can eliminate suffering? No—he said that life is always, by definition, suffering, because humans and all other beings cling to mistaken ideas that we and our physical world exist as we see them. This insight is what makes Buddhism truly radical; it goes to the root of the problem, our own emotions of anger, greed, and apathy. Indeed, a Buddhism that finds the cause of suffering in our own minds and hearts is more radical than any revolutionary credo that merely tries to improve the outside world could ever be.

It was not an accident that Tibet, the world's most complete buddhacracy, had as its greatest heroes neither enlightened rulers nor great social reformers, but uncompromising meditators such as Milarepa. After a life of worldly troubles, Milarepa sought a qualified spiritual master and then retreated to a cave to meditate, alone. When he was with others, he never stopped teaching that worldly affairs were a waste of precious time that could be better spent in meditation. "Life is short and the time of death is uncertain, so apply yourself to meditation," he exhorted.

There is a lesson here. And it is not that all Buddhists should retire from the world as Milarepa did. The lesson is a more subtle one, and I believe that it is this: If we reduce Buddhism to yet another philosophy of improvement to spawn yet more social programs, whether Tibetan nationalism or world peace, we drain it of its vitality. As the *Dhammapada* puts it, "The gift of the dharma surpasses all gifts; the taste of the dharma surpasses all tastes; the joy of the dharma surpasses all joys; extinguish desire, and all suffering passes."[4]

Where Are They Now?

Thaye Dorje is finishing his studies at the Karma Shri Diwakar Institute of Higher Buddhist Studies in Kalimpong, in the eastern Himalayas just south of Sikkim. He spent the summer of 2005 teaching in Europe, and made news by appearing at an interfaith ceremony with the Bishop of London. He hopes to make a trip to the United States in the next two or three years to teach at centers established by Shamar Rinpoche and by the Nydahls.

Shamar Rinpoche continues to lead the effort of the Karmapa Charitable Trust to regain Rumtek. In July 2004, after six years of hearings in a case that his current lawyers say was badly mishandled by earlier attorneys, major preliminary issues were resolved in Shamar's favor by the Indian Supreme Court (see the text of its decision in appendix B). It seems likely that the main case will soon be heard by the District Court in Gangtok.

Khenpo Chodrak teaches at the Karmapa International Buddhist Institute in New Delhi. The school was closed for renovations starting in mid-2005 and will reopen in Fall 2006 to international students seeking to study Karma Kagyu Buddhism.

Ogyen Trinley is finishing his studies at Gyuto Tantric College in Sidbhari in Himachal Pradesh in northwestern India while presenting teachings and meeting with devotees. The Indian government continues to prevent him from traveling abroad and restricts his travels in India. In 2004, he attended the funeral of Bokar Rinpoche at Mirik just over the state line from Sikkim and only a few hours from Rumtek. But the Indian government refused to let him go into Sikkim or to Rumtek. In the last couple years, as we have seen, he has had contact with Shamar

Rinpoche. Shamar is confident that the young lama, whom he refers to as "Ogyen Trinley Rinpoche," will turn out to be a strong advocate among the Tibetan exile leadership for the interests of the Karma Kagyu.

Tai Situ Rinpoche lives at his monastery Sherab Ling in Himachal Pradesh, not far from Ogyen Trinley.

Gyaltsab Rinpoche lives at his monastery Ralang, a few hours from Rumtek in Sikkim.

APPENDIX A:
BUDDHISM AND THE KARMAPAS

Chronology of Buddhism and the Karmapas

Glossary

Who Recognized the First Sixteen Karmapas?

CHRONOLOGY OF BUDDHISM AND THE KARMAPAS

Fifth century B.C. Shakyamuni Buddha reaches enlightenment while sitting under the Bodhi Tree in present day Bodh Gaya, India.

779 A.D. Padmasambhava, a missionary from India, establishes Samye, the first Buddhist monastery in Tibet.

1110 The first Karmapa Dusum Khyenpa is born.

1185 Dusum Khyenpa founds Tsurphu monastery and the Karma Kagyu school.

1358-1642 Pagmotru, Rinpung, and Tsangpa Dynasties rule Central Tibet under the tutelage of the Kagyu school and the Karmapas.

1408 Chinese Ming Dynasty Emperor Chengzu presents the Black Crown to the fifth Karmapa.

1642 The fifth Dalai Lama assumes the throne of Central Tibet with military backing of the Qoshot Mongols under Gushri Khan. The new government forcibly converts hundreds of Nyingma and Kagyu monasteries to the Dalai Lama's Gelug order.

1792 The tenth Shamarpa dies in Nepal and the Qianlong emperor of China bans his future reincarnations. Many of his monasteries are confiscated and his monks forcibly converted to the Gelug order.

1924 The sixteenth Karmapa Rangjung Rigpe Dorje is born.

1950-51 The Chinese People's Liberation Army invades and conquers Tibet.

1959 Nearly a hundred thousand Tibetans, including the Dalai Lama, the sixteenth Karmapa, and other high lamas flee Tibet.

1962 The Karmapa Charitable Trust is formed to manage the assets of the Karmapas after the death of the sixteenth Karmapa and until the seventeenth Karmapa reaches adulthood.

1966 The sixteenth Karmapa opens Rumtek monastery in Sikkim as his seat-in-exile.

1964-1973 Gyalo Thondup tries to unite all five religious schools of Tibet under his brother the Dalai Lama through the United Party initiative.

1974 First visit of the sixteenth Karmapa to Europe and the United States. While the Karmapa is away, Tai Situ leaves Rumtek to start his own monastery.

1975 Thrangu Rinpoche resigns as Rumtek abbot and leaves to start his own monastery.

November 5, 1981 The sixteenth Karmapa dies at age fifty-eight in a cancer hospital outside of Chicago.

May 6, 1983 Birth in Lhasa of Tenzin Khyentse, whom Shamar Rinpoche later recognizes as the seventeenth Karmapa, giving him the name Thaye Dorje.

June 26, 1985 Birth in rural Kham of Apo Gaga, whom Tai Situ later recognizes as the seventeenth Karmapa under the name Ogyen Trinley.

September 1989 As he would later claim, Tai Situ discovers the letter written by the sixteenth Karmapa predicting his rebirth.

March and November 1990 The Karmapa Search Committee holds two meetings in New Delhi. Situ Rinpoche does not present his letter at either meeting.

March 19, 1992 Situ presents his Karmapa prediction letter to a meeting of the Karmapa Search Committee at Rumtek. Shamar, Jamgon, and Rumtek General Secretary Topga express doubts about its authenticity and call for testing.

April 1992 With permission of the Chinese government, Situ and Gyaltsab send out two search parties to find the boy in Tai Situ's prediction letter.

June 9, 1992 The Dalai Lama confirms the recognition of Ogyen Trinley as Karmapa.

June 29, 1992 The Chinese government approves the recognition of Ogyen Trinley as the "Living Buddha Karmapa."

September 22, 1992 Ogyen Trinley is enthroned at Tsurphu monastery. No representative from either Rumtek or the Karmapa Trust is present, but thousands of devotees and dozens of Chinese officials attend.

August 2, 1993 With assistance from the state government of Sikkim, Situ and Gyaltsab take over Rumtek monastery and expel the monks of the sixteenth Karmapa and officials of the Karmapa Trust.

January 26, 1994 Shamar announces that he has found his own Karmapa candidate, Thaye Dorje, in Tibet.

March 17, 1994 The Karmapa Institute in New Delhi hosts a welcome ceremony for Thaye Dorje that is·disrupted by a violent protest by supporters of Ogyen Trinley.

August 2, 1994 While traveling abroad, Tai Situ is banned from reentering the country for "Anti-India activities."

July 31, 1998 The Karmapa Trust files its first civil case to regain possession of Rumtek and its valuables.

August 1998 The ban on Situ returning to India is lifted. But soon afterwards the government issues a permanent order excluding him from nine northeastern states, including Sikkim, on national security grounds.

December 1999 Thaye Dorje makes his first trip abroad, visiting Southeast Asia and Europe.

January 2000 Ogyen Trinley arrives in India with a story of escape from the Chinese authorities. The Indian press challenges major details of his account.

2003 Thaye Dorje completes his formal education and prepares for a career of teaching and traveling.

July 5, 2004 The Indian Supreme Court decides the major preliminary issue in the case over possession of Rumtek in favor of the Karmapa Trust. Soon after, the Trust asks a Sikkim court to restore Rumtek to its management.

May 30, 2005 In New Zealand, the High Court in Auckland decides in favor of followers of Thaye Dorje in a property rights dispute with supporters of Ogyen Trinley.

GLOSSARY

bodhisattva (Sanskrit, lit., "enlightenment being") An advanced spiritual practitioner who remains in the physical world to help others, or, more generally, any person who promises to achieve enlightenment for the benefit of others.

Buddha (Sanskrit, lit., "Enlightened One") A person who has realized the nature of reality and has full knowledge of the open, dynamic nature of all phenomena. Buddhists believe that there have been numerous Buddhas in the past and that others will follow, but that the Buddha for our era was Shakyamuni, "the sage of the Shakyas," who lived in northern India around the fifth century B.C.

Chogyal (Tibetan, lit., "King of Dharma") The title of the Namgyal dynasty rulers of the tiny eastern Himalayan kingdom of Sikkim from 1642 until India annexed Sikkim in 1975.

Dalai Lama The effective leader of the Gelugpa order (though its formal leader is the Ganden Tri Rinpoche). The Dalai Lamas controlled the government of Central Tibet from 1642 until the current fourteenth Dalai Lama Tenzin Gyatso fled the Chinese in 1959. Since 1959, the Dalai Lama has run the Tibetan Government-in-Exile based in Dharamsala in the Himalayan foothills of northwestern India.

dakini (Sanskrit) A female meditational deity, sometimes called a Buddhist angel, representing the inspiring power of consciousness.

dharma (Sanskrit, lit., "carrying, holding") The teachings of the Buddha, comparable to the Christian term "Gospel." More generally, phenomena.

Ganden Phodrang (Tibetan) The formal name of the Dalai Lama's government of Central Tibet from. 1642 until 1959. Since 1959, the term has been applied to the Dalai Lama's Tibetan Government-in-Exile in Dharamsala, India.

Gelug (Tibetan, lit., "Joyous Way" or "Ganden Way") The last of the four main schools of Buddhism founded in Tibet. Begun in 1409 by Tsongkhapa, the school later produced both the Dalai Lamas and the Panchen Lamas. Its three large monasteries of Sera, Drepung, and Ganden came to dominate Lhasa after the fifth Dalai Lama took control of the government of Central Tibet in 1642.

Gyalwa (Tibetan, lit., "Victorious") An honorific term applied to the Karmapas.

Kagyu (Tibetan, lit., "Hearing Lineage") The third of the four major schools of Buddhism founded in Tibet. It originated in the eleventh century with the householder yogi Marpa the Translator (1012-1097). The Kagyu developed at least twelve separate lineages, most originating with Gampopa (1079-1153).

Karma Kagyu (Tibetan, lit., "Hearing Lineage of the Karmapas") The largest sub-school of the Kagyu, established by the first Karmapa Dusum Khyenpa in 1185 when he founded Tsurphu monastery, which became the seat of the Karmapas.

Karmapa (Tibetan, lit., "Man of Enlightened Activity") The highest lama of the Karma Kagyu lineage and the first reincarnate lama or tulku of Tibet, whose line began in the eleventh century with the first Karmapa Dusum Khyenpa (1110-1194.)

Kham (Tibetan) A large, fertile area located in the borderland between central Tibet and China, traditionally independent from both governments. Since 1642, when the Dalai Lama took power in Central Tibet, Kham has served as the power base of the Karma Kagyu. Today, the western section of Kham is included in the Tibet Autonomous Region while eastern Kham has been absorbed into the Chinese provinces of Sichuan, Yunnan, and Qinghai.

khata (Tibetan) A silk offering scarf, usually woven with traditional religious symbols.

khenpo (Tibetan) A degree awarded by traditional schools of Buddhist philosophy equivalent to a Ph.D. or doctor of divinity in the Kagyu and other religious schools of Tibet. Equivalent to a geshe in the Gelug school.

KIBI The Karmapa International Buddhist Institute, a school in New Delhi to train international students in Buddhist philosophy. It was started by the sixteenth Karmapa before his death in 1981 and completed by Shamar Rinpoche.

KTC The Karmapa Charitable Trust, established by the sixteenth Karmapa in 1962 to manage his assets after his death and before his next reincarnation—the seventeenth Karmapa—would be found and reach the age of twenty-one.

labrang (Tibetan) Originally the personal household of a high lama, it came to refer to the monastic corporation that held the assets of a line of reincarnate lamas after the death of one incarnation and until the majority of the successor.

lama (Tibetan, lit., "none above") A religious teacher. Lamas can be either monks or laypeople.

lineage A succession of teachers who have passed down oral teachings to their students, usually originating with Shakyamuni Buddha or with a meditational deity seen by an advanced practitioner in a vision. Buddhists value an unbroken oral lineage because its teachings carry invaluable blessings of all the previous masters in that lineage that only a qualified lineage master can convey to his or her students.

Mahamudra (Sanskrit, lit., "Great Seal") In the Kagyu school, the most advanced practice of meditation, or more generally, the path to enlightenment.

Mahayana (Sanskrit, lit., "Great Vehicle") The type of Buddhism practiced in East Asian countries including China, Korea, Japan, and Vietnam as well as in the Himalayas, where it is called the Vajrayana. It is the path of the bodhisattva, where practitioners try to reach enlightenment not only for their own benefit, but to help all beings. Often contrasted with the Theravada ("The Way of the Elders") Buddhism of Southeast Asia, or with a straw-man version of the Theravada known as the Hinayana ("The Lesser Vehicle"), both of which Mahayana adherents see as paths to individual enlightenment only, without helping others.

Madhyamaka (Sanskrit, lit., "Middle Way") A philosophical view usually expressed in the negative, as a position between two extremes of positivism (that everything exists the way it appears to the mind and the senses, a view that can lead to complacency) and nihilism (that all phenomena are illusory, a view which can lead to despair or megalomania).

Nalanda Institute The monk's college at Rumtek, named for the first Buddhist university which operated in northern India during the Middle Ages.

-pa (Tibetan) Suffix that can be attached to a proper noun to make it refer to a person, for example Gelugpa (a member of the Gelug school) or Khampa (someone from Kham).

PLA The People's Liberation Army of Communist China.

puja (Sanskrit) A ritual prayer ceremony. In Tibetan Buddhism, a puja may involve visualizing a bodhisattva or meditational deity and reciting mantras or a liturgy.

Rinpoche (Tibetan, lit. "precious one" or "precious jewel") A title of respect for lamas who are considered to have achieved a high level of spiritual realization. Sometimes the title is recognized as purely honorary.

Rumtek The monastery founded in Sikkim by the sixteenth Karmapa after his escape into exile in 1959.

samadhi (Sanskrit, lit., "establish, make firm") A state of deep meditative concentration said to be peaceful and joyful.

samaya (Sanskrit) An advanced vow in the Vajrayana, a bond between a teacher and a student of serious tantric practice. The vow should only be taken after careful consideration, since to break it can lead to lifetimes of suffering. Often misunderstood, ordinary devotees are not bound by samaya.

samsara (Sanskrit, lit., "journeying") The state of physical existence, described as a cycle of an unending cycle of birth, death, and rebirth entailing various degrees of suffering.

sangha (Sanskrit, lit., "crowd, host") The community of ordained Buddhist practitioners, primarily monks and nuns. In the West, the term is often used more generally to refer to people who practice Buddhism.

shamatha (Sanskrit, lit., "dwelling in tranquility"; Tibetan, shi'nay) Mental-calming or tranquility meditation considered preliminary to higher forms of meditation and spiritual practice in Tibetan Buddhism.

Shakyamuni (Sanskrit, lit., "Sage of the Shakya Clan") Epithet of Siddhartha Gautama, the historical Buddha, who lived in northern India in the fifth century B.C.

TAR The Tibet Autonomous Region, the government of the central area of Tibet established by the Chinese in 1965 to cover most of the geographic area ruled by the Dalai Lama's Central Tibetan government before 1959.

thangka (Tibetan) A religious painting done on a scroll and usually framed by silk.

tulku (Tibetan, lit., "transformation body") Generally, a reincarnate lama, though it can also refer to a religious object such as a statue or a painting that has been blessed so that it is considered to contain the spirit of the deity it portrays. Like "rinpoche," tulku is often given as an honorary title.

Vajra Mukut (Sanskrit and Tibetan) Also known as the Vajra Crown or the Black Crown of the Karmapas. Originally given to the fifth Karmapa Deshin Shegpa (1384-1415) by the Chinese Ming dynasty emperor Chengzu, also known as Yongle (1403-1424), in the fifteenth century. Later, in the seventeenth century, the king of Li Jiang gave a replica of the crown to the tenth Karmapa Choying Dorje.

Vajrayana (Sanskrit, lit., "Diamond Vehicle") The form of Mahayana Buddhism practiced in the Himalayas, sometimes called Tantric Buddhism and known for powerful practices that can help a person achieve enlightenment in a single lifetime.

vipashyana (Sanskrit; Pali, *vipassana*; Tibetan, *lhaktong*) Insight or analytic meditation, considered an advanced practice in the Tibetan tradition.

Yarney (Tibetan) Annual rainy season retreat begun by Shakyamuni Buddha and continued by many Buddhist traditions to this day. In the Himalayas, the retreat begins with an opening ceremony, reserved for ordained monks only, known as the Sojong.

WHO RECOGNIZED THE
FIRST SIXTEEN KARMAPAS?

The Karmapas were the first reincarnate lamas, or tulkus, of Tibetan Buddhism. They began this tradition in the twelfth century, nearly three hundred years before the appearance of the Dalai Lamas. The lamas who recognized the Karmapas always came from the Kagyu school, and usually from the Karmapa's own Karma Kagyu sub-school. The lamas who recognized the most Karmapas were the Shamarpas, with six recognitions, five alone and one with another lama, Tai Situ. The Tai Situs recognized the second highest number of Karmapas: two alone and two more working with other lamas, for a total of four. Gyaltsabs recognized two Karmapas working alone.

No Dalai Lama or other lama from the Gelugpa order or one of the other schools of Tibetan Buddhism ever recognized a Karmapa in the past.

The table below lists each Karmapa through the sixteenth along with the lama who recognized him. This information is taken from a chart submitted in 2004 by Geoffrey Samuel, professor of anthropology at the University of Newcastle in Australia, as part of an affidavit in the case of *Lama vs. Hope and Ors.* in the High Court of New Zealand, Auckland Registry. Samuel's primary source was the 1976 book *Karmapa: The Black Hat Lama of Tibet* by Nik Douglas and Meryl White. "For the first thirteen Karmapas," Samuel wrote, "their account is based on the *Zla ba chu Shel gyi phreng ba* ('Moon Water Crystal Rosary') by the 8th Situ, Chokyi Jungne (1700-74), supplemented by two earlier sources. For the 14th to 16th Karmapas, it is based on the spoken commentary of the 16th Karmapa. Both sources should be acceptable to all parties in the present dispute."

KARMAPA	RECOGNIZED BY
1st Dusum Khyenpa (1110-1193)	Gampopa
2nd Karma Pakshi (1204-1283)	Pomdrakpa
3rd Rangjung Dorje (1284-1339)	Urgyenpa
4th Rolpe Dorje (1340-1383)	Konchok Rinchen
5th Deshin Shegpa (1384-1415)	2nd Shamar Khacho Wangpo
6th Tongwa Donden (1416-1453)	3rd Shamar Chopal Yeshe
7th Chodrag Gyamtso (1454-1506)	1st Gyaltsab Goshir Paljor Dondrub
8th Mikyo Dorje (1507-1554)	3rd Situ Tashi Paljor
9th Wangchuk Dorje (1556-1603)	5th Shamar Konchok Yenlak and 4th Situ Chokyi Goha
10th Choying Dorje (1604-1674)	6th Shamar Mipham Chokyi Wangchuk
11th Yeshe Dorje (1676-1702)	7th Shamar Yeshe Nyingpo
12th Changchub Dorje (1703-1732)	8th Shamar Palchen Chokyi Dondrub
13th Dudul Dorje (1733-1797)	7th Gyaltsab Kunchok Oser
14th Thegchog Dorje (1798-1868)	9th Situ Pema Nyinge Wangpo
15th Khakyab Dorje (1871-1922)	9th Drukchen Mingyur Wong Gi Dorje
16th Rangjung Rigpe Dorje (1924-1981)	11th Situ Pema Wangchuk Gyalpo and 2nd Jamgon Kongtrul

APPENDIX B:
ANALYSIS OF ORIGINAL DOCUMENTS

Decision of the Indian Supreme Court

Analysis of Tai Situ's Prediction Letter

**Rao Report to the Indian Cabinet on
the Coup at Rumtek Monastery**

DECISION OF THE INDIAN SUPREME COURT
July 5, 2004

This decision was the culmination of the case that the Karmapa Charitable Trust filed in 1998 to regain control of Rumtek monastery. In this decision, given in the case of *Tsurphu Labrang vs. Karmapa Charitable Trust and Ors.*, announced in New Delhi on July 5, 2004, the court refused to hear the appeal of the Tsurphu Labrang, a group created by Gyaltsab Rinpoche and Tenzin Namgyal to represent the claims of followers of Ogyen Trinley to manage Rumtek in legal proceedings. The court rejected their Special Leave Petition to this effect. By thus refusing to interfere in the earlier decision of the Sikkim District Court and a subsequent confirmation by the High Court in New Delhi, the Supreme Court allowed the original decision to stand—meaning that the Tsurphu group had no legal claim to Rumtek, and that the Karmapa Charitable Trust was the only group recognized to manage the monastery.

SLP(C)No. 22903 OF 2003
ITEM No.41 Court No. 5 SECTION XIV
A/N MATTER

SUPREME COURT OF INDIA

RECORD OF PROCEEDINGS

Petition(s) for Special Leave to Appeal (Civil) No.22903/2003
(From the judgement and order dated 26/08/2003 in WP 5/03
of The HIGH COURT OF SIKKIM at Gangtok)

TSHURPHU LABRANG Petitioner (s)
VERSUS
KARMAPA CHARITABLE TRUST & ORS. Respondent (s)
(With Appln(s). for permission to place addl. documents Vol.III
to VI and exemption from filing O.T. and clarification and
directions and with prayer for interim relief and office report)

Date : 05/07/2004 This Petition was called on for hearing today.
CORAM :
HON'BLE MR. JUSTICE S.N. VARIAVA
HON'BLE MR. JUSTICE ARIJIT PASAYAT

For Petitioner (s) Mr. A.B. Saharya, Sr. Adv.
Mr. Sudarshan Misra, Sr. Adv.
Mr. Naresh Mathur, Adv.
Mr. Sudarsh Menon, Adv.
For Respondent (s) Mr. Parag Tripathy, Sr. Adv.
Mr. Parveen Agarwal, Adv.
Mr. Somnath Mukherjee, Adv.
Mr. S.S. Hamal, Adv.
Mr. Kamal Jetely, Adv.
Mr. Gurpreet Singh, Adv.
Mr. Jayant, Adv.
Mr. Harish N. Salve, Sr. Adv.
Mr. Deepak K. Thakur, Adv.
Mr. K.V.Mohan, Adv.

Mr. Brijender Chahar, Adv.
Mrs. Jyoti Chahar, Adv.
Mr. Ashok Mathur, Adv.

UPON hearing counsel the Court made the following
ORDER
Mr. B.S. Chahar, learned counsel states that the State of Sikkim does
not desire to file affidavit.
We see no reason to interfere. The Special Leave Petition is dismissed.
We, however, clarify that the trial court will not take into consideration
any observations made in the impugned order or in the order of the
District Judge dismissing the application.

(K.K. Chawla) Court Master
(Jasbir Singh) Court Master

Analysis of Tai Situ's Prediction Letter

At a meeting of the Karmapa Search Committee held at Rumtek on March 19, 1992, Tai Situ Rinpoche presented a letter that he claimed was given to him by the sixteenth Karmapa before his death. After the meeting, the Rumtek administration made a detailed study of the letter to determine its authenticity. Below are their major findings, as published in *The Karmapa Papers*, 71-73.

Analysis of the Prediction Letter

As mentioned earlier, there have been doubts expressed about the letter presented by Situ Rinpoche on March 19, 1992. Is it the authentic testimonial letter of H. H. the 16th Gyalwa Karmapa?

Unfortunately, we only had a copy of *the* letter, not the original. Nevertheless we examined the copy to see what might have brought about these doubts. Some seem to suspect Situ Rinpoche of having written *the* letter himself, so we included in our analysis those of his letters available to us.

General remarks about the letter:

In several places the text seems to be damaged by humidity. Traces of a vertical fold can be seen in the middle of the paper. Horizontally the letter seems to have been folded in at least three places: below the third and the eighth line of the text and above the seal. This last fold can also be deduced because traces of the seal are found above it.

Although the writing in the part above the seal is blurred to such an extent as to be illegible, there seem to be no traces of ink on the seal itself.

Fortunately, we had more than 30 letters handwritten by H. H. the 16th Karmapa dating from the 1970's to 1981, shortly before he passed away. We asked several Tibetans for comparison who confirmed that *the* letter, at first sight, looked as if it were written by His Holiness. But this impression seemed to vanish the more they went into details, especially for people very familiar with H. H. the 16th Karmapa's handwriting. What follows are comparisons as to: 1) the *signature,* 2) the *handwriting* and *spelling,* 3) the *letterhead.*

1) Signature:

The signature on *the* letter is almost entirely covered by the seal. From what little was visible on our copy, the signature might be different from those we found on H. H. the 16th Karmapa's letters. This impresssion is strengthened when the signatures are superimposed by computer.

Signature on *the* prediction letter   Examples of Karmapa's signature as found on his letters

2) Handwriting and Spelling:

Only a forensic test of the original letter could definitely prove whether the handwriting on the letter is that of H. H. the 16th Karmapa or not.

- Nevertheless we compared the handwriting of the letter with that of Karmapa and Situ Rinpoche: There seem to be differences between the script in the letter and the handwriting in Karmapa´s letters we had. On the other hand, one could find similarities when comparing the letter´s script with Situ Rinpoche's handwriting (see two examples in the tables below; the syllables used for comparison are marked in the respective letters).
- For differences in the spelling of the word "drub" see table below: In line #6 of the letter, this word is written with the second postscript "sa". We did not find this misspelling in any of H. H. Karmapa's letters, whereas it is to be found in a letter by Situ Rinpoche (see Doc T5)

	as written by H. H. the 16th Karmapa	as written by Situ Rinpoche	as written in "the" letter
• the syllable "phyogs"			
• two examples of the vocal "e"			
• the syllable "drub"			

The above examples were taken from the letters below (see part D, 4 for enlarged reproductions):

The letter

Letter by Situ Rinpoche

Letter by Situ Rinpoche

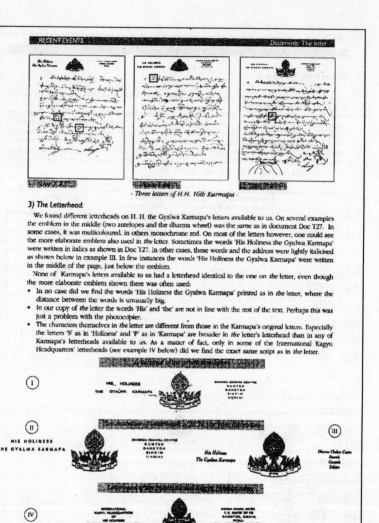

- Three letters of H.H. 16th Karmapa -

3) The Letterhead:

We found different letterheads on H. H. the Gyalwa Karmapa's letters available to us. On several examples the emblem in the middle (two antelopes and the dharma wheel) was the same as in document Doc T27. In some cases, it was multicoloured, in others monochrome red. On most of the letters however, one could see the more elaborate emblem also used in *the* letter. Sometimes the words 'His Holiness the Gyalwa Karmapa' were written in italics as shown in Doc T27. In other cases, these words and the address were lightly italicised as shown below in example III. In few instances the words 'His Holiness the Gyalwa Karmapa' were written in the middle of the page, just below the emblem.

None of Karmapa's letters available to us had a letterhead identical to the one on *the* letter, even though the more elaborate emblem shown there was often used:

- In no case did we find the words 'His Holiness the Gyalwa Karmapa' printed as in *the* letter, where the distance between the words is unusually big.
- In our copy of *the* letter the words 'His' and 'the' are not in line with the rest of the text. Perhaps this was just a problem with the photocopier.
- The characters themselves in *the* letter are different from those in the Karmapa's original letters. Especially the letters 'S' as in 'Holiness' and 'P' as in 'Karmapa' are broader than in any of Karmapa's letterheads available to us. As a matter of fact, only in some of the International Kagyu Headquarters' letterheads (see example IV below) did we find the exact same script as in *the* letter.

RAO REPORT TO THE INDIAN CABINET ON THE COUP AT RUMTEK MONASTERY

On May 24, 1997, K. Sreedhar Rao, an Indian government official stationed in Sikkim, submitted a fourteen-page report to the secretary of the Indian cabinet in New Delhi, T.S.R. Subramaniam. The report was marked "secret" on each page and its subject was the situation at Rumtek and its implications for relations between India and China. Rao began his term as chief secretary during N.B. Bhandari's final term as chief minister of Sikkim. But unlike officials of the local government, Rao was not elected by Sikkim

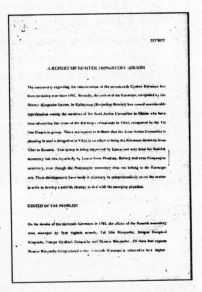

voters or appointed by Bhandari. Under India's federal system, a chief secretary serves as the representative of the central government in each of India's twenty-eight states, and the office is filled by appointment from New Delhi. Thus, as a federal appointee, Rao was independent of the local Sikkim administration and was able to criticize its behavior when he concluded that it threatened the national security interests of the country as a whole. The text of his report is reproduced in full below, staring with Rao's original cover letter.

K. SREEDHAR RAO, IAS
CHIEF SECRETARY

CAMP: Government of Sikkim
Sikkim House
12, Panchsheel Marg
Chanakyapuri, New Delhi-110021

No. SM/4(2)/CS/
Dated: 24.5.1997

Dear Shri

I had sent a brief report to you on the Rumtek situation on 10.12.96. Taking into account certain recent developments I have carried out a more detailed assessment outlining possible options before us. I am sending herewith this assessment for your kind perusal. I am endorsing copies of this both to the DIB and the Chairman JIC with whom I have discussed this matter.

Yours sincerely,
Sd/-
(K. SREEDHAR RAO)

SHRI T.S.R. SUBRAMANIAM,
Cabinet Secretary,
Government of India,
NEW DELHI.

A REPORT ON RUMTEK MONASTERY—SIKKIM

The controversy regarding the reincarnation of the seventeenth Gyalwa Karmapa has been persisting ever since 1992. Recently, the arrival of the Karmapa, recognized by the Shamar Rinpoche faction, in Kalimpong (Darjeeling District) has caused considerable apprehension among the members of the Joint Action Committee in Sikkim who have been advocating the cause of the Karmapa reincarnate in Tibet, recognized by the Tai Situ Rinpoche group. There are reports to indicate that the Joint Action Committee is planning to send a delegation to Tibet in an effort to bring the Karmapa incarnate from Tibet to Rumtek. This group is being supported by Lamas not only from the Rumtek monastery but also reportedly by Lamas from Phodong, Ralang and even Pemyangtse monastery, even though the Pemyangtse monastery does not belong to the Karmapa sect. These developments have made it necessary to comprehensively assess the matter in order to develop a suitable strategy to deal with the emerging situation.

Genesis Of The Problem

On the demise of the sixteenth Karmapa in 1981, the affairs of the Rumtek monastery were managed by four regents, namely, Tai Situ Rinpoche, Jamgon Kongtrul Rinpoche, Tsurphu Gyaltsab Rinpoche and Shamar Rinpoche. Of these four regents Shamar Rinpoche being related to the sixteenth Karmapa is believed to be a higher reincarnate Lama occupying a position next only to the Karmapa himself, whereas the other regents occupy lower position in hierarchy. While the monastery's affairs with respect to religious practices were to be looked after by these four regents, the temporal affairs of the monastery were to be looked after by a trust. Before the demise of the sixteenth Karmapa he was the sole trustee and after his demise, a body of seven trustees was constituted and duly registered to manage the affairs of the monastery and its property. Shamar Rinpoche, Tai Situ Rinpoche, Jamgon Kongtrul Rinpoche and Jigdal Densapa (a former Additioinal Chief Secretary of Govt. of Sikkim), Mr. Gyaltshen (another ex-bureaucrat), Topga Yugyal from Bhutan, a representative of Dabur and Company and Gyan Jyoti from Nepal were all the trustees. This body of trustees used to meet regularly after the demise of the Gyalwa Karmapa and the affairs of the monastery and its properties were being administered in an organized manner. This trust consisting of the above mentioned trustees continues to exist and has been as mentioned above duly registered in India.

The task of finding the seventeenth reincarnate Gyalwa Karmapa however was the collective responsibility of the four regents mentioned above.

In March, 1992 Tai Situ Rinpoche appears to have declared that the letter of prediction about the reincarnation left behind by the Gyalwa Karmapa has been found and the regents should take action to find the reincarnation in accordance with the letter. The regents had apparently met and studied the letter and informed some lay people as also the trustees, of the discovery. However, it is reported that even at that point of time the authenticity of the letter was questioned by some of the trustees and more particularly by Shamar Rinpoche who had pointed out that the letter was not in the handwriting of the sixteenth Gyalwa Karmapa, that there are a number of grammatical and other errors and there could be doubts whether the letter was written prior to the demise of the sixteenth Gyalwa Karmapa. It appears that in view of this doubt the regents resolved to consider the matter further and postponed a decision on the identification of the reincarnation for about seven months. In fact a demand seems to have been raised that this letter supposedly left behind by the sixteenth Karmapa should be subjected to a forensic test but Tai Situ was evasive about this.

In spite of the agreed waiting period mentioned above, taking advantage of the absence of Shamar Rinpoche, the Tai Situ group seems to have organized an expedition to Tibet to identify the reincarnation. This was a violation of the collective responsibility that had been cast upon the four regents to find the reincarnation. In the meanwhile one of the regents, namely, Jamgon Kongtrul met with an accident and died allegedly under suspicious circumstances. It is also alleged that the Government of Sikkim did not conduct a proper inquiry into the matter. Normally, the identification of a reincarnation is apparently a fairly detailed and lengthy procedure involving a number of tests. Reportedly the whole identification in Tibet was carried through in Tibet within a very short while and the reincarnation was taken from the village Bakor in the Kham province of Tibet where the identification took place, to Lhasa and then on to Tsurphu monastery, the original seat of the Karmapas, and formally installed with the active assistance of the Chinese authorities. It is also reported that the reincarnation accompanied by Tai Situ Rinpoche was given a highly visible, ostentatious reception by the Chinese in Lhasa as well as in the Tsurphu monastery.

Having installed the reincarnate in Tsurphu monastery, a message was sent to His Holiness the Dalai Lama who was then in Brazil attending the Rio Earth Summit. The Dalai Lama accepted the discovery as the reincarnation of the sixteenth Gyalwa Karmapa possibly because it was claimed that the reincarnation had been identified unanimously and there was no controversy whatsoever.

The reason as to why His Holiness the Dalai Lama approved the reincarnation in a hurried manner and that also without adequate evidence and proper verification needs to be analyzed. It is possible that a small coterie around him had been influenced by the Chinese. This belief is reinforced by the fact that this small group has influenced His Holiness to continue to support the Tai Situ group even though the Dalai Lama himself has been briefed about the controversy and the lack of unanimity with respect to the reincarnation. The second explanation could be that Dalai Lama was at that point of time carrying on delicate negotiations with the Chinese with respect to Tibet and he was influenced to think that such a recognition may go in his favor during his further discussions with the Chinese. A third explanation put forth by the religiously inclined is that the Dalai Lama heads the Gelug Sect which is not favorably inclined towards the Kagyu sect particularly because of the growing influence of the Kagyu sect. (After the establishment of the Dharma Chakra Center in Rumtek in the early 1960s, the Karmapa sect has opened not less than 600 centers all over the world). The fourth explanation is that the recognition given by the Dalai Lama is not a religious recognition but basically a temporal act placing the Karmapa in a hierarchy next to the

Dalai Lama and the Panchen Lama. It is an act which need not be given any religious significance. While this matter needs to be studied in more detail, what is important to note is that following the recognition of the Karmapa in Tibet and its approval by the Dalai Lama, the People's Republic of China put their seal of approval on the reincarnation. This is perhaps the first time that the People's Republic of China has given such an approval and is possibly calculated to demonstrate to the world the decisive say that the People's Republic of China have in the affairs of the Tibet both spiritual and temporal.

It would appear from the above analysis that the Tai Situ Rinpoche group had managed to get their candidate approved by the Dalai Lama as well as the PRC in spite of the fact that there were fundamental doubts about the correctness of the so-called instructions left behind by the sixteenth Gyalwa Karmapa. Since then the Tai Situ Rinpoche group has been influencing local opinion in Sikkim to continuously pressurize the authorities for bringing the Karmapa reincarnate to Rumtek and formally install him in the monastery.

The Chinese Connection And Role Of Tai Situ Rinpoche

It would appear from the above that Tai Situ Rinpoche group had wittingly or unwittingly played into the hands of the Chinese. However, reports indicate that the Tai Situ who is a Tibetan national had been visiting Tibet on and off and in 1984-85 he traveled extensively and drafted a program for so-called development of his country. He records that "at the end of 1984 and beginning of 1985 I visited for four months my country (meaning China) after 26 years abroad and traveled to the areas of Sitron Tsongol, Gangsheo Yunnan and Shingkjang." The development program includes education, healthcare, culture, handicrafts, increase in income and living standards, etc. What is noteworthy is that throughout his report he talks about friendly connections between the Chinese and the people of other countries, study of the Chinese language and study of Chinese medicine. He talks about Chinese in the most friendly terms referring to the Chinese as Chinese brothers. He talks about Chinese brothers living abroad as well. He talks about the autonomous region of Tibet and indicates that his plan has the honest intention to benefit the people of China and in particular the autonomous region of Tibet, Sitron, Yunnan, Gangshuo, etc. He profusely thanks the two leaders of China, namely, Hu Yao Ban and Deng Xiao Peng as well as other leaders of China for their excellent political stance. The report of Tai Situ Rinpoche is addressed to the Director of Chinese Communist Government. All this indicates that Tai Situ had built up a good relationship with the Chinese possibly from 1984.

It would be appropriate to consider the Chinese interest in this entire matter at this stage. From the time of Chinese occupation and indeed after the departure of Dalai Lama from Tibet, the Chinese have been strengthening their control over Tibet in a variety of ways. Apart from the well established efforts to reduce the religious influence of the Dalai Lama and changing the demographic composition of Tibet by large scale influx of Han Chinese into Tibet it would appear that China having got their own Panchen Lama, have by formally recognizing the seventeenth Gyalwa Karmapa extended their control over the religious consciousness of the Tibetans. It is also very much possible that the Chinese are preparing to get themselves into a position of strength in the post Dalai Lama Tibet. It is not inconceivable that having established their right to recognize the reincarnates, the Chinese would not hesitate to identify the successor to the present Dalai Lama, when the time comes. This would complete their hold on the religious consciousness of the Tibetans both within and outside Tibet. The Chinese may not attach too great an importance to the declaration by the Dalai Lama that there will be no more reincarnation of His Holiness. It is important from our point of view to take note of this. It is also important to note that along the entire Himalayan belt right from Ladakh to Arunachal Pradesh the influence of Tibetan Lamaistic Buddhism is extensive with a string of monasteries. It is reported that the Chinese have been making efforts to penetrate into these monasteries and as of now no less than eleven monasteries are headed by Lamas who can be considered as protégés of China. It would be most undesirable to allow the Chinese to extend their influence in this manner and it is in this context that the present situation in Rumtek needs to be carefully viewed.

The Contending Parties

It has been mentioned above that while the regents who are responsible for the religious affairs of Rumtek, it is the trustees who are really the inheritors of the trust constituted by the late sixteenth Gyalwa Karmapa.

No doubt three out of four regents were members of the trust and with one of them dying in an accident only two namely, Tai Situ Rinpoche and Shamar Rinpoche continue to be members of the trust.

After the so-called discovery of the reincarnate in Tibet, Tai Situ Rinpoche has been avoiding attending the trust meetings and in any case after 1993 he had not been permitted to enter India. He therefore seems to operate through Gyaltsab Rinpoche who continues to be in Rumtek. For some strange reasons though he is also a Tibetan refugee (as indeed are Tai Situ Rinpoche and Shamar Rinpoche), Gyaltsab's permit to remain in Sikkim is renewed by the State Government year after year whereas Shamar Rinpoche has not been allowed to enter Sikkim for some time now.

A group of individuals consisting of Kunzang Sherab, an ex-bureaucrat not particularly known for integrity or efficiency and who for some time was the Secretary of Ecclesiastical Department of the Government of Sikkim, Namkha Gyaltsen, an MLA who represents the Sangha Constituency, Sonam Topden, brother of Mr. Karma Topden, Member of Parliament and few others have formed a Joint Action Committee and have been keeping the issue alive and influencing the local population in Sikkim to subscribe to the view that the reincarnated Karmapa in Tibet is the only real incarnate. They have been able to capture the loyalty of the local Bhutia Lepcha population to a large extent because of the seal of the approval given by Dalai Lama and to a certain extent because of the fact that they do not hesitate to use strong-arm tactics where necessary. They are also supported by some local politicians such as Thuckchuk Lachungpa who is currently with the Congress but was earlier with the Sikkim Sangram Parishad and who specializes in agitational politics. It is due primarily to the Joint Action Committee that an ugly situation was created in the monastery itself, as a consequence of which the two groups fought each other and the group of Lamas owing allegiance to Shamar Rinpoche was physically thrown out of Rumtek monastery. This group of Lamas have been given shelter near the monastery but have not been allowed to enter the monastery itself. The presence of Gyaltsab Rinpoche and the fact that the group owing allegiance to Tai Situ Rinpoche is in physical possession of the monastery, has enabled them to claim that the monastery already belongs to the seventeenth Gyalwa Karmapa reincarnate from Tibet and he should be brought from Tibet and be enthroned in Rumtek. The Joint Action Committee keeps issuing pamphlets, monograms, cassettes all calculated to establish that the Tibetan reincarnation is the only correct reincarnation. This propaganda has no doubt had an impact on the local population. It needs also to be highlighted that the local bureaucracy and the police have also been heavily influenced by this strong propaganda. Attempts by the Shamar Rinpoche's followers to enter the monastery even for the purpose of worship have been beaten back by use of force by the group in occupation of the monastery.

As mentioned before, a legally established trust exists and it was functioning in a normal fashion until the controversy erupted in 1992. Even thereafter, in spite of the trust being for all practical purposes boycotted by Situ Rinpoche, the trust continued to meet right up till 1995. The resolutions taken by the trust from time to time have appealed for moderation, for settlement of dispute by adopting the middle path and dialogue. The efforts of the trust for bringing about a rapprochement have been dismissed somewhat derisively by the Joint Action Committee possibly inspired by the Tai Situ group. In fact the Joint Action Committee seems to have organized something called an International Kagyu gathering and had gone to the extent of calling for the resignation of the trustees. They also made an effort to replace the present trustees with a trust of their own but this was not successful. Because of the possession of the monastery by Tai Situ group the trustees have not been able to occupy their official position within the monastery nor have they been able to perform their functions in a proper manner.

Role Of The State Government

It has been reported that the then Chief Minister Sri Nar Bahadur Bhandari had developed links with Tai Situ Rinpoche and his attitude towards the Rumtek controversy was to a large extent influenced by the Tai Situ group. Reports also indicate that his election campaign was financed by Tai Situ Rinpoche. It is possible that Sri Bhandari wanted to keep his hold over the Bhutia/Lepcha voters who he thought were inclined towards the Tai Situ group. Bhandari's own political history indicates that he was opposed to the merger of Sikkim with India and he has not hesitated from taking anti-India stances whenever it suits his political convenience.

What needs to be highlighted however is that when the controversy erupted and developed into a law-and-order problem the Sikkim Govt.

officers who went to the monastery to control what was basically a law-and-order situation seem to have exceeded their authority. Whether they did this because of express instructions by Sri Bhandari or not is unclear but having arrived on the site to control the situation created by warring groups of lamas aided generously by outside elements reportedly gathered by the members of the Joint Action Committee, the then Home Secretary and the Inspector General of Police seem to have also got hold of the keys to the monastery. They did not take care to make an inventory of the articles in the monastery. What is more important is that the keys were handed over not to the duly constituted trust or to any member of the trust but to the Tai Situ group. By this act of the State Govt. intentionally or otherwise the State Govt. handed over the possession of the monastery to the Tai Situ group who since then are prohibiting the other group from entering the monastery. The trustees have not been able to enter the monastery either and perform their duties and have been writing to the State Govt. to take corrective action in the matter and the Shamar Rinpoche has also been trying to impress upon the Govt. that they should also be given access to the monastery. An attempt was no doubt made to get the monks of the Shamar group back into the monastery but in the face of violent opposition from the Tai Situ group from within the monastery, the attempt was given up. The trustees have not met after 1995 but the Shamar group is now attempting to take recourse to legal remedies. The State Govt. has received two notices from the legal firm M/S Dada Chandji asking for restoration of possession of the monastery and its properties giving a list of articles that are supposed to be a part of the monastery. On expiry of the statutory period it is possible that the matter may be taken formally to a court of Law.

The Joint Action Committee is now stepping up its demand for permitting Tai Situ Rinpoche to come back to Rumtek and is reportedly also intending to send a delegation to Tibet if necessary via Nepal for bringing the Tibetan reincarnate Karmapa to be formally installed in the Rumtek monastery. They are displaying a certain sense of urgency in the matter as they are apprehensive that the reincarnate Lama recognized by the Shamar group who is already now in Kalimpong for approximately a month or so and who intends to be in Kalimpong for about five months, may be brought into Sikkim and attempts may be made to install him in Rumtek. The Joint Action Committee has been urging the Government of Sikkim to lift the ban on the entry of Tai Situ and give permission to bring the reincarnate from Tibet to Rumtek while at the same time not allowing Shamar Rinpoche to enter Sikkim. On the other hand the Shamar group not only wants to re-enter the monastery from which they have been thrown out but would like Shamar to be allowed to come back and indeed the reincarnate identified by him to be installed in Rumtek. A potential conflict of interests is definitely brewing.

Current Concerns And Proposed Courses Of Action

Taking into account the fact that the Chinese Govt. is actively interested in the Rumtek affairs and the emerging situation described above, it would be necessary to anticipate events and consider possible courses of action. The Sikkim Government right now would be hesitant to act because of the belief that a large proportion of the Bhutia/Lepcha population is inclined to accept the Tibetan reincarnation, primarily because of the blessings given by the Dalai Lama and would not like to do anything which can be construed as offending the sentiments of Bhutias/Lepchas. However, given the fact that Sikkim occupies a strategic position it would be most undesirable to have a situation where a Tibetan reincarnation, who is basically a Chinese National recognized by the Chinese, formally occupies a position in a monastery in Sikkim. The Karmapa reincarnate if at all is brought into Sikkim will not come alone and may be accompanied by a very substantial entourage. Such an event can lead to consequences quite unpredictable and may affect the security interests of the country very substantially. Clearly we cannot allow a situation where a Tibetan reincarnate is brought into Sikkim, however vociferous such a demand may become.

The problem can assume complex dimensions because the regents as well as the trustees lose their official authority the moment the Karmapa reincarnate attains the age of 21. We will have to consider steps well before this time. We therefore have to take note of:

(a) The clear intention of the Chinese to expand their influence on the religious consciousness of not only the Tibetans but also of the population in the entire Himalayan region.

(b) The fact that the Chinese are possibly preparing themselves for the post Dalai Lama situation.

(c) The demand for installation of the Tibetan Karmapa in Rumtek which can become more strident as time goes by.

(d) The fact that the Chinese have not recognized Sikkim as part of India.

(e) The possible reaction of the local Bhutia/Lepcha to any steps that may be taken to deny access to the reincarnate from Tibet or alter the present situation in Rumtek.

(f) On the other hand while keeping our security interests in mind also recognize the fact that the legitimate trustees have been disallowed from functioning from the monastery by an act of the State Government and that within the next five or six years both the regents and the trustees will lose their status as religious and temporal authorities of Rumtek once the Karmapa reincarnate attains the age of 21.

Two courses of action that can be suggested in this context are:
• Whether Dalai Lama can be influenced to recognize the second reincarnation and –
• Whether steps can be taken to restore the trustees their legitimate control over the monastery.

The two actions may have to be taken simultaneously and for this the full cooperation of the State Govt. is absolutely essential. The monastery itself has to be cleansed of all unruly elements and of offensive material which can be used to prevent entry by anyone else and which can crate an ugly law-and-order situation.

The above issues require detailed consideration and a careful assessment of both possibilities and consequences.

Notes

Preface

1. Among its other topics, Jeffery Paine's 2004 book *Re-Enchantment: Tibetan Buddhism Comes to the West* discusses the problems caused by romantic relationships between dharma students and three teachers in the Tibetan tradition: two Tibetan men (Kalu Rinpoche and Chogyam Trungpa) and one American woman (Catherine Burroughs). The latter is also the subject of Martha Sherrill's 2001 book *The Buddha from Brooklyn*. In addition, *Shoes Outside the Door: Desire, Devotion, and Excess at San Francisco Zen Center* put out by Michael Downing in 2002 tells the story of an American Zen master, Richard Baker Roshi, who ran into problems partially because of liaisons with devotees.

2. Four books were published in 2003 and 2004 on the Karmapa, all taking the side of the Dalai Lama's candidate Ogyen Trinley. The first of these was Michele Martin's 2003 biography of the young lama, *Music in the Sky: The Life, Art & Teachings of the 17th Karmapa Ogyen Trinley Dorje*. In 2004, three books on the Karmapa controversy followed: *Karmapa: The Politics of Reincarnation* by Lea Terhune, *The Dance of 17 Lives: The Incredible True Story of Tibet's 17th Karmapa* by Mick Brown, and *Wrestling the Dragon: In Search of the Boy Lama Who Defied China* by Gaby Naher. An earlier book, *Rogues in Robes* published in 1998 by Tomek Lehnert, discussed the controversy from the experience of a follower of Shamar Rinpoche. I will occasionally refer to these books in my discussion.

INTRODUCTION

1. The titular head of the Gelug school is known as the Ganden
    Tripa (or Tri) Rinpoche, the abbot of Ganden monastery. The
    post is filled on a rotating basis by high lamas in the school, but
    never by the Dalai Lama himself. The current throne-holder, the
    101st Ganden Tri Rinpoche, Khensur Lungri Namgyel, is a French
    national. Now in his seventies, he was appointed by the Dalai
    Lama in 2003.

2. Dalai Lama, "Human Rights and Universal Responsibility."
    Address to the United Nations World Conference on Human
    Rights, Vienna, Austria, June 15, 1992, http://www.tibet.com/DL/
    vienna.html, accessed September 12, 2005.

3. P. Christiaan Klieger, *Tibetan Nationalism*, 89.

4. *Flight of A Karmapa*. Directed by Yoichi Shimatsu. Hong Kong:
    Nachtvision, 2001.

5. Rumtek Sangha Duche. *Proceedings of the International Karma Kagyu
    Conference*. New Delhi, 1996.

6. *Karmapa Charitable Trust vs. the State of Sikkim and Gyaltsab Rinpoche*,
    Civil Suit No. 40 of 1998 in the Court of the District Judge, East
    and North Sikkim in Gangtok.

7. "Affidavit of Geoffrey Brian Samuel," *Lama vs. Hope and Ors*, CIV-
    2004-404-001363, High Court of New Zealand Auckland Registry,
    November 11, 2004.

8. Dhoring Tenzin Paljor, *True Account of the Dhoring Gazhi Family*. The
    edition I used (with the help of Tibetan translators) was published in
    1988 in Tibetan by People's Publications of the Tibet Autonomous
    Region in Lhasa. In the Wylie system of transliteration, the title is *Ga'
    bzhi ba'i mi rabs kyi byung ba brjod pa zol med gtam gyi rol mo zhes bya ba
    gzhugs so.*

9. Compared to other major religions, Buddhism is the fastest
    growing in the United States. According to a 2001 study, since
    the previous survey held in 1990, Buddhism had grown 12%
    versus 11% for Christianity and 10% for both Judaism and Islam.
    Interestingly, Buddhism grew overall 33%, but at the same time
    shrank 23%, making it one of the "high turnover" religions in
    the study. See Egon Mayer, etal., *American Religious Identification*

Survey, City University of New York, 2001, http://www.gc.cuny. edu/faculty/research_briefs/aris/key_findings.htm, accessed June 28, 2005.

1 BAYONETS TO RUMTEK

1. "Protector Practices," http://www.kadampa.org/english/practice/ protector_practices.php, accessed July 24, 2005.

2. "The Dharma Protector Dorje Shugden," http://www.kadampa. org/english/tradition/dorje_shugden.php, accessed July 24, 2005.

3. Stephen Bachelor, "Letting Daylight into Magic: The Life and Times of Dorje Shugden," *Tricycle: The Buddhist Review*, Vol. 7 No. 3, Spring 1998.

4. Parvathi Menon, "Of the Dalai Lama and a Witch-hunt," *Frontline*, Vol. 17 Issue 26, December 23 to January 5, 2001.

5. Jeffery Paine, "Reply to Jay Landman," *Washington Post Book World*, August 1, 2004.

2 THE PLACE OF POWER

1. Gaby Naher, *Wrestling the Dragon*, 207.

2. Rumtek monastery website, http://www.rumtek.org, accessed July 10, 2005.

3. Gaby Naher, *Wrestling the Dragon*, 207.

4. Rumtek Sangha Duche, *Proceedings of the International Karma Kagyu Conference*, 44. My discussion of Rumtek before and during the takeover relies heavily on testimony presented at the 1996 event, the International Karma Kagyu Conference. Billed as "A Gathering of the 16th Karmapa's Devotees Organized by the Rumtek Sangha Duche [monk's body]," the meeting was held at the Karmapa Institute in New Delhi from March 28 through March 30, 1996. Shangpa Rinpoche, the leader of Karma Kagyu centers in Singapore, organized the event, which featured speeches by Shamar, Topga, and Khenpo Chodrak. In addition, monks living at the monastery gave first-hand, eyewitness accounts of what they had experienced and seen during the takeover of Rumtek in

August 1993. More than three hundred supporters attended the conference, including lamas and monks from Rumtek and other Karma Kagyu monasteries, and lay people from East Asia and Western countries. The hundreds of centers founded by Ole and Hannah Nydahl were particularly well represented at the event, with devotees coming from as far away as Australia, Spain, Japan, and Venezuela.

5. Lea Terhune, *Karmapa: The Politics of Reincarnation*, 198.

6. Rumtek Sangha Duche, *Proceedings of the International Karma Kagyu Conference*, 45.

7. A remarkable woman, Bedi was known in India as the mother of Bollywood heartthrob Kabir Bedi and the grandmother of talk-show host Puja Bedi.

8. Christopher Hitchens, "Blaming bin Laden First," *The Nation*, October 22, 2001.

3 AN ANCIENT RIVALRY

1. Tsepon W.D. Shakabpa, *Tibet: A Political History*, 50-56.

2. John T. Davenport has translated the *Sakya Lekshe* as *Ordinary Wisdom: Sakya Pandita's Treasury of Good Advice*, published in 2000.

3. Tsepon W.D. Shakabpa, *Tibet: A Political History*, 65.

4. In *The Religion of Tibet*, 81, Sir Charles Bell wrote that the order's original name was *Ga-luk*, the "Ganden Way," after the sect's main monastery outside of Lhasa, Ganden, which means "the Joyous." But since "this seemed to suggest the way of pleasure, a slight change was made, and it became *Ga-luk*, 'The Virtuous Way.'"

5. Shakabpa's text, *Tibet: A Political History*, is the standard modern source on the history of Tibet in both its Tibetan original and its English translation. However, the two-volume Tibetan version contains much information that has been edited out of the single-volume English translation. The translation leaves out emotional prose that is acceptable in Tibetan works but that might offend Westerners, as well as numerous historical facts that conflict with Shakabpa's thesis that Tibet was independent of China

throughout most of its history or that might impugn the reputation of the Dalai Lamas.

6. The primary sources for the conflict between the Tsangpa kings and the Karma Kagyu on one side and the *Depa* or Duke of Lhasa, the Mongols, and the Gelugpa on the other are two works by the fifth Dalai Lama, his autobiography and a history of Tibet, as well as Shakabpa's own two-volume history of Tibet in the original (but not in its single-volume English translation, which omits mention of the Duke of Lhasa).

7. Called the *Bod Kartso Chig Gyur*, this system of government would have given Tibet a level of centralization that such European powers as France and England were beginning to achieve at the same period.

8. Fifth Dalai Lama, *Autobiography*, vol. 1, 255-256. See also Tsepon W.D. Shakabpa, *An Advanced Political History of Tibet*, vol. 1, 392. Both of these works are in Tibetan language. I use translations courtesy of Shamar Rinpoche.

9. Fifth Dalai Lama, *Autobiography*, vol. 1, 201.

10. These figures come from Khenpo Chodrak Tenphel.

11. Dawa Norbu, *Tibet: The Road Ahead*, 265.

12. Quoted by Elliot Sperling in "Orientalism and Aspects of Violence in the Tibetan Tradition," included in *Imagining Tibet* edited by Thierry Dodin and Heinz Räther, 319. Sperling uses this passage from the *Autobiography* of the fifth Dalai Lama to explain the pitfalls of taking historical material out of context and applying contemporary standards to it: "One may say with some confidence that the Fifth Dalai Lama does not fit the standard image that many people today have of a Dalai Lama, particularly the image of a Nobel Peace Prize laureate."

13. Sir Charles Bell, *The Religion of Tibet*, 107.

14. Isabel Hilton, *The Search for the Panchen Lama*, 63-75.

4   THE ORIGIN OF THE KARMAPAS

1. Nik Douglas, *Karmapa: The Black Hat Lama of Tibet*, 33.

2. Karma Thinley, *The History of the Sixteen Karmapas of Tibet*, 42.

3. In his book *History as Propaganda: Tibetan Exiles versus the People's Republic of China*, John Powers discusses in great detail the conflicting interpretations of tribute missions by lamas, among other topics, as part of the ongoing argument over the historical relationship between Tibet and China.

4. Karma Thinley Rinpoche, *The History of the Sixteen Karmapas of Tibet*, 74.

5. The rest of the story comes from a version told to me by Shamar Rinpoche.

6. Lea Terhune, *Karmapa: The Politics of Reincarnation*, 111.

7. Mick Brown, *The Dance of 17 Lives*, 34. Later, in July 2005, Brown apologized to Shamar Rinpoche for making this claim and promised to remove it from future editions of his book.

5 A Lull in Hostilities

1. Patrick French, *Tibet, Tibet*, 14.

2. I draw on two main sources for information about the United Party initiative and the sectarian conflict that followed it: Anil Maheshwari, *The Buddha Cries!*, 19-21, and "Division and Reunification of Chushi Gangdrug," http://www.chushigangdruk. org/history/history12.html, accessed December 28, 2004.

3. Dawa Norbu, *Tibet: The Road Ahead*, 266.

4. Anil Maheshwari, *The Buddha Cries!*, 20-21.

5. Namgyal Shastri, "Situ Rinpoche: Fully Satisfied," *Dharamsala Tibetan Review*, August 1992.

6. Chodrak told me that his source for the story was a book published by Topga Rinpoche in Tibetan in New Delhi in 1994, *Tam natshok kun tog ge rimo* or *Assorted Tales on the Art of Thinking*. Topga's book in turn was based on records kept by the general secretary at the Karmapa's Tsurphu monastery in the 1920s.

7. This chart of Karmapas is taken from information submitted by Professor Geoffrey Samuel of the University of Newcastle in Australia in a 2004 court case in neighboring New Zealand: "Affirmation of Geoffrey Brian Samuel," *Lama vs. Hope*

and Ors, CIV-2004-404-001363, High Court of New Zealand Auckland Registry, November 11, 2004.

6   EXILE, DEATH, AND DISSENT

1. Melvyn Goldstein, A History of Modern Tibet 1913-1951, 34.

2. Nik Douglas in Karmapa: The Black Hat Lama of Tibet lists fifty-two major objects along with sixteen manuscripts, some in multiple volumes, preserved at Rumtek monastery as of the early 1970s.

3. There were seven other lamas in Shamar's hotel room at the time that Shamar agreed to Situ's request. Three of them are still alive as witnesses—Shamar's brother Jigme Rinpoche, Lama Karma Thinley, and Jamgon Kongtrul's attendant Trinley Ngodrup.

4. Mick Brown, The Dance of 17 Lives, 80.

7   THE TRADITIONALIST

1. Drukchen Rinpoche later told the story of his discussion with the Karmapa to Shamar when the two met at the Ashoka Hotel in New Delhi in 1985. Later, Drukchen retold the story to a group of Western devotees at the Dhagpo Kagyu Ling center in Dordogne, France in 1994.

2. Gaby Naher, Wrestling the Dragon, 260-261.

3. This prediction came from the fifth Shamarpa Konchok Yenlak (1525-1583) and was quoted by Anil Maheshwari, The Buddha Cries!, 206.

4. Yeshe Dronma, The Kunzig Shamarpas of Tibet, 19. Interestingly, Shamar received his physical red crown fifty years or more before the Ming emperor Chengzu would present Rolpe Dorje's successor, the fifth Karmapa Deshin Shegpa, with his own physical crown during his stay in Nanjing.

5. Tim McGirk, London Independent, March 18, 1994.

6. Lea Terhune, Karmapa: The Politics of Reincarnation, 147.

7. Tsepon W.D. Shakabpa, Tibet: A Political History, 157.

8. There are four primary Tibetan sources for the life of the tenth

Shamarpa and the Tibet-Gorkha War of the eighteenth century: *The Golden Lineage* by the Great Eighth Tai Situ Chokyi Jungne (early reincarnations); another text by the eighth Situ, his autobiography entitled *The Crystal Mirror* (the first half of the tenth Shamar's life); the autobiography of Kathog Rig Dzin Chenmo (the end of the Shamarpa's life); and the family history of Tibetan government minister Dhoring Tenzin Paljor (extensive detail about the Gorkha War and the role of the Shamarpa). Aside from the slimmed down English version of Shakabpa's book, an English-language source for the history of the war and the role of the tenth Shamarpa is an article by Ramesh K. Dhungel, "Nepal-Tibet Cultural Relations and the Zhva-Dmar-Pa (Shyamarpa) Lamas of Tibet" in *Contributions in Nepalese Studies*, vol. 26, no. 2, July 1999.

9.   There is no historical basis for the oft-told story that Shamarpa's Red Crown was buried beneath the floor of this courthouse. This tale is a confusion of Shamarpa's story with that of the great Sakya master Gorampa Sonam Sengye, whose book *Clearing Away Wrong Views* challenged the Gelugpa view of the Madhyamaka and incurred the wrath of the Dalai Lama's administration. The government banned both Gorampa's text and his future incarnations and buried the original of the text along with Gorampa's crown under the entranceway to the Jokhang temple in Lhasa.

10. Yeshe Dronma, *The Kunzig Shamarpas of Tibet*, 42-44.

11. Anil Maheshwari, *The Buddha Cries!*, 22-23.

8 THE MODERNIZER

1.   Raveena Aulakh, "Holy Hum," *Hindustan Times Sunday Magazine*, May 2, 2004.

2.   Lea Terhune, *Karmapa: The Politics of Reincarnation*, 7.

3.   Mick Brown, *The Dance of 17 Lives*, 90.

4.   Gaby Naher, *Wrestling the Dragon*, 115.

5.   K. Sreedhar Rao, *Report to Shri T.S.R. Subramaniam, Cabinet Secretary, Government of India*, 5.

6. Government of India Ministry of Home Affairs, Lookout Circular 10/98, August 5, 1998.

7. Mick Brown, *The Dance of 17 Lives*, 96.

8. Rumtek Sangha Duche, *The Siege of Karmapa*, viii.

9. Gaby Naher, *Wrestling the Dragon*, 112.

10. Julian Gearing, "Struggle for Tibet's Soul," *Asiaweek*, October 20, 2000.

11. "H.H. XVII Gyalwa Karmapa Found," *Song of Fulfillment*, newsletter of Kagyu Droden Kunchab Buddhist Center (San Francisco), Summer/Fall 1992.

12. Lea Terhune, *Karmapa: The Politics of Reincarnation*, 131.

13. The full text of this exchange is reproduced from an audio recording made of the meeting in Michel Nestorenko, etal., *The Karmapa Papers*, 159. Five European devotees of Shamar Rinpoche, Alexander Draszczyk, Martina Draszczyk, Anne Ekselius, Michel Nestorenko, and Hannah Nydahl, put out this publication at Shamar's request in October 1992. Compiled in Paris, written in English, and distributed from Hong Kong, the publication brought together original documents relating to the Karmapa controversy, with analysis by the editors. The book's highlight is a detailed analysis of Tai Situ's prediction letter, reprinted in appendix B of this book. After its publication, *The Karmapa Papers* was sent to government officials and opinion leaders in the state of Sikkim, where it helped sway opinion towards Shamar's position.

9 A Prentender to the Throne

1. In rare cases, a tulku could be recognized before the death of a particular Buddhist master as a *ma-dey* tulku. For many Tibetans, such tulkus carried little credibility.

2. Nestorenko, etal., *The Karmapa Papers*, 50.

3. All quotes from monks at Rumtek concerning the events of the takeover of the monastery come from *Proceedings of the International Karma Kagyu Conference*, March 1996, unless otherwise indicated.

4. This letter is reproduced in appendix B of this book.

5. *The Karmapa Papers*, 34.

6. Michelle Martin, *Music in the Sky*, 18-19.

7. Topga Rinpoche, *Tam natshok kun tog ge rimo* or *Assorted Tales on the Art of Thinking*, New Delhi, 1994.

8. Lea Terhune, *Karmapa: The Politics of Reincarnation*, 164.

9. Mick Brown, *The Dance of 17 Lives*, 113.

10. Alexander Berzin, *Relating to a Spiritual Teacher*, 42.

11. "Affirmation of Geoffrey Brian Samuel," *Lama vs. Hope and Ors*, CIV-2004-404-001363, High Court of New Zealand Auckland Registry, November 11, 2004. Samuel went on to write that even once the Dalai Lamas came along, the Karmapa's labrang at Tsurphu never asked for permission from the Dalai Lama to choose a Karmapa, except in the one exceptional case of the recognition of the sixteenth Karmapa in the late twenties. In that case, as we have seen, the thirteenth Dalai Lama originally supported the son of his council minister Lungshar as a candidate, but the Tibetan leader later backed down and was forced to concede that the Karma Kagyu could recognize its own choice, who became the sixteenth Karmapa Rangjung Rigpe Dorje.

12. *The Politics of Reincarnation*. Directed by Yoichi Shimatsu. Hong Kong: Nachtvision, 2001.

13. Mick Brown, *The Dance of 17 Lives*, 172.

14. Department of Information and International Relations, Central Tibetan Administration, "H.H. Dalai Lama Recognizes Karmapa's Reincarnation," July 3, 1992.

15. Since this time, some of Shamar's supporters have claimed that the Dalai Lama simply misunderstood the situation, and did not realize that Shamar had not agreed with Situ and Gyaltsab. Once the Tibetan leader discovered his error, it was too late for him to withdraw his support for Ogyen Trinley without losing face. "This point seemed quite important at the time," Shamar told me. "But now it is clear that the Dalai Lama's office had already determined to support Ogyen Trinley, and that it would have found one way or another to do so."

16. K. Sreedhar Rao, *Report to Shri T.S.R. Subramaniam, Cabinet Secretary, Government of India*, 4-5.

10 Abortive Skirmishes

1. Lea Terhune, *Karmapa: The Politics of Reincarnation*, 192.

2. Mick Brown, *The Dance of 17 Lives*, 166.

3. In his book on the Karmapa controversy, Mick Brown quoted a layman who held a low-level post at Rumtek with a version of the argument that Situ's followers have often made against testing the prediction letter: "'Why did Shamar say the prediction letter should be analyzed?' says Ngodrup Burkhar. 'This is a point in his favor to the modern Western audience, who will think, why not? There's no harm. It's an appeal to rationalism; not blind faith. But the second thing is he knew this test could never be done, and that would again be in his favor. He could say "Look, I am asking for something very straight, very plain, something the whole world acknowledges, and they're not going to do it!" But he knew that nobody would plunge themselves into hell by desecrating the letter.'" See Mick Brown, *The Dance of 17 Lives*, 171.

4. Tomek Lehnert, *Rogues in Robes*, 166.

5. The day after Shamar put out his letter in Tibetan, Situ had one of his American devotees, Michelle Martin (who would later write the 2003 biography of Ogyen Trinley *Music in the Sky*) release a translation that was much more affirmative than Shamar intended. This translation interpreted him as saying "now I have attained complete confidence in Situ Rinpoche, and the contents of this letter, according to which the reincarnation has definitely been discovered and further confirmed by His Holiness the Dalai Lama as the incarnation of His Holiness the Gyalwang Karmapa. I offer my willing acceptance and henceforth, I will no longer pursue the matter of examining the sacred testament, etc."

The next day, July 18, Shamar issued his own translation, worded more tentatively:

> On March 19th, 1992, at a meeting with Jamgon Rinpoche, Gyaltsab Rinpoche and myself, Situ Rinpoche presented

a handwritten prediction letter from his protection pouch, claiming it was the written instructions of H.H. the 16th Karmapa (indicating his reincarnation). I had some doubts (about the letter's authenticity). At this point, I rely on Situ Rinpoche (giving me correct information about H.H. the Dalai Lama's decision). Relying on our confidential discussion, I go along with the decision made by H.H. Dalai Lama that a reincarnation has certainly been found as reincarnation of H.H. the Gyalwa Karmapa. Hence, I suspend my demands such as having the handwritten prediction letter being subjected to a (forensic) test.

6. By the early nineties, the Karmapa Charitable Trust board consisted of J.D. Densapa and T.S. Gyaltshen, former officials of the Sikkim state government; Ashok Burman, a New Delhi businessman; Gyan Jyoti Kansakar, a Kathmandu businessman; and Rumtek general secretary Topga Rinpoche. These board members were all appointed in 1962 when Shamar was a child of seven years old, so he could have had no influence over their selection. The only new members were Shamar, Situ, and Jamgon Rinpoches, all appointed by the other trustees in 1984.

7. Rumtek Sangha Duche, *Proceedings of the International Karma Kagyu Conference*, 60.

8. K. Sreedhar Rao, *Report to Shri T.S.R. Subramaniam, Cabinet Secretary, Government of India*, 9.

9. Lea Terhune, *Karmapa: The Politics of Reincarnation*, 193.

10. Article 26, Freedom to Manage Religious Affairs, declares that "every religious denomination or any section thereof shall have the right (a) to establish and maintain institutions for religious and charitable purposes; (b) to manage its own affairs in matters of religion; (c) to own and acquire movable and immovable property; and (d) to administer such property in accordance with law." See http://indiacode.nic.in/coiweb/coifiles/p03.htm, accessed May 2, 2005.

11. Mick Brown, *The Dance of 17 Lives*, 212.

11 THE YARNEY PUTSCH

1. Dalai Lama, *Human Rights and Universal Responsibility*. Address to the United Nations World Conference on Human Rights, Vienna, Austria, June 15, 1992, http://www.tibet.com/DL/vienna.html, accessed September 12, 2005.

2. The meeting was reportedly held at a farmhouse in the Matang Valley, according to numerous Indian newspaper accounts. Without obtaining prior permission to enter the neighboring state of West Bengal, a car from the Sikkim state government picked up Chen at Bagdogra airport beforehand and brought him to Sikkim. At the meeting, Chen allegedly gave Bhandari a suitcase containing $1.5 million.

3. Anil Maheshwari, *The Buddha Cries!*, 122.

4. "Pro-China Coup in Gangtok Monastery," *Hindustan Times*, August 6, 1993.

5. Anil Maheshwari, *The Buddha Cries!*, 103.

12 UNDER OCCUPATION

1. Anil Maheshwari, *The Buddha Cries!*, 99.

2. Rumtek Sangha Duche, *Proceedings of the International Karma Kagyu Conference*, 56-57.

3. "I will rule like Hitler: Bhandari," *Siliguri Telegraph*, November 24, 1994.

4. K. Sreedhar Rao, *Report to Shri T.S.R. Subramaniam, Cabinet Secretary, Government of India*, 13.

5. Lea Terhune, *Karmapa: The Politics of Reincarnation*, 223-224.

6. Anil Maheshwari, *The Buddha Cries!*, 120-121.

7. Rumtek Sangha Duche, *The Siege of Karmapa*, 73-74.

8. Topga Rinpoche, *Letter to Gyaltsab Rinpoche*, September 15, 1995.

9. K. Sreedhar Rao, *Report to Shri T.S.R. Subramaniam, Cabinet Secretary, Government of India*, 9.

13 LAMAS ON TRIAL

1. "Shamar Rinpoche Files Defamation Suit against Controversial Karmapa Book," http://www.karmapa-issue.org/politics/lawsuit_terhune.htm, accessed July 27, 2005.

2. Lea Terhune, *Karmapa: The Politics of Reincarnation*, 231.

3. Judge S.W. Lephcha, *Order in Civil Suit No. 40 of 1998*, the Court of the District Judge, East and North Sikkim at Gangtok, date of decision October 17, 2001.

4. Rezaul Lascar, "Pro-China Monk Let Into India," *Asian Age*, September 6, 1998.

5. Government of India Ministry of Home Affairs, *Lookout Circular 10/98*, August 5, 1998.

6. David Rennie, "Boy Lama Flees Across Himalayas to Escape Chinese," *London Telegraph*, January 7, 2000.

7. Arthur Max, "Young Monk May Emerge As Leader," *San Francisco Examiner*, January 15, 2000.

8. Brahma Chellaney, "Chinese piece in Karmapa jigsaw remains a puzzle," *Hindustan Times*, January 17, 2000.

9. *Flight of A Karmapa*, directed by Yoichi Shimatsu, Hong Kong: Nachtvision, 2001.

10. Mick Brown, *The Dance of 17 Lives*, 223.

11. Gaby Naher, *Wrestling the Dragon*, 262.

12. Martin Brauen, *Dreamworld Tibet*, 79.

13. Ibid., 67.

14. Dhiman Chattopadhyay and Amalendu Kundu, "Court Order on Rumtek Treasure Opens Pandora's Box," *Times of India*, March 25, 2002.

15. "Missing Dorje with Ugyen Trinley," *Gangtok Weekend Review*, July 12-18, 2002.

16. Julian Gearing, "India, Sikkim, China and a vexing Tibetan lama," *Asia Times Online*, www.atimes.com/atimes/China/FG21Ad06.html, accessed July 21, 2004.

17. Jefferson Penberthy, "Battle of the Future Buddhas," *Time*, April 4, 1994.

14 THE SECRET BOY

1. The entire letter was reproduced and interpreted by Topga Rinpoche, *Tam natshok kun tog ge rimo* or *Assorted Tales on the Art of Thinking*, New Delhi, 1994.

15 THE RETURN OF THE KING

1. Anil Maheshwari, *The Buddha Cries!*, 112.

2. Lea Terhune, *Karmapa: The Politics of Reincarnation*, 222.

3. *The Attack*. Directed by Thule Jug. Vienna: Vienna Dharma Projects, 1994.

4. Lea Terhune, *Karmapa: The Politics of Reincarnation*, 222.

5. Tim McGirk, "Buddhist Factions Come to Blows," *London Independent*, March 18, 1994.

6. "Rumtek Chief Crowned Amid Violence," *Indian Express*, March 18, 1994.

7. "Karmapa Controversy 'Unfortunate'," *The Hindu*, April 5, 1994.

8. Vijay Kranti, "Newsmaker: Tenzin Khyentse," *India Today*, April 15, 1994.

9. Interview with Lama Dorje Drolma, January 5, 2000, unpublished.

10. Tina Draszczyk, "An Interview with Trinley Thaye Dorje, the 17th Gyalwa Karmapa," *Buddhism Today*, Vol. 8, 2000.

11. Gosia Pellarin, etal., "Buddha in Silicon Valley," *Buddhism Today*, Vol. 13, Fall/Winter 2003.

12. Interview with Lama Dorje Drolma, January 5, 2000, unpublished.

16 CONCLUSION

1. In this section, many quotes from Thaye Dorje come from two articles: Tina Draszczyk, "An Interview with Trinley Thaye Dorje, the 17th Gyalwa Karmapa," *Buddhism Today*, Vol. 8, Summer 2000; and Gosia Pellarin, etal., "Buddha in Silicon Valley," *Buddhism Today*, Vol. 13, Fall/Winter 2003.

2. Gosia Pellarin, etal., "Buddha in Silicon Valley," *Buddhism Today*, Vol. 13, Fall/Winter 2003.

3. *Dhammapada*, "Desire," verse 21.
4. E. Gene Smith, *Among Tibetan Texts*, 268-269.

BIBLIOGRAPHY

During my research, certain books proved particularly informative and useful. I have placed a star by these works in the list below. I have not listed the numerous newspaper and magazine articles that I have cited in this book or that I have consulted as background since they are not widely available to the general reader.

Avedon, John F. *In Exile from the Land of Snows: the Definitive Account of the Dalai Lama and Tibet Since the Chinese Conquest.* New York: HarperPerennial, 1997.

Bell, Sir Charles. *The Religion of Tibet.* New Delhi: Book Faith India, 1998.

Berzin, Alexander. *Relating to a Spiritual Teacher: Building a Healthy Relationship.* Ithaca: Snow Lion Publications, 2000. *

Brauen, Martin. *Dreamworld Tibet: Western Illusions.* Martin Willson, trans. Trumbull, CT: Weatherhill, 2004.

Brown, Mick. *The Dance of 17 Lives: The Incredible True Story of Tibet's 17th Karmapa.* London: Bloomsbury, 2004.

Crossette, Barbara. *So Close to Heaven: The Vanishing Buddhist Kingdoms of the Himalayas.* New York: Knopf, 1995.

Dalai Lama, Fourteenth, Tenzin Gyatso. *Freedom in Exile: the Autobiography of the Dalai Lama.* New York: HarperPerennial, 1991.

Dodin, Thierry and Heinz Räther. *Imagining Tibet: Perceptions, Projections and Fantasies.* Boston: Wisdom Publications, 2001.

Dronma, Yeshe. *The Kunzig Shamarpas of Tibet.* Hong Kong: Dorje and Bell, 1992.

Douglas, Nik and Meryl White. *Karmapa: The Black Hat Lama of Tibet.* London: Luzac, 1976. *

French, Patrick. *Tibet, Tibet: A Personal History of a Lost Land.* New York: Knopf, 2003. *

Gampopa. *The Jewel Ornament of Liberation: The Wish-fulfilling Gem of the Noble Teachings.* Trans. Khenpo Konchog Gyaltsen Rinpoche. Ithaca: Snow Lion, 1998.

Goldstein, Melvyn C. *A History of Modern Tibet, 1913-1951.* Berkeley: University of California Press, 1989.

_____. *The Snow Lion and the Dragon: China, Tibet, and the Dalai Lama.* Berkeley: University of California Press, 1997.

Grunfeld, A. Tom. *The Making of Modern Tibet.* Armonk, NY: M.E. Sharpe, 1987.

Harrer, Heinrich. *Seven Years in Tibet.* Trans. Richard Graves. New York: Putnam, 1996.

Hilton, Isabel. *The Search for the Panchen Lama.* New York: W.W. Norton and Company, 2000.

Hyde-Chambers, Frank and Audrey, trans. *Tibetan Folk Tales.* Boston: Shambhala, 2002.

Jamgon Kongtul Lodro Thaye. *Enthronement: The Recognition of the Reincarnate Masters of Tibet and the Himalayas.* Trans. with a foreword by Ngawang Zangpo. Ithaca: Snow Lion Publications, 1997.

Karma Thinley Rinpoche. *The History of the Sixteen Karmapas of Tibet.* Boulder: Prajna Press, 1980. *

Klieger, P. Christiaan. *Tibetan Nationalism.* Berkeley: Folklore Institute, 1992.

Lehnert, Tomek. *Rogues in Robes.* Nevada City, CA: Blue Dolphin, 1998.

Lhalungpa, Lobsang P. *The Life of Milarepa.* New York: Compass, 1979.

Lopez, Donald S. *Prisoners of Shangri-La: Tibetan Buddhism and the West.* Chicago: University of Chicago Press, 1998. *

Maheshwari, Anil. *The Buddha Cries!: Karmapa Conundrum.* New Delhi: UBSPD, 2000.

Martin, Michele. *Music in the Sky: The Life, Art & Teachings of the 17th Karmapa, Ogyen Trinley Dorje.* Ithaca: Snow Lion Publications, 2003.

Naher, Gaby. *Wrestling the Dragon: In Search of the Boy Lama Who Defied China.* London: Rider, 2004.

Nestorenko, Michel, etal. *The Karmapa Papers.* Paris, 1992. *

Norbu, Dawa. *Tibet: The Road Ahead.* London: Rider, 1998.

Nydahl, Ole. *Riding the Tiger: Twenty Years on the Road: The Risks and Joys of Bringing Tibetan Buddhism to the West.* Nevada City, CA: Blue Dolphin, 1992.

_____. *Entering the Diamond Way: Tibetan Buddhism Meets the West.* Nevada City, CA: Blue Dolphin, 1999.

Paine, Jeffery. *Re-enchantment: Tibetan Buddhism Comes to the West.* New York: W.W. Norton, 2004.

Penick, Douglas, trans. *The Warrior Song of King Gesar.* Boston: Wisdom Publications, 1996.

Powers, John. *History as Propaganda: Tibetan Exiles versus the People's Republic of China.* New York: Oxford University Press, 2004. *

Ray, Reginald A. *Indestructible Truth: The Living Spirituality of Tibetan Buddhism.* Boston: Shambhala, 2000.

_____. *Secret of the Vajra World: the Tantric Buddhism of Tibet.* Boston: Shambhala, 2001.

Richardson, Hugh. *Tibet and its History.* Boston: Shambhala, 1984. *

Rumtek Sangha Duche. *Proceedings of the International Karma Kagyu Conference: A Gathering of the 16th Karmapa's Devotees Organized by the Rumtek Sangha Duche.* New Delhi, 1996. *

_____. *The Siege of Karmapa.* New Delhi, 1999.

Sakya Pandita. *Ordinary Wisdom: Sakya Pandita's Treasury of Good Advice.* Trans. John T. Davenport. Boston: Wisdom Publications, 2000.

Schell, Orville. *Virtual Tibet: Searching for Shangri-La from the Himalayas to Hollywood*. New York: Metropolitan Books, 2000.

Shakabpa, Tsepon W.D. *Tibet: A Political History*. New York: Potala Publications, 1984. *

Shakya, Tsering. *The Dragon in the Land of Snows: A History of Modern Tibet since 1947*. New York: Columbia University Press, 1999.

Sherrill, Martha. *The Buddha from Brooklyn: A Tale of Spiritual Seduction*. New York: Vintage, 2001.

Smith, E. Gene. *Among Tibetan Texts: History and Literature of the Himalayan Plateau*. Boston: Wisdom Publications, 2001.

Terhune, Lea. *Karmapa: The Politics of Reincarnation*. Boston: Wisdom Publications, 2004.

Thurman, Robert. *Inner Revolution: Life, Liberty, and the Pursuit of Real Happiness*. New York: Riverhead Books, 1998.

Trungpa, Chogyam Rinpoche. *Born in Tibet*. Boston: Shambhala, 2000.

_____. *Cutting Through Spiritual Materialism*. Boston: Shambhala, 2002.

Weatherford, Jack. *Genghis Khan and the Making of the Modern World*. New York: Crown Publishers, 2004.

Tibetan Works

Dalai Lama, Fifth, Ngawang Lobsang Gyatso. *Autobiography*. Vol. 1. Lhasa: Tibetan People's Publications, 1989.

Dhoring, Tenzin Paljor. *A True History of the Dhoring Gazhi Family*. Tibetan People's Publications, 1988.

Shakabpa, Tsepon W.D. *An Advanced Political History of Tibet*. 5th edition. Vol. 1. Kalimpong: W.D. Shakabpa House, 1976.

Yugyal, Topga. *Assorted Tales on the Art of Thinking*. New Delhi, 1994.

INDEX

India, Supreme Court, 206, 210, 255,
  262, 268, 277-278
International Karma Kagyu Conference,
  298-300, 305, 308-309

Jamgon Kongtrul Rinpoche, 28, 37,
  81-84, 105-106, 112, 115-116,
  119, 123-124, 127, 129-131,
  133-134, 145, 212, 218, 246, 267,
  275, 287-289, 303, 307-308
Jigme Rinpoche, 115, 244, 303
Joint Action Committee, 122, 131, 140,
  150, 152, 156, 160, 167-168, 177,
  184-186, 189, 205-206, 237, 287,
  292-294
Juchen Thubten Namgyal, Tibetan exile
  official, 126, 138, 147

Kagyu International Assembly, 158-159,
  161
Kagyupa school, 104-109, 112, 114-116,
  119, 121-122, 127, 134-138,
  145-147, 156, 158-159, 161,
  164, 166, 173, 175-177, 195, 206,
  211-213, 218, 223, 226, 229, 236,
  241, 244, 246-247, 249-251, 254,
  257-260, 262-263, 266, 270-271,
  274, 289, 293, 298-301, 303,
  305-306, 308-309
Kalimpong, India, 88-90, 221, 245, 262,
  287, 294
Kalu Rinpoche, 36, 110, 112, 213, 297
Kangyur, 23, 104
Karmapa, 14-15, 18-24, 26-38,
  44-48, 51, 53, 57, 59-69, 71-99,
  101-114, 116-117, 119-145,
  147-150, 152-160, 163-167,
  169-173, 175-185, 188-189,
  191-197, 199-201, 203-213,
  216-217, 220, 222-224, 226-233,
  235-246, 248-252, 254-260,
  262, 266-268, 270-275, 278, 281,
  287-292, 294-304
Karmapa, fifth, 46, 60-62, 64, 77, 273,
  303
Karmapa, second, 60, 90-91
Karmapa, seventeenth, candidates, 18,
  20-21, 88, 92, 101, 109, 121-122,
  126, 139, 145, 147, 155, 170-171,

176, 211, 213, 227, 229, 235-236,
  242, 251, 257, 266-267, 271
Karmapa, tenth, 51, 176, 273
Karmapa, third, 20, 90
Kham province, Tibet, 57, 59, 68-69,
  74-75, 77, 89, 104-105, 107, 122,
  218-220, 230-231, 267, 270, 272,
  289
Kublai Khan, Mongol chief, 44, 62
Kundun, 42, 253
Kyichod Apel, Duke of Lhasa, 48-49, 301

Lehnert, Tomek, 297, 307
Lhasa, Tibet, 1, 5, 8-9, 14, 27, 35, 42,
  46-54, 59, 67, 69, 74-76, 78, 89,
  92-97, 103-105, 133, 135, 159,
  184, 192, 194-195, 203, 215-221,
  223-228, 230-231, 258, 267, 270,
  289, 298, 300-301, 304
London Independent, 236, 239, 303, 311
Lungtog Dawa, 155-156, 158, 160, 167,
  171, 189-190
Lungshar, Tsepon, Tibetan official, 74-76,
  306

Madhyamaka, 32, 223, 271, 304
Mahamudra, 59-60, 63, 271
Mahayana, 271, 273
Maheshwari, Anil, 98, 168, 172, 237,
  302-304, 309, 311
Marpa, 44, 246, 247, 270
Martin, Michelle, 125, 297, 306-307, 309
Milarepa, 44, 58, 261-262
Mipham Rinpoche, 216-220, 222-228,
  230-231
Mongols, Qoshot band, 49, 266
Monlam, 46-47, 223

Naher, Gaby, 23, 26, 88, 102-103, 108,
  194, 200, 297, 299, 303-305,
  309-310
Nationalism, 298
Nepal, 20, 25, 34, 69-71, 88, 93-96, 111,
  115, 120, 123, 132, 150, 158-159,
  176, 184, 195-197, 199, 228-229,
  231, 266, 288, 294, 304
New Zealand, 10, 268, 274, 298, 302-303,
  306
nirvana, 2